During a visit to a monthly meeting of the Caudill Camp, during the first year of our existence, John B. Wells III told the story of how Colonel Caudill said he wanted a flag with a blue field bearing a white Christian Cross. The design was the same as the historic St. George's Cross, which was used as the flag of England as early as the 1200's. Colonel Caudill's reasoning for choosing a flag fitting this description was that he wanted opposing soldiers to realize they were fighting an army that had God on its side. Mr. Wells also reported that the words "CAUDILLS ARMY" were added to the flag with the "A" in "ARMY" located where the white bars crossed. The flag of the 13th Cavalry survived the war; but, was lost in a Knott County house fire in 1910.

13th Kentucky Cavalry C. S. A.

"Caudill's Army"

Copyright 2013 by
Col. Ben E. Caudill Camp No. 1629, SCV

All rights reserved

ISBN : 978-0-578-13867-1

Published by
Col. Ben E. Caudill Camp No. 1629, SCV
P. O. Box 1102
Whitesburg, KY 41858

Front Cover: Colonel Benjamin E. Caudill, C.S.A., ca. 1864
Back Cover: Richard Brown photo, by permission

This book, and the efforts that made it possible, are dedicated to the memory of Colonel Ben E. Caudill, to the loyalty and courage of the men who followed him, and to their proud descendants.

Colonel Ben E. Caudill, C. S. A.
(Reconstructed Image by Lacey Hale)

v

Table of Contents

Foreword..	1
Acknowledgements...	3
Prologue..	5
Map of Recruits' Homes..	7
History of the 13th KY Cavalry: 1862 – 1865...	8
Battle of Leatherwood: October 19, 1862...	10
Battle of Poor Fork: October 21, 1862..	11
Battle of Wallins Creek: November 19, 1862..	11
Battle of Mill Cliff: December 1, 1862...	13
First Battle of Whitesburg: December 13, 1862.......................................	14
Skirmish at Camp Cumberland: March 15, 1863......................................	16
"Ben Caudill's Army": July 3, 1863...	19
Battle of Gladeville: July 7, 1863..	21
Battle of Blue Springs: October 10, 1863...	27
Battle of Henderson's Mill: October 11, 1863...	29
Battle of Rheatown: October 11, 1863...	30
Battle of Pugh's Hill: October 11, 1863...	30
Battle of Blountville: October 14, 1863...	31
Everette's Raid: November – December, 1863..	33
First Battle of Jonesville: January 3, 1864...	37
Second Battle of Jonesville: January 28 – 29, 1864................................	39
Battle of Chavies: May 2, 1864..	42
Battle of Cove Mountain..	43
Battle of Colley Creek: May 13, 1864...	44
Morgan's Last Raid: June, 1864...	46
Battle of Mt. Sterling: June 8 – 9, 1864..	47
Skirmish at Lexington: June 10, 1864..	49
Battle of Cynthiana: June 11 – 12, 1864..	50
A Letter Home: July 1, 1864..	53
Morgan's Withdrawal: August, 1864...	53
Blue Springs Battle Revisited: August 21, 1864.......................................	54
Pushed Back to Jonesboro: August 23, 1864..	54
Death of General Morgan: September 4, 1864..	56
Prelude to Saltville: October, 1864...	57
Battle at Laurel Gap: October 1, 1864	57
First Battle of Saltville: October 2, 1864...	58
Trip to Shenandoah Valley: October 18 - December 9, 1864..................	60
Battle of Crane's Nest: November 9, 1864...	62
Battle of Bull's Gap: November 11 – 13, 1864..	64
Battle of Marion: December 17-18, 1864...	65

    Battle of Harlan County Courthouse: March 20, 1865........................ 69
    Ending of the War: Spring, 1865... 72
    Battle of Wytheville: April 4, 1865... 73
    Near the End of the War: April, 1865... 74
    Second Battle of Whitesburg: April 16, 1865.................................. 76
    Continuing the Trail to Surrender: April, 1865................................ 77

Reflections:
    William "Banger" "Groundhog" Fugate.. 91
    The Branson Slayings... 93
    Daniel Noble's Medal of Honor... 96
    Five Breathitt County Soldiers.. 99
    Ezekial Brashear Brought Home... 101
    Stephen Sumner.. 101
    The Execution of Gilbert Creech... 102
    The Influence of Ben Caudill.. 103
    Wesley Sumner... 105
    Hooker's Scapegoat.. 107

Photographs... 114

Roster of the 13th KY Cavalry.. 130

Epilogue.. 275

Personal Reflections.. 285

Bibliography.. 288

Foreword
By Richard Brown

More than one hundred and fifty years ago, our great-great grandfathers, their brothers, their cousins, and other relatives were faced with a frightening decision. The so-called Civil War had deeply divided the Commonwealth of Kentucky, and this was particularly true in the eastern part of the state. It was not an easy chore for these men to make a decision that they knew would almost certainly pit them against their brothers and neighbors. This book was compiled to honor one group of men from the mountains of Eastern Kentucky who chose to support the Confederate States of America. The 13th Kentucky Cavalry was born from their decision. Their regiment was first organized as the 10th Kentucky Mounted Rifles and would be known by that name until late in the war, when the regiment's designation was changed to the 13th Kentucky Cavalry. This name change took place in order to clear up confusion with its sister regiment, the 10th Kentucky Cavalry. These two regiments served throughout most of the war, side by side.

Unfortunately, many historians do not acknowledge this regiment, with some even implying that the regiment never contributed to the Confederate cause. It is hoped that this book might change that direction of thought. These sturdy mountain men made good soldiers, though it is acknowledged that many of them sought to stay and fight in the Appalachian Mountains. The regiment was known as "Caudill's Army", a nickname attributed to their commander, Colonel Ben E. Caudill, a well-known preacher; and thirty-three other Caudills who served in his regiment. The respect for the Colonel's character also led to the design of the battle flag that was carried by the regiment, a Christian flag, blue with a white cross. The name, "Caudills Army", was emblazed across the white cross.

This book contains a roster of these brave soldiers, as well as a history of their engagements during the war. They fought mostly in skirmishes and battles in southwestern Virginia, southeastern Kentucky, and northeastern Tennessee. However, they did travel through the Shenandoah Valley as far north as Winchester, Virginia; and they fought in the Battles of Mt. Sterling and Cynthiana in the Bluegrass portion of Kentucky during Morgan's last raid. Also, within these pages are photos of several of the 13th veterans as well as some revealing stories of certain individuals. This regiment was one of the last Confederate regiments to surrender at war's end.

The men of this regiment served under several well-known and respected commanders, including Generals Humphrey Marshall, John S. Williams, William Preston, John C. Breckinridge and John Hunt Morgan. Having served under General Morgan entitled them to go down in history as being part of "Morgan's Men". They also served under Colonel Henry Giltner, whom many believe should have been promoted to General for his outstanding leadership. Whether they were under the command of Marshall, Williams, Preston, Breckinridge Morgan or Giltner, the brave men of Caudill's regiment fought, suffered and died, just as much as any other Confederate regiment. They earned the respect and love of all commanding officers with whom they served.

Acknowledgements

This book would not have been possible without the efforts of many dedicated individuals. Some spent countless hours in libraries poring over military, pension and census records. Others were just as diligent in their efforts in area courthouses, where they dissected marriage and property records. Still others drove many miles to visit the final resting places of Caudill's men, so that these men might be properly honored and remembered. And, a few of the most dedicated took part in all these activities. Here, we would like to thank a few of these individuals and make a sincere apology to anyone we may have inadvertently omitted:

John & Nancy Wright Bays, Stephen D. Bowling, Carlos Brock, Wendell Brown, Mark Carroll, Buford Caudill, Larry Combs, James Epling, J. B. Francis, Rokie Frazier, Dorothy Amburgey Griffith, Atlas Hall, Mack Holliday, Dorothy Hunter, Creda Isaacs, Bill James, Barry Johnson, Stephen D. Lynn, Harold & Henrietta McKinney, Randall Osborne, John David Preston, James M. Prichard, Joe Skeens, Brandon Slone, Jeffrey C. Weaver, John B. Wells III, and Jeanette Whitaker.

The years of research that preceded this publication did not take place in a vacuum. To all those organizations and agencies that provided their resources and their facilities, we are grateful. There were many, and even a partial listing would have to include the following:

Adjutant General Report of the Confederate Army, Adjutant General Report of the Union Army, Brandon Trucking of Isom, Chicago Historical Society, Breathitt County Public Library, Department of Military Affairs, Records & Research; Frankfort, Kentucky, Frankfort Military History Museum, Johnson County Public Library, The Kentucky State Archives in Frankfort, Kentucky; Letcher County Historical Society, Manufacturers' Supply of Hazard, The National Archives in Washington, D. C.; and the Perry County Public Library.

4

Prologue

A pair of old torches, as much as any saber, musket, or moth-riddled shell jacket of the era, may represent the nature of Civil War conflict in the mountain counties of southeastern Kentucky. After a half-day search on a spring day in the early 1960s, 2 chunks of pine bark measuring approximately 2 inches thick by 3 or 4 inches wide by 15 inches long were retrieved from a cavity beneath a rock, high on a Letcher County hillside. The reason for the search was that an old-timer had told a pair of young men that during the Civil War, the people who lived on Blair Branch, a few hundred feet below the "torch rock", "sided" with the Union. He continued by telling us that up in the woods, above the cleared fields, the Union-sympathizing locals kept pine torches hidden under a rock for use in emergencies when Caudill's Confederates were thought to be in the vicinity.

Half a mile or so further around the mountain from the location of the "torch rock" is an over-hanging rock cliff, not unlike many others in the area that gave the main creek the name of Rockhouse. The story, as handed down by the old mountaineer, was that stock belonging to Unionist residents was kept under the cliff during the war, safe from prying Secessionist eyes. Anyone who felt the need to escape to the safety of the remote "Bull Rocks" on summer nights could use the torches to safely complete the journey. The fleeing Lincolnite would have to climb through the cleared ground of the hillside gardens and pastures without a light, but once in the timber, he could put fire to a pine torch for use in negotiating the steep, copperhead-infested ground that lay between him and the "Bull Rocks".

The "head" of neighboring Spring Branch, a creek which sent several men to Colonel Ben Caudill's command, lies scant feet to the west of the "Bull Rocks". These Spring Branch Confederates must have known the area well-enough to predict where their Blair Branch neighbors were hiding their stock. Their reluctance to inform their Confederate superiors may have been indication that mountain loyalties trumped even their sworn allegiance to the armed forces of the Confederacy. Even so, it would appear that the Union-sympathizing neighbors on Blair Branch dared not flaunt their secret and call the Secessionist hand by climbing boldly in broad daylight to their "hidden" stock.

The Recruits' Homes

These men of the 13th Kentucky Cavalry came from 47 counties in three states. This map shows the counties as they existed in 1860:

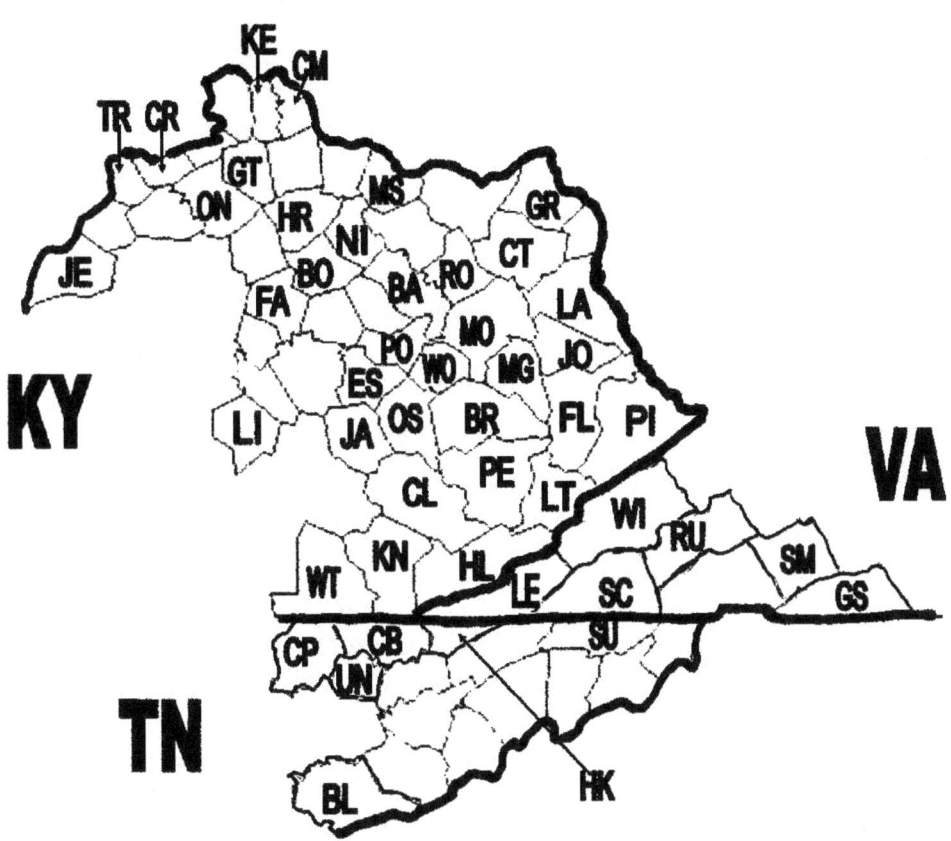

In Kentucky, those 1860 counties included Bath (BA), Bourbon (BO), Breathitt (BR), Campbell (CM), Carroll (CR), Carter (CT), Clay (CL), Estill (ES), Fayette (FA), Floyd (FL), Grant (GT), Greenup (GR), Harlan (HL), Harrison (HR), Jackson (JA), Jefferson (JE), Johnson (JO), Kenton (KE), Knox (KN), Lawrence (LA), Letcher (LT), Lincoln (LI), Magoffin (MG), Mason (MS), Morgan (MO), Nicholas (NI), Owen (ON), Owsley (OS), Perry (PE), Pike (PI), Powell (PO), Rowan (RO), Trimble (TR), Whitley (WT), and Wolfe (WO).

Of course, some came from southwest Virginia. Their home counties were Grayson (GS), Lee (LE), Russell (RU), Scott (SC), Smyth (SM), and Wise (WI).

And finally, some called northesast Tennessee home in 1860. They lived in Blount (BL), Campbell (CP), Claiborne (CB), Hancock (HK), Sullivan (SU), and Union (UN).

History of the 13th Kentucky Cavalry

When the War Between the States began, in April of 1861, the residents of Letcher County, in southeastern Kentucky, attempted to stay out of the fighting. At first, there were no recruiting stations for either Union or Confederate soldiers in Kentucky, forcing anyone who wanted to enlist in either army to travel out of the state. For the first few months, the men of the mountains managed to continue their normal way of life, but that was soon to change. As both armies began to enter Kentucky, the issue of which side to support was forced upon these mountaineers. Since Letcher County bordered Virginia, a state which had joined the Confederacy, the majority of the residents supported the Southern cause. In addition, most of the early pioneers of the county had migrated there from Virginia and North Carolina, a kinship that was hard to ignore.

By September of 1861, a recruiting office for Confederate soldiers was established in Whitesburg, the county seat. The majority of these new troops joined the 5th Kentucky Infantry, which was commanded by Colonel John S. Williams, a Kentuckian. A local farmer and preacher, Ben E. Caudill, began to organize some of his neighbors and relatives into Company F of this new regiment. Recognizing his ability of leadership, the men of the fledgling company elected him captain. This, plus the unique closeness and kinship of the company, earned them the nickname "Caudill's Army", which would follow them throughout the war.

The newly formed 5th Kentucky Infantry began to drill and train in Whitesburg and on Rockhouse Creek, near the mouth of Colley Creek. The regiment eventually was accepted in the Army of Eastern Kentucky, a newly formed Confederate department under the command of General Humphrey Marshall. While in Letcher County, a large outbreak of disease including measles, mumps and dysentery ran through the army. A military hospital was built near the mouth of Sandlick Creek near Whitesburg. Unfortunately, the hospital was soon overrun with patients, forcing local citizens to take the sick into their homes. Dozens of soldiers died during this time and were buried in the Sandlick Cemetery in plots donated by John A. Caudill, father of Ben Caudill. During this time, the general ordered the army to move to Paintsville, Kentucky, in order to gain new recruits and to threaten the Union recruiting station established at Louisa, in Lawrence County.

Company F and the remainder of the Army of Eastern Kentucky soon were in their first major battle at Middle Creek in Floyd County. Here the Confederate Army tangled with the Union Army under the command of Colonel James Garfield, future President of the United States. The battle forced the Confederates to retreat back to Whitesburg and Pound Gap. Later, they moved into southwestern Virginia, to be stationed there. Traveling north, they were engaged in the Battle of Princeton, which was a Confederate victory. In September of 1862, they marched back into Kentucky and served as the rear guard during the Battle of Perryville. It was during this time that Captain Caudill requested permission from General Marshall to begin raising a troop of mounted soldiers. Realizing that the one-year enlistment would soon be up, the general relented and promoted the captain to colonel, giving him the authority to begin recruiting.

During the march of the 5th Kentucky out of Kentucky in October of 1862, the enlistment time for most of the men ran out. This occurred while the army was camped near Hazel Green, Kentucky. While there, General Marshall asked the men to rejoin the 5th Kentucky; or, at least join the newly forming 10th Kentucky Mounted Rifles, which was the regiment that Colonel Caudill was organizing. Some of the soldiers did rejoin the 5th Kentucky but most decided that they had enough of marching and wanted to be mounted troops. Therefore, many joined the fledgling mounted regiment stationed in Whitesburg. Much later, in March of 1865, the regiment would be reorganized and renamed the 13th Kentucky Cavalry. The nickname of "Caudill's Army" would stay with the regiment throughout the war.

1862

During October of 1862, the 10th Kentucky Mounted Rifles drilled and trained in the same locations, Whitesburg and Rockhouse, as had the 5th Kentucky when they were stationed in Letcher County. The majority of the training took place in the large bottoms just west of Whitesburg. These bottoms were owned by John A. Caudill, father to Colonel Caudill. Men from throughout southeastern Kentucky came to Whitesburg to join the mounted regiment, most bringing their own mounts. Some men from neighboring Virginia joined the regiment as well.

The fledgling regiment had not trained long before it received its first assignment. General Marshall ordered Colonel Caudill to send some men to Brashearville, in Perry County, to guard the salt works there. The salt wells produced a very important commodity that was important to both armies. Salt was the only way to preserve meat during the time period that included the war. These wells were owned and operated by Robert Brashears, an uncle to Colonel Caudill. The colonel sent Company B, under the command of his brother, Captain David J. Caudill, to the salt works.

Captain Caudill and his men camped in the bottom adjacent to the salt works and began to forage for supplies. Meanwhile, a newly formed Union State Guard regiment, the Harlan County Battalion, was organized and drilled on the Cumberland River, not far from Letcher County. Many of these new Union recruits were from Letcher County. This regiment was under the command of Major Benjamin Blankenship. While in the process of training his men, the major received word that several men from the Leatherwood area of Perry County, near Brashearville, were interested in joining the battalion. In addition, he was informed about the Confederates guarding the salt works.

Realizing he could possibly complete two jobs with a single effort, the major ordered Captain Morgan to take the best equipped men of Companies A and B to the Leatherwood area. There, he was to link up with the prospective soldiers, then travel down Leatherwood Creek and attack the Confederates at Brashearville. The fight between neighbors and kin was about to begin in earnest.

The Battle of Leatherwood
October 19, 1862
(Map on Page 80)

In the early afternoon of October 19, Captain Morgan and his men met the prospective soldiers on Leatherwood Creek. The local men told the captain where the Confederates were camped and volunteered to help attack them. A decision was made to use the local men as both guides and soldiers; then attack their enemy. Following their new comrades down the creek, the Union soldiers slipped up on the unsuspecting Rebels. A part of Captain Caudill's men was in a garden alongside the creek, foraging for food. The Union soldiers were able to approach the Confederates across the creek without being seen. When in position, the Yankees fired a ragged volley across the creek. The surprised Rebels instinctively took cover on their side of the creek and began to return fire.

Hearing the shooting, Captain Caudill and the remainder of his men left the camp and ran upstream to help their comrades. Arriving at the scene, they took cover along the creek bank and began helping their comrades return fire. Recognizing some of their adversaries, taunts and curses began to swap sides as well as bullets. The beginning of neighbor fighting neighbor had begun in earnest. Both sides had particularly good cover, as dozens of trees lined both sides of the creek. This apparently helped prevent many of the shots from finding their mark. The ragged firing seemed to go on forever, with neither side giving ground. The stalemate was finally broken when Captain Caudill was wounded. With their commander out of action, the remaining Rebels began to retreat downstream toward their camp. Mounting their horses, the boys in gray began riding upstream along the Kentucky River toward their base camp at Whitesburg, taking their wounded with them.

Captain Morgan and his Union soldiers swarmed across the creek but did not chase the Confederates any further than their original camp. Here, they stopped to confiscate everything of value. They were surprised to find one gigantic pone of cornbread that had been made in one of the large salt kettles. Afraid that the Confederates would return with reinforcements, Morgan and his men left the salt works intact and returned to the Cumberland River Valley.

From "War of Rebellion": On November 18, 1862, General Humphrey Marshall stated in a letter to James A. Seddon, Secretary of War, that Caudill had enlisted nine companies. He says "the men at Whitesburg have been consistantly engaged with the home guards (about 600 strong) and I hear successfully engaged generally, though the other day a party of forty came into Whitesburg and murdered several of the citizens, burned the houses of Capt. Caudill and of his father and brothers, and carried his wife off a prisoner. I mention these things to show you that in the border counties of Kentucky the war is deadly and fiercely waged, although the participants are all mountaineers, and their numbers are comparatively small." -Gen. Humphrey Marshall

Battle of Poor Fork
October 21, 1862

Captain Caudill's men returned to Whitesburg with the wounded captain. News of the fight angered Colonel Ben Caudill and he immediately sent a large number of troops to the salt works to confront the enemy. However, when they arrived, the camp was deserted. Locals in the area told the Rebels that the Yankees had returned to Poor Fork (now the City of Cumberland) in Harlan County. With this knowledge, Colonel Caudill decided to take the fight to the enemy and attack them in their camp at Poor Fork. Leaving Whitesburg on October 20, the 10th Kentucky traveled across Pine Mountain to the Cumberland River Valley. Realizing that they could not make it to Poor Fork before dark, Colonel Caudill ordered his men to dismount and make camp.

At daybreak on October 21, the Confederates mounted and began their travel toward Poor Fork. Having been informed about pickets being posted outside of town, the colonel ordered his men to gallop into town, pushing the pickets aside. Telling the rear guard to take care of any pickets on their flank, Colonel Caudill and his men galloped into town, firing as they charged. The men and officers of the Harlan Battalion were taken by surprise by the assault. Firing few shots in return, the Yankees fled into the nearby mountains, abandoning the majority of their gear. Amazingly, the attack was over in minutes.

Colonel Caudill allowed his men to pillage throughout the abandoned camp. They were soon surprised to find most of the equipment and other baggage that had been taken from Captain Caudill's camp at Brashearville, only two days previously. In addition, the Union quartermaster's supply building was full of desperately needed military supplies. This forced Major Ben Blankenship of the Harlan Battalion to request additional supplies from Union headquarters in Frankfort.

The colonel and his men stayed in Poor Fork for the next three days until an early winter snowstorm started brewing. This stay ensured that the Harlan Battalion had a hard time regrouping. Both sides now realized that either group could inflict hardships and casualties on the other.

The Battle of Wallins Creek
November 19, 1862
(Map on Page 81

After having been routed by the 10th Kentucky Mounted Rifles, Major Blankenship began to gather again at their base camp in Poor Fork. Short on supplies, the major decided to raid the Confederate camp at Whitesburg in hopes of confiscating anything there that might be useful to his army. On November 11, the Union soldiers rode out of Poor Fork and started for Whitesburg. Word swiftly raced across the mountain that the Harlan Battalion was heading for the Letcher County area.

Colonel Ben Caudill had sent part of his army to Brashearville to guard the salt works and part was on patrol in southwestern Virginia, leaving a small detachment to guard the camp at Whitesburg. Upon receiving word that the Harlan Battalion was heading their way, the soldiers in the Confederate camp knew that they were too few to resist Blankenship's men. They wisely loaded as many supplies as they could and hid the remainder. Then, they vanished into the mountains.

On the morning of November 12, Major Blankenship and his men stormed through Whitesburg and on to the Confederate camp located just beyond. They were soon surprised to find an empty camp. To make things worse, hardly anything of value could be found in the abandoned camp. The same was found to be true of the small town of Whitesburg when the Union soldiers returned there to look for supplies. Dejected, the major and his men had a long, cold ride back across the mountain to Poor Fork.

Upon their arrival at camp, their spirits were lifted when they were met with the news that much needed supplies, including arms, were waiting for them in Manchester, Kentucky. Major Blankenship ordered Captain Ambrose Powell to take Company B to pick up the supplies. On November 15, the captain and his men left with a wagon to travel to Manchester.

Word of the trip soon reached Colonel Caudill in Whitesburg. The colonel decided to ambush the wagon load of supplies to help arm some of his own men. He hoped to intercept the supplies somewhere between Mt. Pleasant (now the City of Harlan) and Cumberland Ford (now the City of Pineville). Union scouts informed Major Blankenship that a column of Confederate cavalry was reported riding toward the Cumberland River area. The major immediately suspected the reason for the Rebel soldiers' mission was to capture his supplies. Taking his best armed and equipped troops, Major Blankenship managed to get to Wallin's Creek, which was about seven miles west of Mt. Pleasant, ahead of the Confederates. The ford where Wallin's Creek emptied into the Cumberland River provided an ideal ambush site.

On the evening of November 19, 1862, the Union soldiers soon lined the woods overlooking the ford, waiting for the approaching Rebels. Colonel Caudill had scouts riding in front of the column and when they started crossing the ford, Blankenship's men opened fire. Dropping from their horses and finding protection behind the large trees lining the river bank, the Confederates began to return fire. Colonel Caudill and his men rushed forward to respond to the gunfire. Arriving at the ford, they began to return fire as well at the concealed Yankees. Volleys of gunfire echoed up and down the river, as neither side could get the upper hand on the other. The firing kept constant until the evening sun began to set behind the tall mountains. With darkness now at hand, Colonel Caudill withdrew his men. Not knowing how many soldiers faced him, and realizing they could no longer surprise the supply wagon, the colonel decided to withdraw back to Rebel Rock. Using the darkness of night as cover, Caudill and his men left the riverbank and rode back upstream.

Major Blankenship and his men did not know if the Confederates were going to stay and fight again at morning light. Laying on their arms, the Union soldiers stayed in position throughout the night. The next morning, the soldiers were delighted to learn that the Confederates had left the area. Not sure of Caudill's intentions, Major Blankenship took his men to meet the wagon load of supplies and escort them back under guard to their camp. Meanwhile, Colonel Caudill and the 10th Kentucky Mounted Rifles returned to their camp at Whitesburg. They would have to obtain more weapons elsewhere.

The Battle of Mill Cliff
December 1, 1862
(Map on Page 82)

The 10th Kentucky Mounted Rifles continued to send out patrols and scouting parties throughout southeastern Kentucky and southwestern Virginia. During this time, the Harlan Battalion continued to harass both citizens and Confederate soldiers in the Whitesburg area. Colonel Caudill decided to attack the Union Camp at Poor Fork in hopes of ridding the country of them. On the morning of November 30, the colonel and some of his regiment rode out of town with their sights on Poor Fork. By evening, they arrived at Rebel Rock in Harlan County. It was determined that there was not enough daylight to continue on their raid, therefore the 10th Kentucky camped at the infamous rock overhang.

Early on the morning of December 1, the Confederates continued their trip to Poor Fork. Arriving just outside the town, Colonel Caudill prepared his men to charge. With a Rebel yell, the gray-clad column charged into town. Unfortunately, there was only a small detachment of Union soldiers guarding the town. These Yankees were soon sent scurrying into the nearby woods, firing only a volley or two. The colonel was informed that the Harlan Battalion had moved to Mt. Pleasant the previous day.

Deciding to continue carrying the fight to the Union soldiers, Colonel Caudill decided to ride down the Cumberland River Road to Mt. Pleasant. Before leaving Poor Fork though, he allowed his men to eat the breakfast that the Yanks had begun cooking. Unfortunately for the colonel and his men, this gave some of the Union soldiers from town enough time to ride ahead of the Confederates and warn Major Blankenship. The major sent two companies of his men to ambush the Rebels as they traveled downstream. The Union officers chose to ambush the Confederates at Mill Cliff, which is about two miles west of Rebel Rock. This site was a perfect ambush site as the road and the Cumberland River ran closely together. In addition, the Mill Cliff was a spur of the mountain that overlooked the road. Hiding their horses, the Union soldiers climbed up on the spur and began to wait.

After allowing his men to rest and eat at Poor Fork, Colonel Caudill ordered the column to continue toward Mt. Pleasant. As the forward scouts of the the column rode under the spur at Mill Cliff, the Harlan Battalion soldiers began to fire. Luckily for the Confederates, shooting downhill caused the Yanks to shoot high, with most rounds missing their targets. The main Confederate column moved rapidly forward and began to engage the Union soldiers hidden in the hills above them. Colonel Caudill and his men used the trees lining the riverbank for protection. A general engagement began with neither side attempting to move from their position. The shooting soon began to ease up, with only sporadic firing letting each side know the other was still in place. This stalemate continued until the Confederates were able to withdraw under the cover of darkness. Knowing he had now lost the advantage of surprise; Colonel Caudill ordered his men to begin the journey back to Whitesburg. His men found some comfort just in being able to return with the supplies confiscated at Poor Fork.

Typical of most mountain battles, the casualty rate was low. The 10th Kentucky Mounted Rifles had suffered at least one killed and several wounded. The Harlan Battalion had suffered several wounded as well.

The First Battle of Whitesburg
December 13, 1862
(Map on Page 83)

During the first couple of weeks of December, portions of Colonel Caudill's regiment were in at least three different areas. Several companies of the 10th Kentucky were stationed at the mouth of Leatherwood, guarding the salt works. At least two more companies accompanied their commander in a scouting party into southwestern Virginia. The rest of the soldiers were encamped at Whitesburg. These men were under the command of Lieutenant George Houck.

Many of the men stationed in Whitesburg were sick and were in a military hospital that had been constructed there. The hospital was located near where the Sandlick Creek emptied into the North Fork of the Kentucky River, on land owned by John Caudill, father of Colonel Caudill. This hospital had been built in 1861 when the 5th Kentucky Infantry and other regiments were stationed there. Tragically, dozens of soldiers died in this hospital, with many of them being buried in the Sandlick Cemetery, which was also owned by John Caudill. The hospital was eventually burnt by marauding Union soldiers.

Major Blankenship of the Harlan Battalion was soon aware of the 10th Kentucky Mounted Rifles being in separate areas. Knowing this had weakened the force at Whitesburg, he decided to take advantage of the opportunity and attack them. Leaving his encampment on the Poor Fork of the Cumberland River on December 12, the major and several companies of his men began to travel toward Whitesburg. Arriving in the evening, on the northern side of Pine Mountain, not far from the small town, the major decided to wait until first light of the next morning to attack. No fires could be built, in order to keep their location a secret.

On the morning of December 13, the Harlan Battalion quietly assembled and made their way toward the sleeping little town of Whitesburg. The Union soldiers rode through the town and made their way to the ford of the river just beyond. Leaving their horses on the riverbank near the ford, the boys in blue made their way on foot toward the Rebel camp.

Fortunately for the Confederates, their young officer in charge, Lieutenant George Houck, took his command seriously and took precautions to avoid being surprised. He established pickets on both sides of the camp, far enough away to give the encampment warning of any surprise attack. In the early morning dawn, the men of the Harlan Battalion stumbled into the pickets, who immediately fired a volley at the Yanks. The firing alerted the Confederate camp, allowing Lieutenant Houck time to organize his men and rush them toward the shooting. Meanwhile, the pickets were being slowly pushed back toward the main camp. Both armies collided in the river bottoms near the mouth of Sandlick Creek, just upstream from the hospital.

Both sides found cover behind split rail fences that separated the bottom. Several volleys were exchanged before men on both sides began to recognize their opponents. Soon curses and insults were added to the melee of battle. Tragically, the fighting of neighbor against neighbor, and even brother against brother was in full force in the war in the mountains. Tired of the stalemate, Lieutenant Houck jumped the fence and urged his men to join him in charging the Union line. The sight of the charging Rebels caused the men of the Harlan Battalion to retreat. Luckily for them, Major Blankenship and his officers were able to restore order among the startled men and began a more orderly withdrawal.

Slowly, the Yankees were forced back through the river bottoms toward Whitesburg. Each time the Union soldiers managed to make a stand, the Rebels would charge, forcing them to retreat again. This type of fighting continued until the boys in blue found themselves back at the ford in the river where their horses were being kept. Realizing that they were in serious trouble, Major Blankenship ordered his men to mount and retreat. In minutes, the Harlan Battalion was galloping through the dusty streets of Whitesburg as they began their journey back across Pine Mountain to the safety of their camp. Lieutenant Houck was disappointed that the enemy was getting away, but all the Confederates could do was watch, as the Yanks rode off. The Confederates' horses were way back at camp, too far to have a chance of getting to them in time to catch the hard-riding Yanks. The young lieutenant had to be pleased with the performance of his men, as well as himself. Though official army records of the battle were lost, it is known that several men on both sides were wounded, with at least two Union soldiers killed.

Soon after the fight at Whitesburg, Colonel Caudill returned. Now that the war had arrived in southeastern Kentucky, more men began to come to Whitesburg to enlist in the 10th Kentucky Mounted Rifles. The colonel continued to use the bottoms outside of town to train and drill his growing regiment. By the end of December, General Humphrey Marshall sent orders for the colonel to maintain patrols in three areas: The Pound Gap area of southeastern Kentucky, the Three Forks area near Booneville in Owsley County, and the Big Sandy area between Pikeville and Louisa. Of course, the main threat in the Pound Gap area was from the Harlan Battalion. In the Booneville area, the 14th Kentucky Cavalry was beginning to make their presence known. And in the Big Sandy area, the 39th Kentucky Mounted Infantry was beginning to patrol and harass southern sympathizers. To maintain a Confederate presence in these areas, the colonel reluctantly divided his regiment into three forces.

Before long, Major Blankenship of the Harlan Battalion became aware of the diminished presence of a Confederate force in the Whitesburg area. Taking advantage of this, the major and his men raided Letcher County, easily pushing out the small number of soldiers guarding the area. In addition to destroying the Confederate camp outside of Whitesburg, they also burnt down Colonel Caudill's house and barns, as well as those of his father and brothers. The brazen rouges went as far as to kidnap the colonel's wife, but thankfully, released her later, unharmed. These acts of violence against Confederate sympathizers were so severe that General Marshall reported the incidents in his reports to Confederate headquarters in Richmond, Virginia. The year of 1862 had ended on a sour note for the colonel and many of his men of the 10th Kentucky Mounted Rifles.

On December 31, 1862, General Marshall wrote Seddon again, explaining that he had given Ben E. Caudill at Whitesburg orders to man Pound Gap and all the other mountain gaps along his front and to resist the egress of the enemy.

1863

During the early months of 1863, the 10th Kentucky Mounted Rifles continued their patrolling in the three areas that General Marshall had ordered. Angered by the deprivations placed on his relatives and friends back in the Whitesburg area, Colonel Caudill hoped to soon be able to combine enough of his regiment to attack and do away with the Harlan Battalion. He would soon get his chance as the Commonwealth of Kentucky started running short on money. One of the first things they did was to cut funding to the Kentucky State Guard, of which the Harlan Battalion was a part of. Word soon spread that the Harlan Battalion would no longer be funded after the end of February 1863. This resulted in several of their soldiers leaving and going home. But to Major Blankenship's credit, he was able to convince a considerable number of them to stay and fight.

With the Harlan Battalion weakened, Colonel Caudill felt that he could gather enough men to attack the Union camp. Recalling companies from both the Booneville and Big Sandy areas, the colonel had enough men to feel confident of success in routing the Union soldiers on the Poor Fork of the Cumberland River.

The Skirmish at Camp Cumberland
March 15, 1863

In hopes of keeping the proposed attack a secret, Colonel Caudill did not inform his men until the evening of March 14. At this time, he ordered them to be issued ammunition and provisions that would last for three days. The colonel waited until dark before ordering his men to saddle their mounts and prepare to move out. He hoped that keeping the mission quiet would allow them to catch more of the Harlan Battalion in their encampment near the community of Poor Fork. The Union men called their encampment "Camp Cumberland". Traveling in the dark of night, the 10th Kentucky Mounted Rifles arrived a few miles upstream of Camp Cumberland around midnight.

Wanting to attack the encampment in the daylight, Colonel Caudill ordered his men to dismount. He also ordered that no fires were to be lit in hopes of keeping the regiment's location a secret. On March 15, 1863, as the rising sun began to brighten the dark, morning sky, the Rebel soldiers quietly mounted their horses and began to ride toward their objective.

Riding through the morning mist that was rising off the river, the gray column approached Camp Cumberland. The eager, Confederate soldiers just knew that they were about to attack an unsuspecting Yankee camp. Unfortunately, as luck would have it, several Union soldiers from the encampment had picked this time to go out on patrol. This blue-clad patrol ran head long into the front of the gray column, surprising both armies. Firing a desperate volley, the Yanks fled into the nearby woods at break-neck speed, hoping to save their lives.

Colonel Caudill knew that the sound of gunfire would alert the Union camp, giving the Yanks time to either prepare for battle or to flee. The colonel hoped the Yankees would choose to stay and fight; but he knew that either way, the Confederates must act quickly. Sounding the charge, Caudill and his men raced toward Camp Cumberland at a gallop.

At the sound of the gunfire echoing through the mountain valley, the sleepy encampment quickly came to life. Grabbing their rifles, the Union soldiers began to mill around in confusion. Major Blankenship and his officers began to shout and curse at the men, trying to regain some semblance of order. The major almost had the men formed into a battle line when the first Confederate horsemen came charging wildly into view. Unfortunately for the major, the sight of the yelling and firing Rebel soldiers terrified the Yanks, creating more panic than before. As the Rebel horsemen thundered through the tents and huts that comprised the camp, most of the Union soldiers fled into the nearby woods.

To their credit, several Yanks managed to make a stand for a short time, firing ragged volleys at the galloping Rebels. The determination of the Union soldiers to stay and fight quickly faded however, when they observed what seemed to be an endless line of gray-clad soldiers, splashing up the river. No number of threats or pleadings could convince the last hold-out of blue-clad soldiers to stay and fight. Discarding anything that would slow them down, including their rifles, the Yanks quickly disappeared into the dense underbrush outside camp.

In just a few minutes the shooting was over. The hard-riding Rebels could not find any targets to shoot at as the last of the Yankee occupants vanished from the camp. No attempt was made chase the fleeing Yanks into the woods. Prior experience had taught the soldiers of both armies never to follow a wounded enemy into the woods.

The triumphant Confederates began to scour the camp for booty, but to their dismay, discovered that their blue-clad counterparts did not have much to prize. The hardships of the war had been tough on the Union soldiers as well. One bright spot was the discovery of a large cache of bacon. With anything of value confiscated, the order to burn the camp was given. With the mission now complete, the 10th Kentucky Mounted Rifles returned to Whitesburg.

The raid had the effect that the colonel had hoped for, as the discouraged soldiers of the now defunct Harlan Battalion had enough of fighting for the moment. Though Major Blankenship attempted to hold the battalion together, his men wanted no more part of it. Most returned home but would later join other Union regiments in the area.

Upon their return to Whitesburg, Colonel Caudill once more divided his men and sent them back to their previous missions. The colonel was with some of his men at the salt works on Leatherwood Creek when new orders from General Marshall arrived. The 10th Kentucky Mounted Rifles were to report to southwestern Virginia and begin to patrol in that area. By May 14, most of the regiment was in Virginia. From May until July, they were constantly on patrol in both southeastern Kentucky and southwestern Virginia. Due to their intimate knowledge of both sides of the border, General Marshall depended on them for any warning of a probable invasion of Virginia. The regiment was now transferred out of the Army of Eastern Kentucky and placed in the Army of Tennessee under the command of General William Preston.

From "War of Rebellion":

Headquarters of Union 9th Ohio Voluntary Cavalry, Manchester, Ky.

May 21, 1863

To Brig. General Willcox
Commanding District of Central Kentucky
Lexington, Ky.

"On Thursday last I was informed by reliable citizens that 1,300 of the enemy under Col. Campbell Slemp and B. E. Caudill were advancing on Manchester to drive me out. I immediately sent out a scouting party of 20 men to watch their movements and selected a very strong position five miles in advance of my camp upon which to meet them. Slemp's 64th VA regiment crossed the Cumberland Mountains at Crank's Gap near Jonesville on Friday last, as I learn from a couple of spies whom I caught last Tuesday."

Major W. D. Hamilton
9th Ohio Cavalry

The following story appeared in the Abingdon Virginian newspaper on Friday, July 3, 1863. This newspaper kept up with events occurring during the war in southeastern Kentucky and southwestern Virginia. Most of the troops who guarded the area around Abingdon consisted of Kentuckians. To help maintain morale, the newspaper attempted to keep news from eastern Kentucky in their publication. Copies of the paper were sent to the army camps and read aloud to the soldiers.

"Ben Caudill's Army"
<u>Abingdon Virginian</u>
July 3, 1863: Volume 24

"Who has not heard of Ben Caudill's Army? Will anybody anywhere acknowledge himself so far behind the times, and so little posted in the history of this revolution, as to deny the knowledge of the existence of Ben Caudill's Army?

Now I happen to be acquainted with the history of Ben Caudill's Army, and would consider myself as having wronged the public as well having neglected my imperative duty, were I not to place said history on record. That the reader may understand why this noted command bears the title at the head of this communication, I will give the origin, by referring to the winter of 1861-2, when the 5th Kentucky Regiment, then under command of Colonel (now General) John S. Williams, was experiencing the severe campaign of that winter in its endeavors to hold possession of Eastern Kentucky.

It must be known that Captain Benjamin E. Caudill commanded one of the companies of that regiment, which company was composed principally of men from the county of Letcher. During one of the 'masterly retreats' of this regiment from Kentucky, and while passing down one of the pent in streams of Letcher County, the roads along which were at no time more than four feet deep with mud, an elderly matron appeared in the door of one of the cabins which present themselves at every point where there is a sufficiency of bottom land and level hill sides 'to justify a crop' and addressed herself in the following manner to the soldiers as they plodded along: 'Is this Mister Williams's Company?' Upon being answered in the affirmative, she continued to ask, in her anxiety once more to behold a son or husband, 'Can you tell me where Ben Caudill's Army is?'

These questions were received by the boys with great delight, and manifestations of that lively appreciation of the ridiculous which can always be seen in soldiers and has since afforded the foundation of many a good joke on 'Ben'.

In the month of August 1862, when the 5th Kentucky was in Tazewell County, Virginia, "Ben" was granted the privilege of proceeding with his company to its native county of Letcher. There he remained during the campaign of the remainder of the Brigade in the interior of Kentucky that fall, and when the army of General Bragg and the army of everybody else any ways Southern was under the necessity of evacuating the State, 'Ben' remained, despite the master efforts of the Home Guards to force him from 'the land of his birth'.

'Ben' has never been troubled with the regular, genuine, blue-bellied Yankees, to any great extent, but has had more contentions with the Home and State Guards than anybody.

By this time, the army under 'Ben' had grown to considerable size, so large, indeed, was it, that the old women were astonished at its tremendous proportions, and were constrained to exclaim 'Well, now, I do declare, Old Kaintucky has done powerful well in this war!' But, notwithstanding the pride which they all felt in the reflection that the men of the good State of Kentucky had rallied to the standard of Southern Rights in such astounding numbers, the said old women could not help thinking that it would have been far better for the peace of the land had 'Ben' remained at home and never instigated the war!

But to the record, I have said that 'Ben' had many ups and downs with the Home Guards- principally ups. Well, he did. Pardon the expression. But (altho' 'Ben' was a preacher of the gospel and a ferment man) he "raised particular H_ll" amongst the said Home Guard fraternity, and finally succeeded in almost entirely ridding the country of them-that is, the country which he proposed to hold, viz: the line of the Kentucky River from Pound Gap to Jackson, Breathitt County.

Indeed, so great was the fear of 'Ben' that whenever the 'Suits' heard of his coming, they invariably stampeded. The Cincinnati Gazette styles him 'The Great Mountain Guerilla Chieftain'.

If at any time 'Ben' should be absent from camp scouting the hills or visiting the fair sex, (for he is not a hater of women) the command would fall upon Major Chenoweth, from whom Home Guards obtain no favors, and who at all times and under all circumstances administers the severest justice to said Home Guards.

Since the time of his first entrance into Kentucky, 'Ben' firmly held his ground, and continued to recruit his 'Army', until ordered out by General Preston, or rather by Colonel Trigg, who, it is said, was at that time Acting Brigadier, for the purpose of organization and review.

'Ben' is now a real 'Simon Pure' Colonel and has at this time a regiment of nine companies, which musters about 350 of as good soldiers as the army can produce. This regiment is styled the 10th Regiment Kentucky Volunteer Infantry. With a few more weeks of drill and discipline, it will compare favorably with any other regiment.

Notwithstanding the disposition of not a few of the 'enlisted men' to stay at home and enjoy the sweets of domestic tranquility, (in the bushes!) and at the same time 'fight for Kentucky', the ranks of this command will be full in a short time, say when the corn is laid by, and more particularly when authority is given enforce conscription in Kentucky, and it is sincerely hoped that the time is not far distant."

One of Ben's Army.
Camp at Gladeville, June 21, 1863.
(note: Gladeville was later changed to Wise)

The Battle of Gladeville
July 7, 1863

On June 27, having returned from a patrol in Kentucky, Colonel Caudill sent a report to Confederate headquarters that he believed more than two thousand Union troops in the Cumberland Gap area might move into southwestern Virginia with hopes of attacking the salt works at Saltville, Virginia. General Samuel Jones considered the threat serious and ordered regiments in the area to be ready to come to Colonel Caudill's aid, but the overall commander, General William Preston, overruled the order, considering it only a rumor. Later events would prove Colonel Caudill's assessment correct.

On July 6, 1863, the 10th Kentucky Mounted Rifles and the 7th Confederate Cavalry made camp in Gladeville (now the City of Wise), Virginia. The small town consisted of several nice homes, stores, a courthouse, and hospital used to treat soldiers. The townspeople were glad to have the soldiers present; and, to show their gratitude for fighting for their country, asked if they could sponsor a southern ball for them. It was considered to be a belated Fourth of July celebration. Colonel Caudill and his officers agreed to the offer, and also volunteered their musicians and cooks to help. Quickly, the women of the town began decorating and preparing food. By evening, the town was in full party mode.

Meanwhile, a large Union army under the command of General Julius White was making its way through the Big Sandy area. His orders were to probe into Virginia and discourage the Confederate Army from having a presence in southeastern Kentucky. When near Pound Gap, the general ordered Major John Mason Brown to take the 10th Kentucky Cavalry and the First Ohio Cavalry (a force of approximately 450 soldiers) and make a raid on the railroad in Virginia by way of the gap. General White would continue downstream toward Pikeville with most of his troops. He did this both to divert attention away from Brown's excursion and to attempt to engage any Confederate forces in the Big Sandy area. His plan worked; Confederate scouts reported back to headquarters in Virginia that the Union army was moving toward Pikeville, missing the departure of Brown's army altogether.

Major Brown's army was led by scouts of the 39th Kentucky Mounted Infantry, who were from the Pound Gap area. Traveling by dark across the gap on the evening of July 6, the Union cavalry column was spotted by Confederate scouts. However, these scouts assumed the column was a regiment of Confederate cavalry that was supposed to return to Virginia through the gap, and did not sound an alarm, a tragic mistake. To make matters worse, the 39th Kentucky scouts captured a local Virginia resident who informed them of the ball being conducted in Gladeville. With the assistance of these local scouts, the major easily surrounded the town just before daybreak.

Meanwhile, in Gladeville, the ball had been a tremendous success. Enlisted men and officers alike had taken part in dancing, eating and wonderful music until the late hours of night. Most of the officers were invited to spend the night in residents' houses in town. Though pickets had been set out to surround the town and guard it, most of them had slipped back into town to partake of the party. Colonel Caudill was unaware that his command was now practically unguarded.

With the first light of dawn on July 7, hundreds of blue-clad cavalrymen swept into the sleeping town. In a first-hand account of the attack, Private John Wright, a teen-aged soldier of the 10th Kentucky Mounted Rifles, recounted in a newspaper interview: "There were 15 of us in one tent and before we knew it, they had us surrounded and we had to surrender". With the enemy converging all around, Private John J. Amburgey and a fellow soldier ran to a hiding place, perhaps in some brush. While silently waiting, the soldier with John Amburgey put his hand on top of a poisonous snake and his subsequent loud scream gave their position away. Several Rebel soldiers managed to organize a limited resistance, with many using the courthouse as a rallying point. There, they managed to hold off several determined attacks by the Yanks, wounding several. Luckily for the Confederates, the early morning mist mixed with the black powder smoke from hundreds of rifles, limited visibility; allowing many of Colonel Caudill's men to escape into the nearby mountains. Drawing back, the Yanks informed the barricaded men in the courthouse that they would burn them out if they did not surrender. Before the torches could be thrown on the building, the Rebels reluctantly agreed to surrender. The same process was used to capture the many officers holed up in houses throughout the town.

Colonel Ben Caudill and most of his staff officers began to surrender, handing over their swords and small arms. Eighteen officers and ninety-nine enlisted men of the 10th Kentucky Mounted Rifles and 7th Confederate Cavalry were now prisoners of war. Within minutes they had a netted an astounding number of Caudill's top officers including Captain Hiram Stamper, Captain George Hogg, Captain W.S. Landrum, Captain Anderson Hays, Captain J. C. Walker, Captain Sam Brashear, Lieutenant Isom Collier, Lieutenant Wilburn Amburgey, Lieutenant Aaron Bentley, Lieutenant John Craft, Lieutenant Ed Grigsby, and Lieutenant Henry Caudill. The commander of the 1,100-man regiment and his best officers were being rounded up and tied with ropes like so many head of cattle. Sadly, many of these prisoners would never return to their homes, dying in prisoner-of-war camps in the north, both from starvation and disease. Fortunately, several officers were able to escape, along with most of the enlisted men.

Major Brown, giddy with the success of his attack, decided to take his prisoners and return to Kentucky, rather than to continue with his original plan of destroying the railroad bridges near Bristol. His report to General White stated, "The presence of superior forces of the enemy prevented further progress toward the railroad". He ordered his men to destroy and burn all the Confederate baggage, tents and ammunition that could be found around Gladeville. Guessing correctly that a rescue party would soon be organized, Major Brown and his men immediately began to travel back toward Pound Gap and to Kentucky.

General Julius White sent the following after-action report to Major General Ambrose Burnside:

Headquarters District of Eastern Kentucky
Beaver Creek, July 11, 1863

"Colonel: I have the honor to submit the following report of the recent operations of this command:

On the 3rd instant, I marched from this station with six companies of the 65th Illinois Infantry (two mounted) 10th Kentucky Cavalry, one squadron of Ohio Volunteer Cavalry, one company of 14th Kentucky Infantry (mounted) and two mountain howitzers, under command of Lieutenant Wheeler of Company M, 2nd Illinois Light Artillery. At Pikeville, 20 miles south of this, I was joined by a part of the 39th Kentucky Infantry mounted in all about 950 men. From Pikeville, I proceeded up the Louisa Fork of Sandy River with about half the entire force, directing that the 10th Kentucky Cavalry and the Ohio Squadron proceed by a rapid march through Pound Gap or Sounding Gap to Gladeville, Virginia and demonstrate upon or attack the force of the enemy at that place, under Colonel Caudill; thence up to the railroad at or near Bristol, and destroy so much of it should appear too hazardous an undertaking. This command reached Gladeville (after some skirmishing with the enemy along the way) completely surprising and carrying the place by storm, beating in the doors and windows, from which the enemy were firing, with axes and compelling his surrender after fifteen minutes of close and desperate fighting, during which the loss of the enemy was 20 killed and 30 wounded. Eighteen commissioned officers, including Colonel Caudill, commanding the regiment, were surrendered, with ninety-nine enlisted men. The camp equipage, stored arms, and ammunition of the command were destroyed. Major Brown, 10th Kentucky Cavalry, commanding this detachment, then returned to camp at Pikeville, thence this place, with his prisoners, safely, the presence of superior forces of the enemy preventing farther progress toward the railroad."

Very respectfully, your obedient servant,
Julius White
Brigadier General, commanding

The captured Confederates were marched from Gladeville, Virginia toward Pikeville, Kentucky. Word of the capture quickly spread throughout Wise County and a man named Delano Bowling decided to gather a group of fourteen local men armed with flintlock rifles to ambush the Union troops and free the Confederate prisoners, in particular his nephew, Jessie Bowling. Scouts were sent out to monitor their movement and the procession was sighted; the Southern soldiers on foot, bound with a rope, walking in front of the Union troops on horseback. At the rear of the procession four mules were pulling a large Union supply wagon.

By nightfall, the party had reached Indian Creek near its confluence with Virginia's Pound River where they set up camp. On Indian Creek, the mountain laurel grew thick up to the edges of the road; and the one prisoner the Yankees most wanted to contain, "Bad" John Wright from Company G, watched for his chance and silently stepped out of line into the laurel and escaped. The prisoners were under heavy guard and no opportunity arose during the night for Bowling's team to free them. Bowling's men chose to move three miles closer to the Kentucky line at Horse Gap where they waited on a high bluff throughout the night.

The next morning, July 8, 1863, the Confederates were awakened to resume their march in front of the Union troops with Bowling's party waiting for them to reach Horse Gap. Bowling had given his men the order to fire after he did. He told them to shoot behind the prisoners. When the Union soldiers were spotted coming around a sharp curve marching up a steep hill, Bowling opened fire. Immediately, the prisoners heard thirteen other rifle shots ring out as two mules with the supply wagon were killed. A black man with the supply wagon and a Union soldier were killed and two other Union soldiers were seriously wounded, retreating into the brush.

The Yankees quickly jumped out of the road and took cover in the woods, returning heavy fire in the area of the bluff where Bowling's men were reloading. With bullets splitting timber and rocks all around them, four of Bowling's group were wounded from musket fire.

Bowling wisely retreated to a spot where the men could treat their wounds and still be able to view the soldiers. However, they were unable to mount another attack because the Union soldiers were now using the Confederate prisoners as human shields. The Union troops replaced the dead mules with a couple of saddle horses to help pull the supply wagon. They hauled the two dead bodies with them and moved the Confederate prisoners to the rear of the wagon.

The march of the prisoners continued up the steep mountain over the Fincastle Trail that many of the Confederates knew well, through Pound Gap and down the mountain into Letcher County, Kentucky. Just on the Kentucky side of the gap, the march halted, and a camp was set up. Plans were made to spend a second night near Pickett's Rock. The Union soldiers rapidly constructed a pen about ten feet high to enclose the Confederate prisoners for the night.

Guards were placed around the pen to keep prisoners from escaping. Shortly after dark a bugle sounded and the command to fall in was heard. A report had arrived at the camp that a regiment of Confederate troops was on the way from Saltville, Virginia in an attempt to overtake the Union forces. The prisoners were awakened and instructed by the northern troops to mount horses. The camp was abandoned, and the Union troops walked alongside the horses to prevent the prisoners from escaping. The following morning, July 9, 1863, brought a change in strategy with the daylight. Colonel Caudill and the prisoners were instructed to get off the horses and walk beside them while the Union soldiers rode. The procession reached Pikeville, Kentucky, and continued its slow march north. From Pikeville they walked to Prestonsburg. Here they made camp for three days and nights under heavy guard awaiting the arrival of a large flatboat on the Big Sandy River.

Private William Collins, among the prisoners, said, "We had no shelter and were compelled to sleep on the ground, without blankets. From this place we were taken on a flatboat to Catlettsburg, Kentucky. From this point we were taken by steamboat to Cincinnati".

It took nine days to reach Cincinnati from Gladeville, Virginia. The Confederate prisoners were forced to make the journey by walking, horseback, flatboat and finally steamboat. They were marched down the steamboat plank at the docks in Cincinnati, on the Ohio River, on July 18, 1863. The Confederates were taken from the river port to Kemper Barracks and imprisoned for the night.

The capture of Colonel Caudill and his men sent a sobering ripple of fear through the Confederate command of Virginia. The vulnerable salt works at Saltville were ultimately, if belatedly, reinforced. Colonel Caudill and his compatriots would spend several months, even years, in prisoner-of-war camps in the North, awaiting parole or exchange. The colonel and some of his men were eventually exchanged before the war ended, but others were not so lucky. Dozens of these "Caudill's Army" men would die in Camp Douglas and other camps.

As a result of this raid, General Preston would ultimately request that southwestern Virginia be transferred out of the Army of Tennessee, since "I feel assured that it would be more rapid, simple and efficient than to defend the district and transact the business through Chattanooga." The area was then designated the Department of Southwestern Virginia (later it was renamed the Department of Southwestern Virginia and East Tennessee). This incident involving Caudill's Army was recognized as one of the first indicators that the Confederacy would have serious trouble protecting southwest Virginia from Union invasion from Kentucky. Unfortunately, the men of the 10th Kentucky Mounted Rifles would have to pay the price for this wake-up call.

Brigade Commander Henry L. Giltner stated to General John S. Williams on August 25, 1863 that Major Chenoweth was in command of the 10th (13th) at Whitesburg, which was down to about 133 men as of August 23, 1863. Chenoweth's command, along with Prentice and Fields' Partisan Rangers were ordered to Castlewood, Virginia on August 25, 1863.

With the withdrawal of Major Brown and his Union troops, the men of both Caudill's Army and the 7th Confederate Cavalry began to regroup. Surprisingly, enough men from both regiments had escaped to form a viable fighting force. With Colonel Caudill now a prisoner, Major Thomas Chenoweth was placed in command of the 10th Kentucky Mounted Rifles. The major was a native Kentuckian from Mason County. General Samuel Jones ordered the major and his men to continue their patrolling of southwestern Virginia. Their headquarters were now at Abingdon, Virginia.

On August 25, 1863, Colonel Giltner of the 4th Kentucky Cavalry informed General Williams of the distribution of his troops. The 501-strong 4th Kentucky Cavalry was at Lebanon in Russell County, Virginia. Prentice's command, meanwhile, was near Pound Gap and was composed of about 200 men. Prentice was joined at the Gap by Captain Fields' Kentucky Partisan Ranger Company with 76 men. Captain Davidson's Lynchburg Artillery was near Abdingdon with 91 men. Major Chenoweth of the 10th Kentucky Mounted Rifles was at Whitesburg, in Letcher County, Kentucky with 133 men. Giltner ordered Chenoweth, Fields and Prentice to fall back. Chenoweth and Fields complied. Prentice did not.

By late summer, General John S. Williams was assigned to command the small army in southwestern Virginia. The men of the 10th Kentucky Mounted Rifles were glad to have him in command; many of them had fought for the general while serving in the 5th Kentucky Infantry. The general formed his army into two brigades. The First Brigade was commanded by Colonel Henry Giltner and consisted of the 4th Kentucky Cavalry, 10th Kentucky Cavalry, and the 10th Kentucky Mounted Rifles. The Second Brigade was commanded by Colonel James E. Carter and consisted of the 1st Tennessee Cavalry, 16th Georgia Cavalry and the 21st Virginia Cavalry. The artillery consisted of two mountain howitzers, two parrot guns and four William's guns. This force had a combined strength of approximately seventeen hundred men, all seasoned veterans.

In late September, General Williams received orders to move his army into East Tennessee. Confederate officials hoped that Williams and his men could relieve some of the pressure being placed on the Confederate army in Knoxville by General Ambrose Burnside and his large Union army. The men of the 10th Kentucky Mounted Rifles would soon be very far from their Kentucky homes.

The first week of October found General Williams and his men at Blue Springs, near Mosheim, a small town in Green County, Tennessee. It is located in the Nolichucky River Valley, just north of Greenville, Tennessee. The East Tennessee and Virginia Railroad and the old Knoxville Road ran through this area. This portion of East Tennessee supplied many soldiers for the Union Army.

The plan worked; General Burnside decided to move approximately 5,000 of his men toward this new threat. In addition, he sent 2,500 cavalrymen under the command of Colonel John W. Foster in a sweeping movement that was intended to flank Williams' Confederate army. On October 4, 1863, Burnside's scouts encountered Williams' pickets that were posted outside of the main Confederate camp.

The following morning, Burnside ordered the 2nd Tennessee Infantry to attack. Crossing the large fields, the Tennesseans easily pushed the Confederate pickets back. Colonel Giltner led a charge of the First Brigade across the field and drove the Union soldiers back. Just as the Yankees were on the verge of being routed, the Union artillery opened up, stopping the hard-charging Rebels. The 10th Kentucky Mounted Rifles and the rest of the First Brigade had to pull back to their original defensive positions. For the remainder of the day, both armies were content with holding their positions and firing at each other. Around 4 P.M., the Union army pulled back toward their main camp, ending the day's fighting. General Williams had his men fall back to the ridge that ran between the railroad and the road. Here, he ordered them to construct breastworks overlooking the fields below. Holding the high ground now gave the smaller Confederate army an advantage.

The following day, a Yankee squad approached the Confederates under a flag of truce. Union commanders requested permission to enter the field of the previous day's skirmish and retrieve their dead and wounded. General Williams granted his permission, allowing another day to pass without fighting. Unbeknownst to the Confederate general, the Union commander was using the time to allow the remainder of the main Union army to arrive on the scene, which now greatly outnumbered the Rebels. It was also allowing time for Colonel John Foster to bring his Union cavalry around to the flanks of the dug-in Confederates. On October 9th, the remainder of Burnside's infantry arrived. He immediately ordered the large army to march and drill in front of the band of Rebels. With drums and bugles playing the massive army marched back and forth across the large field. General Burnside believed that after seeing they were outnumbered, the Confederates would retreat. But he underestimated the Rebel's resolve; they continued to hold their position.

The Battle of Blue Springs
October 10, 1863
(Map on Page 84)

As dawn began to lighten the early Saturday morning sky, General Williams began to position his men for the attack that was sure to come. Knowing that Burnside would try to flank the much smaller Rebel army, Williams tried to minimize the problem by spreading his men thinly along the breastworks. Colonel Giltner and the First Brigade occupied the left side of the line, while Colonel Carter and the Second Brigade occupied the right. Lieutenant Lloyd and his two mountain howitzers were positioned on the right of the road, while Lieutenant Graham and his two parrot guns were on the left. Captain Schoolfield and his four Williams guns were stationed in the center of the breastworks. The 10th Kentucky Mounted Rifles, under Brigade commander Colonel Henry Giltner, spent the remainder of the morning strengthening their position on the left. Their partial brigade also included Diamond's 10th KY Cavalry and the 4th KY Cavalry bringing their total strength to around nine hundred.

General Burnside was confident that his larger army would easily push the Confederates out and took his time lining up for battle. At 10 A.M., the Union general finally gave the order for the attack to begin, two and a half miles from Blue Springs, Tennessee. Both artilleries opened up on each other; and, though outgunned, the smaller Confederate force, with a total strength of around 1,700, held the advantage of the high ground. With much fanfare, the Union army began to march across the open fields toward the Confederates. The entrenched Rebels waited until they were in gunshot range before opening fire. The withering fire stalled the Union line, and eventually caused it to fall back, just out of range. At this time, the 34th Virginia Cavalry, under the command of Colonel Vincent Witcher, arrived on the scene. Though outnumbered, the determined cavalrymen charged past the breastworks and managed to push the Yankee line back. General Burnside had to send in reinforcements to stop the attack, pushing Witcher's men back to the Confederate line of defense.

Massing more troops in the center, Burnside ordered his men to attack again. The much larger Union army began to realize that they were on the verge of routing the Rebels; but, instead of capitalizing on their success, the Union officers stopped to line their men up for a final push. This overconfidence allowed the Rebels to reinforce the center; and also allowed Schoolfield and his Williams guns time to cover the area. As the long line of Union soldiers crossed between the rifles and the Williams guns, they came under a terrific volley of firing, including grape and canister. This unexpected turn of events demoralized the Union line, and they began to retreat, in panic. The evening sun was beginning to set; therefore, Burnside decided not to attempt another attack. Knowing that Colonel Foster should soon be on the Confederates' flanks, possibly as early as the next morning, he ordered his army back to camp. Though neither side realized it at the moment, with neither claiming a real advantage, the Battle of Blue Springs was over by nightfall. Confederate Adjutant E. O. Guerrant estimated that between seventy-five and a hundred Confederates were either killed, wounded, or missing.

While General Williams was back in Greenville telegraphing his commanders, Colonel Giltner received word from Confederate scouts that a large Union cavalry force was in the area. After conferring with his officers, the colonel decided to retreat, back in the direction of Bristol. Leaving a rear guard to burn fires to keep the Union from knowing their plans, the Confederates retreated to Greenville, marching alongside their many wagons, all night. There, the small army was delighted to see General Alfred Jackson and approximately five hundred soldiers; ready to join forces with them. General Williams took back command and ordered the army to march toward Henderson's Mill, several miles away. Jackson's troops took the lead, with the Second Brigade behind them, and the First Brigade assigned the rear guard. Quietly, the long gray column moved out of Greenville. The 10th Kentucky Mounted Rifles had survived a terrible fight.

The Battle of Henderson's Mill
Early Sunday Morning
October 11, 1863

Unfortunately for General Williams' Confederates, Colonel John Foster and his twenty-five hundred Union cavalrymen had managed to maneuver themselves in front of them. Foster and his men had raided Bristol and burned a portion of Blountville. While in this area, a courier from General Burnside arrived, informing Foster that he was to march toward Greenville in hopes of attacking the Confederate flank. By nightfall of October 10, Foster and his men arrived near Henderson's Mill and went into camp, expecting to move on to Greenville the next day.

Just as dawn was beginning to brighten the morning of October 11, the forward elements of Williams' army collided with the pickets of Foster's Union cavalry, hidden in the heavy timber along the Jonesboro Road. General Jackson and his men charged the woods, believing that they were being fired upon by bushwhackers. But, at the sound of Union cannon, they realized that they faced the Union army. Williams' artillery immediately began to return fire into the misty woods, creating more fog and restricting the visibility for Caudill's Army. General Williams and his mounted soldiers raced to join General Jackson in their charge of the enemy. This charge took Foster and his men by surprise; the combination of the early morning fog and the gray-clad Rebels, charging wildly out of it toward them, was more than the Union soldiers could stand, and they began to retreat. A running fight had begun.

Colonel Foster and his officers managed to regroup their men, only to have the hard-charging Rebels force them to retreat again. This scenario repeated itself several times for almost three miles along the road toward Kingsport. Near a road intersection, General Williams decided to stop his men, while Foster's men fled toward Kingsport. Though it was only 8 A.M., the running battle that had started near Henderson's Mill was over. Williams' men began to regroup, with each man trying to locate his own regiment. Major Chenoweth managed to gather the men of the 10th Kentucky Mounted Rifles and fell back to be the rear guard as General Williams ordered the army to continue toward Bristol. Their path led them toward Rheatown, a small town east of Henderson's Mill. No doubt, the men and horses were exhausted as they had enjoyed neither rest nor hot food since the morning before. The Confederate army arrived at Rheatown around 9:30 A.M. Not being as exhausted as the cavalrymen, General Jackson, and his men, along with Lloyd and Graham's artillery, moved on through the town without stopping. The First and Second Brigades were ordered to stop in town and go into camp to rest.

The Battle of Rheatown
Mid-Sunday Morning
October 11, 1863

While dismounting and going into camp, General Williams and his men were unaware that General Shackleford and his Union army had managed to approach the town and were concealed in the nearby woods. At the sound of the Union artillery opening up, the Yankee soldiers fired into the Second Brigade; the closest Rebels to them. It was now the Confederate's turn to retreat; the Second Brigade raced back through the First Brigade's camp. Colonel Carter managed to rally about three hundred of his men to confront the charging Yanks. This gave Colonel Giltner time to align his men on the left of Carter's. In addition, Schoolfield's battery of Williams guns began to fire canister at the attacking enemy. This stemmed the flow of Yankees and both sides began to exchange fire from their respective positions. A large contingent of Union soldiers bravely charged into the center of the Confederate's defensive line, allowing more Yanks to move toward flanking the Rebels. This gave the Confederates no choice but to run for their lives and survival. Colonels Giltner and Carter managed to keep the men from fleeing in a panic, forming an orderly retreat.

Continuing on the road toward Bristol, the Confederate cavalry caught up with General Jackson's men and the remainder of the artillery. Scouts informed the beleaguered Rebels that a hill that was about two and a half miles away would make a good defensive position. The name of the hill was Pugh's Hill.

The Battle of Pugh's Hill
Sunday Afternoon
October 11, 1863

General Jackson and his infantry, along with Lloyd and Graham's Batteries, passed the hill and continued their retreat. The mounted soldiers and Schoolfield's Battery climbed to the top of Pugh's Hill and began to construct breastworks. The First Brigade dug in on the right side of the ridge, while the Second Brigade took positions on the left. Schoolfield and his small band of guns were placed in a position that had a commanding view of the fields below. As the battle began, General Williams collapsed to the ground from complete exhaustion. Colonel Giltner was now in charge.

The fight began with a duel between the opposing artillery. One exploding shell landed close to one of Schoolfield's guns, killing several men and horses. The Union army then marched out of the woods and began crossing the field. The long columns of blue-clad soldiers charged toward the hill. For several minutes, the Confederates managed to keep the Yanks from climbing the hill. But soon, the greatly outnumbered Rebels could not hold back the swarming flood of Union soldiers. The Second Brigade began to retreat as the Union soldiers neared the crest of the hill. With the Second Brigade now gone, it left only the 4th Kentucky Cavalry, the 10th Kentucky Cavalry, the 10th Kentucky Mounted Rifles and the 34th Virginia Cavalry to hold the hill. Just when the 4th Kentucky was about to be overrun, a remarkable feat of bravery was performed. The 34th Virginia stormed out of their position and charged downhill at the approaching Yanks. Caught up in the moment, the three remaining regiments also joined in the seemingly senseless charge. The Union Infantry was completely caught off guard and retreated in the face of the onslaught of "crazy" men screaming toward them. Having temporarily stopped the Union attack, Giltner and his officers ordered his men to fall back to their horses and retreat. Schoolfield and his brave battery stayed in place long enough to fire a broadside of grape and cannister into the Yankee lines. This afforded Giltner's men the time needed to find their horses. Giltner allowed Schoofield and his battery to speed past them before allowing his men to retreat.

General Williams' small army continued their retreat toward Jonesboro, Tennessee in an orderly fashion. During the retreat, the 10th Kentucky Mounted Rifles, acting as rear guard, skirmished with Union cavalry. The main Union army was satisfied with stopping on Pugh's Hill to rest, giving the Confederates time to move away. As the evening sun was about to set, the exhausted army marched into Jonesboro. The bone-weary soldiers dropped from their horses without being ordered to do so. The longest two days of these soldiers' lives had finally ended. In two days, they had fought in four battles and marched thirty-five miles, without the benefit of food or rest. Though badly outnumbered, they had managed to bloody the Union Army that had tried to destroy them. However, they were still not out of danger, as the Union Army was still in striking distance of them. On October 13, the 10th Kentucky Mounted Rifles and the remainder of Williams' army began their march for Blountville, Tennessee.

The Battle of Blountville
October 14, 1863

General Williams' army arrived at Blountville on Wednesday, October 14, to a welcome sight. The long-awaited reinforcements that the general had requested had finally arrived. These included the 51st Virginia Infantry, 30th Virginia Sharpshooters and two more batteries of artillery. The battle-weary troop's elation did not last long as scouts raced in with information that a large regiment of Union soldiers was approaching. Even with the reinforcements, they were still outnumbered.

Williams gave orders to prepare for the upcoming fight. General Jackson and his men were ordered to construct breastworks on the left wing while General Wharton and the new reinforcements moved to the center of the defensive line. General William Jones took command of the First and Second Brigades and began to prepare the right wing breastworks. Each of the artillery batteries unlimbered and set up on the small hills in the rear. The small Confederate army was ready for the attack.

General Shackleford formed his Union troops in line of battle, ordering them to fix bayonets. The long line of blue-clad soldiers began to march across the open fields while both Confederate and Union batteries of artillery opened up, shaking the ground. Though outnumbered, the well-entrenched Rebels held their ground, forcing the Yanks to pull back. After reforming, the long, blue line started across the field of battle again. This time, Shackleford sent a large number of troops around the Confederates to attack their flanks. General Williams saw what was happening but did not have any reserves to send to meet this new threat, as he barely had enough men to meet the frontal attack. Reluctantly, the general ordered his men to retreat. This retreat was done in an orderly fashion, allowing the outnumbered Rebels to fall back toward the small town of Zollicoffer. Once again, Williams' army, including the 10th Kentucky Mounted Rifles, was able to escape.

Early on Thursday morning, October 15, Williams and his men passed through Bristol. Later that day, the army marched into Abingdon, Virginia. Having received more reinforcements, General Williams decided to make a stand here. The small hills in the area made a strong defensive position. Breastworks were built along the hills as the Confederates prepared for a last stand. Colonel Giltner and the First Brigade were placed in front of the defensive line and were expected to slow down the Union advance. General Shackleford was an experienced officer and could see that the defensive line was very strong. He ordered his men to form a battle line back in the woods, just out of rifle range. The artillery was then brought up and opened fire on the Rebel defensive line. Upon seeing that the threat of artillery was not going to dislodge the Confederates, Shackleford pulled his men back and went into camp. This would give him time to study the situation. For the next two days, both armies were content with preparing defensive positions and warily watching one another. The only action was skirmishing between pickets, as each army probed the others defense. On Saturday, October 17, General Shackleford received orders to fall back toward Knoxville. As the Union army began to fall back, both sides breathed a sigh of relief.

General Williams and his men would spend the remainder of October in the Abingdon and Blountville areas. Other than minor skirmishing, no major fighting took place in the area during the remainder of October. For the men of the 10th Kentucky Mounted Rifles and the rest of the Army of Southwestern Virginia, the end of the month had not come soon enough. Though forced to retreat from eastern Tennessee, they could feel some satisfaction in having fought the much larger Union army to a standstill. And, they had managed to avoid being destroyed as a viable fighting force.

By November of 1863, Company K of the 13th Kentucky Cavalry (10th Kentucky Mounted Rifles) was detached to Colonel Slemp's 64th Virginia Infantry, operating in Lee County, Virginia. On November 12, 1863, eight of the Company K soldiers; Andrew Angel, Harrison Barrett, Chadwell Brittain, Wickliffe Crawford, Alfred Evans, George B. Lyttle, Andrew J. McKee, and Jacob McKee were captured in the Cumberland Gap area of Lee County, a little less than tree months after they had enlisted.

Both Field's Kentucky Partisan Rangers and Chenoweth's 10th Kentucky Mounted Rifles were present with Williams' Brigade at Blountville, Tennessee on October 31, 1863. Fields was still in camp on November 3rd. His company was issued clothing by the brigade quartermaster on November 13th at "Hix Crossroads, probably in Tennessee. Chenoweth however, had marched to Wise County, Virginia, where he defeated Alf Killen's Unionists at the Crane's Nest on November 9, 1863; and then wento into camp at "Wise Court House" (per Abingdon Virginian, November 20, 1863). On November 21st, Chenoweth was in Abingdon. His adjutant and quartermaster were issuied forae in Abgindon on December 6th, Chenoweth requested salt in Abingdon on December 31st and the battalion was mustered in while camped in Lee County, Virginia on December 31st.

(From "Pioneers of Dickenson County" …as told to E. J. Sutherland by Henry Keel at Clintwood on May 25th, 1922): "While there were several persons killed in the county (then part of Wise County) in several small skirmishes or bushwhacking engagements, there was only one real fight in the county."
"In November 1863, about 200 Confederates, under Major Chenoweth, were camped on Cranesnest River, just opposite the present home of Allen Powers. Captain Alf Killen, a Unionist, collected about forty Union sympathizers in Wise County, with the intention of surprising the Rebel encampment; but they were the ones that got surprised. Major Chenoweth got news that the Yankees were on the way and when they made the attack at daylight, they found the Rebels awake and ready for them. Sam Caldwell took a detachment of Confederates to a nearby gap through which it was certain the Yankees would retreat, but found, on arriving there, that the enempy had passed through not over five minutes before. In this skirmish the Rebels suffered only one casualty, a Wright from Kentucky was wounded. The Federals lost nine killed."

Captain Peter Everette's Raid into Kentucky
November and December of 1863

At the conclusion of the East Tennessee Campaign, Major Chenoweth and the 10th Kentucky Mounted Rifles were stationed with the rest of Giltner's Brigade in Abingdon. From this location, they could rush to defend the salt works at Saltville or the lead works at Wytheville. They could also defend against a Union invasion from East Tennessee or West Virginia.

General Samuel Jones was now the commander of the district that included the Department of Southwestern Virginia and made his headquarters at Abingdon. On October 25, he ordered Colonel Giltner to take his brigade to Moccasin Gap, near the Virginia and Tennessee border. When the column rode out, Major Chenoweth and the 10th Kentucky Mounted Rifles led the way. Many of the men of the 10th knew about Moccasin Gap as they had been stationed there during their time with the 5th Kentucky Infantry. Several of their comrades were buried by the hospital in Holston Springs. On October 27, Giltner received orders to move to Blountville, Tennessee.

While stationed there, General Jones received word that General Stephen Burbridge was massing troops in southeastern Kentucky for an invasion of Virginia. He sent word for Colonel Giltner to send a regiment to that area to check out the rumor. The colonel chose the 10th Kentucky Mounted Rifles. By the first week of November, Major Chenoweth and the 10th Kentucky were in Castlewood, Virginia. Scouting into Kentucky, they soon discovered that the report was just a rumor.

While the major and his men were scouting in southwestern Virginia, a daring plan that would include them was being devised back in Abingdon. The plan to conduct a raid into the Bluegrass section of Kentucky was the brainchild of Captain Peter Everette, commander of the 1st Battalion Kentucky Rifles. Captain Everette was well known for his daring and successful raids into enemy-held territory. The captain presented the plan to General Robert Ransom, the newly appointed commander of the Department of Southwestern Virginia. The general saw merit in the plan and sent Everette to see General Samuel Jones. When the general met Everette, he liked the plan; the thought of a raid tying up Union forces in Kentucky could possibly delay any Yankee plans for an invasion of Virginia. The general gave his consent; on the condition that only a small force would be used. The captain chose his regiment, the 1st Battalion Kentucky Rifles, the 10th Kentucky Mounted Rifles and the 7th Confederate Cavalry to go on the raid. Major Chenoweth wanted to accompany his men as well; but he had to agree to allow Everette to be in command.

On November 21st, the raiding party rode out of Castlewood, carrying as much provisions as they could without using pack animals. They crossed into Letcher County, Kentucky, through Pound Gap on November 23rd. While in Letcher County, the party replenished their provisions. Many of the men of the 10th Kentucky Mounted Rifles were from this area and took advantage of the return home. Now rested, the party returned to the Pound Gap-Mt. Sterling Road and continued their journey toward central Kentucky.

On November 30th, some of Captain Everette's scouts informed him that at least two companies of Yankee cavalry were at Salyersville, a small town in Magoffin County, along the road that the raiders were traveling. Conferring with the other officers, Everette decided to attack the Yanks. He divided his men into two groups, surrounding the town. At the sound of his pistol, the Rebel raiders charged into town. (During this fight, Captain Everette noticed that the men of the 10th Kentucky Mounted Rifles' version of the "Rebel Yell" sounded like they were saying "yahoo"; so, from then on, the captain referred to them as the "Yahoos".) The Union cavalrymen were taken by surprise; but, managed to put up a limited defense. After several minutes of lively gunfire exchange, the Yanks who could reach their horses did so, and raced out of town. At least thirty surrendered, and several were killed. With no way to manage prisoners, Captain Everette paroled them all.

The Confederate raiders stayed in Salyersville long enough to eat some of the Yankee's provisions; and, to restock their haversacks. Worn-down or broken-down horses were replaced with captured Union horses. The captain knew that the Yankee soldiers who had escaped would immediately report the attack to their commanders. In order for their original plan to be successful, the raiders would have to travel the sixty miles from Salyersville to Mt. Sterling before the garrison there could be alerted. To accomplish this, the men rode hard all day on December 1st, arriving outside Mt. Sterling around midnight. Scouts reported that Union soldiers of the 40th Kentucky Mounted Infantry, approximately 540 men, were encamped on the Ticktown Road just outside Mt. Sterling. Also, several companies of Yanks were in the town, many of them occupying the courthouse.

Everette knew that he would have to keep the 40th Kentucky out of the fight in town if he was to succeed in capturing the Union commissary. He selected Lieutenant Isaac Coffin, who was a local, to lead the 10th Kentucky Mounted Rifles (approximately one hundred and twenty-five men) to get in position to attack and block the 40th Kentucky. Their objective would be to keep the Union cavalry from entering the town, preventing the reinforcement of the garrison stationed there, a daunting task. The remainder of the raiders would storm into town and surround the courthouse. The crack of the captain's pistol was the signal for the attack to begin.

At approximately 2 A.M. on December 2nd, Captain Everette fired his pistol. The men assigned to take the courthouse quickly raced into position, firing into the government building. The awakened Yanks in the building began to fire blindly into the streets, hoping to stop the onslaught of Rebel fire.

Meanwhile, Lieutenant Coffin and the 10th Kentucky Mounted Rifles began pouring a murderous fire into the camp of the 40th Kentucky. Many of the terrified Union soldiers scrambled away from the gunfire, while others attempted to rally to their officer's pleas. A combination of the yelling and firing from the Rebel raiders confused the Yanks, creating the illusion that they were being attacked by a superior force. Whatever troops remaining in the camp were content with forming a defensive line and were not interested in entering the town to investigate the shooting heard there. This part of the plan was working well.

But the fighting at the courthouse had become a stalemate. The Yankee defenders refused to surrender, and the Rebel raiders could not storm the building without enduring great loss of life. Rather than take a chance on losing any of his men, Captain Everette decided to set the courthouse afire. When torches began to fly through the air and land on the courthouse, the Union soldiers immediately asked to be allowed to surrender. Everette gave orders for his men to accept the offer.

With the town completely under Confederate control, the raiders broke into the commissary building. To their delight, they discovered it to be full of provisions, ammunition and artillery shells. Officers immediately had the men load as many of the provisions and ammunition that the extra horses could pack. And this was a substantial amount; there had been more than two hundred horses confiscated from the Union corral. Due to the large number of artillery shells in the building, the raiders could not safely burn the building to destroy those they couldn't carry. Regrettably, they would have to leave the building intact, along with its contents.

Captain Everette knew that, sooner or later, the 40th Kentucky would realize that the invading force was relatively small; and then, they would attack. He therefore sent couriers to order Lieutenant Coffin to return with the 10th Kentucky Mounted Rifles. A few men would stay behind to keep the Union soldiers at bay. At 4 A.M. In the morning, two hours after the attack began the column of gray-clad soldiers rode out of Mt. Sterling.

The raiders made good time along the road and soon arrived at Hazel Green, stopping to discuss the situation. Everette and his fellow officers were confident that Union officials in eastern Kentucky were now aware of the raiders' presence. Expecting to be ambushed along the Mt. Sterling-Pound Gap Road, they decided to turn off the road and take a different route back to Virginia. The raiders began to travel along the Rebel Trace, the rugged road through the Kentucky River Valley. This road would be much tougher to travel but the chance of encountering Union cavalry would be slim.

On December 4th, scouts reported to the captain that a Union garrison of approximately one hundred soldiers had fortified the town of Jackson in Breathitt County. After a quick conference among the officers, it was decided to attack the town. Several men were chosen to watch over the captured horses and provisions while the remainder attacked the town.

The plan was the same as used at Salyersville; divide into two columns, surround the town, and charge at the signal. Staying in the woods to avoid detection, the columns soon had the town surrounded. At the crack of the captain's pistol, the men yelled and charged into town, catching the Yanks by surprise. The garrison was overrun before they knew what was happening. Most threw up their arms and surrendered; but, several tried to fight back. The outnumbered Union soldiers fired several feeble volleys before being overwhelmed, forcing them to surrender. The fight had lasted only minutes, sparing both sides any major casualties.

After gathering the prisoners into a large group, Confederate officers began to write out their paroles. Everette and the other officers were afraid that it would be difficult to transport them back to Virginia. Checking the town for provisions and contraband, soldiers soon found a herd of two hundred hogs, meant to be used by the Union Army. Knowing they could not transport the hogs back to Virginia, Captain Everette ordered them to be killed. Any meat that could not be carried away by the soldiers was given to local citizens, who had also been suffering from a shortage of food.

When the captured horses and provisions were brought into town, the captain ordered the column to continue their march. Before leaving Jackson, he allowed his men to set fire to the Union fortifications and structures. With smoke billowing in the background, the raiders began traveling southeast toward the relative safety of Virginia.

Two days later, the hard-riding cavalrymen entered Letcher County. The weary soldiers of the 10th Kentucky Mounted Rifles felt much safer, being back in familiar territory. When the column reached the old campground of the 5th Kentucky Infantry at the confluence of Colley Creek and Rockhouse Creek, the men of the 10th Kentucky asked Major Chenoweth to obtain permission for them to stay for a while and visit their families. When Chenoweth asked Captain Everette about the request, the captain consented, but decided to continue to Virginia with the other two regiments, taking the horses with them. The captain did allow his men to stop for a short time in Whitesburg. The raid for the men of the 10th Kentucky Mounted Rifles was officially over.

The raid had been very successful; all of the raiders were now well-mounted with captured Union horses. And, they had captured many much-needed provisions and supplies.

Finally, they had alerted Union officials, causing them to deploy their troops throughout the area, in hopes of discouraging another raid. This delayed any Union plans of an invasion of Virginia through Pound Gap. Probably one of the most beneficial effects of the raid was the restoring hope in the residents of Kentucky that the southern army had not given up on them.

The 10th Kentucky Mounted Rifles could not stay long in Letcher County. General William "Grumble" Jones was now commander of the Department of Southwestern Virginia. The general sent orders for Major Chenoweth and his men to report back to Virginia. Back in Virginia, the 10th Kentucky began scouting again, in all areas of southeastern Kentucky, southwestern Virginia and northeastern Tennessee. In late December of 1863, Captain David J. Caudill was ordered to take one hundred men of the 10th Kentucky Mounted Rifles and reinforce Colonel Pridemore and the 64th Virginia Infantry at Jonesville in Lee County, Virginia.

1864

Battle of Jonesville
January 3, 1864
(Map on Page 85)

Jonesville is a small town located in the Powell Valley in Lee County, Virginia. The valley is known for its fertile and productive fields. Unfortunately for the farmers in the area, both Confederate and Union officials were well aware of that fact. Both would forage in the area to maintain the survival of their soldiers. The Union had a stronghold on Cumberland Gap and Tazewell, Tennessee, not far to the west of Jonesville. The nearest Confederate stronghold was at Rogersville, Tennessee, not many miles south. In addition, all local roads intersected in the area of Jonesville, much like the hub of a wheel.

The Union commander of the region was Colonel W. C. Lemert, with headquarters in Tazewell. His next-in-command was Major Charles Beeres, who usually stayed in the Cumberland Gap area. The major was considered by the local citizens as being a supporter of total warfare, much like General Sherman. His troops burnt the courthouse in Jonesville for no apparent reason. He later allowed his men to burn the Franklin Academy on the pretense that it was a Confederate hospital. Most of the residents of the Powell River Valley despised and feared him. Confederates in the area hoped to catch him on a foraging party and exact revenge upon him. They soon got their wish when the major left Cumberland Gap with the 16th Illinois Cavalry and 22nd Ohio Battery, a force of approximately four hundred and fifty men, under orders to attack the small garrison of Confederates at Jonesville.

General William Jones, at his headquarters in Rogersville, received a courier on December 31st from Colonel Auburn Pridemore of the 64th Virginia Infantry informing him of Beeres' plan to attack Jonesville. The general immediately ordered the 8th, 21st, 27th and 37th Virginia Battalions to move from Rogersville to support Pridemore at Jonesville. On a bitterly cold day on the 31st of December, the Confederates began their march to help. The 64th Virginia had recently been reinforced with Captain Caudill and one hundred of the 10th Kentucky Mounted Rifles. Though it was bitter cold, Pridemore ordered his small army to construct breastworks to face the expected invasion. The colonel knew that General Jones was coming to his aid, and he hoped to trap the Yankees between them.

Major Beeres knew that there was a small garrison of Rebel soldiers facing him in Jonesville but was unaware of the advance of General Jones. On the bitterly cold morning of January 3, 1864, Beeres ordered the artillery to set up on the hill just west of town near the Harlan Road. The Illinois cavalry were formed in line of battle in front of Pridemore and his men. After a few volleys of cannon fire, the Union soldiers advanced on Pridemore's position. Major James Richmond commanded the 64th Virginia on the right side, while Captain David Caudill led the 10th Kentucky on the left. After several ragged volleys of gunfire, the Confederates were ordered to charge the Yankees. With a resounding Rebel yell, both regiments surged forward, pushing the surprised Union soldiers back. Amazingly, the outnumbered Confederates pushed the Yanks back so quickly, that they overran and captured the Union artillery.

At this point in the battle, Major Beeres managed to stop his retreating troops and got them back under control. His counterattack was successful, as they recaptured their artillery pieces. Pridemore and his officers stopped their retreating soldiers and managed to, once again, stop the advancing Yanks. At this time, General Jones and his men arrived on the flanks of the Union army. Seeing that he was trapped between the two armies, Major Beeres tried to escape on the Harlan Road towards Kentucky. Unfortunately for him, Colonel Pridemore had anticipated this movement and ordered some of his men to move quickly and cut off the escaping Yanks. Now surrounded, the major had no choice but to raise a white flag.

The casualties of this frigid fight were high for Major Beeres and his men; approximately three hundred and fifty men were captured, including forty-eight wounded and at least twelve killed. The Confederates had twelve wounded and at least four killed. Both armies also reported losing men to the extreme cold; some suffering from frost bite and others freezing to death.

From "War of Rebellion":

Lt. Col. Auburn L. Pridemore, 64th Virginia Cavalry

To: Captain Martin, Assistant Adjutant General

"On the morning of January 3, 1864, I received an order from Brig. General W. E. Jones to press the enemy on the north of the road east of Jonesville. I drew up in line, dismounted, took possession of the hill east of town and opened fire. In ten minutes, we had possession of the town. I received an order to attack the enemy – now driven by force below – from Milburn's – to a position on a high hill west of twon in a line perpendicular to the valley road. Just as my line of attack was formed, Capt. Caudill (D. J.) with 100 men of the 10th (13th) KY came up making my whole strength about 230. Major Richmond had command of the right, Captain Caudill on the left wing. We now

commenced to advance through an old sage field under fire of their artillery. We moved to within 250 yards of the enemy's line and battery and opened a well directed fire on his front. After a few rounds, I observed that his lines might be easily flanked. I took command of the right wing leaving Major Richmond that of the left and Capt. Caudill's men. I had with me about 50 men. I soon took possession of a small ridge in the enemy's rear, having previously driven the enemy's sharpshooters off of the same ridge. Then ordered intention to unite my whole force and charge the battery, but before I could reorganize the line, the enemy surrendered – 240 in number, 3 pieces of artillery, 405 wagons, all of their arms and horses. Soldiers from all the regiments coming up who had won honors in the morning and fought with us, now and justly entitled to share with us, joined in collecting the spoils. The 64th VA and 10th (13th) KY, both officers and men, acted gallantly. Four non-commissioned officers and privates in the 10th (13th) were wounded."

The Second Battle of Jonesville
January 28 and 29, 1864
(Map on Page 86)

After the fight on January 3rd, General Jones decided to leave the 27th Virginia Cavalry with Colonel Pridemore's 64th Virginia and 10th Kentucky Mounted Rifles. The addition of these men increased the small army's number to roughly five hundred soldiers. On January 27th, Pridemore and his men were encamped at Ewing, a small community about fifteen miles west of Jonesville. Part of their mission was to observe and harass Union forces stationed at Cumberland Gap.

General Theophilus Garrard was now commander of the Union forces in the Cumberland Gap region. In order to maintain Union control in the area, he established outposts throughout the area. One of these outposts was at Mulberry Gap in Hancock County, Tennessee, about eleven miles southwest of Jonesville. The Union force stationed at Mulberry Gap was under the command of Colonel S. Palace Love and consisted of the 11th Kentucky Infantry, 27th Kentucky Infantry and the 11th Tennessee Infantry.

On the morning of January 28th, Colonel Love ordered Captain Newport to take fifty men of Company E of the 11th Tennessee and scout in the vicinity of Jonesville, in hopes of learning the location of the Confederates. Captain Newport ordered his men to draw provisions for one day and began to march toward Jonesville.

At approximately the same time, Colonel Pridemore ordered his men to break camp at Ewing and begin to move back to Jonesville. Having not encountered any Union activities, he decided to move back closer to his supply base. Colonel Pridemore and his staff were at the front of the column with the 64th Virginia leading the way. The 10th Kentucky Mounted Rifles were in the middle while the 27th Virginia acted as rearguards. Neither army knew that they would soon collide in battle.

The First Day of Battle
January 28, 1864

Captain Newport and his column began traveling in a northeast direction, soon crossing into Virginia. Shortly after entering Virginia, they crossed Wallen Ridge into the Powell River Valley. After crossing the Powell River, Newport allowed his men to dry their clothing and eat before continuing their march toward Jonesville. He was aware the cold temperature and wet clothing would make his men miserable, dulling their alertness.

Colonel Pridemore and his column traveled east up Indian Creek. At the head of Indian and Hardy Creeks, they turned south, riding down Hardy Creek into the Powell River Valley. At this time, scouts returned with information of a Union patrol in the valley traveling toward Jonesville. Pridemore immediately ordered his men to advance on the double quick toward Jonesville in an effort to intercept the Yankees.

Close to mid-afternoon, Captain Newport and his patrol were a short distance west of Jonesville. At this time, his advance guard observed a large contingency of Rebel cavalrymen advancing toward them. The guard raced back to the main column of Union soldiers and gave the alert. The captain knew he was outnumbered; therefore, he looked for a strong defensive position. Finding a strong wooden fence nearby, he had his men form a defensive line behind it. In addition, he sent back a courier asking for reinforcements.

Seeing that the Yanks had formed a strong defensive position, Colonel Pridemore ordered his men to stop and dismount. He was not sure of the number of troops facing him and decided to approach them cautiously. The gray-clad line advanced across the large field, only to be met with a withering fire. The colonel allowed his men to find cover and return fire. The outnumbered Yanks were managing to hold off the Rebels. Captain Newport knew that the Confederates would soon realize that they outnumbered the Yanks and decided to conduct an orderly withdrawal. His men began to fall back, keeping two columns, one to shoot, while the other retreated. In order to inspire his men, the captain exposed himself several times to the Confederate fire. This act of bravery worked for the first mile before tragedy struck when the captain was severely wounded. With their leader out of commission, the Yanks panicked and began to run for their lives.

Fortunately for them, they soon ran into the reinforcements that Captain Newport had requested. Colonel Love had ordered the 11th and 27th Kentucky Infantries and the remainder of the 11th Tennessee Infantry to rush to the rescue. The Federal soldiers now outnumbered their Confederate counterparts. As the evening sky began to darken, Colonel Pridemore ordered his skirmishers to probe the long Union defensive line. The night sky and bitter cold encouraged both sides to cease hostilities. The 10th Kentucky Mounted Rifles and their comrades had endured the first day of battle; but not many would sleep during the night, knowing that the enemy was so near.

The Second Day of Battle
January 29, 1864

At first light, Colonel Pridemore ordered his men to form into a battle line with the 64th Virginia in the center, the 10th Kentucky on the right and the 27th Virginia on the left. With his men in position, the colonel ordered his men to fire upon the Yankee defensive line. For the first two hours of battle, neither army seemed willing to take the initiative and attack the other. Becoming impatient, Pridemore decided to push the Yanks out of their breastworks. At approximately 10 A.M., the order to charge was given. With a determined Rebel yell, the boys in gray charged across the open field. The sight and sound of the screaming soldiers was more than the Union soldiers could stand; they began to retreat. The Union officers managed to keep the men from turning the retreat into a panic stricken one and got them to begin an orderly withdrawal. Every mile or two, the Yanks would stand their ground and fire back at the constantly advancing Rebels.

By 1:30 P.M, the boys in blue had retreated for more than five miles back toward Ewing. Having found a strong defensive position on Indian Creek, the Union officers were able to rally their men. Realizing the cost of attacking a strong defensive position, Colonel Pridemore ordered his men to construct breastworks of their own, facing the Yanks. Both armies were content to fire random volleys at each other, while they strengthened their fortifications. The second day of battle appeared to have come to a close.

During the night, Colonel Love ordered his men to construct several campfires in order to convince the Confederates that they were staying in place to do battle the next day. Leaving a few men to maintain the ruse, the colonel and his men quietly began a retreat; back to their stronghold at Wireman's Mill, which was close to reinforcements at Cumberland Gap. Before daybreak, the few remaining Union soldiers slipped away, hurrying to join their comrades.

At daybreak, Confederate skirmishers advanced on the Union breastworks, only to find the enemy gone. Wary of being tricked into an ambush, Colonel Pridemore sent a patrol to scout the Union army. The scouts returned to inform the colonel that Colonel Love and his men were back in their fortifications at Wireman's Mill. Knowing that the Yanks could easily be reinforced from Cumberland Gap, the colonel decided to return to Jonesville. The 10th Kentucky and their comrades had managed to be victorious over the Union army once more.

Captain William J. Hall's service records state that Caudill's Battalion headquarters was located in Washington County, Virginia on January 7th, 1864. On February 29th, 1864, Major Chenoweth signed a supply requisition at Rogersville Junction, which indicates that he returned to the brigade about that time.

The Battle of Chavies
May 2, 1864

For the remainder of the winter, the 10th Kentucky Mounted Rifles continued to be divided throughout the area. With provisions and forage hard to find, it was easier to supply the regiment's needs while stationed in several different locations. So, Major Chenoweth allowed one company to go to Whitesburg to camp. This would allow the men to gather supplies from a friendly area; and it would keep them apprised of any nearby Union activities. In April, the men in Letcher County knew that they would soon have to return to Virginia and began to look for reasons to prolong their stay. A reason became available when they were informed that Major John Eversole of the Union 14th Kentucky Cavalry and some of his fellow soldiers, with their enlistment time completed, had returned to their homes at Chavies, in Perry County.

Many of the 10th Kentucky knew of the major from previous fights with him; and several men were related to him and his family. Major Eversole's mother, Lucy, and Colonel Ben Caudill's mother, Rachel, were daughters of pioneer, and Revolutionary War veteran, William Jesse Cornett. Several of William's grandsons, as well as other relatives, were serving in the 10th Kentucky. In spite of, or perhaps because of this, the Confederates in Whitesburg were eager to capture the major and any other Union soldiers that might be with him.

On May 1st, 1864, the company of the 10th Kentucky Mounted Rifles rode out of Whitesburg and headed for Chavies. While on their way, word of the planned attack swiftly traveled to the major. Though he did not know when the Confederates might attack him, Major Eversole called all of the local Union soldiers that were now home to gather at his home at Chavies. His house was a large, two-storied cabin that was constructed of thick logs, making it a perfect fortress. If he was attacked, the major was confident he could defend himself.

The Rebel raiders arrived in the Krypton area, near Chavies, on Sunday evening, just as darkness filled the sky. No campfires were permitted; they hoped to keep their presence a secret, knowing that the element of surprise could be the difference between success and failure.

As the sun began to rise on May 2nd, 1864, the Rebel raiders began to creep toward the formidable cabin. When all were in position, the crack of a rifle signaled for all to begin firing. Volleys of gunfire began echoing up and down the river valley. The Union soldiers that had gathered with Major Eversole returned fire from the cabin and the barn. During the early stages of the attack, the major was mortally wounded when he exposed himself from the second floor of the cabin. In addition, his brother, Joseph, also a Union soldier, was killed when shot while going by a window. The thick logs easily absorbed the heavy lead bullets, but some did find openings and cracks.

During a lull in the fighting, the major's wife informed the Rebels of the death of her husband and brother-in-law. With their lust for revenge gratified and vengeance fulfilled, the Confederates began to pull back from the cabin. Though it was only mid-day, the fight was over. Mounting their horses, the men of the 10th Kentucky Mounted Rifles began their long ride back toward Letcher County.

The Battle of Cove Mountain
May 10, 1864
(Map on Page 87)

By the first week of May in 1864, General John Hunt Morgan, "Thunderbolt of the Confederacy", had been placed in charge of the Department of Southwestern Virginia, which included the 10th Kentucky Mounted Rifles. Now, these mountain soldiers would forever-more be able to recall that they were once a part of "Morgan's Men". The small army was once again divided into two brigades. The First Brigade was commanded by Colonel Henry Giltner and consisted of the 4th Kentucky Cavalry, 10th Kentucky Cavalry and the 10th Kentucky Mounted Rifles. The Second Brigade was commanded by Colonel R.A. Alston and consisted of the 1st Kentucky Cavalry, 2nd Kentucky Cavalry, and the 6th and 7th Confederate Battalions.

On May 7th, 1864, General Morgan decided to have a grand review of his troops; but it was not intended to be considered a contest between the two brigades. Of course, this would not be the case as each brigade did its best to outshine the other. This review was performed at Saltville before many officers and local politicians, whom the general had invited. The Second Brigade claimed to have won the review because they had better-looking uniforms and better equipment than the First Brigade. Of course, the First Brigade argued otherwise.

The following day, on May 8th, all of Morgan's men who were not mounted were ordered to travel by train to Dublin, near Cloyd's Mountain, to reinforce General Albert Jenkins. The general's small army was being attacked by General George Crook's Union army. The mounted men of Morgan's army began riding toward Dublin on their horses. Colonel D. Howard Smith was appointed commander of the dismounted men riding the train. This group consisted of some of the men of the 10th Kentucky Mounted Rifles.

The Battle of Cloyd's Mountain was fought on May 9th, 1864 and was a defeat for the Confederacy. Colonel Smith and his dismounted men arrived at Dublin just in time to serve as a rear guard during General Jenkins' retreat. These brave men, though not in the main Battle of Cloyd's Mountain, were credited with saving the Confederate artillery. Part of Morgan's Men had been involved in their first fight under their new commander.

Meanwhile, also on May 9th, General Morgan and his mounted men were riding toward Wytheville when they learned that General William Averill and his Union cavalry were approaching the town. The small Confederate army rode for a couple of hours into the night before Morgan gave the order to dismount and go into camp.

The following morning, May 10th, Morgan's men began to ride toward Wytheville, with the 1st Brigade, including the 10th Kentucky Mounted Rifles, leading the way. The lead column rode into the rustic town in the afternoon. Part of the town had been burnt in a previous Union raid; and now, the townspeople were afraid it was about to happen again.

Upon arriving in Wytheville, General Morgan was informed that Colonel Crittenden and his infantry (known as Jones' Brigade) were engaged with General Averill's Union army at Cove Gap on Cove Mountain. These men were entrenched in the gap and holding off the attack by Averill's cavalry. They were greatly outnumbered, and without help, would soon have to retreat, leaving Wytheville vulnerable to the Yankees. By road, Cove Mountain was six miles from Wytheville, but going through the woods, the distance was only four miles. Knowing this, Morgan ordered Giltner and Alston to turn off the road and thus approach the right flank of Averill's forces. Colonel Giltner was given command of the two brigades while the general took command of Jones' Brigade at the gap. Due to the forest cover, Averill had no idea that Morgan's men were in the area. Reaching the open grassy field that led to Averill's men entrenched on top of the hill, Giltner ordered his men to dismount. Still undetected, the Confederates formed into a battle line on the edge of the forest with the First Brigade on the left and Second Brigade on the right.

At 5 P.M., bugles signaled for the two brigades to charge out of the forest. With Rebel yells echoing up the valley, both brigades charged across the open bottoms and up the hill. At first, the Union line charged down the hill to meet the oncoming Rebels; but soon, it stopped and began to retreat, back up the hill. At this time, a popular Confederate officer, Major Nathan Parker, fell, mortally wounded; causing the two brigades to storm the Union position with revenge on their minds.

Meanwhile, Morgan and Jones' Brigade began to charge the middle of the Union battle line, while another group of Confederates attacked Averill's left flank. Averill was now being attacked on his right, front and left, leaving him no choice but to sound the retreat. With darkness aiding them, the Union cavalry broke and ran down Cove Mountain in all directions. The paths down the mountain were dangerous to travel in the dark; so, Morgan decided not to endanger his men by pursuing the fleeing Yanks. Besides, the Confederates were exhausted from both the hard ride and from the fighting. The victorious Rebels moved back to Wytheville. Morgan and his men had prevented the Union cavalry from destroying the lead works at Wytheville; and had pushed the Yankee invaders out, for the time being.

Battle of Colley Creek
May 13, 1864
(Map on Page 88)

While most of the 10th Kentucky Mounted Rifles were in southwestern Virginia with General John Hunt Morgan, one of their companies remained in Letcher County, doing scouting duty. At first they stayed in Whitesburg but when provisions were depleted, they decided to move to their old camp at the mouth of Colley Creek, where it empties into Rockhouse Creek. Here many of the men were near their families and could expect help with supplies.

While using the old campground as a base from which to scout, the Confederates were unaware that a Yankee patrol was coming, looking for them. This patrol was made up of the 11th Michigan Cavalry and a company of the 39th Kentucky Mounted Infantry. The 11th was superbly equipped with the new Spencer repeating rifles, a vast improvement over the muzzle loading rifles that the Confederates carried. Major Charles Smith of the 11th Michigan Cavalry was in command of the patrol, which was operating out of Louisa, in Lawrence County. At Pound Gap, the major was informed that a company of the 10th Kentucky Mounted Rifles was encamped at Colley, below Whitesburg.

Early on the morning of May 13th, the Yankee patrol slipped through the sleeping little town of Whitesburg; and, guided by some of the 39th Kentucky, traveled down the rugged trail known as the Rebel Trace toward Colley Creek. The Yanks were able to slip up on the unsuspecting Confederates as they lounged around their camp, before going out on patrol themselves. When close to the camp, the Yankee cavalry dismounted and quietly approached the Rebels. They opened fire with their new Spencers, creating the impression that a huge number of Union soldiers were firing.

Though surprised, the Rebels did not run; but immediately began to fight back. Firing from both armies echoed up and down the valley, with neither side giving ground. After several minutes of this exchange of gunfire, the Confederates knew that they were outgunned and could not push the Union soldiers out. The boys in gray rushed into the woods to their horses and raced further into the surrounding woods, riding in all directions to hopefully prevent pursuit. Before the Yanks could get back to their horses, the Rebels were long-gone.

The Union soldiers entered the abandoned camp, hoping to find anything of value. But they were disappointed to find that the poor Rebels had left nothing behind of any consequence. The long years of war had depleted the area of everything of value, including provisions. Learning that more Confederate soldiers were coming to the Whitesburg area, Major Smith wisely decided to return to his base in the Big Sandy area; to report upon his success at defeating the local Confederates. After his departure, the men of the 10th Kentucky Mounted Rifles who had hit the hills began to reform and regroup; they were used to this sort of Yankee attacks and were not discouraged by it. They would continue to scout the area until recalled to southwestern Virginia.

From "War of Rebellion":

11th Michigan Cavalry, Louisa, KY

May 16, 1864

"I proceeded with my command of two squdrons of 11th MI. Cav., Cos. A & F and one company 39th KY Mtd. Inf., Co. B, from this point on Monday the 9th – I moved to Pound Gap, passing inside of rebel breastworks in gap. Finding that a rebel force was on Rockhouse Creek and numbering some 45 men, I moved to that place marching from

sunrise until 1 am, resting two hours, and pushing on again at 4 am. Charged the enemy's camp about 11 am on the 13th. We ran some three miles capturing one captain, one lieutenant and five horses with equipment and killing one horse. On my return I learned that Chenoweth was one mile and a half beyond Whitesburg with about 75 men, but my horses were unable to move farther in that direction and I also learned that there was no forage to be procured on that route."

Major Charles E. Smith, 11th Michigan Cavalry

Morgan's Last Raid into Kentucky
June of 1864

General Morgan was now in full charge of the Department of southwestern Virginia, with his main objectives to protect the salt works at Saltville and the lead works at Wytheville. Word arrived in late May of 1864 that Union General Stephen Burbridge was forming a large army to invade southwestern Virginia. Knowing that this Yankee army would be much larger than his own, the Confederate general decided to take the fight to the enemy, hoping to change their plans of invading. This would be a risky gamble as it would leave the area practically undefended.

Morgan divided his invading force into three brigades. The First Brigade, commanded by Colonel Giltner, consisted of the 4th Kentucky Cavalry, 10th Kentucky Cavalry, 1st Kentucky Mounted Rifles, 2nd Kentucky Mounted Rifles, 10th Kentucky Mounted Rifles and the 6th Confederate Battalion. The Second Brigade, commanded by Colonel D. Howard Smith, consisted of the 1st Kentucky Cavalry, 2nd Kentucky Cavalry, and the 3rd Kentucky Cavalry. The Third Brigade, commanded by Colonel Robert Martin, consisted of about eight hundred men, who were dismounted, from all of the above regiments. It was hoped to mount these men with Union horses not long after they invaded Kentucky. The three brigades consisted of a total of approximately 2,300 men.

On Tuesday, May 31st, the small army left Abingdon and began their march toward Kentucky, passing through Castlewood and Gladeville. The long column arrived below Pound Gap on the Virginia and Kentucky border on June 2nd. A large army of several hundred Union soldiers was holding the gap, hoping to prevent the entry of the Confederates into Kentucky.

General Morgan ordered his men to dismount and charge up the hill toward the entrenched Union soldiers. The boys in blue tried to hold their positions but the wave of gray coming toward them was more than they could stand. They began to retreat and flee into the surrounding mountains. The Kentuckians were poised upon reentering their home state. With the soldiers remounted, the column moved into Kentucky and continued down the road to the foot of the mountain. Knowing that Union officials would expect him to come along the Mt. Sterling-Pound Gap Road, Morgan decided instead to travel by the rugged Rebel Trace. Knowing that they were from the area and that they knew the rugged road first-hand, the general ordered Major Thomas Chenoweth and the 10th Kentucky Mounted Rifles to the front of the column and told them to lead the way.

The trail was rough on the horses and men, and it took until June 6th for the column to arrive at Hazel Green. Almost two hundred men were added to the ranks of the Third Brigade due to having their horses give out on the rugged trail. Local residents informed General Morgan that a large Union army of approximately three thousand men had passed through Hazel Green on their way to the Kentucky border; the two armies had passed each other on parallel roads. The following day, the 7th of June, the weary soldiers of the Third Brigade arrived in Hazel Green, having almost kept up with the horses; an admirable feat. While waiting for these rugged soldiers, the general ordered Major Chenoweth to take the mounted men of the 10th Kentucky Mounted Rifles to ride to Paris and destroy the railroad there. He sent other regiments to destroy railroads in other areas as well, hoping to thwart reinforcement efforts from central Kentucky. The remainder of "Morgan's Men" would charge into Mt. Sterling to dislodge the Union defenders there.

The Battle of Mt. Sterling
(The First Day)
June 8, 1864

Moving quietly to the outskirts of Mt. Sterling during the night, the Confederate raiders prepared to attack. At 4 o'clock on Wednesday morning, June 8th, Morgan's men charged the two Union camps in and around the town. The larger camp consisted of two hundred or more men, while approximately one hundred men occupied the smaller camp. The attack pushed the Union soldiers back into town where they took refuge in the buildings there. These buildings proved to be a formidable stronghold for the Yankee soldiers. But, when torches were brought up to burn the soldiers out, they began to surrender to their Confederate counterparts. The Union suffered ten killed, twelve wounded and two-hundred and fifty prisoners taken. The Confederates suffered five killed and fifteen wounded. The dismounted men of the 10th Kentucky Mounted Rifles had been part of a significant victory.

The victorious Rebels began to pilfer through the captured Yankee plunder, finding badly needed items such as clothing and shoes. Unfortunately, some of Morgan's men were not satisfied with the Union plunder and began to go through stores stealing things. At this time, some of the soldiers robbed the local bank of $75,000. Though only a few of the men participated in this thievery, it made them all look like thieves and vagabonds.

At this time, General Morgan made an ill-advised decision to allow a portion of his army to stay in town, while the remainder continued toward Lexington. Morgan took the Second Brigade and moved out, leaving what remained of the First and Third Brigades. This was probably due to his overconfidence that General Burbridge and his Union cavalry were still in the vicinity of Virginia combined with his desire to allow the dismounted men to rest from their forced march. Unbeknownst to the general was the fact that General Burbridge pushed his men relentlessly back to Mt. Sterling.

Colonel Giltner was placed in charge of the men left in Mt. Sterling, with orders to destroy all Union supplies that could not be transported, and then continue on to Lexington the next day. Orders were given to place pickets at least a mile from the camp. However, these orders were not carried out, as pickets were only established a few hundred yards from town. Underestimating the enemy usually is unwise, as it would prove to be in this case.

The Battle of Mt. Sterling
(The Second Day)
June 9, 1864

In an outstanding forced march, General Burbridge pushed his cavalry mercilessly to Mt. Sterling. They covered the last ninety miles in less than thirty hours, a killing pace for man and beast. In the pouring rain, the Union cavalrymen arrived outside Mt. Sterling. Giving them no time to rest, Burbridge ordered them to charge the sleeping Confederates. Many of the first Rebel casualties were inflicted while the men were in tents and wagons. Though surprised by the brutal attack, the Rebels did not panic and formed a resistance. Colonel Martin managed to rally a counterattack, charging the Union cavalrymen and capturing their cannon. Using superior numbers, the Union soldiers also counterattacked, retaking their cannon.

Colonel Giltner rallied the First Brigade and fought their way to the Third Brigade, which was greatly outnumbered. The two brigades managed to push the Yankees back. After fighting their way to join with Colonel Martin and his troops, the Rebels were ordered by Colonel Giltner to charge the Yanks. This surprised the Union soldiers and Burbridge, who had expected to easily overrun the Confederates. The two brigades pushed the surprised Union troops back into Mt. Sterling, where they took refuge in houses and other buildings. This strong new position allowed the Yanks to halt the Confederate attack.

Realizing that the Union soldiers were content with holding their defensive line in and around the buildings in town, Giltner ordered his men to move toward Lexington. With the First and Third Brigades joined together, the colonel left a small rearguard to keep the Yanks pinned down. About ten miles down the road to Lexington, Giltner and his men met with the returning General Morgan and the Second Brigade. Angered at the loss of some of his men, the general wanted to return to Mt. Sterling and renew the attack. But Giltner informed him of the strong defensive position that the Yankees occupied; and that it would probably take artillery to dislodge them. Seeing the wisdom of this advice, Morgan ordered his men to travel on to Lexington.

The second day of battle had been costly for the small Confederate army, with at least fourteen officers and forty enlisted men killed. At least eighty men were wounded, and another hundred or more taken prisoner. Several men of the 10th Kentucky Mounted Rifles, with Captain David Caudill commanding, were a part of these casualties.

Morgan ordered his dismounted men to double up behind a mounted comrade and continue to Winchester. There, he had a welcome surprise for them; they had captured approximately three hundred horses and mules from Union supply depots. They also borrowed several wagons for moving their wounded. While the men of the First and Third Brigades rested along the road, Morgan and the Second Brigade went to Lexington, arriving at dark. Here, they attacked the Union defenders, pushing them into the center of town. The Rebels set fire to a large depot where hay had been stored for Union horses. This destroyed the supplies and gave the Confederates light to see by in the dark of night.

Meanwhile, Major Chenoweth and the 10th Kentucky Mounted Rifles returned from their raid on Paris, reuniting with Colonel Giltner's command outside of Winchester. Having been deep inside horse country, these resourceful soldiers had replaced their worn-out horses with beautiful racehorses. Descendants of Oliver Halcomb, a member of the regiment, still tell of him returning to Line Fork Creek, riding a thoroughbred and leading two others.

Now regrouped, Giltner ordered his column of men to move toward Lexington. This column was a real spectacle, as it consisted of wagons and buggies carrying soldiers, as well as soldiers riding everything from racehorses to mules. In addition, the Union prisoners-of-war tramped along in line with the column. It truly would have been strange sight!

The Skirmish at Lexington
June 10, 1864

Giltner and his men arrived on the outskirts of Lexington just before daybreak on June 10th, guided by the fire still burning at the Union depot and stables. In order to prevent looting again, as was done in Mt. Sterling by a few, all of the soldiers were under orders to stay together. A portion of the men were sent forward to help the Second Brigade attack the Union fortifications in town. A spirited exchange of gunfire erupted up and down the streets of town. Hoping to maintain their position, and not surrender, the Yankees began to shell the town where the Confederate invaders were located. A combination of the strength of the Union fortifications, plus the thoughts of the Yanks destroying the beautiful town with cannon fire, persuaded Morgan to quit pressing the attack. Leaving a few men to harass the fort and keep the defenders holed up, the general ordered his men to move out on the road to Georgetown. Some of the men of the 10th Kentucky Mounted Rifles had now been in three fights in as many days.

The colorful caravan began their march to Georgetown, with Giltner's Brigade in the lead. While riding along, several soldiers of the Second Brigade began to brag about their looting skills, of which the other brigades began to make fun of them, calling them names. This led to several fist fights breaking out before calm and order were restored. To the relief of their officers, the column reached Georgetown without any more fights breaking out.

While resting in Georgetown, Morgan received word that a large Union army was forming in the Frankfort or Danville area. Hearing this, the general ordered his men to saddle up and move on toward Cynthiana. As the column moved toward their new destination, Morgan sent some men back to Lexington to attack the town again, hoping to confuse the enemy with their intentions. All through the evening and night, the long column plodded toward Cynthiana, the county seat of Harrison County. Just before daylight, the lead elements of the tired army arrived; three or four miles outside of town.

The Battle of Cynthiana
(The First Day)
June 11, 1864

The Covered Bridge

Due to casualties suffered and units sent on various missions, Morgan now had approximately twelve hundred men available for battle. Across the Licking River from them, 300 men of the 168th Ohio Infantry and 200 men of the Harrison Home Guards were entrenched. The general ordered the Second Brigade to travel up the road to the right, cross the river, and strike the Union flank. The First Brigade formed across from the main Union line in the vicinity of a covered bridge. With part of the brigade laying down a covering fire, several companies of mounted men rushed across the bridge. The sight of the yelling Rebels alarmed the Union defenders and they immediately fell back into town. As the remainder of the First Brigade crossed the covered bridge, Giltner ordered Colonel Trimble to take the 10th Kentucky Cavalry to Keller's Bridge, which was below the town, in an effort to cut off the Yankee retreat. To the Rebel's dismay, the Unions soldiers took cover in the town's buildings. Without artillery, the Rebels could not manage to dislodge the Yankees. Reluctantly, Morgan gave the order to set fire to one of the buildings. At this time, the Union commander, Colonel George Berry, was killed. The combination of the prospects of being burned out, and the loss of their commander, convinced the Union soldiers to surrender. Morgan's men had now captured another four hundred prisoners, but unfortunately, one of the buildings was burnt down.

Keller's Bridge

While the celebration of the fall of the town began, Trimble and his men came under attack at Keller's Bridge by a large unit of Union soldiers. This unit was comprised of approximately 800 men of the 171st Ohio National Guard, under the command of General Edward Hobson. Hobson and his men had just arrived by train at the burnt railroad bridge. Trimble sent a courier back to Morgan with a plea for help. Upon receiving the message, Giltner immediately rushed the First Brigade to help the hard-pressed 10th Kentucky.

Joining with Trimble, Giltner now had a force of approximately five hundred men. Facing the long blue battle line were the 4th Kentucky Cavalry on the left, the 1st and 2nd Kentucky Mounted Rifles in the center and the 10th Kentucky Cavalry with the 10th Kentucky Mounted Rifles on the right. Colonel Giltner gave the order to charge, and the gray line surged forward with an unnerving Rebel yell. The Union line managed to fire two volleys before they began to retreat. They retreated down the gentle slope toward the Licking River to the vicinity of the cliffs, where Union officers rallied them into making a stand.

The Union soldiers now began to exchange volleys with the Confederates. This exchange continued for more than a half hour, with neither side giving an inch. Colonel Giltner once more ordered a charge, which broke the Union line. They retreated through a railroad cut and into the bend of the river, which was a strong defensive position. The colonel now had another problem; his men were running out of ammunition. Luckily, General Morgan and the 2nd Brigade had ridden around the Union line and approached their flank. General Hobson now was surrounded and decided to surrender his men. Combined with all other prisoners taken previously, Morgan now had more prisoners than he had soldiers!

General Morgan decided to send General Hobson to Cincinnati in hopes of exchanging him for one of his officers. He sent Major Chenoweth and Captain Cal Morgan as escorts to take Hobson up north. This left Captain David Caudill in charge of the 10th Kentucky Mounted Rifles. Aware that most of his men were out of ammunition, Morgan ordered them to exchange their two-banded rifles for the Springfields just captured from the Union troops. These guns had plenty of available ammunition. In a decision that later came back to haunt them, the soldiers did not follow orders; simply because most did not like the long, three-banded Springfield rifles.

Scouts arrived to tell General Morgan that General Burbridge was approaching Cynthiana with almost three thousand troops, a force more than twice that of Morgan's. To make matters worse, some of these Yankee troops were armed with the repeating Spencer rifles. Even though the Confederates were greatly outgunned, Morgan decided to stand and fight; a decision he would later regret.

The Battle of Cynthiana
(The Second Day)
June 12, 1864

At daybreak on June 12th, General Burbridge ordered his men to approach the entrenched Confederates. Ironically, Trimble and Caudill's men faced their old adversaries; the 39th Kentucky Mounted Rifles and the 11th Michigan Cavalry. After exchanging several volleys with the Rebels, Burbridge ordered his men to charge. Amazingly, the thin Rebel line managed to withstand the charge and drive the Yankees back. Regrouping, Burbridge's men charged once more, only to be driven back for a second time. Having underestimated his enemy, Burbridge then sent his reserves to attack the Confederate flanks.

This strategy began to succeed as the greatly outnumbered Confederates protecting the flanks were driven into the main Rebel battle lines. They fell back along the Paris Road and once more took up positions, only to be charged again by the long, blue line of soldiers. Now greatly outnumbered and running out of ammunition, Morgan ordered a retreat along the Augusta Road. However, the First Brigade was now cut off and would have to retreat along the Leesburg Road. Giltner and his men fought their way to the bridge that crossed the Licking River only to find it in possession of the Yankees. They were now trapped between two enemy forces.

Not considering surrender, the men of the First Brigade spurred their horses down the steep banks to the river. As they surged across the river, many were shot and killed by Union soldiers lining the bridge. Amazingly, many of the men made it across the river and up the opposite bank, only to face another Union force. Summoning a scream available only to desperate men, the Confederates charged the Yanks and pushed their way through. Then, they began to ride hard for Georgetown, with a Union force on their tails. After a chase of about three miles, the Union pursuers gave up and returned to Cynthiana. Giltner and his men, mostly now unarmed, continued their retreat. Meanwhile, Morgan and the men with him retreated along the Augusta Road and headed back toward Virginia as well. Both groups of men returned to Virginia where they regrouped.

The raid had been successful since it delayed the invasion of Virginia for several months, but that came at a great cost. Confederate casualties were approximately 80 killed, 125 wounded and 450 missing or captured.

From "War of Rebellion":

Headquarters, Dept. of Western Virginia & East Tennessee
Abingdon, VA

July 20, 1864

"After consulting with General W. E. Jones, who was then commanding the department, it was decided that I should move at once into Kentucky and gain the rear of the forces moving in this direction, believing the small force I commanded could offer but a feeble resistance in their front without pursuit and thus being diverted from their raid in this direction. On the first of June my advance was met by a force of the enemy twelve miles this side (east) of Pound Gap, being the advance of the Federal forces. We drove them back rapidly before us and succeeded in remounting some of the dismounted men upon horses that were taken upon the gap, which point was gained just at night fall. We from 22 to 27 miles per day, the dismounted men making that distance over mountain passes that troops had never traveled before. **Upon the morning of the 7th Major Chenoweth with 50 men (was detached) to destroy railroad between Paris and Covington upon Lexington & Covington Railroad to prevent reinforcements from Ohio.** *(On June 11th) General Hobson and staff were sent, at their own request, under a flag of truce to Cincinnati to try and arrange with General Heintzelman for an exchange. Major Chenoweth, Surgeon (R. R.) Goode and Calvin C. Morgan accompanied the flag. These officers I understand are held as prisoners of war by Federal authoriites. The next morning (12th) we were attacked by 5,200 infantry, cavalry, nd artillery under General Burbridge."*

General John H. Morgan

A Letter Home

Private William Brashear of Company H, 10th Kentucky Mounted Rifles, wrote this letter home after the raid.

July 1st, 1864

"Dear Mother, Sister, and Brother,

I take this opportunity of writing you a few lines. I have not been well for some time but I have been going all the time until now. I am resting and is getting well. I hope these lines may find you all in good health. I would be glad to see you all but times does not permit of my coming to see you all.

Father and Isaac Brashears are well at this time. I will now tell you something about our Kentucky march. We was on a hard march for twenty days and during that time had four fights, one at Mt. Sterling, one at Lexington, and two at Cynthiana. We lost some of our boys at Mt. Sterling, some was killed, some was captured. Sampson Brashears was captured. He was left on the battlefield and we have not heard from him since. S.A. Brashears was left on the battlefield at Cynthiana. I think is just wounded. S.B. Smith wounded in the left thigh, left in the hospital. James Brashears and Little William Brashears is all right, came out safe and sound. I had one ball pass thru my pants but never touched the hide. We fought on Saturday about 6 hours, all the time in close distance. We captured 1273 Yankees in the 6 hours fight and the same night following captured 1,000 more and one train of guns and all of its storage. We lost but few men in all that captures. The Yankee loss was heavy. I must now tell how we faired and how the people treated us while we were in Kentucky. The citizens give us vittles, tobacco, whiskey and many other things to many to mention and treated us with all kinds of respect and hollowed Hurrah for Jeff Davis.

I must bring my letter to a close
Write me the first chance,

W. Brashear"

Morgan's Withdrawal into Tennessee
August 1864

The raid into Kentucky was now a part of the ever-growing legend of General John Hunt Morgan, known as the Thunderbolt of the Confederacy. The general's command spent the last part of the summer of 1864 gathering stragglers that had escaped capture during the raid. The combination of men slowly returning from Kentucky and the addition of new recruits had brought the small army close to pre-raid numbers. Once again, the morale and confidence were high among the men of the Department of Southwest Virginia and East Tennessee.

Learning that a large contingent of Yankees under the command of General Alvin Gillem was in East Tennessee, Morgan immediately began planning to push them out. In early August, he ordered several of his regiments to move to Jonesboro, Tennessee. In hopes of keeping appraised of Union plans for an invasion into Virginia, he ordered the 10th Kentucky Mounted Rifles to patrol the Kentucky and Virginia borders. Captain David Caudill was commander of the regiment as Major Chenoweth had been captured and was being held as a prisoner-of-war.

Caudill and his fellow mountaineers were eager to move back into the mountain ranges near their homes. Knowing the land very well, they were adept at the task at hand. But the time of being near their families was short-lived as orders arrived on August 16th for them to report to Colonel Giltner in east Tennessee. The courier did not bring all bad news; he informed Captain Caudill that Colonel Ben Caudill, his brother, had been exchanged on August 3rd and had arrived in Abingdon on August 15th. However, the popular colonel was very weak from his long incarceration as a prisoner-of-war and would not be able to take command of the regiment until nearly a month later.

Blue Springs Battlefield Revisited
August 21, 1864

The 10th Kentucky Mounted Rifles arrived in Jonesboro, on August 20th, at which time they were informed that Giltner's Brigade was now in Greeneville, Tennessee. The brigade was under the command of Colonel Trimble as Colonel Giltner had been recalled to Abingdon. Continuing their march, the 10th Kentucky arrived at Greeneville on August 21st. From there they were rushed to the old Blue Springs battlefield as Colonel Trimble and the brigade were preparing for a fight. The men of Caudill's Army marched on to Blue Springs, arriving at midday to a warm welcome. The outnumbered Confederates needed all the help they could get. Captain Caudill and his men were placed on the right of the 10th Kentucky Cavalry. By two o'clock the men had completed building breastworks and were expecting a Union attack.

At three o'clock the Union army attacked, driving in the Confederate pickets, before being stopped by the main battle line. The two opposing armies were content with exchanging volleys from a distance, as the Yanks realized that the Rebels had a strong defensive position. The rest of the evening was spent with sporadic gunfire being exchanged. Finally, the Unions soldiers returned to their camp, much to the delight of the Confederate defenders. For the remainder of the night, the Rebels slept on their guns.

Pushed Back to Jonesboro
August 23, 1864

Colonel Trimble received word that Colonel Giltner had arrived back at Greeneville with about 350 soldiers of Vaughn's Brigade. Aware of the Union presence, Trimble posted pickets in all directions, a decision that later proved prudent. General Gillem's Union force greatly outnumbered Trimble's. He sent the 10th Michigan Cavalry with their Spencer repeating rifles to hit Trimble's flank.

At one-thirty, Gillem ordered the attack to commence. The attack was two-pronged, as planned, but the pickets set out by Trimble alerted the colonel of the presence of the 10th Michigan. This gave him time to send reinforcements to stop that part of the attack. Meanwhile, Gillem sent a large number of soldiers to attack the main Confederate battle line. Knowing he could not hold out long against two fronts of attack, Colonel Trimble decided to retreat to Greeneville. Fighting furiously to hold the Union line at bay, the colonel organized an orderly retreat. The Rebel cavalrymen would retreat for about a mile, then dismount and fight for a while, then remount move out again, doing this for about three miles until the Yanks had enough and quit the pursuit.

Colonel Giltner and Vaughn's Brigade joined with Trimble just as the brigade entered Greeneville. The Union artillery soon began to shell the Confederate's position, resulting in Giltner ordering the army to move to Jonesboro. After arriving there and building additional breastworks, Giltner was informed that Gillem and the Union army had reversed course and fallen back toward Bull's Gap. The following morning, General Morgan arrived, as well as General Vaughn and the remainder of his brigade. Morgan, before returning to Abingdon, ordered the army to go back to Greeneville and set up a camp. The next few days were uneventful except for the 10th Kentucky Cavalry and 10th Kentucky Mounted Rifles chasing after bushwhackers.

On August 28th, General Morgan returned to resume command of the small army at Greeneville. On September 1st, Morgan ordered Giltner's Brigade to accompany him to Jonesboro, arriving there in the evening. Scouts arrived the following day informing Morgan that General Gillem had moved his Union troops back into the Bull's Gap area. General Morgan decided to confront this new threat, and to be nearer the enemy, made plans to return to Greeneville.

On the morning of September 3rd, Giltner's Brigade began to march back to Greeneville. Captain James Rogers and company D of the 10th Kentucky Mounted Rifles were given the honor of riding at the front of the column with General Morgan. The general had made the statement that Captain Rogers was "One of the most gallant and daring officers in the army". The column arrived back in Greeneville in the evening during a rainstorm. Making his headquarters at the home of Mrs. Alexander Williams, Morgan ordered Captain Rogers to remain in town and instructed the remainder of Giltner's Brigade to camp on the Rogersville Road, about two miles from town. A portion of Vaughn's Brigade was camped on the Bull's Gap Road, while Clark's Battalion was encamped on the Jonesboro Road. The 16th Georgia Cavalry was ordered to camp on the Warrensburg Road below its intersection with the Newport Road. Unfortunately, they passed the intersection up due to the rain and darkness, leaving the Newport Road unguarded. Someone rode to Gillem's headquarters with this information.

The Death of General Morgan
Sunday Morning
September 4, 1864

Before daylight on Sunday morning, General Gillem ordered Captain Charles Wilcox and company G of the 13th Tennessee Cavalry to by-pass the Georgia Cavalry by taking the Newport Road into Greeneville. Wilcox's orders were to surround the Williams house and capture or kill Morgan. To create a diversion, Gillem would attack Vaughn's Brigade on the Bull's Gap Road. The 13th Tennessee was the perfect company for the job as most of the men in it were from the area and could easily find the Williams house in the dark. Around 6:30 AM, Gillem attacked on the Bulls Gap Road. Hearing the gunfire, Wilcox charged into town, surrounding the Williams house. They easily defeated the guards there and demanded that Morgan surrender.

Morgan, hearing the gunfire, grabbed his pistols, threw on his clothes, and ran out of the house into the vineyard, joined by Captain Rogers and Captain L.E. Johnson. The three men ran out of the vineyard and hid under the nearby church. Hearing the Yankees tearing the doors off the church, they ran back into the vineyard. While here, Mrs. David Fry, a Union sympathizer, hollered and told the location of the trio. At that time a soldier in a brown jean cloth jacket rode up to the vineyard; and, thinking he was a Confederate soldier, the trio stepped out to meet him. They were mistaken; however, he was Private Andrew Campbell of the Union 13th Tennessee, and he once was a Confederate soldier.

Rogers and Johnson stepped toward other Union soldiers, who ran up to them, while holding up their hands. They saw Morgan hold up his hands; then heard a gunshot and someone say, "I've killed the horse thief". The Thunderbolt of the Confederacy was now dead.

Meanwhile, Giltner's men, including the 10th Kentucky Mounted Rifles, heard the shooting both in Greeneville and along the Bull's Gap Road. Giltner ordered his men to mount and prepare for battle. He sent Captain David Caudill and the 10th Kentucky Mounted Rifles to take the wagons around Greeneville to the Jonesboro Road, while he and the remainder of the men rode into Greeneville. On their way, a courier met them with orders to travel around Greeneville as fast as possible and join Colonel D. Howard Smith, who had assumed command of the army, on the Jonesboro Road.

Arriving at the road, near Rheatown, Giltner met Captain Caudill who told him that he thought an attack on the wagons was imminent and had abandoned them. Lt. George Houck managed to save the mules pulling the wagons but burnt the ammunition. Nothing seemed to be going right for them. Giltner sent a flag of truce by a captain into Greeneville to find out what had happened. The captain was informed of Morgan's death and was allowed to take the body back to Rheatown. The men of the 10th Kentucky Mounted Rifles, as well as the rest of Morgan's men, were devastated to hear the tragic news. They were also informed of the capture of Captain Rogers. Later, Rogers escaped by jumping off a moving train and traveling by foot, for hundreds of miles, to rejoin his regiment.

The Department of Southwest Virginia and East Tennessee was now under the command of General John Echols. The general kept the majority of the small army in the Jonesboro area for the remainder of September. Meanwhile, he sent the 10th Kentucky Mounted Rifles back into southwestern Virginia to scout the area. Their previous commander, Major Chenoweth, had been exchanged, and had returned to take command of the regiment.

Prelude to Saltville
The Salt Capital of the Confederacy
October 1864

Before the end of September of 1864, Major Chenoweth and the 10th Kentucky Mounted Rifles were called back to report and help defend the salt works at Saltville, Virginia. Word had arrived that General Stephen Burbridge and approximately five thousand Union troops were planning a double angle attack. General Gillem was to come up from Bulls Gap to help Burbridge, who was to come through Pound Gap, with his attack. Ironically, the majority of Burbridge's troops were Kentuckians. It would be another case of brother against brother; the majority of troops guarding the salt works were Kentuckians as well.

General Burbridge was delayed in leaving Kentucky and changed his route to go by the Big Sandy River. General Gillem left Bulls Gap, only to be attacked along the way by General Vaughn and others. At this time, Gillem received orders to report back to the Bulls Gap area. Couriers were sent to inform Burbridge of this change, but they could not find him to deliver the message. Burbridge would be on his own; but he still had many more men than the Confederates who were guarding the salt works.

The Battle at Laurel Gap
October 1, 1864

Taking the battle to the enemy, Colonel Giltner spread his brigade out on the slopes of the Clinch Mountain, overlooking Burbridge's men camped about three miles away. At 10:00 a.m., the Union soldiers approached the foot of the mountain. To the entrenched Confederates, the long line of blue soldiers seemed endless. The road up the mountain meandered back and forth, giving the Confederates several targets to shoot at with their first volley. The 4th Kentucky Cavalry and the 10th Kentucky Mounted Rifles were stationed above the road, looking down on the Yankees. After the first volley, the Yanks dismounted and began to fight their way up the slopes toward the Rebels. After an intense battle that lasted for about half an hour, the Confederates retreated up the mountain. In an effort to slow the Yankees down, the Rebels cut down trees across the road.

Upon reaching the top of the mountain, the 10th Kentucky Mounted Rifles were joined by the 64th Virginia Cavalry. Together, they hastily dug in and prepared breastworks in hopes of holding off the swarm of Union soldiers. At approximately 2:00 PM, the Yanks came charging up the hillside, once more greatly outnumbering the Rebels. After several minutes of fighting, Colonel Giltner reluctantly ordered his men to fall back to Laurel Gap, a strong defensive position. The 4th Kentucky and the 10th Kentucky Mounted Rifles were on the left of the gap, while the 64th Virginia lined the right side. The 10th Kentucky Cavalry was to prevent the Confederates from being flanked.

At 5:00 PM, the Union line attacked in large numbers. At first, the thin gray line held; but soon, another large number of Union soldiers managed to flank the 64th Virginia and attack them, forcing them to retreat. This threatened the collapse of the left side of the line, forcing Colonel Giltner to sound retreat once more. Realizing the futility of staying and fighting against overwhelming odds, the colonel ordered his men to fall back, down to the Holston River. Amazingly, Burbridge allowed his men to stop and go into camp, not pushing the fight. The general was confident that he would easily attack the salt works defenses and defeat them the next day. The fighting for the day had ended.

The First Battle of Saltville
October 2, 1864

The delaying tactics that Giltner's Brigade had fought on the previous day proved to be the turning point of the battle. General John S. Williams had pushed his troops all night; and, by early Sunday morning of October 2nd, they began to arrive in Saltville. If Burbridge had kept up the attack on Saturday evening, he probably would have been successful in his destroying the salt works. Now, the Confederates had received reinforcements. Regardless, the Rebels were still outnumbered almost two to one. In addition, the Yankees were better armed; the 11th Michigan carried Spencer repeating rifles and the 5th U.S. Colored Troops were armed with the Starr breech-loading rifles.

The sporadic firing of pickets ended on Sunday morning as the Union troops attacked in full force, pushing the 4th Kentucky back, with the 10th Kentucky charging the Union lines to give them time to do so. The two regiments then joined the 64th Virginia and the 10th Kentucky Mounted Rifles at the top of Sanders Hill. While preparing breastworks there, they saw a welcome sight as General Felix Robertson arrived on Chestnut Ridge behind them with at least two-hundred and fifty men. To the right of Robertson, some Tennessee troops had also arrived to take up position.

The large Union line charged Giltner's troops, forcing them off of Sanders Hill, pushing them back to Robertson's breastworks. Here, Giltner and his men formed to the left of Robertson, placing the 10th Kentucky on the bluffs overlooking the river, and to their left was the 10th Kentucky Mounted Rifles in the cemetery. To their left was the 64th Virginia and the 4th Kentucky. Colonel William Breckinridge with the 1st and 9th Kentucky formed up on their far left. Facing them was Union General Edward Hobson and his troops, as well as Colonel Charles Hanson and his troops, all Kentuckians.

At 11:00 AM, the Union line charged all across the front, with the Union colored troops charging General Robertson's position. Seeing the black troops infuriated his men, and they fought with crazy ferociousness. A Tennessee battery had arrived to assist Robertson, helping to mow down the attacking Yankees.

Meanwhile, the battle between the Kentuckians had also begun. General Hobson led his men across the river through Broddy's Bottom under the withering fire of Giltner's Brigade. The main assault struck Trimble's 10th Kentucky Cavalry and began to push them back. Colonel Giltner rushed the 10th Kentucky Mounted Rifles and the 64th Virginia to Trimble's aid. Even with the reinforcements, the Union line was too strong to hold back, which pushed the brigade back into the cemetery. The 4th Virginia rushed up to help, only to fire one volley and fall back. Straightaway, Colonel Trimble led a charge into the Union lines, breaking their attack. However, the brave colonel paid for his heroic act with his life, being shot down while charging with his sword. The Confederate line had held at the edge of the cemetery. To Giltner's left, Colonel Breckinridge was holding the high ground on the bluffs above the river. Colonel Hanson and his boys in blue were finding it difficult to attack the area. Each attack was beaten back. Trying to encourage his men, Hanson exposed himself to the gunfire at the front of the attack, only to be seriously wounded. The loss of their leader took most of the fight out of the Yankees at this location.

At approximately 3:00 PM, Captain Bart Jenkins and his Confederate cavalry hit Burbridge's flank, using hit and run tactics. To offset this attack Burbridge sent most of his reserves to defend the flanks, taking away needed men from the front. The last charge of the day almost succeeded for the Union soldiers that were still trying to dislodge Robertson from Chestnut Ridge. The 12th Ohio finally breached the middle of the line, to be joined by the 11th Michigan and the 5th Colored troops. The Confederates fell back to another line of trenches where they held until the Union troops ran out of ammunition and had to retreat. The last sign of hope for a Union victory seemed to be dashed as General John C. Breckinridge and Vaughn's cavalry arrived just at sundown, to the cheers of the embattled Confederates. The stage was set for a Union disaster.

General Burbridge ordered his men to regroup and camp on the opposite side of the Holston River. Burbridge knew of the hatred that the Kentucky troop had for him and did not want to fall into their hands. Therefore, he turned over command to General Hobson and left for Kentucky. During the night, Hobson had several big fires built to give the Confederates the impression that they were staying to fight the next day. Under the cover of night, the once-confident Union army retreated back toward Kentucky, leaving their wounded and dead on the battlefield. They retreated back through Pound Gap, leaving dead horses and wounded men all along the way.

The following morning, the Rebels woke to find themselves in complete control of the battlefield. They had succeeded in forcing a superior number of troops to retreat. That morning however, several soldiers went onto the field and supposedly murdered some of the wounded black Union troops. This cowardly act was contributed to the Tennessee troops under General Robertson. The 10th Kentucky Mounted Rifles were never accused of the crime. Unfortunately, when word of the crime reached Union newspapers, they whipped the public up to the point where another invasion was imminent. Another Union commander with a terrible reputation was sent to punish the Confederates and the area around Saltville. His name was General George Stoneman, a name that would forever be remembered in southwestern Virginia.

A Trip to the Shenandoah Valley
October 18th through December 9th, 1864

After the successful defense of Saltville, Richmond officials kept General John C. Breckinridge as commander of the Department of Southwest Virginia. With a shortage of men, they knew that they needed the best officer that was available. On October 16th, Breckinridge ordered Giltner's Brigade to move from Saltville to Wytheville where they would continue to scout for Union incursions. The brigade consisted of the 4th Kentucky Cavalry, 10th Kentucky Cavalry and the 10th Kentucky Mounted Rifles. The brigade had been in Wytheville only a couple of days when they received orders to move once more. General Breckinridge received a dispatch ordering him to send the brigade and Cosby's Brigade to aid General Jubal Early in the Shenandoah Valley. Reluctantly, the general agreed to send them. The dismounted troops of both brigades were to be left behind, which included men of the 10th Kentucky Mounted Rifles. As Colonel Caudill had returned and took command of the regiment, Major Chenoweth was to remain as commander of the dismounted men. Later, in November, these men would be involved in battles at Cranes Nest and Bulls Gap.

On Tuesday, October 18th, General Cosby, commander of the two brigades, left Wytheville and began traveling East toward the Shenandoah Valley. The Cosby Brigade consisted of the 1st and 2nd Kentucky Cavalry, 64th Virginia Mounted Infantry, 6th Confederate Cavalry and Jenkins Cavalry.

Along the way, General Cosby stopped at Natural Bridge to allow them to see one of nature's great wonders. They then stopped in Lexington, Virginia, to allow them to visit General Stonewall Jackson's grave. It was hoped that these visits would reduce their concerns about leaving their home area. Sadly, the next sight was of unbelievable destruction. As they neared Staunton, they encountered hundreds of burnt fields and farms, all done by General Sheridan.

General Cosby and his men arrived at New Market on Saturday, October 29th, and immediately reported to General Early. In order to make communications easier, Early named the regiment "Cosby's Cavalry Brigade" and placed them under the command of General Lunsford Lomax. He earned the men's respect by showing them he was appreciative of their arrival. Unfortunately, the soldiers from the mountains soon fell out with the commander of the division stationed next to them; General John Pegram. This officer, when observing them, commented that the Yankee cavalry would run all over them with their pistols and sabers, as the mountain troops were armed mostly with two-banded Enfields, a longer-range weapon than those of the Yanks.

Cosby was informed that General Sheridan's army was stationed twenty miles from the Confederate camp at Strasburg, Virginia. On November 5th, Cosby's Cavalry Brigade saw their first action when Yankee cavalry probed the brigade's pickets. The men of the brigade immediately charged forward and forced the Yankee cavalry to retreat. General Lomax, showing his respect for their initiative, sent word of his approval to the camp. In a show of his respect, Lomax ordered them to be pickets for the main army.

On November 11th, Cosby's Brigade was ordered to move to the Battle of Cedarville battlefield (eight miles south of Winchester). At this location, Lomax's division formed the right wing of General Early's line of battle. General Sheridan and his Union army were formed into line of battle three miles away at Newtown. The following morning, General Cosby received orders to go to Early's left wing to support General Rosser, who was being severely pressed by the Union army. In an effort to speed up their arrival, the brigade was ordered to cross in front of the main battle line at the double-quick. This line was two miles long and was an awesome sight to the mountaineers. They could hear the sound of the cannon balls going over their heads from the artillery duel. When it was observed that the Yanks had pulled back from this portion of the battlefield, Lomax ordered the brigade to return to the right wing. Once more, the brigade rode in front of the two-mile-long battle line.

Upon arriving back at their previous position, the brigade prepared for the large attack that seemed certain to come. However, both armies were reluctant to instigate the fight and were satisfied with holding their line of battle. The men of both armies spent the night sleeping on their weapons, expecting a charge that never came.

The following morning General Early ordered his army to fall back. Cosby's Brigade was ordered to maintain their position to protect the flanks. While holding their position, General Gordon's infantry division began to pass by. Naturally, the infantrymen began to poke fun at the mountaineers as they passed by. The catcalls and insults quickly died down however, when the infantry was informed that these mountaineers were "Morgan's Men". Even in the Army of Northern Virginia, the tales of Morgan's exploits gained respect.

The next day, the brigade was halted and formed into a line of battle once more. General Early hoped that Sheridan would conduct a frontal attack on the strengthened Confederate line. By November 21st, the men of the brigade had concluded that the Yankee army had left. They soon changed their minds when a blue line of Union Cavalry attacked their position. Fending off the short-lived attack, they were informed by a captured Yank that General George Custer commanded the attacking force. Custer was probing the area, looking for a gap in General Early's line of battle.

The next morning, during a thunderous volume of cannonading, General Custer engaged the brigade once more. Again, the fight was short and furious as the brigade took advantage of their long-range rifles (the ones that General Pegram had ridiculed) and drove the Yankee cavalry back before they could come within pistol range. Twice in two days the brigade had thwarted an advance by the infamous Custer.

The next two days were quiet and peaceful along the line of battle when word arrived that Sheridan and his army had pulled back to the North. General Early thought that the danger of an attack was over, for the time being, and decided to send the brigade back to southwestern Virginia. The general had received word that a Union invasion from Kentucky and northeastern Tennessee was suspected. Early knew that General Breckinridge would need Cosby's brigade to help fend off the threat, and on November

24th, he gave General Cosby permission to return the brigade to their home territory. That same day, Cosby's Cavalry Brigade began marching toward southwestern Virginia. Several men were now without a mount and would have to travel by railroad. Captain David Caudill of the 10th Kentucky Mounted Rifles was in charge of getting these dismounted men home. The men traveling by horseback arrived in Wytheville on December 9th, 1864.

From "War of Rebellion":

Major General Breckinridge
Morristown, TN

November 23, 1864

"Have you received my letter in regard to Colonel Caudill's command? Shall it be ordered up? It is at Castlewood (VA). Colonel Giltner is here. As forage is getting scarce he proposes that it would be best to move into one of the southwestern counties, Scott or Lee, off the railroad where it is abundant.

J. Stoddard Johnston, Asst. Adjutant General
Wytheville, VA

During this trip to the Shenandoah Valley, the men who had been left at Abingdon had also seen action. Major Chenoweth and the dismounted men of the 10th Kentucky Mounted Rifles had been combined with the 7th Confederate Cavalry, under the command of Colonel Clarence Prentice.

The Battle of Cranes Nest
November 9, 1864
(Map on Page 89)

During the fall of 1864, an effort by the 39th Kentucky Mounted Infantry was made to recruit soldiers for the Unionarmy from the Clintwood area of Wise (now Dickenson) County, Virginia. This regiment was stationed in southeastern Kentucky; and the new group of recruits were referred to as "home guards". The company of approximately seventy recruits elected a local resident, Alf Killen, as their captain.

The Home Guard met on the Long Fork of the Cranes Nest River, due to several Union sympathizers living in that portion of the county. The main objective of the company was to protect local citizens from deprivations inflicted by both bushwhackers and Confederate supporters.

General John Breckinridge had learned of the company and decided to send troops to disband it. He chose Colonel Prentice to lead the excursion. The colonel would use his 7th Confederate Cavalry as well as the men of the 10th Kentucky Mounted Rifles that had been attached to it. These Kentuckians were commanded by Major Thomas Chenoweth.

The Confederate detachment of approximately three hundred soldiers arrived near the head of Cranes Nest River on the morning of November 8th. Continuing to travel northward along the river, the gray-clad column stopped to camp in a bottom just below Powers' Mill, a bucket-wheel gristmill. At approximately mid-day, Prentice ordered his men to set up tents, post pickets, and send scouts out into the surrounding countryside.

Meanwhile, the Home Guards were drilling in a churchyard on Long Fork, about two miles north of the Confederate encampment. Within an hour of the Confederate's arrival, a local resident informed Captain Killen that the Rebels were setting up camp at the mill. Immediately, they began making plans to attack the larger group of soldiers. Killen believed that, though he was outnumbered, the element of surprise would help them defeat the Confederates. The men of the Home Guards were from the area and knew it very well. One of them suggested traveling down the river to Horseshoe Branch, leave the river, and climb up Harm Ridge. There was a low saddle in the ridge that was above the Confederate encampment. Before daylight, the Union soldiers could easily travel down the hollow and shoot into the unsuspecting camp. Killen and his men approved the plan and began to travel down Long Fork. After making their way up to the gap on Harm Ridge, they quietly made a cold and dark camp. The plan that Killen and his men had devised was a sound one, with the chance of success very high. Unfortunately for them, there were also men of the 7th Confederate Cavalry from the area. One of these men was part of the scouting party sent out by Prentice. A local resident, possibly thinking the scouts were Union men, told them about the plans. The scouts now knew the Home Guards plan and returned to the Confederate camp to inform their leader.

Armed with this valuable information, Colonel Prentice prepared to ambush the ambushers. He quietly placed men on both sides of the hollow that the Union men would be coming down. They were ordered not to fire until all of the Yankees arrived at the camp site. To keep the campsite looking normal, three or four men were selected to sit around and tend the campfires. The stage was now set for the suspected morning attack.

As the first hint of daylight began to brighten the dark morning sky, on Wednesday morning, November 9th, the men of the Home Guard began slipping down the hollow from the gap in Harm Ridge. When they were all in position around the supposedly sleeping Confederate camp, Captain Killen fired his pistol to signal the beginning of the attack. The Yanks fired a ragged volley into the camp, killing one Confederate and wounding another. Just as the Yanks started charging the camp, a tremendous volley of gunfire from the Rebels lying in ambush lit the dawn sky.

The gunfire caught the attacking Yankees by surprise, dropping several of them in their tracks. The sight of the charging Rebels was more than the Home Guards could stand. Those still on their feet began running down the river in an attempt to save their lives. Union officers managed to rally their men for a few volleys before continuing the retreat. The fighting was over in minutes. Luckily, the Yanks knew the area and were able to escape. This, along with poor visibility of the early morning hour, allowed the surviving Home Guards to elude the Confederates, averting a complete disaster.

When the powder smoke and fog lifted that morning, a scene of death and destruction became visible. Lying in the river and in the bottom were the bodies of eight Union soldiers. Another saga of "brother against brother" had played out. Tragically, many of the combatants were related to each other. Some of the very Confederates, who had only moments earlier tried to kill the Union men, were now carefully burying the dead Unionists in the bottom.

The battle ended the high hopes of the men of the Union Home Guard that they would be a force to be reckoned with. The remnants of the group moved into southeastern Kentucky, where many had relatives. Prentice and Chenoweth, along with their men, moved back to Abingdon, having concluded their mission successfully.

The Battle of Bull's Gap
November 11 through 13, 1864
(Map on Page 90)

Back in Abingdon, Major Chenoweth and his dismounted troops of the 10th Kentucky Mounted Rifles, were combined with the dismounted soldiers of the 10th Kentucky Cavalry, under the command of Lieutenant Colonel Robert Alston. General John Breckinridge had received word that General Alvan Gillem's Union troops had returned to the Bull's Gap area of eastern Tennessee. He sent orders for General Basil Duke and his cavalry to travel to Carter's Station. He also sent the dismounted men under the command of Lieutenant Colonel Alston (including the men of the 10th Kentucky Mounted Rifles) by train to the station to meet them. Here they also met up with Vaughn's Brigade. On November 10th, the small army moved out on the road to Jonesboro, Tennessee.

The cold and muddy column marched through Jonesboro and on to Greeneville. They spent the night near Rheatown on a muddy field; and the next morning, November 11th, rose and began marching toward the enemy, passing through Greeneville. When within a mile of Bull's Gap, a battle line of blue-clad soldiers was seen approaching the Confederates. Duke's and Vaughn's brigades attacked the Yankees, with Alston and the dismounted men protecting the flanks and used for reserves. The Rebel cavalry was successful in driving the Yankees back into their fortifications at Bull's Gap. During the night, Alston's men and the artillery were brought up to the front lines facing the gap. Throughout the night, the artillery from both sides sparred back and forth.

At daybreak on November 12th, General Breckinridge could see the formidable breastworks of the gap. The strength of the fortifications convinced the general that a frontal attack would be suicidal. An attack from all sides was devised with Alston's men joining some of Duke's men for an attack on the right side. The remainder of Duke's men was to attack the front of the fortifications. Vaughn's Brigade was to attack the rear of the gap. The attack from the right was considered the main attack; hoping the demonstrations in the front and rear would divert the Union defender's attention. General Breckinridge would lead the attack on the right himself. The attack went well at first; the right side of the attack managed to take the breastworks, but the left side stalled due to heavy resistance from the Union defenders. Soon, the attack on all sides was stalled and came to a standstill. Realizing that the attack would cost too many of his soldier's lives, the general ordered his men to retreat into the woods facing the gap.

As the evening sun began to set, the sound of drums was heard, as a column of approximately five hundred North Carolina troops under the command of Colonel Palmer arrived. This was a welcome sight to the weary Confederates but an alarming one to General Gillem and his Union troops defending the gap. General Breckinridge guessed that the arrival of the reinforcements would result in the Union soldiers retreating back toward Morristown; and began to move his troops, hoping to cut off the retreat. His hunch proved to be correct as word arrived that Gillem's men had abandoned the fortifications of Bull's Gap.

Breckinridge immediately ordered Vaughn's Brigade to move to Russelville, which would be in front of the retreating Yanks. Duke's Brigade was sent to their left in an attempt to fall on Gillem's flanks. Alston and his men joined the North Carolina troops commanded by Colonel Palmer, using them to push the Union soldiers. Gillem's men encountered Vaughn's men and pushed through them, forcing a fight in the woods. By this time, it was past midnight, and the day was November 13th. Four miles outside of Morristown, Gillem and his men formed a battleline. Several volleys were exchanged as both armies stood toe to toe. Finally, Vaughn's men hit the flank of Gillem's force, resulting in a general retreat. Reaching Morristown, Gillem was relieved to see a regiment of Union soldiers and some artillery arrive on the train. With these added reinforcements, Gillem formed once again to do battle. However, the delay had allowed Palmer and Alston to double-quick their men into lines alongside Duke's and Vaughn's. The combined group of Confederate soldiers was more than the Union line could stand and they broke and ran, disappearing into the darkness of night.

When daylight lit the sky of November 13th, the Confederates were delighted to find the Union soldiers all gone, leaving behind lots of much-needed supplies. Though it was a victory for the Confederates, it was only a minor setback for the Union as thousands of additional soldiers were rushed to the area, forcing Breckinridge to fall back into Virginia. The dismounted men of the 10th Kentucky Mounted Rifles had marched their legs off; but had been part of a much-needed victory.

The Battle of Marion
December 17-18, 1864

The town of Marion was located on the Middle Fork of the Holston River in Smyth County, Virginia. It was strategically located midway between the salt works at Saltville and the lead works at Wytheville. The town and outlying farms had escaped most of the destruction that so many areas of Virginia had suffered, probably due to the mountains and its geographic location. Unfortunately, the town's luck of avoiding damage would finally run out.

Major General George Stoneman had been made commander of all Union forces in Kentucky and Tennessee; and, like others before him; he began planning a raid into southwestern Virginia. He believed in the concept of total warfare; the destruction of anything that could help the Confederate cause, whether it be civilian or not. He sent word for General Stephen Burbridge to bring his army of four thousand Union troops through Cumberland Gap and meet him in Tennessee. There, they were joined by General Gillem and another fifteen hundred troops. On the 13th of December, they easily pushed General Basil Duke's cavalry aside near Rogersville and pushed on to Kingsport. There, the Union general started his application of total warfare, destroying everything in his path. On December 14th, Duke once more tried to stop him but was pushed back toward Abingdon. The next day, Stoneman and his men went into camp about thirteen miles west of Marion. He would start his devastating trip toward Marion on December 16th.

General John C. Breckinridge oversaw what was left of Confederate forces in the area and stationed them in Saltville to protect the salt works located there. His small army was comprised of Giltner's Brigade; made up of the 4th Kentucky Cavalry, 10th Kentucky Cavalry, 10th Kentucky Mounted Rifles, and the 64th Virginia Cavalry. In addition, he had General Duke's cavalry, General Cosby's cavalry and the 34th Virginia Cavalry. The destruction in southwestern Virginia forced Breckinridge to choose whether he should continue to protect the salt works or go to the rescue of Marion. He decided to help the people; and, in the early morning hours of December 17th, the brigade moved out toward Marion.

The First Day of Battle
December 17, 1864

Breckinridge had the 10th Kentucky Mounted Rifles, under the command of Colonel Ben Caudill, to ride at the front of the column. As Caudill and his men neared the covered bridge that crossed the Middle Fork of the Holston, they saw Withcer's cavalry come racing toward them with the 11th Michigan Cavalry on their heels. Caudill's men immediately dismounted and fired a volley into the Union cavalry, emptying several saddles and causing them to retreat.

As the rest of Breckinridge's troops began to arrive on the scene, Colonel Caudill noticed that Stoneman's men had secured the high hill overlooking the river. Realizing this was the strongest defensive position in the area, Caudill immediately ordered his men to charge the hill to dislodge the Yankee soldiers. Seeing what Caudill was attempting to do, the rest of Giltner's Brigade charged, helping the colonel dislodge the Yanks and forcing them to retreat.

With the best defensive position now his, Breckinridge faced another problem; he did not have enough men to form a defensive line against the much larger Union army. To compensate, he ordered every sixth man to hold and guard the horses, instead of the customary fourth man. This allowed Breckinridge to line the hill with a long, thin line of soldiers. The 4th Kentucky constructed breastworks in front of the covered bridge, with the 2nd Kentucky to their right and the 64th Virginia, 10th Kentucky and Caudill's Army to their left. Duke and Withcer's men made up the far right of the defensive line.

General Burbridge began forming his men into columns to attack the Rebel position, staggering the 5th and 6th Colored Cavalry between the white regiments. As soon as they were in position, the large line surged forward, charging in unison. The thin Confederate line fired volley after volley, while Major Richard Page and his small battery of four cannons opened up. The intensity of the firing stunned the Yankees, causing them to fall back. Union officers rallied their men and once more charged but were beaten back as well. As the sun began to set, the Union soldiers were ordered to charge for the third time. This charge was also beaten back as the thin gray line held again. The days battle was now over as both armies were content with hunkering down and trying to stay warm.

The Second Day of Battle
December 18, 1864

Rainfall greeted the two armies at daybreak, adding more misery to their ranks. General Burbridge waited for the fog to lift and the rain to cease before attacking again. About mid-morning, he decided that the light rain would probably not stop falling and decided to continue the attack. The Union soldiers charged across the muddy field, trying to fight both the mud and the Confederates. The combination of black and white troops managed to push the 4th Kentucky and Cosby's men back, but their general was able to rally his men and push the Yanks back, retaking their positions.

On the far right, General Duke was being pressed hard by a heavy column of Union soldiers. Seeing this, Colonel Giltner sent the 2nd Kentucky to reinforce Duke. Now that Duke had the 2nd Kentucky to take their place in line, he combined with Withcer's men and attacked the flanks of the enemy, completely routing them. Seeing his flank being driven back shook Burbridge and his men, resulting in a disorderly retreat. The Rebels had held once more. But the victory had come at a cost; the men had shot up almost all of their ammunition. Most Confederate defenders had shot at least seventy-five rounds, some as much as one hundred.

At approximately 4 P.M., the firing became sporadic as the Yanks stopped their charging across the muddy fields. At this time, the Rebels saw a long line of blue-clad cavalry coming down the road to join their comrades. This was General Gillem and his Tennessee troops, whom Stoneman had called back from their raid on Saltville. The unexpected fighting capabilities of the small Confederate army had temporary created a reprieve for the salt works.

As darkness began to engulf the battlefield, each army began to hunker down behind their breastworks. The men from both sides were cold, muddy, weary and hungry. Learning that the boys in gray did not have anything to eat, the citizens of Marion sent as much food as could be spared to try to help out. Both sides had to build fires as the men became numb and insensitive due to the cold.

General Breckinridge sent officers around to all the men to get an idea of what shape they were in. The news was not good, as the number of wounded and killed had depleted the already outnumbered force. In addition, the men had no more than ten rounds of ammunition apiece. At 11 P.M., the general reluctantly ordered his men to begin withdrawing. A small contingent of men were left to keep the fires burning and to occasionally fire rounds to keep the Yanks from knowing that they were pulling out. Scouts informed the general that Union cavalry blocked the road before them, causing the army to leave the road and start crossing the mountain range to safety.

The next day, December 19th, Stoneman's men woke to find that they alone on the battlefield. General Stoneman continued to Saltville and attempted to destroy the salt works there, but in his haste, left enough intact for continued use. Stoneman and Gillem fell back into Tennessee while Burbridge and his men returned to Kentucky by going through Pound Gap.

Though the battle at Marion was declared a Union victory, Breckinridge and his men had accomplished several things. Their fighting capability had convinced Stoneman to return earlier than planned to the safety of his main camp, which contributed to his inability to totally destroy the salt works. In addition, the Rebels had inflicted heavy casualties on the Yankee army and fought them to a standstill. The 10th Kentucky Mounted Rifles had survived another terrible battle.

1865

Headquarters, 10th KY Mounted Rifles
Turkey Cove, VA
Jan. 23, 1865

Col. H. L. Giltner
Commander Brigade

"Colonel, I arrived in camp yesterday, but had little success. I find the community much imposed upon by stragglers and absentees. Capt. Jones' Company (Prentice's command) has recently murdered three soldiers said to belong to my regiment. The soldiers were arrested by the party and taken to Jones' camp. Their horses, clothing, boots too are now in the company and the men missing. What disposition must I make of Capt. Herd? I find plenty of cover in this vicinity and my men are coming in. The bushwhackers have been stealing horses and committing other degradations in the Cove and station. Tis reported that they are now in the Crab Orchard twelve miles from my camp. Send me a newspaper.

Respectfully,

B. E. Caudill
Colonel, Commanding Regimen

The Battle at the Harlan County Courthouse
March 20, 1865

On Sunday, January 1st, 1865, the men of the 10th Kentucky Mounted Rifles and the remainder of Giltner's Brigade were camped in Washington County, Virginia. The first day of the New Year arrived during a cold snowstorm. Their commander, Colonel Giltner, had spent the last few weeks attempting to re-equip his ragged army. Many of the men were almost naked as their uniforms were worn out. He did manage to acquire a shipment of unbleached jean wool pants, which, to give them some color, were dyed a brown color using walnut hulls and alum. On January 2nd, the colonel decided to travel to the Shenandoah Valley to beg for supplies, leaving Colonel Ben Caudill in charge of the brigade.

Before leaving, Giltner ordered Caudill to move the brigade to Lee County, Virginia. There were two reasons for this move. The first was that the possibility of obtaining forage for the horses was greater in Lee County. Also, it was thought that any new movements of Union forces would come through there. Colonel Caudill prepared to move on January 3rd but had to delay his departure due to a snowstorm. The men hunkered down and weathered the storm until the 6th of January, when they moved out toward their new camp. Colonel Caudill gave the honor of leading the column to his regiment, the 10th Kentucky Mounted Rifles. Slowly, the column trudged through the snow, arriving there three days later.

The new camp was established near Jonesville, Virginia, in a sheltered valley known as Turkey Cove. Colonel Caudill immediately ordered the men to construct shelters to protect them from the cold. Utilizing tents and logs cut from the nearby forest, they soon constructed dozens of crudely-built huts. These shelters were critical; every day of the month of January was cold and snowy. Despite the cold weather, these men still had a duty to perform. Each day, the colonel sent out patrols toward Kentucky and Tennessee to watch for enemy activities. Luckily, the cold conditions had taken the fight out of their Union counterparts, resulting in no fighting.

The first week of February brought the same weather pattern as January; colder and more snow. During this week, Colonel Giltner returned to take over command of the Brigade. Doctor George Whipple, Surgeon of the 10th Kentucky Mounted Rifles, informed Colonel Giltner that the health of the men was remarkably good, despite the harsh winter. Another piece of good news was the return of Captain Jim Rogers of the 10th Kentucky Mounted Rifles, who had been captured when General Morgan was killed. He entertained his fellow soldiers with the tale of his escaping from the Yankees.

With Valentine's Day rapidly approaching, Colonel Caudill was beset with numerous requests to perform marriage ceremonies. His reputation as a preacher was well known among both soldiers and civilians. The unusually high number of marriages was primarily due to most couples becoming resolved that the war would never end. Many had been waiting for the end of the war to marry.

During late February and early March, a new conscription law began to be enforced by appointed "conscription officers". This law required all men between the ages of 17 to 50 who were physically able to fight be conscripted into the Confederate Army. This was commonly referred to as the "cradle and grave law". Regardless of this new conscription, Colonel Giltner sent Colonel Caudill and a portion of the 10th Kentucky Mounted Rifles to Kentucky with orders to recruit more men.

All events during this time period were not gloomy. The men of the Brigade received word from General Echols that he had submitted a request to Richmond officials recommending that Colonel Henry Giltner be promoted to the rank of brigadier general. Unbeknownst to the men of the brigade, Richmond officials would grant the promotion, but the war would end before it took effect.

The best news, however, was the announcement that a thousand of Morgan's men, who had been captured throughout the war, had arrived in Wytheville and Abingdon. Union officials had finally agreed to an exchange of prisoners. Most of these men belonged to the 4th Kentucky Cavalry, 10th Kentucky Mounted Rifles and the 64th Virginia Mounted Infantry. These men were eager to rejoin their comrades; but unfortunately, the war would end before the majority could. This was due to the emaciated condition that most of them were in, as well as the dates of their probations. On March 16th, 1865, a large party was held to welcome the soldiers back.

The men of the brigade awoke Sunday morning of March 19th to unseasonably warm weather. Most soldiers spent the day soaking up the sunshine and taking it easy. A hard-riding scout arrived in camp in the evening that brought them back to the reality of war. He reported to Colonel Giltner that a large group of Union soldiers was in the Harlan County area, near Mt. Pleasant (now the city of Harlan). Upon hearing the report, Captain Rogers immediately asked permission to take his company of the 10th Kentucky Mounted Rifles to confront the enemy. The colonel granted his request and ordered him to take along twenty-five men of the 64th Virginia to supplement his force. Within an hour of the receipt of the report, Captain Rogers and his men were on their way to Kentucky.

Although it was dark, the column of gray-clad cavaliers managed to cross the high mountain range by traveling along the familiar Harlan Road. Passing through Crank's Gap into Harlan County, they silently traversed down the mountain road to where it met Crank's Creek Fork. This large stream flowed through their objective of Mt. Pleasant, the county seat of Harlan County. Realizing that daylight was about two hours away, the captain ordered to halt and dismount. Moving off the road, and setting pickets, the tired soldiers were soon curled up asleep.

As dawn began to lighten the morning sky, Captain Rogers sent scouts to observe the Yanks in Mt. Pleasant. The scouts returned with word that there appeared to be at least forty enemy soldiers in town. Most wore blue uniforms though some were irregularly dressed. Their description appeared to suggest that these men were probably bushwhackers or home guards. Regardless, Rogers knew that they needed to be defeated and driven away.

Captain Rogers gave orders for his men to prepare for battle and to quietly approach the small town. Using the forest to hide their movements, the cavalrymen slowly moved to the outskirts of town. With his men in position, the captain gave the order to charge. With an alarming Rebel yell, the men charged forward. Though surprised by the attack, the Yanks immediately formed a battle line, many of them taking cover in buildings surrounding the courthouse.

As the captain and his men attempted to force the stubborn Yankees from their cover, a mixture of yells and the crack of firearms filled the morning air. Adding to the confusion of battle, the swirling of dozens of horses racing through the dirt streets soon raised a large cloud of dust. A combination of this dust and gunpowder smoke soon created a fog that obscured the two sets of combatants. Taking advantage of this cloud, the hard-pressed Yanks managed to get to their horses and began to scatter into the thick forest near town. The Confederates pursued them into the woods for a short distance but soon lost them.

Returning to the courthouse, the victorious Rebels soon lost their exuberance. The clearing of the fog of battle exposed the still body of a gray-clad cavalry soldier lying in the dusty street. It was Private Andrew Jackson (known as Jack) Reasor, an 18-year-old youth, who was well-liked by his comrades. Reasor had the distinction of being the last known soldier of the 64th Virginia to be killed in action. Two Yanks also lay in the street, one dead and the other seriously wounded.

With the battle over, Captain Rogers established pickets around town and sent scouts to ensure that the Yankee horsemen were gone. Interviewing some of the inhabitants of the town revealed that the men occupying it were bushwhackers who claimed to be members of the Home Guard. Most of the men were deserters from both armies, explaining the irregular dress. They were a dangerous band of armed men and most of the townspeople were glad to see them go.

Scouts returned to the town with news that no other Yankee activity could be located in the area, and that the bushwhackers were all long-gone. Upon hearing this report, Captain Rogers ordered his men to load the body of young Jack on his horse and moved out of town. Without any fanfare, the solemn column began to retrace their steps back to Lee County, Virginia.

Arriving back at the Brigade's camp, the captain ordered Jack's body to be taken to his family's farm in nearby Turkey Cove. He then reported to Colonel Giltner, who ordered the captain to take the 10th Kentucky Mounted Rifles to camp between Turkey Cove and Cranks Gap to see if an enemy patrol had followed them. Though the mission was considered a success, the loss of Jack made brought sadness to their camp.

The Ending of the War
Spring of 1865

On Wednesday, March 22, 1865, the 10th Kentucky Mounted Rifles were encamped at Jonesville, Virginia, with Giltner's Brigade. That morning, the camp was welcomed to the sight of Colonel Ben Caudill riding in with fifty men who had been recently exchanged. Old comrades greeted each other energetically, with stories of battles and prisoner-of-war camps being swapped. During the excitement, a telegram arrived from General Echols ordering the brigade to move eastward until they were within a six-hour march of Abingdon. The move was scheduled for the next day as the Confederate Inspector General, General Davidson, was there to inspect the troops. At the end of the inspection, Davidson informed the men that he thought they were a "splendid brigade". He also said that he would recommend the promotion of Colonel Giltner to brigadier general; a notice received warmly by the men.

The brigade arose the following morning and began their march toward Abingdon, stopping long enough at Stickleyville for the men to vote in the Confederate elections. Though most of the men of the 10th Kentucky Mounted Rifles were Kentuckians, they were allowed to vote for representatives in southwestern Virginia. Two men running for office were well known by the Kentuckians: Colonels Slemp and Pridemore. Both had been officers in regiments attached to the brigade. After voting, the men rode from Lee County into Scott County and went into camp.

At daybreak on the morning of March 24th, the brigade began marching toward Nickelsville. At Rye Cove, in Scott County, they were ordered to stop, and to conduct the execution of Private Henry Bishop, a deserter from the 64th Virginia Infantry. Twelve men from regiments other than the 64th were chosen at random to conduct the execution (four weapons were loaded with bullets, the rest with blanks). Everyone else in the brigade was ordered to witness the execution. At the order to fire, the young private fell to the ground, mortally wounded. Even the toughest of soldiers thought it was a sad and solemn spectacle. The camp was quiet for the remainder of the evening.

The men awoke the next morning and were in a hurry to get moving, hoping to leave the awful memory of the execution behind. They crossed the Clinch River and traveled through an area desolated by war. The long column passed through Nickelsville, and into Russell County. They camped there and traveled on to Hansonville the following day.

Early on the morning of March 27th, the brigade formed to continue the march; with the order of march being the 7th Confederate Cavalry, 10th Kentucky Mounted Rifles, 4th Kentucky Cavalry, 64th Virginia Cavalry, 10th Kentucky Cavalry and Jenkins Cavalry. Riding most of the day, the brigade arrived outside of Abingdon at 2:30 P.M. There, they were ordered to go into camp.

On Tuesday, March 28th, a courier delivered a dispatch from Confederate headquarters in Richmond. The dispatch stated that the 10th Kentucky Mounted Rifles was being reorganized and now would be known as the 13th Kentucky Cavalry. This was due to the confusion with the 10th Kentucky Cavalry. Commanding officers of the 13th Kentucky were Colonel Ben Caudill, Lieutenant Colonel David Caudill and Major Thomas Chenoweth. The regiment would be known as the 13th Kentucky Cavalry for the remainder of the war.

The brigade would spend the next few days in the Abingdon area, constantly sending out patrols. The Confederate command did not know where the Union Army would attack next; but several reports of General Stoneman's cavalry being in northeastern Tennessee and North Carolina came in daily. During this time, the 25th Virginia Cavalry was transferred to Giltner's Brigade.

On Monday, April 3rd, Colonel Giltner ordered the 13th Kentucky to Marion to check out rumors of Union activity in that area. Not long after the 13th left, word arrived in that Richmond, Virginia, had been evacuated. Also, General Echols sent a report that Union cavalry was attacking Wytheville. The brigade immediately left for Marion, to join up with the 13th Kentucky already there. The men were going to rush on to Wytheville, in hopes of saving the town.

Battle of Wytheville
April 4, 1865

The brigade arose on the morning of April 4th and began to ride to Wytheville. The column arrived in Mt. Airy at 8 A.M. and was informed that a force of approximately four hundred soldiers of the 15th Pennsylvania Cavalry was in Wytheville. Colonel Giltner immediately sent Colonel Caudill with the 4th and 13th Kentucky Cavalries to investigate the report. The rest of the brigade was to follow, taking one battery (Lynch's Battery) with them.

When Colonel Caudill and his men reached the turnpike bridge over Reed Creek, three miles from Wytheville, they found it on fire. The only other way across the creek was the railroad bridge which also was on fire. This bridge was not as damaged as the turnpike bridge; therefore, the colonel ordered the 13th Kentucky to charge across it. They had no sooner crossed it when it became impassable, due to the fire. At this time General Echols and Colonel Giltner arrived with the remainder of the brigade. The general ordered the 4th Kentucky to cross the ford at the turnpike bridge. He also ordered the 64th Virginia and the 10th Kentucky to cross the ford at the railroad bridge to join the 13th Kentucky. The 25th Virginia and Lynch's Battery were held in reserve to protect the crossing and to put out the fires to save the bridges.

The 4th Kentucky had just crossed the creek when they encountered a small force of Union cavalry. With a rousing Rebel yell, they immediately charged the surprised Yankees. The Yanks turned and raced away with the 4th Kentucky on their heels. The other three regiments joined in the chase and rode on to Wytheville. As the Confederate cavalrymen neared town, they ran into a battle line of approximately five hundred Yankee soldiers, mostly dismounted. The 4th Kentucky took the brunt of the charge until the remainder of the brigade arrived. They then formed a battle line of their own, with the 13th Kentucky in the center, the 10th Kentucky on the right, and the 4th Kentucky and 64th Virginia on the left. Firing a volley in unison, the Confederate battle line charged forward.

The long, blue line held their position momentarily until panic set in, forcing them to flee. Using their swords and threats, Union officers were able to rally their men into another line of defense. This second battle line was close to town at the intersection of the main road and the road that led to the lead mines.

Once more the Confederate battle line surged forward, with another Rebel yell. The Pennsylvania soldiers were completely terrified of the army charging them. Many dropped their guns, running for their lives, ignoring the pleas and threats of their officers. They had discovered it was much easier to push around women and children than seasoned Rebel soldiers. Fortunately for them, they were able to get to their horses and race away before they could be captured.

The hard-charging Rebels pursued the fleeing Yankees through town but could not catch the mounted soldiers. Union officers managed to rally some of their men at the top of a small hill on the opposite side of town and formed a battle line. The 64th Virginia was the first regiment to reach the new Union battle line and charged ferociously. For the third and final time the results were the same, as the Yankee line broke and fled in panic. By 5 P.M., all organized resistance was over. Some of the 10th Kentucky who had recovered their horses chased the fleeing Yanks for a short distance. That evening, General Echols ordered each regiment to camp near Wytheville on the several roads leading into town. The excitement soon ebbed as the soldiers were worn out, with all but the pickets sleeping soundly throughout the night. The men deserved the rest as they had prevented the Yankee invaders from destroying the town and the nearby lead mine. What the sleeping men did not know, at the time, was that this would be the last major fight for them; the end of the war was approaching fast.

Near the End of the War
April 1865

The next morning, General Cosby's Brigade rode into town to reinforce Giltner's Brigade. Not long after Cosby's arrival, Vaughn's Brigade arrived outside of town. If General Stoneman's cavalry returned to fight now, the odds were in the Confederate's favor. By 11 A.M., General Echols realized that there would be no Union attack; scouts returned with word that Stoneman's Cavalry had left the area. At this time, he ordered Colonel Giltner to take his brigade to Newbern to scout for enemy activity. Giltner and his men rode into Dublin, just a few miles from Newbern, on April 6th.

Colonel Giltner sent back word to General Echols that the Newbern area was secured and that there was ample campground for the remainder of the army. The general then issued orders for his army to march to Newbern, arriving there on April 8th, with a force of approximately three thousand men. When reports began to arrive that General Robert E. Lee's army was in trouble, General Echols decided to take his army to help. He sent out orders for all detachments in southwestern Virginia to gather at Newbern. Colonel Ben Caudill and a detachment of men from the 13th Kentucky Cavalry were sent to Lee County, Virginia and eastern Kentucky to bring all unattached men who could be found.

Crossing the New River without incident, Echols' army marched to Christiansburg. The general delayed the march there to give stragglers time to catch up. Many of his men had just returned from prisoner-of-war camps and were badly worn out.

While at Christiansburg on April 10th, the general received word that General Lee had surrendered on the previous day. Not believing the report, he decided to push on to Richmond. Giltner's Brigade was ordered to lead the column toward Roanoke. As they reached the Roanoke River, they encountered dozens of soldiers. Thinking them deserters, the colonel ordered them held. When the numbers grew to about a thousand men, Giltner decided the war was actually over and ordered the men released.

The sad and broken-hearted army camped that night on the bank of the Roanoke River, finally admitting that the news of Lee's surrender was true. Many of the men, in later years, would remember that night as the saddest one of the war. While sitting around the campfire, many of the mountain warriors shed tears while reliving dozens of battles fought during the previous few years.

Orders to fall back to Christiansburg were given the next morning. When arriving there, the officers consulted on what to do next. The consensus was to allow each brigade to decide whether to disband, return home or attempt to reach General Joseph Johnston's army in North Carolina. The infantry regiments all elected to disband; therefore, General Echols furloughed them for sixty days with the understanding that, if necessary, they could be called back to duty. Generals Echols and Duke decided to attempt to reach Johnston's army with any cavalry that volunteered to go. Approximately one hundred men from Giltner's Brigade, including some from the 13th Kentucky Cavalry, volunteered to go with Echols. Colonel Diamond of the 10th Kentucky Cavalry was appointed commanding officer of this group. The majority of Duke's men chose to go with the general; the rest would ride with Colonel Giltner and General Cosby back to Kentucky. The 25th and 64th Virginia Cavalry were going to Lee County, Virginia, and then on to Cumberland Gap, to surrender.

Reaching Liberty Hill, General Cosby elected to leave his men and escape by himself, turning over command of the the two brigades to Colonel Giltner. Realizing that he would have a hard time finding forage for such a large group, the colonel decided to divide his army. The men from Cosby and Duke's brigades were sent across Pound Gap into Letcher County, Kentucky. Giltner's Brigade would enter Kentucky by the Levisa Fork of the Big Sandy. The two groups were to rejoin at Prestonsburg.

While traveling in the Levisa Fork area, Colonel Giltner received word that President Lincoln had been assassinated. When he shared this information with his men, they did not express any satisfaction with it. Most did not approve of the manner of his death and others realized that the man who would replace him would be even harsher to Confederates who had supported the southern cause.

The Second Battle of Whitesburg
April 16, 1865

While most of the 13th Kentucky Cavalry was with Giltner's Brigade in Virginia, a company under the command of Lieutenant George Houck was operating in southeastern Kentucky. He was under orders from Colonel Caudill to round up stragglers and new recruits for the 13th Kentucky. While in Letcher County, he would be involved once again in a fight in Whitesburg, and ironically, his old enemy, now Captain Benjamin Blankenship, would be in command of the Union patrol involved in the battle.

On April 12, 1865, Major Elisha Treadway, commander of the Three Forks Battalion, dispatched Captain Blankenship with a detachment of men from Company F to the Pound Gap area. Their orders were to bring under control a band of bushwhackers operating in the vicinity of southeastern Kentucky and southwestern Virginia. The Yankee patrol entered Wise County, Virginia, and skirmished with the bushwhackers, killing two of their leaders and capturing four of their men. Captain Blankenship returned to his camp of operations in Harlan County, Kentucky, to deliver the prisoners.

The captain and his detachment then continued their mission and rode once again into Whitesburg on the 16th of April. The normal, heavy rains of spring had been falling in the mountains, swelling the streams and river. This made traveling by horseback a muddy and miserable trip for the horse soldiers.

Meanwhile, Lieutenant George Houck and his company of men from the 13th Kentucky Cavalry were doing practically the same mission as their Union counterparts. While on patrol in the Beaver area, the lieutenant heard that bushwhackers were raiding Whitesburg. The Confederate patrol arrived in the small town on April 16th and ran into their Union adversaries. Luckily, the two parties were on opposite sides of the swollen Kentucky River that flowed through the town.

Upon spotting each other, gunfire erupted from all sides, with both companies of men blazing away at each other. Long years of war had hardened these soldiers and now only bullets flew across the river, unlike the previous battle in the town when insults were traded heavily. Both armies used the large trees lining the riverbanks for cover as the firing continued. The superior firepower and better weapons of the Union soldiers started to take its toll on the Rebels, resulting in the wounding of several of them. To gain enough time to withdraw his men, Lieutenant Houck hoisted a white flag. As his men casually started pulling back, the lieutenant pretended to negotiate the terms of surrender. Captain Blankenship soon realized it was just a scheme and ordered his men to continue firing, shooting down the truce flag.

Lieutenant Houck and his men retreated downstream toward the mouth of Sandlick Creek, destroying all skiffs and canoes that they encountered along the river. With no boats available, the Three Forks soldiers could not continue the fight nor pursue the Rebels as the river was swollen out of its banks, allowing no fording. The men of the 13th Kentucky Cavalry made good their escape, removing their wounded with them. A casualty list is not available for this fight; therefore, it was only known that some of the soldiers of both armies were wounded, perhaps fatally.

The Confederate patrol may have been blessed more than they realized by escaping capture. The next assignment that Captain Blankenship and his men received was to escort Confederate prisoners from Irvine to Lexington, Kentucky. On this trip, the captain was accused of allowing his men to murder some of the prisoners. Upon learning that orders for his arrest had been issued, Blankenship moved his men back into the mountains along the Kentucky and Virginia border. Shortly after the war ended, the captain fled the state, evading a trial for murder and disobeying orders. If they had been captured, Lieutenant Houck and his men may have met the same fate as the murdered prisoners.

The lieutenant and his men stayed in the area and rejoined Colonel Caudill, when he and some of the 13th Kentucky Cavalry arrived there, after leaving Giltner's Brigade. Some of the regiment was still with Colonel Giltner as he traveled toward his surrender in central Kentucky.

Continuing the Trail to Surrender
April 1865

On April 23rd, Giltner's army arrived at Salyersville, Kentucky, and was informed that General Joseph Johnston had surrendered his army. Colonel Giltner conferred with his staff and concluded that they would surrender as well. Major Chenoweth of the 13th Kentucky Cavalry was sent with the following message inquiring how to surrender:

Headquarters Confederate States Force
Salyersville, Kentucky
April 23, 1865

To the Officer Commanding Department of Kentucky:

Sir:

"A combination of unfortunate events having separated us from the Confederate Army, we are perhaps driven to the necessity of surrendering ourselves prisoners of war. The object of this communication is to ascertain terms of such surrender. We have waged an honorable warfare, and we will have honorable terms or none. We speak by authority of the men under our command. The officer bearing this letter is instructed to await your reply three days."

Very respectfully,

Henry L. Gilther, Col. Com'dg Brig. Ky. Cavalry
J. Tucker, Col. Com'dg Brig. Ky. Cavalry
Thomas Johnson, Major Com'dg. Brig. Ky. Cavalry

The following answer was received from this communication:

Headquarters United States Forces
Mount Sterling, Kentucky
April 27, 1865

H.L. Giltner
Colonel Com'dg. Div. C.S.A.

"You will be allowed the following terms to surrender your command: Surrender of men to be paroled. All public property and horses and arms to be given up. Officers can retain their sidearms when they are paroled. They must wear citizen dress while in Kentucky. They will be treated kindly. These terms will be given and none other."

By order of Brig. Gen. Hobson
H.N. Benjamin, Maj. 185th Reg't. Ohio V.I.
Com'dg.

On the 29th of April 1865, Colonel Giltner sent the following reply in regards to the surrender of his men:

Major H.N. Benjamin
Com'dg. U.S. Forces at Mt. Sterling

"With the assurances of Capt. Benj. T. Nix and Lt. H.S. Rawls, U.S.A., accompanying escort of the Flag of Truce, of the the immediate parole of all officers, I am compelled to accept the terms of capitulation tendered by Brig. Gen. Hobson. I shall reach Mt. Sterling by 3 P.M. Tomorrow the 30th inst."

Most Respectfully,
Your humble servant,2
H.L. Giltner, Col. Com'dg. Etc.

On Thursday, April 30th, 1865, Colonel Giltner and his men rode into Mt. Sterling, passing through hundreds of Union cavalry lining the sides of the road. Meanwhile, Colonel Ben Caudill and several of his men from the 13th Kentucky Cavalry returned to Letcher County. Arriving at a large grassy field in Mt. Sterling, the tired Rebels came to attention, saluted their officers, and laid down their rifles. After going through the ritual of being paroled, most officers and all of the enlisted men known as Giltner's Brigade quietly left town. Most of these southern warriors immediately headed home to the mountains of eastern Kentucky.

Colonel Giltner and his staff were not allowed to leave and remained in Union custody after their men left for home. General Hobson ordered the colonel and his staff to be transferred to his headquarters in Lexington, Kentucky. The general knew that Colonel

Giltner was highly regarded and respected by Confederate soldiers throughout Kentucky. Taking advantage of this knowledge, Hobson asked the colonel to use his influence to convince groups of soldiers who refused to surrender to turn themselves in. One of these pockets of resistance was Colonel Ben Caudill and the 13th Kentucky Cavalry who were back in eastern Kentucky, operating as a Confederate unit. In hopes of preventing further bloodshed, Colonel Giltner wrote the following letter to Caudill:

Lexington, Kentucky
May 4, 1865

Colonel B. E. Caudill
Commanding 13th Kentucky Cavalrymen

Colonel,

"In the surrender I have recently made of my command to Brigadier General Hobson, I have included you and your men and officers in the surrender.

If you do not come forward and accept the terms, you will be declared an outlaw and treated as such."

H.L. Giltner
Colonel, C.S.A.

Upon receiving the letter, Colonel Caudill conferred with his men and decided to honor Colonel Giltner's request. After turning themselves in to Union officials, the last organized Confederate regiment in southeastern Kentucky had conceded the war was over.

Though the war was officially over, most of the Confederate veterans would still suffer hardships and persecution many years after the war. Most arrived home to find their fields overgrown and their fences torn down. Several found their cabins and barns burnt as well. Neighbors and family members who had supported the Union side did not welcome them home. Many of the veterans moved from the mountains to start their lives anew, hoping to put the persecution faced at home aside. Most of them, however, would stay and rebuild; but it would take many difficult years to put the war behind them.

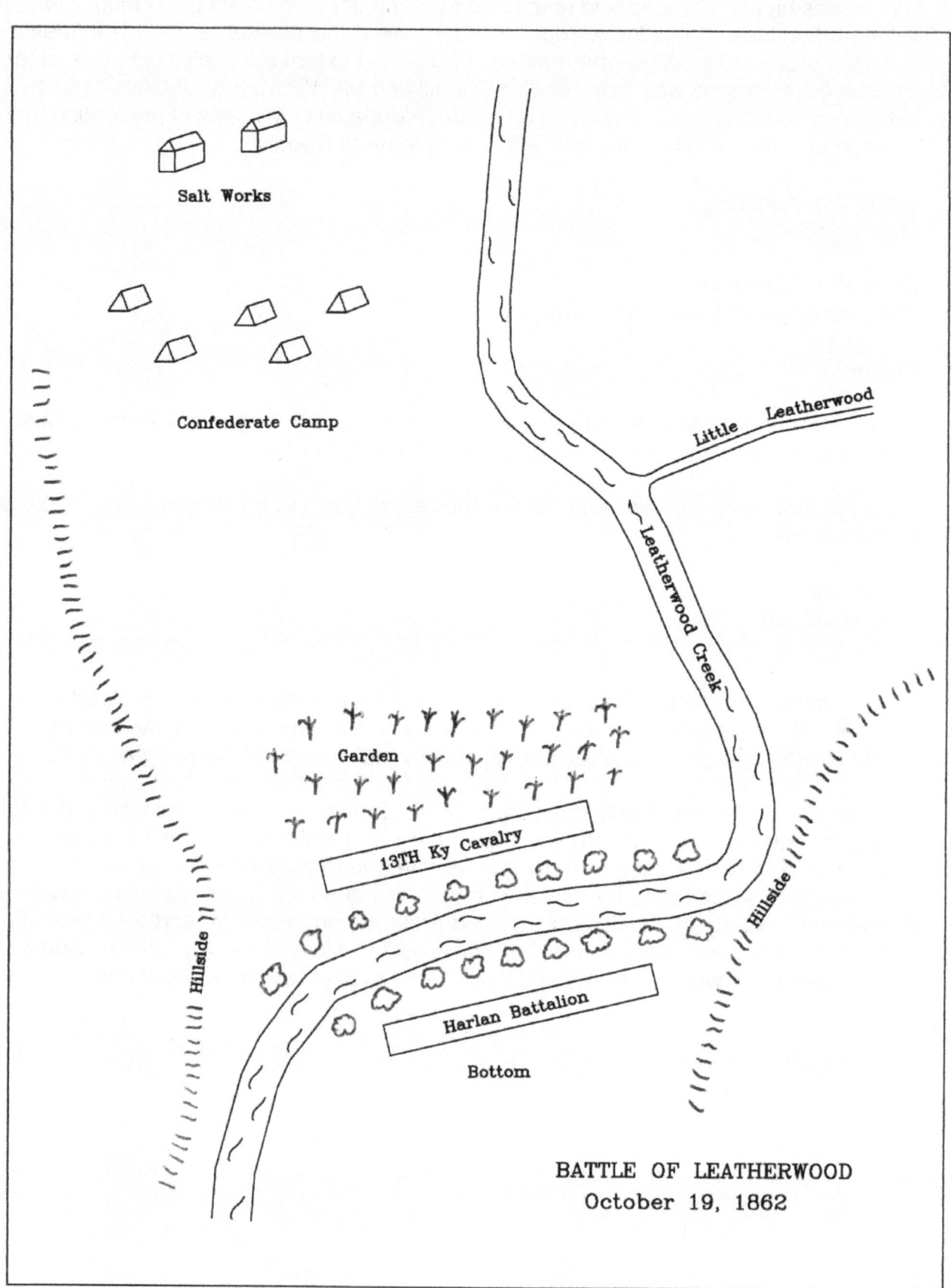

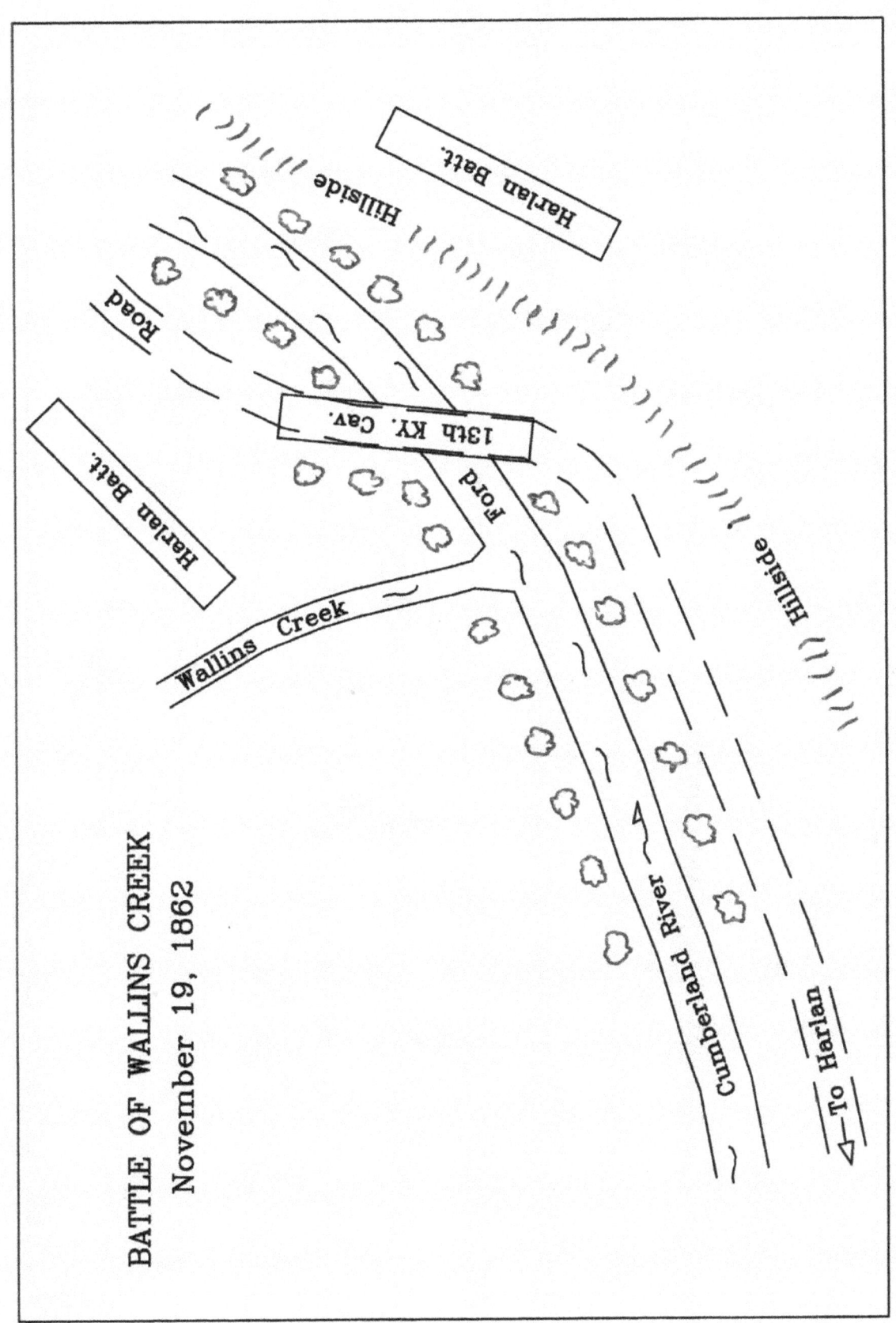

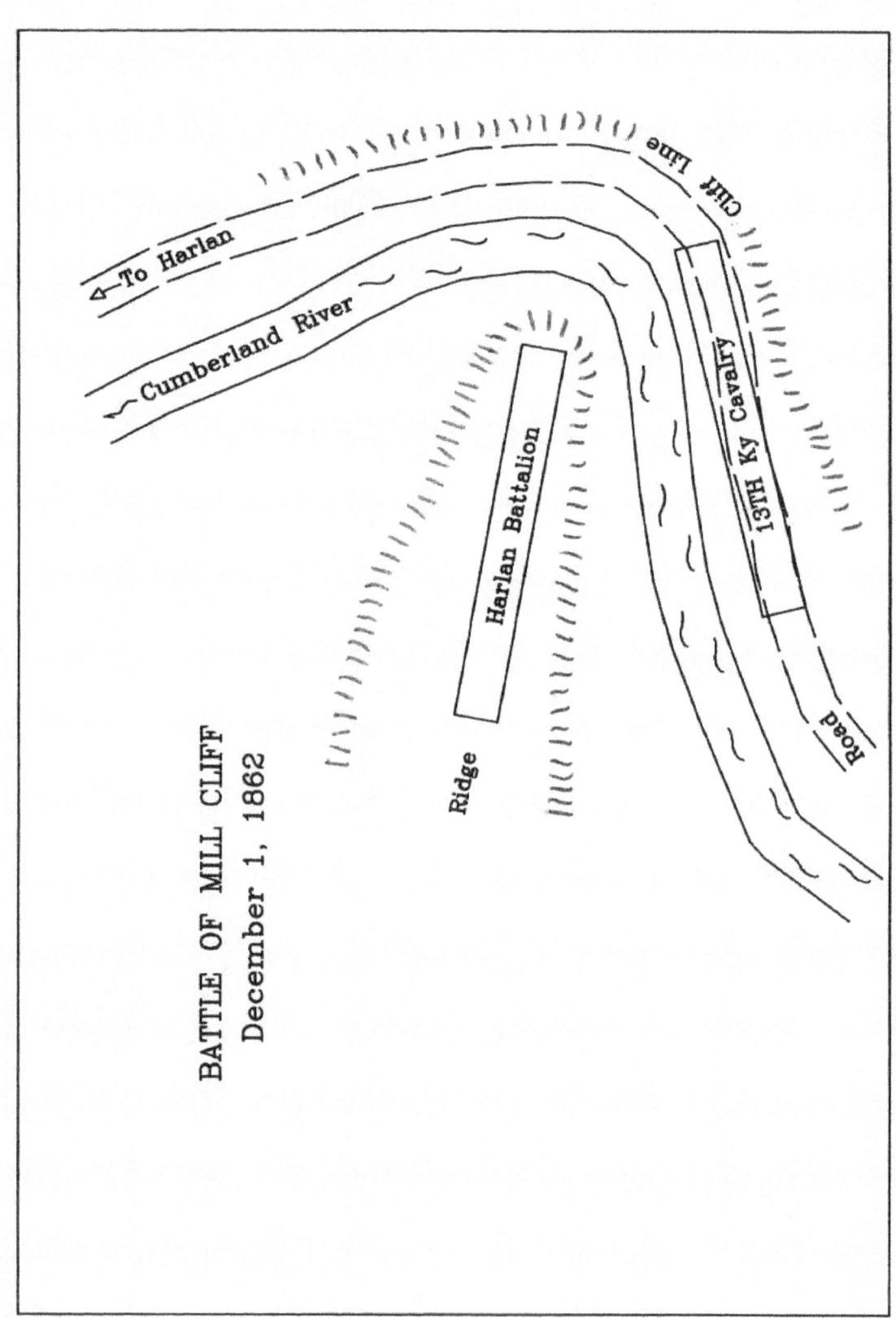

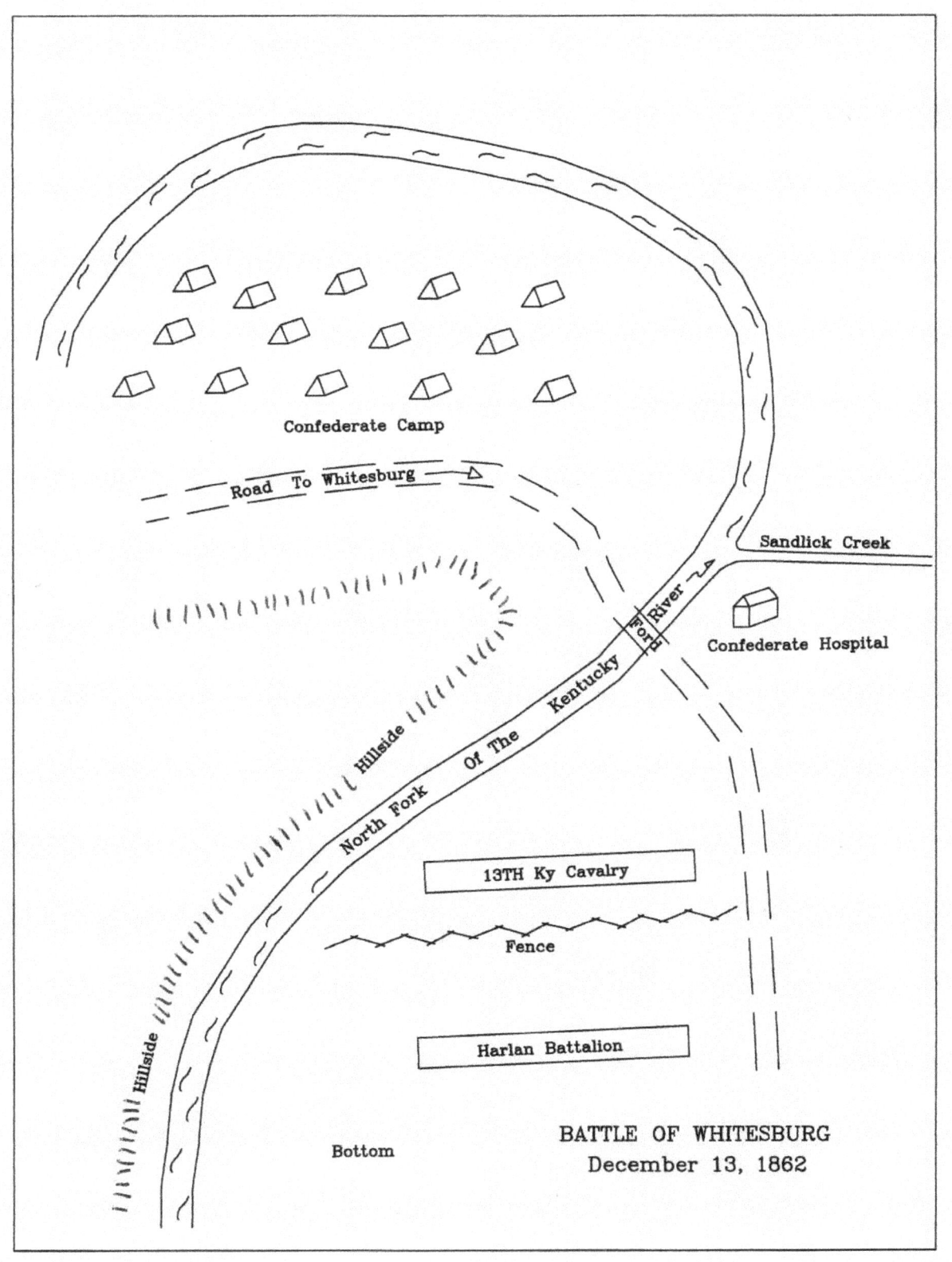

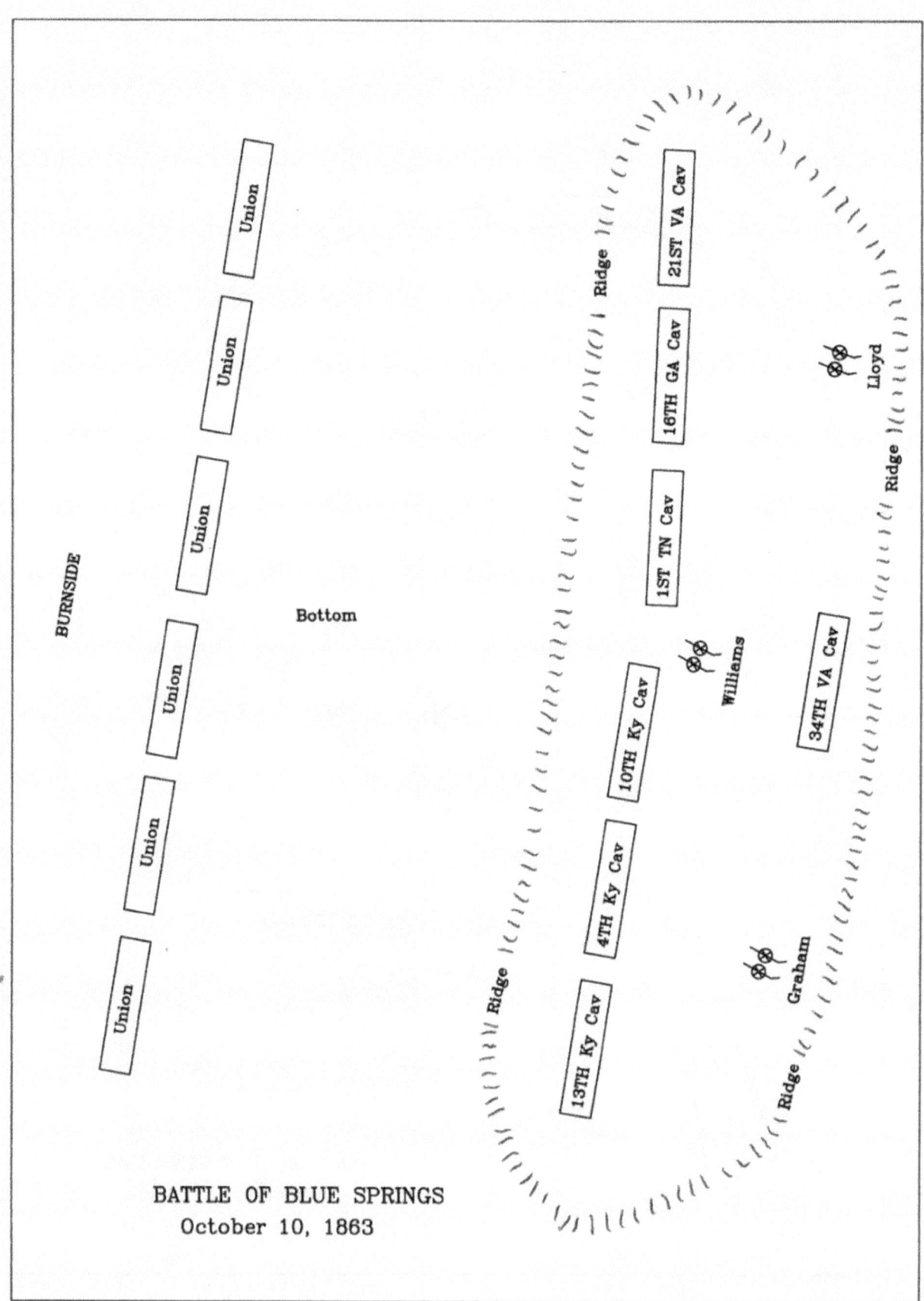

BATTLE OF BLUE SPRINGS
October 10, 1863

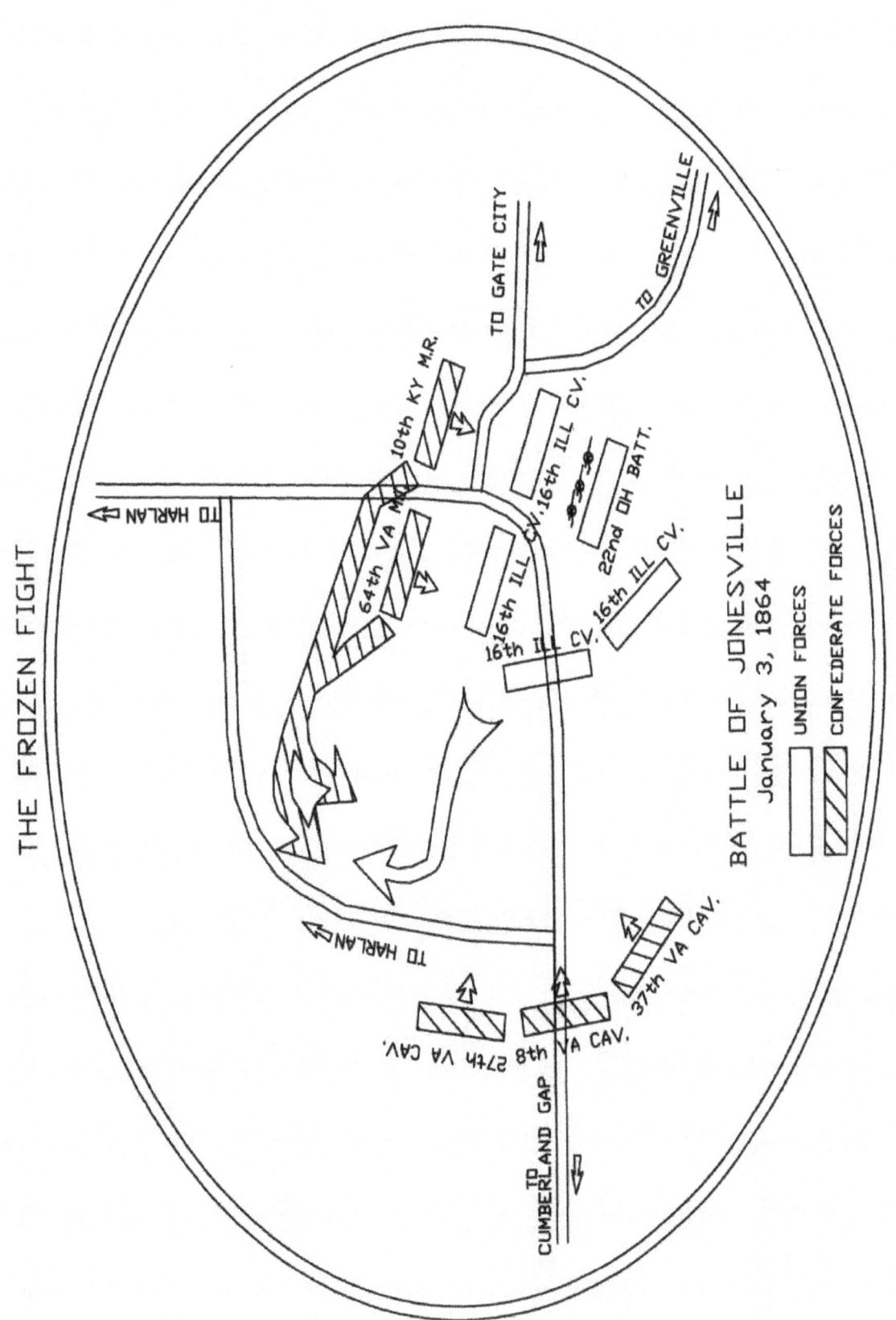

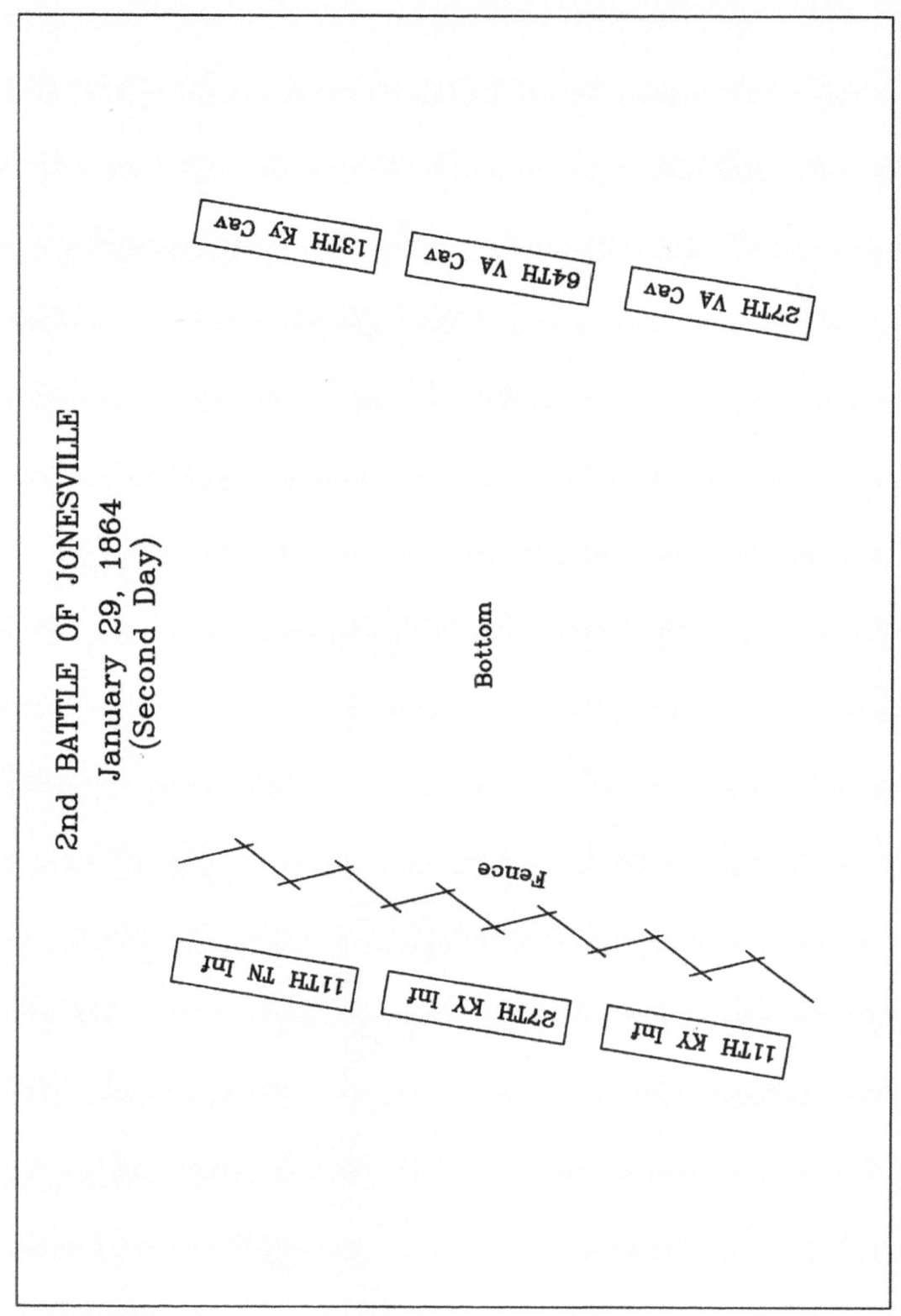

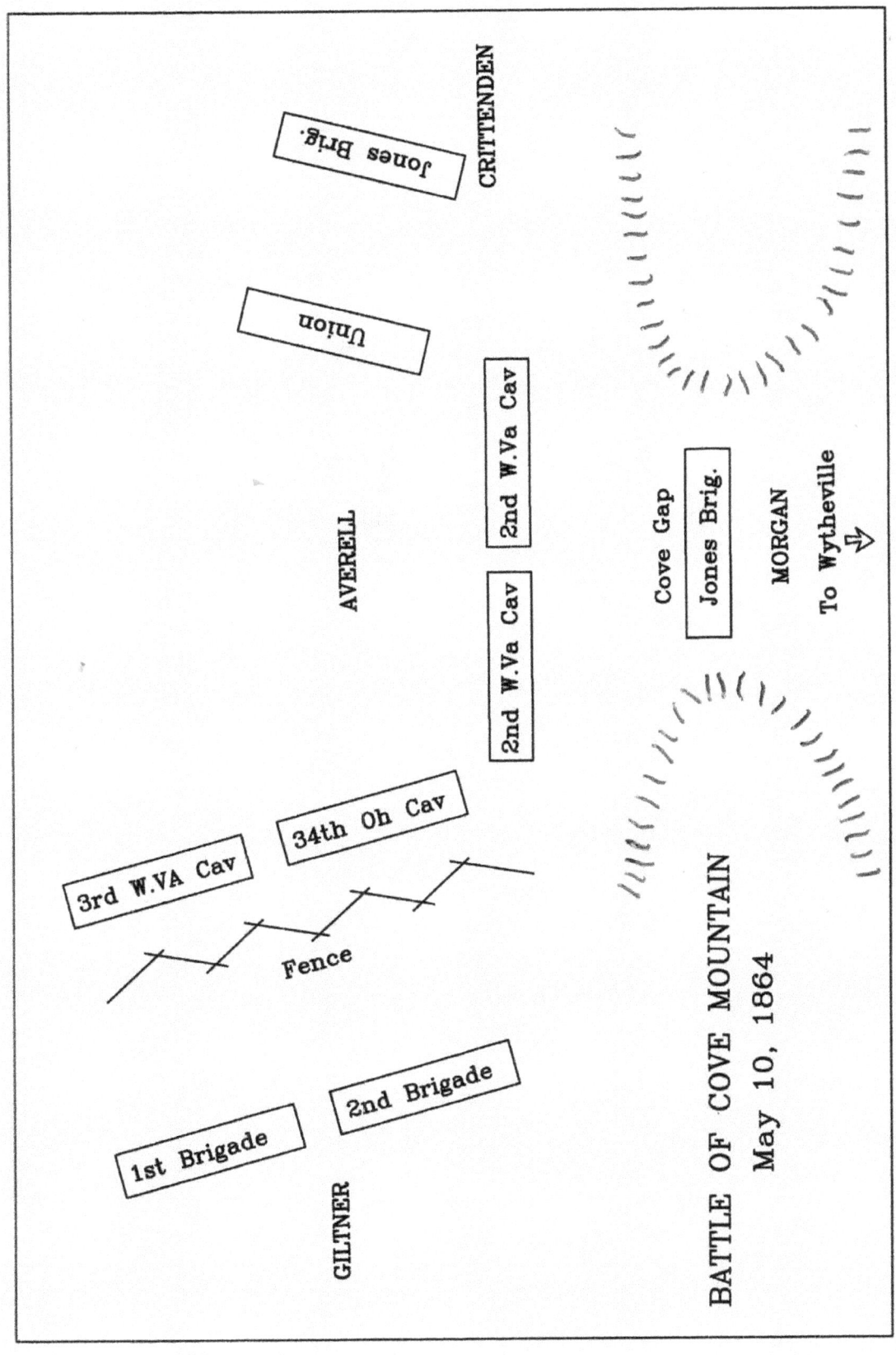

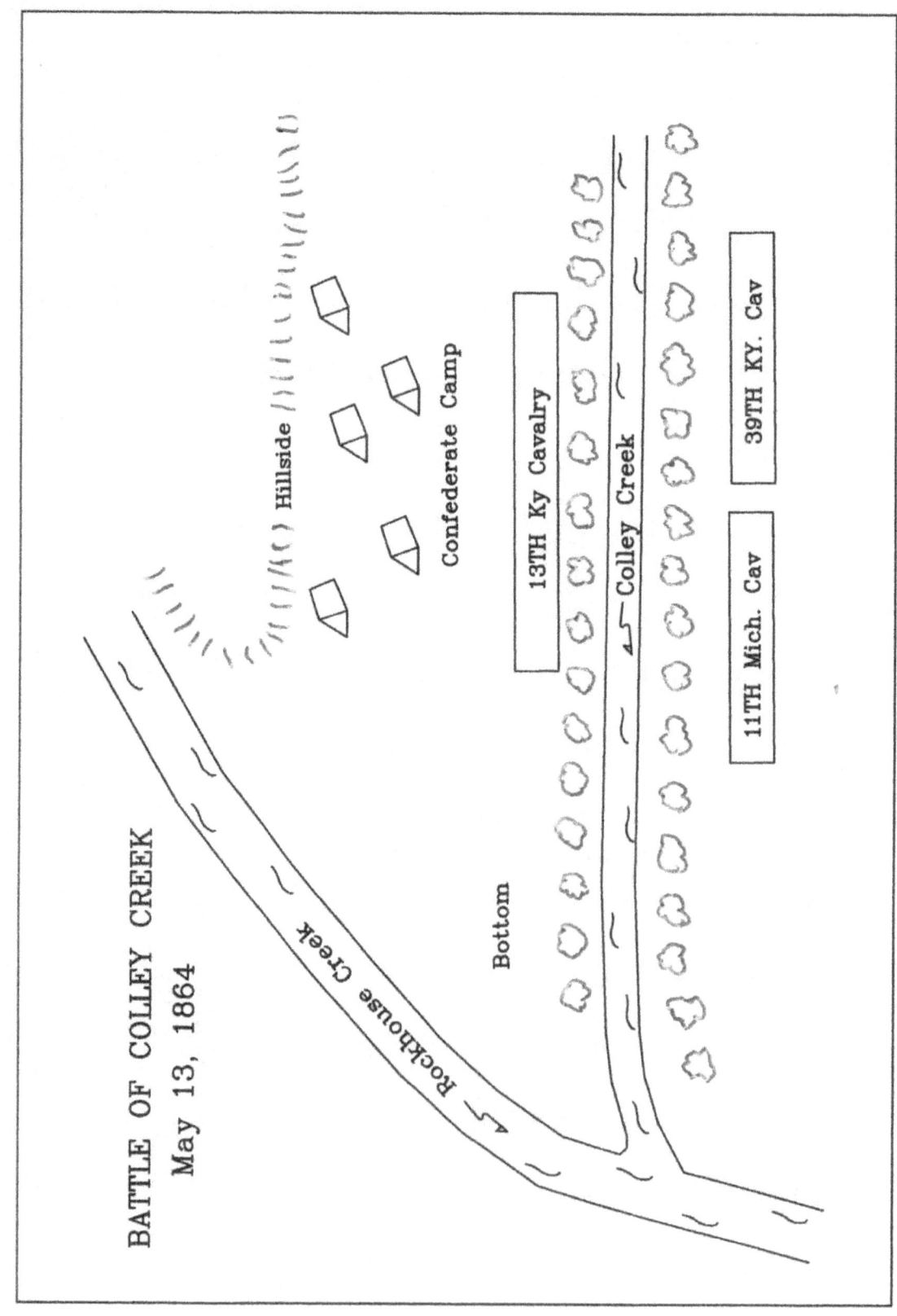

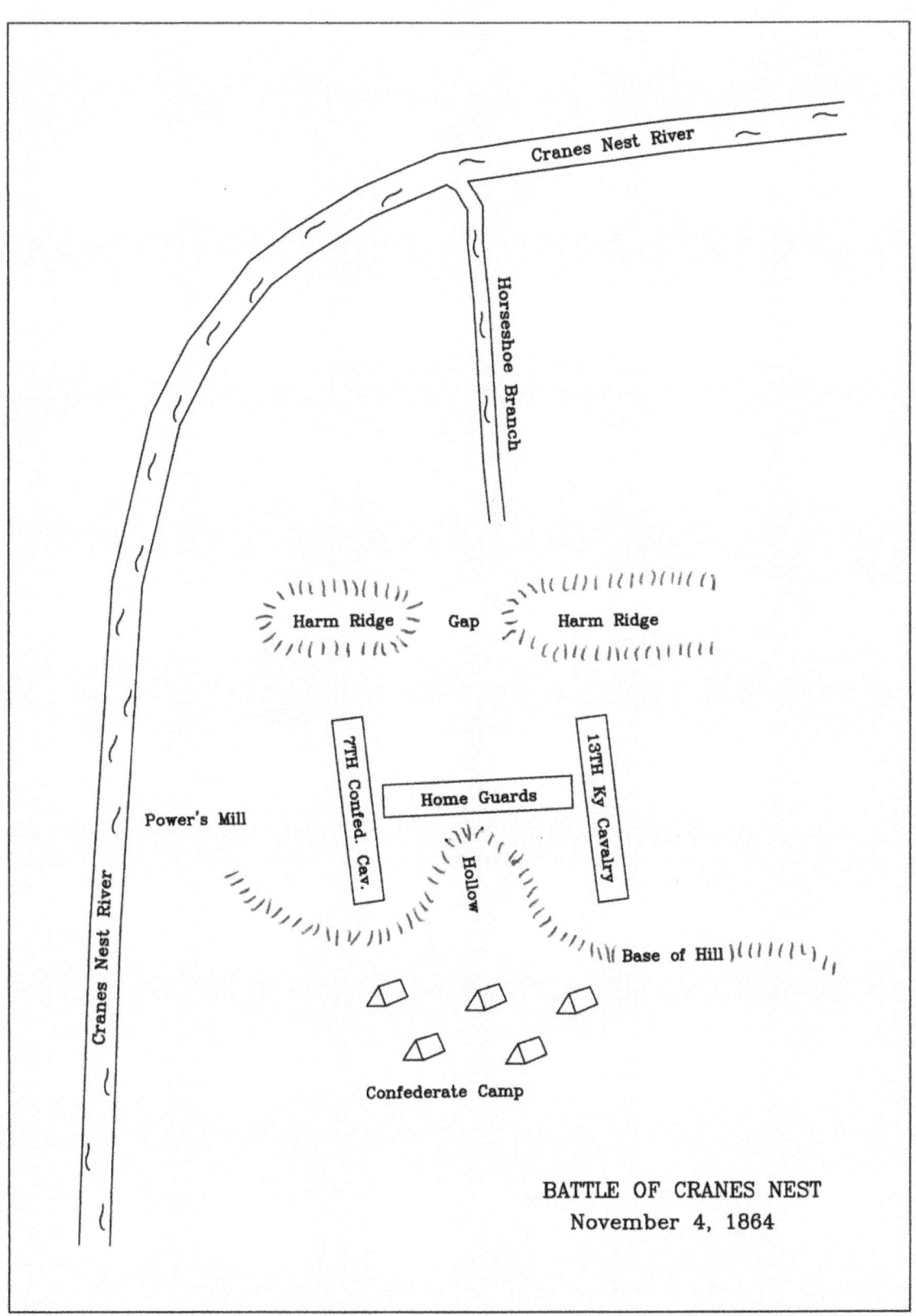

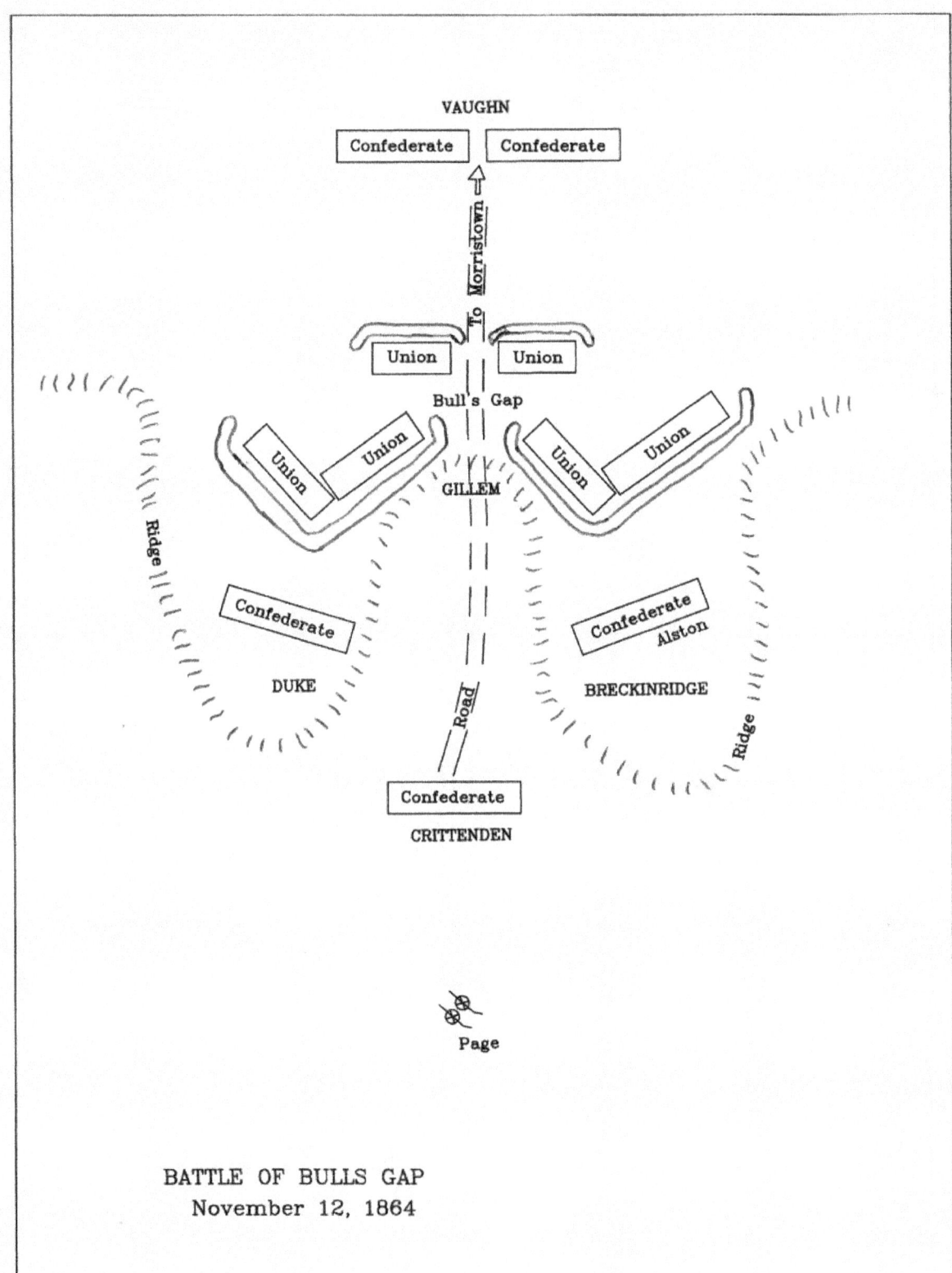

BATTLE OF BULLS GAP
November 12, 1864

Reflections

The war records of the men of the 13th Kentucky Cavalry are kept at the National Archives in Washington, D. C. These service records usually provide the date and place of enlistments; but are often incomplete regarding locations where they camped, their capture and prison records, hospital records, discharge and/or death records. An unfortunate number of Caudill's men enlisted, met muster, and then "disappeared" from the record; their unfortunate fate being unrecorded and perhaps unknown, even to their superiors.

What is known about the prewar and postwar lives of these men is available in public documents; these include census records, marriage records, pension records, property records, and a limited number of death records.

However, in a few rare cases, there is additional information concerning the lives of these Confederates. It may be handed down through the generations, it could come from the printed word, or it may be a combination of other factors. Here are a few such stories:

William "Banger" "Groundhog" Fugate
By Manton Ray Cornett

Fifty years after the beginning of the war, Private George Washington Noble sat down; and, from memory, wrote the book, <u>Behold, He Cometh in the Clouds</u>. The book has two themes; he interfaced his religious testimonials with his personal experiences before, during, and after the war ended.

One of his most often-mentioned personalities was his friend, neighbor, and second cousin, William Fugate. In the years before the war, William may have earned his best-known nickname, "Banger". It is entirely possible that his moniker was due to his fondness for fisticuffs. Noble tells how "Banger fought James Gwin a "pitched battle with Jacob "Rail Jake" Neace serving as "Banger's" second and Drewrey Gwin as James'. In this particular fight, "Banger" lost. On another occasion, "Banger" fought John C. Roberts. James Allen was "Peney's" second, and John S. Noble was "Banger's". This time, "Banger" won the fight.

Early in the war, "Banger", William P. Noble and George W. Noble ran off to join the Confederate Army. They joined the recruiter at the mouth of Combs' Branch, camped at Henry Engle's and marched up and back down Clear Creek the next day. Less than a week later, they took part in the failed attack on the Unionist Eversole cabin on the North Fork of the Kentucky River in Perry County.

After reaching Salyersville, "Banger" deserted, was captured, and then escaped under the cover of darkness, while in his sock feet. He overtook and rejoined the Confederate company the next day.

After tasting real battle at Middle Creek, "Banger", along with several others, deserted again, after learning that their unit was headed out of state, to Virginia. But, when his unit returned to Kentucky, "Banger" and several of the other deserters rejoined the company.

While still in Kentucky, "Banger", George W. Noble, and several others were captured by Unionist troops. "Banger" began to act "crazy" causing Union Colonel Herd to offer to send him home. Unfortunately for "Banger", Union Captain Bill Strong said that he knew "Banger" Fugate; and, that he was the smartest prisoner in the group. Union Lieutenant Marcum then offered "Banger" a chance at freedom if he could outrun their cavalry for 100 yards. At first, "Banger" refused, figuring that if he ran, it would just give the Unionists a chance to shoot him. "Banger" finally believed their promise that they would not shoot him for running. He was given a 10-yard head-start and won the race. Unfortunately for "Banger" the Unionists were not trustworthy; and he was headed off to prison with the other Confederates.

"Banger" and his friends were taken to Lexington and placed on a train. "Banger" began to act "crazy" once again; but received no reward for his efforts. After crossing the Ohio at Cincinnati, they were transported to Camp Chase Prison in Columbus. After a few weeks there, they were transferred to Johnson's Island Prison where they remained for about 5 months. In November of 1863, they were transferred to Point Lookout Prison in Maryland; and there they remained for another five months.

At Point Lookout, "Banger" continued his "crazy" act by spelling the word G-R--O-U-N-D-H-O-G in a variety of ways, but only whenever he was within earshot of the Union Sergeant of the Guard. The guards felt sorry for "Banger" and would take him outside and give him food. "Banger" made friends with Finnigan, the Sergeant of the Guard, who continued to take him outside the prison compound. Finnigan began to call "Banger" by a new nickname; "Groundhog". Sometimes, after being outside, "Banger" aka "Groundhog", would come in at night with enough food to share with his closest friend, George W. Noble. When he was allowed to visit the prison commissary, "Banger" played "crazy" and the workers would throw meat, turnips and carrots at him. He got to keep anything that hit him. "Banger' picked up the food, stuffed it in his bosom, ran away, and shared it later with his friends from "back home".

When the word finally came that some Confederate prisoners would be exchanged, "Banger" cried when his name was not among those that were called. After pleading to go home with George W. Noble, to be with his wife and children that he called by fictitious names, Sergeant Finnigan interceded on "Banger's" behalf. Fortunately for "Banger", Union Captain Patterson agreed with Finnigan and let him go.

On the steamboat to Baltimore, "Banger" pretended to be afraid and threatened to jump into the water. His plan, which he had shared with George W. Noble, was to gain Union sympathy again, and possibly be offered money. Sure enough, Sergeant Finnigan, calmed "Banger" down and gave him $2.00, a tidy sum in those days.

After a brief stay in Baltimore, "Banger" got ahead of George W. Noble on the road to home. But at several locations, Noble and Wiley Miller, his traveling companion, would know that "Banger" had been there. The hired hands that they met were imitating "Banger" by spelling G-R-O-U-N-D-H-O-G.

The Branson Slayings
By Richard Smith

On August 29, 1862, Richard Branson, a son of Henry and Betsy (Howard) Branson, made known his stance concerning Southern secession by enlisting in the Confederate mounted regiment being "raised" by Colonel Ben Caudill at Whitesburg. On an unknown date the next spring, while carrying out the duties of 4th Sergeant in Co. B of Caudill's 13th Kentucky Cavalry, not-yet 40-year-old Richard Branson became a casualty of war in a skirmish on Lost Creek in Breathitt County. The exact nature of his wound is not known, but he survived what must have been a rough ride to Letcher County, where he was transported to let nature take its course. Sgt. Richard Branson succumbed to his wounds on the 11th of June 1863, at his parents' home on Crase Branch.

James, an older brother of Richard Branson who was born about 1828, had been married to Sally Howard since 1846. James was the father of eight children. This may have been a factor that delayed his joining forces with Colonel Caudill's recruits until November 15, 1862. He served as a Private in Co. H and is known to have been present with his regiment on April 30, 1863.

The hand-carved grave marker of Leonard Branson, the oldest of the Confederate sons of Henry and Betsy Branson, bears the inscription, "Killed by the enemy about Sept. 1862, age about 38 years." Branson relative and historian, William Banks, expressed the opinion that the carver of the stone did his work many years after the fact and missed the year of Leonard's murder by one and his age by as much as five. The Branson murders occurred in September 1863 and Leonard was more likely 43 years of age at the time of his passing, as he appears to have been born about 1820. He was married to Elizabeth Brashear. They were the parents of 6 children.

As is the case with many other Confederate veterans, Leonard had no service record. Therefore, his date of enlistment, company, and rank attained are not known. However, every direct descendant and lateral relative that Caudill Camp members have interviewed have maintained, as his head stone suggests, that Leonard was an enlisted Confederate soldier. Perhaps James and Leonard were with Richard when he was wounded, or maybe they were encamped in reasonable proximity to their home when he was brought there, wounded. Whatever their circumstance and considering the loosely organized nature of early-war Kentucky's Confederate regiments, it's conceivable that James and Leonard enjoyed Colonel Caudill's blessing if they stayed home a few days to help tend their dying brother.

Sgt. Richard Branson's death preceded the capture of Colonel Ben Caudill and about 120 of his men at Gladeville by less than a month. Whether James and Leonard Branson had returned to their regiment by the time of that tragedy is unknown. The fact they had, collectively, a dozen and a half hungry mouths to feed at home could never have been far from their minds. If their return to military duty was less-than-prompt, their tardiness may have owed to the growing season being in full swing in Kentucky. Perhaps the fact the Branson brothers were still at home when the tragedy occurred at Gladeville may explain why they were not captured there.

The theory has been expressed in print by John B. Wells III, and other historians who have studied local aspects of the Civil War, that Colonel Caudill's command was in near-total disarray during the months following the Gladeville incident. Throughout late summer 1863, James and Leonard Branson may have remained at home, awaiting orders that never came. Whatever the case, on a September day in 1863, they were paid a visit by Perry County unionists.

There are few accounts in print of the action that took place on Crase Branch that day. One interpretation of the battle can be found in Fess Whitaker's The History of Corporal Fess Whitaker. On page 117, Mr. Whitaker referred to the attack on the Branson cabin as "the only real battle (of the Civil War) fought in Letcher County." Another contributing factor to lead one to believe the fighting may have been intense is that several former dormitory residents of neighboring Stuart Robinson School attest that, well into the 20th Century, following a rain they could pick up "musket balls" in a steep section of the school pasture that borders the area where the Branson cabin was located. The location of the pasture would indicate much return fire came from within the Branson cabin.

The R.B. Caudill papers state, as did Dean Branson, a surviving descendant, that Leonard Branson was caught away from his home and was killed near the mouth of Crase Branch. Mr. Caudill identified the attackers as a group of soldiers led by Major John C. Eversole of Perry County. He also named a Sexton, a resident of Letcher County's Rockhouse Creek, of which Crase Branch is a tributary, as being present and eluded that, since Sexton would have had knowledge of the area and its residents, he likely served as scout for Major Eversole's raiding party. Branson descendants maintain some of Leonard's children were with him and saw their father murdered.

Local historian, William Banks, stated that young Andrew Jackson Crase also witnessed the killing of Leonard Branson. Mr. Banks reported that Crase was seen by the killers but managed to evade them. Mr. Crase is said to have feared for his life, made his escape to Virginia where he joined a Confederate regiment, the 47th Virginia Mounted Infantry, under an assumed name, and served throughout the war. His gravestone verifies his Virginia service as does Stephen Lynn's compilation of pension applications of Kentucky veterans and widows. Author Lynn's book is entitled Confederate Pensioners of Kentucky.

After dispatching Leonard Branson, it seems Eversole's men advanced further up Crase Branch to the site of the Branson cabin where they encountered much stiffer resistance. Fess Whitaker mentioned that the Rebels horded up in the Branson cabin. The students said they collected many battle artifacts from school property. From other testimonials, however, it would appear that the only "Rebel" horded up in the Branson cabin was James Branson. Dean Branson claimed the father of the Confederates, Henry Branson, was present in the house. If the volume of fire indicated by student-found relics is an indicator, and if it is true that James Branson had not appropriated a Yankee-issued repeating carbine, then it may be likely that one or more of the Branson women helped load weapons inside the cabin. If so, Eversole's men must have allowed females to leave at some point late in the fight. The names or numbers of those inside the cabin during the fight will probably never be ascertained.

The shooting apparently lasted for the better part of the afternoon. The bullet holes, some of which would accept a young man's thumb, in the logs of the Branson cabin attested to the number of Union shots fired into its hewn timbers. Fess Whitaker mentioned that bullet holes could be seen in the logs around the door of the cabin in the photograph he used in his book, which we have included here. As a teenager, I was privileged to help re-locate the logs from the Branson cabin to another site, where they later fell victim to a pine straw fire. I've never forgotten the size or volume of the bullet holes.

Fess Whitaker's comparison of the fight at the Branson cabin to that at the Alamo is certainly acceptable with reference to the predictable outcome. It is unknown at what time of day James took the rifle or pistol that disabled or killed him, but it seems likely he was dead by dark. His body was found in the cabin.

The aforementioned Dean Branson stated that just after dark, old Henry managed to escape from the cabin and fled on up Crase Branch to a corn field, on property currently owned by Curt Blair, in which someone had "already shocked some fodder". It was in one of these fodder shocks that Henry Branson, whose only crime appears to have been fathering three Confederate soldiers, hid from his tormentors for the last time. Although this phase of the "battle" was not nearly as drawn-out as the afternoon fight, its outcome was as imminent. The Yankees decided to simply run their bayonets through the few shocks of fodder until they found Henry Branson.

Some have suggested that the murder of the Bransons by a uniformed force commanded by Major John C. Eversole was one of the events that led to the 1864 attack by troops of Colonel Ben Caudill's 13th Kentucky Cavalry on Eversole's Middle Fork home. That action, the second attack of the war on the Eversole dwelling, resulted in the death of the Major and his brother Joseph. Regardless of whether the slaying of the Bransons led to the demise of Major Eversole, it certainly widowed mothers, orphaned children, destroyed property, and gave rise to one of the most often-repeated stories of Civil War atrocities on Rockhouse Creek.

Daniel Noble (1838 – 1903)
Confederate Mounted Infantryman and Union Naval Hero
By Manton Ray Cornett

On Thursday, October 25, 2012, a small gathering took place on a hillside near Gilmore in Wolfe County, KY. The group consisted of three members of the Ben Caudill Camp, Sons of Confederate Veterans; Faron Sparkman, Lawrence Cook and Manton Ray Cornett. Sparkman and Cornett had arrived from Hazard while Lawrence and his wife had travelled from Pike County. The group had come together to place a very special marker on the grave of a man who lived an incredible young life.

Daniel Noble was born in Breathitt County in 1838, the son of Hiram and Sarah "Sally" Francis Noble. Like most young men in the area, he considered himself a farmer. Still single when the 'war between the states' began, he and two of his older brothers, John Whorton and William Palmer, joined the Confederate Army. From September 23, 1862 until July 7, 1863 Daniel would serve as a Private in Company G of Colonel Ben Caudill's Confederate 13th Kentucky Cavalry (designated as the 10th Kentucky Mounted Infantry in 1863). For months, they rode throughout southeastern Kentucky and southwestern Virginia. Then, Daniel's life would take an almost unbelievable turn. While in Gladeville, VA, the town now called Wise, Daniel, and about 120 of his Confederate comrades, including his commanding officer, were captured. A Union force, led by Major John Mason Brown, had pushed through Pound Gap, and caught them by surprise. From Gladeville, the prisoners of war were taken back through Kentucky to the Ohio River. On July 18th, 1863, they arrived at Kemper Barracks in Cincinnati. Two days later, most of the men were transferred to Camp Chase Prison in Columbus, Ohio. After nearly five weeks, Daniel was transferred again; this time to the appalling Union prison in Chicago, Illinois known as Camp Douglas. There were very few ways to leave Camp

Douglas. Many Southern men would die there from disease, deprivation, and exposure; tragically, their remains are still there today.

In December of 1863, part of the U.S. Navy's fleet visited Chicago. One reason for being there was to round up as many new recruits as possible. Daniel, and many others who were healthy enough to be chosen, realized that harsh weather was in store, their shelter was inadequate, food was in short supply, and that this might be their best chance for survival. From December 22 to December 26, eighty Confederate prisoners of war from Camp Douglas were selected to become 'landsmen' in the United States Navy. A 'landsman' is an inexperienced seaman; in today's terms, they might be called landlubbers. Daniel's official date of enlistment was December 23, 1863. On that day, he was described as 23 years of age; a 5' 8 1/2" citizen of Breathitt County, KY with blue eyes, light hair, fair complexion, and having two small scars on his left thigh.

Daniel's first naval assignment was aboard the U. S. S. South Carolina, which was part of the South Atlantic Blockading Squadron, stationed off the coast of Charlestown, SC. The screw-propelled steamer was capable of 12 knots and carried four 8-inch guns and one 32-pounder. Prior to Daniel joining her crew, the South Carolina had seen service from Boston to Mosquito Inlet, Florida. Daniel would remain with the U.S.S. South Carolina until January 25, 1864. While life aboard the South Carolina may have been relatively mundane, Daniel's naval experience was about to become both exceptional and unforgettable. On January 26, 1864, he was transferred to and became a crew member of the U.S.S. Metacomet. This new ship was a side-wheeled steam-powered gunboat, assigned to the West Gulf Blockading Squadron near Mobile Bay, Alabama. She could run at 12 ½ knots and carried four 9-pound guns, one 12-pound gun, two 24-pound guns and two 100-pound guns. (These sizes refer to the weight of the projectiles, not to the weight of the weapon.)

On June 6, 1864, the Metacomet captured the British blockade-runner Donegal, and on June 30, helped destroy another blockade-runner, the Ivanhoe. On August 5, Union Admiral David Farragut led his 17-ship fleet, including the Metacomet, into Mobile Bay, intent on destroying or capturing the two Confederate forts and the ships protecting them. The Battle of Mobile Bay was about to begin.

Upon entering Mobile Bay, the lead ship, the U.S.S. Tecumseh, struck a 'torpedo', better known today as a mine, and began to sink. This prompted Admiral Farragut to encourage his ships' captains to continue the attack by uttering those now-famous words, "Damn the torpedoes, full speed ahead".

As the battle ensued, the Metacomet helped capture the Confederate gunboat C.S.S. Tennessee and the C.S.S. Selma. The crew of the Metacomet was also directed to rescue the crew of the ill-fated Tecumseh. Six crewmen, including Landsman Daniel Noble, were dispatched from the Metacomet in a small boat. Their goal was to rescue as many crewmen from the Tecumseh as possible. Through their heroic efforts, they were able to save ten Union sailors from an almost certain death. For their daring deed, all six crewmen of the Metacomet were recommended for the Congressional Medal of Honor. Soon after the Battle of Mobile Bay, the Metacomet was sent to the coast of Texas, where the crew captured a blockade-runner named Susanna on November 28 and the schooner Sea Witch on December 31. While in New Orleans on January 1, 1865, Daniel deserted the U. S. Navy and began making his way back to Kentucky.

On January 15, 1866, Daniel Noble was awarded the Congressional Medal of Honor. The citation reads: "For the President of the United States of America, in the name of Congress, takes pleasure in presenting the Medal of Honor to Landsman Daniel Noble, United States Navy, for extraordinary heroism in action while serving as Landsman on board the U.S.S. Metacomet. Landsman Noble served among the boat's crew which went to the rescue of the U. S. Monitor Tecumseh when that vessel was struck by a torpedo in passing enemy forts in Mobile Bay, Alabama, 5 August 1864. Landsman Noble braved the enemy fire which was said by the admiral to be 'one of the most galling' he had ever seen and aided in rescuing from death ten of the crew of the Tecumseh, thereby eliciting the admiration of both friend and foe."

We know little about Daniel's life after the war. Since he didn't exactly leave the U. S. Navy on friendly terms, and since he was living in a remote area, making communication with the 'outside world' difficult, it is very likely that he never knew about the Medal of Honor award. We do know that he applied for a Union pension, which was 'Rejected' in 1890. We know that his two marriages produced eight children, and that the family spent most of the post-war years in Wolfe County, near Campton. And finally, we know that Daniel died in 1903 and is buried in the Childers Cemetery at Gilmore, in Wolfe County, KY.

We also know that Daniel received an upright Confederate headstone from Veterans' Affairs in 2007. At that time, local researchers were totally unaware of his experiences beyond Camp Douglas and his enlistment in the U.S. Navy. That new information first surfaced in February 2012, when Mr. Don Morfe, a member of the Medal of Honor Society, contacted Faron Sparkman, one of the researchers who had completed the process that led to Daniel's Confederate headstone being placed on his grave. The Society had attempted to obtain a Union headstone with Medal of Honor recognition and had been refused. The Veterans' Administration informed the Society that the only way they would grant their request would be for the Confederate marker to be removed from Daniel's grave. This seemed undesirable, even unacceptable, to all parties concerned. The only other alternative would be to use private funds to purchase a reasonable facsimile from a private monument company. That option was explored, and eventually, a marker was purchased by the Noble Family Association, produced by Appalachian Monument in Mayking, KY, and placed by members of the Ben Caudill Camp, S.C.V.

Daniel's grave, with his unique combination of headstones, is located on a wooded hillside, east of Highway 1419 in Wolfe County, just north of Lindon Drive. The GPS coordinates are 37° 44.877'N and 83° 21.992'W.

Five Breathitt County Soldiers: Lost no more, after 134 years
By Stephen D. Bowling

It was a great pleasure on Thursday to have the opportunity to mark the graves of five men from Breathitt County who gave their lives while in service to the South more than four months after the war ended.

These five men left their homes during the Civil War and joined the Confederate Army but never made it home; and, for more than 134 years, they were lost to their families and to history. All of that has now been corrected with the installation of five new granite Confederate markers on their graves in Madison County.

The following is an account of the trip on Thursday made by two members of the Ben Caudill Camp:

The Ben Caudill Camp's "Tombstone Express" steamed out of Perry County and made only a brief stop at the Strong Cemetery at Lost Creek in Breathitt County where Carlos Brock and Stephen D. Bowling placed a memorial stone for Private Wiley Oren Davis, (Company G, 13th Kentucky Cavalry). This feat was accomplished in 12 minutes (possibly a new Mountain record).

The "Express" fired up a full head of steam and turned toward Drowning Creek in Madison County to place five new stones.

After approximately 5 years of research by the Caudill Camp and six months of on-the-ground searches, the exact location of five missing Breathitt County men was discovered and proven by several documented sources. The story is as follows:

Emory Allen (Comp. I), John Alfred Allen (Comp. G), Irvine Allen (Comp. G); three brothers in Confederate service, and David Richardson (Comp I, 13th) were all released from prison and were headed home on the "old County Road" in Madison County. They were accompanied by Andrew Fletcher Gwinn, a civilian who was captured while serving as a guide for Company G and a possible member of Company G.

According to G. W. Noble's <u>Behold He Cometh in the Clouds</u> and family oral sources, the party was shot and killed "at the mouth of Drowning Creek in Estill County." Sources from the period support this statement. Col. Lilly (14th and 3 Forks Battalion) had established a line of defensive works that surrounded Irvine and Battalion Head Quarters. One of those sites, which partially stands today, was at the Mouth of Drowning Creek on the Estill County side on a high cliff. Drowning Creek serves as the county line between Estill and Madison; and, as the story goes, many men were shot from ambush "where the old county road makes a sharp turn up in Drowning Creek near its mouth".

According to a local historian, "Lily's men would sit on that high cliff there, up in the woods and shoot Confederates as they staggered home half-starved after the war" (obviously a Southern Historian).

After compiling as much information as we could on the events at Drowning Creek, I set out on this hallowed ground and found the spot, the remnants of the old works high on the cliff; and, more importantly, the landowner who had possessed the land since 1957. After some discussion, the landowner, Shelby Spicer, related to me that he had bulldozed the small point nearest the mouth of Drowning Creek and that it had been covered with "30 or 40, maybe even 50 graves that people later said were soldiers that were killed in battles here on Drowning." He said that he remembered the holes in the ground but thought they were natural.

In accordance with the Allen family's oral tales the graves were "on a low point overlooking the Kentucky River and the mouth of Drowning Creek and the highest point at the mouth." Everything fit into place after my brief visit to the site.

Ecstatic, I returned to Breathitt and Faron immediately ordered stones for the men we knew were killed and buried in Madison County. Only later were we able to piece together the complete story; and we even found railroad vouchers for the transportation of these soldiers to Louisville in late July 1865. Research also uncovered a report that Col. Lily had filed in August stating:

1865, August 9-- encounter at Drowning creek, Estill- 7 armed confederates killed.

Are these our five soldiers and two more?? Who are the other "30 or 40, maybe even 50" soldiers who are lying unmarked in Madison County? Five of those killed by Lilly's men are now marked. Sadly, more than 130 years had passed since their families suffered the pain and anguish of their loss.

Ezekial Brashear Brought Home
By Richard Smith

Many years ago, genealogist and Letcher County historian Bill Banks received a letter from an aged Mr. Sonny Branson of California. The Branson letter contained information concerning east Kentucky Banks/Branson marriages and notes pertaining to Brashear family genealogy.

The Brashear information included the fact that Ezekial Brashear, a son of Sampson and Margaret (Bright) Brashear, and husband of, first, Nancy Cornett and, later, Mary Ann Combs, had served as a Private in Co. B of the 10th Kentucky Mounted Rifles, a Confederate regiment also known as Caudill's Army. Mr. Branson wrote that Private Brashear had accompanied his regiment, while under the command of General John Hunt Morgan, on Morgan's last raid into Kentucky during the early days of June 1864. He further stated that Private Ezekial Brashear served in a manner above and beyond military expectation in action at Mt. Sterling, Kentucky, prior to being killed in that battle.

The Branson letter also related that General Morgan became aware of the bravery Private Brashear had demonstrated in combat at Mount Sterling, and upon learning he was a Kentuckian, ordered that his remains should be removed to his family cemetery for burial. The Branson letter went on to identify the specific burial place of Private Brashear in the Branson Cemetery at the mouth of Pratt Fork, near Letcher Post Office.

Stephen Sumner
By Richard Smith

In a mid-1990's interview, an aged Jasper Sumner of Kodak, KY, revealed that his paternal grandfather, James Sumner, and other family members, had been residents of George's Branch in Perry County since well before the Civil War. Jasper reported that his grandfather had been a bit old for service at the time of the war, and that he had discouraged his sons from taking sides in the conflict.

Younger sons, James and John Wesley, had ignored their father's advice and had cast their lot with the Confederacy by enlisting in Caudill's command. Instead of marching off to war beside his brothers, James' older son, Stephen, had chosen to stay at home and help provide for and perhaps protect the family from Unionists in the area who would be aware of his brothers' allegiance. He busied himself with hillside farming, raised goats, and enjoyed the relative neutrality offered by the remoteness of the head of George's Branch.

Most of their household goods were provided by the land, but, as John Donne had admonished, near the end of winter, 1863, the day came when James Sumner's family members found they had need of their fellow man. When it became apparent that they would have to acquire supplies from a store located near the mouth of George's Branch, son Stephen saddled the family pet, a black saddle mare belonging to his father, and made the normally pleasant ride to "the mouth of the holler".

Upon arriving at the store, Stephen noticed a handful of uniformed men hanging around in the yard. He may have recognized some horses, formerly the property of his neighbors, tied by a common rope and realized he was about to encounter Union stock buyers. Probably realizing that his father's fine example of Kentucky horseflesh had already become the focus of Union attention, he continued toward a hitching rail. By the time he dismounted, one of the Union soldiers grabbed his mount's bridle and another began checking her feet. Although the exact words that were exchanged between Stephen and the Union officer in charge will never be known, it is no great stretch of the imagination to assume they became heated as Stephen tried to explain that the mare didn't belong to him, and that he certainly couldn't sell her.

Escalating tempers will often draw a crowd, and as this one grew in numbers, Stephen recognized some of his neighbors. When he decided he had heard enough and tried to take the mare's reins back from the soldier who held them, the officer who had done most of the talking attempted to draw his side-arm from its flapped holster. A friend, who must have joined the crowd only after Stephen's conversation had distracted the stock buyers, threw him an ancient, but loaded, shotgun. It's likely that Stephen probably caught the gun awkwardly, and with the muzzle very near the officer's face, attempted to swat the big lock back with the heel of his hand. Whatever the case, the old gun accidently discharged its predictable load of birdshot but missed the officer's head by mere inches. He wasn't as lucky, however, with regard to the burning particles of black powder that had propelled the shot from the gun. The tiny coals blinded him, and the blast must have temporarily confused his men.

With little regard for the mental or physical condition of the men in blue, Stephen grabbed the bridle of his father's mare, vaulted aboard, and applied his heels to her ribs. To the tune of Yankee gunfire, he and his father's mare made their escape.

Spurring the mare, perhaps harder than would have been approved by his father, Stephen soon arrived at the Sumner farm in the head of George's Branch. He must have had no desire to tarry, though, since his decision to join Confederate forces had been helped along by angry men who may be immediately to his rear.

Old Jasper Sumner said Stephen left in a hurry and made his way across the ridge that separates the watersheds of Carr's Fork and the North Fork of the Kentucky River. Once he struck the river, he had but to turn upstream a short distance to the mouth of Leatherwood Creek. There, he encountered the encampment of Caudill's men who were guarding the Brashear family salt wells. On March 16, 1863, he joined their cause, enlisting in Company H of Caudill's 10th Kentucky Mounted Rifles.

The Execution of Gilbert Creech

Gilbert Creech, also known as "Scritch", was born in 1815, the son of John Creech, Sr, and Sarah Armstrong Creech. On July 13, 1843, he married Elizabeth Maggard, the daughter of "Old" Sam Maggard, who lived above Hindman, KY. Creech was one of those men who chose to support the Union during the war; he served in Company B of the Harlan County Battalion and became a close associate of the notorious local Unionist, Clabe Jones.

On April 14, 1863, Gilbert Creech, his brother Elijah, and about 50 other Union Home Guards, were captured by Benjamin Caudill's men who were under the command of Major Thomas J. Chenoweth, 13th KY Cavalry, on Leatherwood Creek in Perry County. They were all tried for various crimes and paroled, with the one exception being Gilbert Creech. After being brought to trial at the Confederate camp, it was concluded that he had killed and robbed an elderly man and woman. He was also charged with having "waylaid and shot Confederate soldiers". Gilbert Creech was court-martialed and found guilty of murder, robbery and other crimes. Major Chenoweth asked Creech if he had been guilty of bushwhacking his Confederates. Gilbert answered, "Yes, and I will bushwhack again". Major Chenoweth's simple and straightforward answer was, "It's damned uncertain."

Gilbert Creech was sentenced to be shot by a firing squad of fourteen soldiers, representing seven companies of the 13th KY Cavalry. Major Chenoweth sent for the wife and children of Creech and allowed a last visit. Corporal Isaac Collins, Corporal Benjamin Smith, and Private Daniel Howard, whose brother had been killed by Creech, were among the selected men for the firing squad. Eighteen-year-old Private Franklin Allen volunteered for the ensuing detail. Other participants included Captain Samuel Ray Brashear, Lieutenant George W. Houck, Sergeant David Grigsby, Sergeant Drury S. Godsey, Corporal Daniel Smith, Private James N. Brashear, Private John W. Wright, Private John McKee and William Brashear. Immediately before he was shot, when the firing squad was ordered to take aim, Creech patted himself on the chest and told everyone present that he was ready. It was said, by some who were present, that Gilbert Creech was probably one of the most daring and courageous men ever to face a firing squad. His body was buried in the P. H. Hall Cemetery.

Gilbert Creech was executed on April 14, 1863, at the Brashear Salt Works in Perry County, on the lot where M. C. Cornett's dwelling once stood. The Salt Works were located near the mouth of Leatherwood Creek on Highway 699, just off Route 7. During the war, the area was known as Brashearville; but today, it is called Cornettsville. Postwar indictments were brought, from 1865 to 1867, against the men involved in the execution; but it was found that they acted with proper military conduct and were pardoned by the governor.

The Influence of Ben E. Caudill
By Richard Smith

In the years leading up to the Civil War, John A. Caudill appears to have been known throughout the Cumberlands and beyond as a trusted and revered man of God. He held esteemed positions in a large association of churches. He was a son of one Revolutionary War veteran and nephew to another. Descendants of these Revolutionaries and those of at least two more of their brothers had settled in the area shortly after the turn of the 19th Century. Most of these Caudills had proven themselves intelligent, capable, and adaptable by thriving in the wilderness to the west of the Appalachian divide. They owned tillable land and had propagated.

Early in the Civil War, John A. Caudill's son, Ben, cast his lot with the Confederacy. This, as much as any other event, may have tipped the scales in favor of the Confederacy in the headwaters of the North Fork of the Kentucky and the Elkhorn Fork of the Big Sandy. Ben Caudill was a leader within the large Caudill clan, a respected member of the community, a husband and father who provided well for his family, and a "big" mountain preacher. His early-war service was as Captain of Company F of the 5th Kentucky Confederate Infantry.

In the estimation of his Confederate superiors, Ben Caudill must have fulfilled all they expected of an officer. One of these Confederate powers-that-be may have delved into genealogy and recognized that Captain Caudill might even further serve the Confederacy should he be promoted and sent home to recruit the legion of men who were his kin and acquaintances into the service of the South. The necessary military moves were made, and in August of 1862, Colonel Ben E. Caudill attacked his new assignment by opening a new Confederate recruiting camp on land owned by his father at the mouth of Sandlick in Letcher County.

It would seem reasonable to think that it might have been very difficult to "raise" a regiment as late as August of 1862. The war had been raging throughout the southeastern United States for the better part of a year and a half. Confederate cannon had long-since expelled Kentuckian Major Anderson and his Union forces from Fort Sumpter. Without doubt, the manner in which the Yankees had been forced to skedaddle at 1st Manassas had resulted in many a Southern guffaw and commitment to serve. News of the screams of wounded Confederates in the brush fires of Shiloh, the action at Fort Donelson, and even talk of the death of General Zollicoffer, at not-too-distant Fishing Creek, must have filtered down to the mountain neighborhoods. With the news of conflict at Middle Creek and Ivy Mountain, in neighboring counties, the assumption that all who intended to serve the Confederacy were already doing so.

It was these uncommitted men in the headwaters area of Kentucky that Confederate commanders had in mind when they sent Ben Caudill home to recruit. Their thinking proved correct to the degree that the promotion of Ben Caudill to Colonel might be credited with having been a stroke of genius, as the locals, so hesitant to join until now, were apparently just waiting for one of their own to lead them. According to comparative data tabulated by Owen Wright several years ago, Colonel Caudill's kin, acquaintances, fellow Baptists, and those who had only heard of his reputation flocked to his recruiting camps in numbers that helped boost the per capita average for Confederate service among adult males of Letcher County beyond that achieved in any other community in the South.

Wesley Sumner
By Richard Smith

Abundant evidence exists that John Sumner enlisted as a Private in Co. B of the Confederate command of Colonel Ben Caudill on September 9, 1862, at Whitesburg. According to family history handed down by John's daughter, Celia Sumner Back, within days of her father "jining" Caudill's forces, a band of Union troops showed up at John's Letcher County home and took his only son, Wesley, with them when they left. Granny Celia said she never saw her brother again; and, according to her, none of Wes' relatives or acquaintances who served with Caudill, including her father and husband, ever admitted to seeing him again.

However, Wesley's name shows up on the early-war Company B roster of Caudill's 10th Kentucky Mounted Rifles, although his muster-in site or date has not been found to his date. Neither, to my knowledge, have Caudill Camp members succeeded in finding military information pertaining to Wesley between the time his name appeared on the roster and the July 7, 1863 debacle at Gladeville, Virginia. A Confederate record was found that stated Wes was captured there, along with Colonel Caudill and about 120 of his comrades. His name appears on the list of Confederate prisoners who arrived on August 24 of that year at the Union prison known as Camp Douglas in the Chicago area.

Colonel Caudill's ranks were filled with men who were kin to, friends with, or at least knew Wes Sumner by sight. Surely, one of them would have passed along information pertaining to him had he actually served with the 10th Kentucky Mounted Rifles. The same applies to those who may have been imprisoned with him.

Information that conflicts with the concept that Wesley was captured at Gladeville is to be found on his death certificate that was issued at Camp Douglas. That document states that he was captured at Buffington Island as a member of Morgan's Raiders, died on November 4, 1863 of typhoid fever, and is buried in grave # 792 in Oakwood Cemetery, E. 67th Street, Chicago, (Cook County), Illinois.

This battle at Buffington Island, of course, took place (on July 19, 1863) when General John Hunt Morgan and his troops attempted to re-cross the Ohio River downstream from the mouth of the Hocking River on Morgan's Great Raid into Indiana and Ohio in the summer of 1863. Prisoners captured at Buffington Island could possibly have been shipped by rail to Camp Douglas by the date of Wesley's arrival there.

In summary, after being abducted by Union troops, the scant evidence extant concerning the Confederate service of Wesley Sumner seems to suggest one of three scenarios:

1) Wes escaped from his captors locally, rode with his father and other relatives in Caudill's regiment, was captured at Gladeville, and served in Union captivity from July 7 until November 4, when he died. For unknown reasons, those who knew his fate must never have revealed their knowledge of it. This would include Wes' first cousin, James Sumner, who was captured at Gladeville and arrived at Camp Douglas as a prisoner on

the same day as Wes. James may never have seen Wes while in transport to Douglas or while there, may never have seen him, as the camp was a city unto itself. If he saw Wes, James chose to never reveal his awareness of his presence at Camp Douglas to family and friends. (James survived Camp Douglas but died of typhoid in Perry County in 1880. His widow, Nancy Back Sumner, appears as the head of household on the 1880 Perry Census with 8 minor children in her care.)

2) Wes escaped from his captors locally, joined Caudill's command briefly (explaining the appearance of his name on Caudill's roster) but was sent on detached service with Morgan, during which time he was captured at Buffington Island. He must have never encountered friends or relatives during his Confederate service or during the few months he remained captive.

3) Wes was transported by his captors to an area removed from eastern Kentucky, escaped from captivity, joined Confederate forces convenient to the area of his escape, and served in the ranks of Morgan's Raiders until being captured at Buffington Island. (The appearance of the name Wesley Sumner on Caudill's Co. B roster might be explained away by claiming the name of Wes' first cousin, John Wesley Sumner mistakenly appeared on the roll of Co. B. John Wesley apparently served in Co. H.)

Wesley's sister Celia talked of her need for closure concerning her brother's mysterious disappearance until her dying day in 1924. As the 150th anniversary of Wes' death approaches, the fact is that the few relevant records that have surfaced that pertain to his Confederate service and ultimate death have revealed scant actual detail concerning his fate.

Hooker's Scapegoat
Compiled and edited by Manton Ray Cornett

To qualify as a scapegoat, one must be "a person who is blamed for the wrongdoings, mistakes, or faults of others, especially for reasons of expediency". Synonyms include "whipping boy", "victim", "goat" and "fall guy". In the Bible, it was "a goat sent into the wilderness after the Jewish chief priest had symbolically laid the sins of the people upon it" (Lev. 16).

The following facts and allegations related to Thomas Martin were reported in the pages of Cincinnati newspapers as they transpired and were recently researched and brought to light by Faron Sparkman, Ben Caudill Camp Historian. The opinions and analysis of Thomas Martin's demise were contributed by James M. Pritchard, research room supervisor at the Kentucky State Archives.

May 13, 1863: Unlike most young men, both North and South, Thomas Martin did not enter the war seeking adventure or glory. He took up arms, not to fight for the Union or the Confederacy, but to settle a personal score. After being confronted by Jarius (Jarud) Biggs, a furloughed Union soldier, who accused Martin of stealing his canoe and flourished a gun in his face, Martin borrowed a gun and returned to confront Biggs. Martin later claimed that he met Biggs in the road, and in a fair fight, wounded Biggs in his arm. Biggs notified Union authorities that he had been ambushed by Martin, who was "with a band of guerrillas". Martin, now marked for arrest, fled into neighboring Morgan County. For a time, Martin found refuge in a known haunt of rebel partisans and bushwhackers.

Sometime in the late fall of 1863, Captain Sam Thompson's command, including Thomas Martin, returned, from Virginia to northeastern Kentucky on a scouting mission. Thompson had orders to gather additional recruits and round up deserters. Thompson was regarded by local Unionists to be guerrilla, even though he was a regular Confederate commissioned officer. He had previously commanded a company of "Partisan Rangers", who had killed at least three Home Guards during a foray in March 1863. Thompson had also been associated with the notorious Captain Algernon Sidney Cook, a partisan leader who terrorized northeastern Kentucky in 1863.

September 2, 1863: Captain Sam Thompson and Captain Sid Cook accompanied Captain John T. Williams, another noted mountain partisan, on a raid into Flemingsburg, Kentucky. In addition to emptying the stables and plundering stores, they robbed the local bank.

September 12, 1863: Thomas Martin, a farmhand on his father's farm in Carter County, KY, enlisted in the Confederate army, joining General John S. William's Virginia Brigade. At this time, Martin later claimed, he was sworn in as a private in Captain Samuel W. Thompson's company of the 10th Kentucky Rifles. At this stage in the war, the Kentucky mountains had become contested ground between the cavalry of both sides. Federal forces based in northeastern Kentucky raided railroad lines, lead mines and salt works in southwestern Virginia. Confederate troops frequently dashed out of Virginia on raids that sometimes penetrated deep into north central Kentucky. Deserters and guerrillas from both sides raged a merciless feud in the isolated hills.

September 24, 1863: After a bank robbery in Ashland, Kentucky, Cook's band fled to southwestern Virginia and entered the regular service as Company G of the 7th Confederate Cavalry Battalion.

October 25, 1863: "Cook's Devils" returned to northeastern Kentucky and killed Rowan County Clerk E. H. Logan, who had been active in enrolling men in the Union militia.

November 1, 1863: Joining forces with Captain Sam Thompson, Cook led another raid into Carter County. Approaching Olive Hill, Cook rode to the home of Deputy Provost Marshall William H. Tyree and shouted that he was a Federal officer returning from a scout. Tyree emerged, pistol in hand, and was shot down. Cook also shot a Federal soldier who was attempting to flee from the house. Riding through the night, the raiders seized more horses and plundered several homes of Unionists before they were overtaken by Union cavalry. Driven off after a sharp skirmish, Cook and Thompson escaped into the hills of Morgan County. Thompson apparently returned to Virginia in late 1863, but Thomas Martin straggled behind in northeastern Kentucky.

January 17, 1864: According to the Cincinnati *Enquirer*, Martin was captured at Gladeville, VA by a squad of scouts from the 40th Kentucky Regiment, under Captain William Adams. Martin stated that he belonged to the 10th Kentucky Mounted Rifles under Colonel Benjamin E. Caudill. Caudill was then a prisoner and the Rifles were being commanded by Major Chenoweth. The record in *United States vs. Thomas Martin* states that Martin was captured in present-day Elliott County, Kentucky, by a detachment of the 40th Kentucky Mounted Infantry, on January 8, 1864. Captain Stephen H. Young of the 40th stated that Martin offered to join his company if released. Young refused his request, regarding all of Thompson's men as "die-hard" rebels. At Catlettsburg, Kentucky, Martin was identified by his old enemy Jarius (Jarud) Biggs as the "guerrilla" who had waylaid him the previous summer, even promising Biggs that, given the chance, he would shoot him again.

February 12, 1864: Accused of being a guerrilla, Martin was denied the rights of a prisoner of war and sent to McLean's Barracks in Cincinnati, Ohio. For the next several months he languished in his cell while Federal officials gathered evidence to try him before a U. S. Military Commission.

September 22, 1864: A military commission convened in Cincinnati bringing charges against Thomas Martin, "citizen".

Charge 1: "Being a guerrilla": From May 1, 1863 to February 20, 1864, Thomas Martin was a member of Cook's Guerrillas, "not belonging to any of the regularly organized and authorized forces of the "so called" Confederate States of America. This in the counties of Greenup, Morgan, Boyd, Rowan and Carter in the state of Kentucky". On or about May 31, 1863 in Greenup County, KY, he "shot at and wounded Jarud (Jarius) Biggs, a private of Co. K, 10th KY Cavalry, at that time at home on sick furlough". On October 1, 1863, he "was present with said guerrillas when they killed William E. Tyree, Provost Marshall of Carter, Morgan and Rowan Counties, Kentucky at his residence at Tiger Bridge in Carter County, Kentucky".

Charge 2: Robbery: From about May 1, 1863 to about August 15, 1863, "in company, Thomas Martin robbed Robert Lampton of Star Furnace in Carter County, KY of dry goods from his store and jewelry and other articles from his house, horses, a gold watch, money and other valuables, and breaking and destroying the furniture in his house". In September 1863," along with Cook's guerrillas, he did rob the Ashland Bank in Boyd County, KY of ten thousand dollars, by putting the bank occupants in fear and forcibly taking said money". In the company of Cook's guerrillas, he "robbed Charles Reason of Cannonsburg in Boyd County, KY of a gold watch, large quantities of dry goods and one hundred dollars in money". During the month of November 1863, in company with Cook's guerrillas, he "robbed William Lampton, the owner of Pennsylvania Furnace in Greenup County, KY of two horses and a large amount of goods from his store".

To these charges, the accused pleaded "Not Guilty".

The Commission deliberated and found Martin "Not Guilty" of all specifications that were made in Charge 2. However, even though the commission deleted some of the wording made in Charge 1, Martin was found "Guilty" of all specifications in that charge. In other words, he was guilty only of being a guerrilla and of wounding Jarud (Jarius) Biggs. His affiliation with Captain Samuel Thompson's command, a unit that frequently cooperated with "Cook's Devils" damned him in the eyes of the court. Martin was sentenced to be shot to death with musketry, at such time and place as the Commanding General may direct. After the trial, young Martin was confined in McLean Barracks, on Third Street between Central Avenue and John Street, in total ignorance of his fate. The condemned prisoner spent his days policing the barracks and, according to one source, became a special favorite of Brigadier General August Willich, commander of the district that included Cincinnati and northern Kentucky. By the time of Lee's surrender at Appomattox, Martin was hopeful that his life would be spared. According to a report in the Cincinnati *Gazette*, President Lincoln intended to commute the death sentence to imprisonment. Lincoln's assassination probably sealed Martin's fate; on April 25, 1865, Major General Joseph Hooker, commander of the Northern Department, approved the findings and sentence of the court and ordered Thomas Martin to be executed.

May 2, 1865: Learning of his fate, Martin "was much surprised, but bore the announcement with great fortitude". The sentence was to be executed under the direction of the Commandant of the Post at Cincinnati, Ohio between the hours of 12:00AM and 2:00PM on Friday May 5, 1865. This order was issued "by command of Major General Hooker, O. H. Hart, Lieutenant Colonel and Assistant Adjutant General".

May 3, 1865: The undertaker visited his room and took measurements for Martin's coffin. After asking that his father be notified of his fate, Martin requested that Father Frederick P. Garesche prepare him for death. A correspondent for the Cincinnati *Times* visited

Martin in his cell on the eve of his execution and reported: "We found Father Garesche reading to Martin from the Bible. They were sitting on the prisoner's rough bunk; a crucifix lay on the bed beside Martin. Attached to his leg was a huge ball and chain. Martin appeared to be an ignorant and simple boy, unable to read or write, or even tell his own exact age. He thought he was twenty-one but appeared to be less than twenty. He was tall and lank, had long and coarse brown hair, pale blue eyes, and had a weak, superficial nature, the type that is so easily swayed in any direction."

May 4, 1865: Leading citizens of Cincinnati, learning that a citizen was to be shot to death in their city, sent dispatches to Secretary Stanton at 10:20AM, asking for suspension of the sentence. Mr. Logan, Martin's counsel sent a military dispatch and Colonel Hart, of General Hooker's staff, also forwarded a telegram to General Hooker, who was travelling from Springfield to Cincinnati, after attending President Lincoln's funeral. Hooker replied that the matter was beyond his control and that the new President was the only authority to be addressed. Secretary Stanton replied in like fashion. Telegrams were then sent to President Johnson by Colonel Hart and by leading citizens. Judge Johann B. Stallo, leader of the local German community; George H. Pendleton, Democratic candidate for vice-president in 1864; and Judge W. M. Dickson, related by marriage to Mary Todd Lincoln, sent urgent telegrams to Washington, requesting a stay of execution. According to one source, General Willich was "instrumental in persuading Stallo and others to attempt to intervene".

May 5, 1865: Having slept about four hours, Martin arose early, took a very light breakfast and just before noon, refused to eat any more food, since the time of his death was so near. "He was baptized and received the Sacrament of the Holy Communion from Father Garesche." At 12PM, the twelve companies of the 37th Iowa under Lieutenant Colonel G. R. West and Company A of the 192nd Pennsylvania Regiment under Lieutenant Smith were assembled outside the barracks, waiting for orders. At 1 o'clock and 10 minutes, Adjutant General Booth, of General Willich's staff, rode up and gave orders for the move. The soldiers moved up the hill and formed into a hollow square, where they waited at "rest arms" for the prisoner and his attendants. At precisely 1PM, Martin was informed that he must prepare for the execution. Without hesitation, he rose from his bunk, took up his hat and proceeded to the carriage waiting outside the door. He bid good-bye to the officers of the barracks, thanking them for the many kindnesses they had extended to him, and added, "Boys, I will die like a brave man". Accompanied by Father Garesche and thirty-one convalescent soldiers acting as guard, the procession proceeded through the city. Martin smiled and nodded to the undertaker and bore himself with great firmness until they reached the fatal spot. There, his nature mellowed, and he wept for a few moments. "Comforting words from Garesche and a little whiskey steeled his nerves."

Anticipating word from Washington, a swift horse was in position in front of General Hooker's headquarters, with a messenger ready to carry any dispatch. At 1PM, there still had been no reply. As the prisoner was half-way to the place of execution, with the troopers in position, at twenty-five minutes of two o'clock, the telegraph operator said, "Here is the reprieve". It read: "War Department, Washington, D.C., May 5, 1865, Major General Hooker, Commanding Northern Department: Suspend the execution of Thomas

Martin, to be executed in Cincinnati this day, until further orders. By order of the President. E. M. Stanton, Secretary of War". The telegram was immediately sent to General Hooker's headquarters, and instantly Colonel Hart dispatched Lawrence Sands, Chief Clerk, to the place where the execution was to occur. "Sands dashed through the streets, across fields, over fences, and along by-paths, reaching the spot in seven minutes." The procession was then in sight of the fatal ground. "Receiving the dispatch, the troops were ordered to re-form and return to the barracks, and Martin was ordered to be conveyed back to McLean Barracks. Martin received the announcement with calmness and manifest. He took Father Garesche by the hand and appeared grateful for the action of the President." The crowd appeared satisfied and thankful. Sergeant Hollincamp and the nine men who were detailed to do the shooting seemed to be greatly relieved. There was little doubt then that Thomas Martin's sentence would be commuted to a specified term of imprisonment, or that he would be pardoned after taking the oath of amnesty.

May 10, 1865: But now, a telegraphic order was sent to Major General Hooker that the temporary reprieve should be carried into execution, and that "Thomas Martin should be executed on Thursday, May 11, 1865, between 12PM and 1PM". General Hooker sent word to Martin that he would we shot on Thursday at noon. General Willich, the camp commandant, was directed to carry out the execution. According to the *Enquirer,* Martin, while surprised, received the grim news with "surprising coolness".

May 11, 1865: Martin sent for Father Garesche, who responded by administering to him spiritual comfort. Martin had rested but little on the previous night, and frequently expressed that this time he would surely die. He maintained that he was not guilty of the charges that had condemned him to death, but that he would die like a brave man.

As ordered, Union men of the 37th Iowa and 192nd Pennsylvania formed into column inside Kelton Barracks and marched out to Broadway, down Broadway to Court, and then through Deercreek Valley to a point about halfway up the old road leading to Walnut Hills where they were halted. At that same hour a carriage, carrying Father Garesche and Thomas Martin, with a military guard, left McLean Barracks, and moved to the spot where the Union troops waited. Arriving at the head of Deercreek Road, the carriage was halted, and the procession was formed in the following order: Provost Marshall, Captain McCleary, the band, the firing party consisting of eight privates and one sergeant, Thomas Martin, supported on either side by Father Garesche and a sergeant, and a reserve party of twenty-eight men from McLean Barracks, under command of Lieutenant Millspaugh. Thomas Martin was dressed in light pants, steel-colored vest, a black frock coat, a small necktie, white stockings, brogans and a light-colored slouch hat.

"The procession moved up the hill until it reached the ground selected for the execution. Troops that had preceded the procession were formed into a hollow square, with three sides of soldiers, and the hill forming the background, on the fourth side. As the procession arrived, the band played a mournful dirge and the firing party followed, with arms reversed."

The procession moved through between the columns and the firing party entered the interior of the square, taking their positions. The coffin had been taken to a house near the spot early that morning, and when the procession arrived, was in its place on the ground, waiting for the arrival of its occupant. Thomas Martin took a position near the head of the coffin, and Captain Booth, Adjutant General to General Willich, read General Order 32 and the telegraphic order fixing the hour for the execution. Martin listened attentively to the reading of the orders. When asked if he had any remarks to make, he said merely, "I have nothing to say". He was then led to the rear of the coffin, behind which he knelt, on the ground. Captain McCleary stepped forward to bandage his eyes, but Martin refused, so that he might witness the shooting. He finally consented to the blindfold, but only at Father Garesche's urging. The Father placed a crucifix in his left hand and bade him a final "good-bye". The firing party was just eight paces from the prisoner. Captain McCleary, in charge of the execution, gave the order:

"Attention!"
"Ready – Aim – Fire!"

"Martin instantly fell back without a sound or struggle. He was dead the instant he was struck." His hands were not restrained, and he died as bravely as he had promised that morning. When his body was examined, it was found that "two balls had pierced his heart, one ball entered his right side, one ball passed through his throat, one ball entered his left shoulder, one ball missed him completely, one weapon misfired, and one weapon had fired a blank". Surgeons made the examination and pronounced him dead. His body was placed in the coffin and immediately taken to the Catholic Cemetery and placed in the vault. Thomas Martin's remains rest in the Saint Joseph New Cemetery, 4500 Foley Road, Cincinnati (Hamilton County), Ohio.

Thomas Martin's execution was over at "precisely half past 12 o'clock", and along with the military personnel, was witnessed by about one hundred persons, including men, women and children from the immediate vicinity. "Rain fell throughout the entire proceeding."

Many agreed with the *Daily Enquirer's* condemnation of the affair: "We are satisfied that an awful mistake has been made, and that a life has been needlessly taken that will in no respect sub serve the ends of justice or the public well-being."

What happened between the time of the reprieve and the revocation that sealed Thomas Martin's fate? James M. Prichard made several interesting points in his article that appeared in the *"North and South"* magazine, Volume 6, Number 7:

Captain James Dinkins, a former Confederate officer, claimed in 1903 that Martin's death was the result of General Hooker's rage over Camp Commandant General Willich's interference with his orders. Dinkins alleged that Hooker summoned Willich and others to his headquarters on May 10, upbraided them for their efforts on Martin's behalf, and firmly announced his intention to have the reprieve revoked.

Others argued that Martin was an innocent victim of the bitterness that followed the assassination of President Lincoln. Indeed, the trial of the surviving conspirators involved in Lincoln's assassination began on May 10, the very day Martin's reprieve was cancelled in Washington.

The threat still posed by roving bands of die-hard guerrillas may have been a primary factor in Martin's death. On the night of May 5, the very day Martin's defenders obtained his stay of execution, a large band of heavily armed guerrillas slipped across the Ohio River. At a point some fourteen miles from Cincinnati, in the very heart of General Hooker's military jurisdiction, they attacked a train, robbed the passengers, looted the safe of over $30,000 in government bonds, and disappeared into the hills of northern Kentucky. Hooker could well have sought to make an example of the young "guerrilla", his death serving as a warning to further "guerrilla" activity.

In conclusion, it may appear that Thomas Martin was a victim; a victim of Jarius (Jarud) Biggs' malice, a victim of fear and hatred spread by men such as Captain Sidney Cook, a victim of misguided military justice, and a victim of his own gullibility and naivete.

**Adams,
Randolph Dixon**

**Allen,
Stephen Farris**

Amburgey, John J.

**Adams,
Watson Etchison**

**Allen,
William James**

Back, David

Akemon, John

**Amburgey,
Anderson**

Back, Isaac

Back, James C.

Bentley, Aaron Rice

Brashear, Harvey G.

Back, Lewis Cecil

Bentley, John Q.

Brashear, Jesse

Back, William Cody

Bradley, Jacob

Brashear, Sampson

Brashear, William E.

Burton, Isaac

Caudill, Ben E.

**Brashear,
William Rutledge**

Calhoun, Thomas

Caudill, David D.

**Brashear,
William T. B.**

Caudill, Abel

Caudill, David J.

Caudill, Henry H. "Tush"

Caudill, James Aaron

Caudill, William J. "Stiller Bill"

Caudill, Isaac

Caudill, John M.

Caudill, William W. "Wid"

Caudill, Isham "Ike"

Caudill, Samuel C.

Chaffins, Samuel Nelson

Chenoweth, Thomas John

Combs, Granville

Combs, Ira

Combs, Alfred

Combs, Hanbill

Combs, Jeremiah

Combs, George A.

Combs, Henry Duff

Combs, Nicholas

Combs, Shadrack H, "Rebel Shade"

Cornett, Joseph E.

Crabtree, David Simpson

Cope, William Jackson

Cornett, Russell

Craft, Enoch A. "Chunk"

Cornett, John

Cornett, William A.

Craft, John Linville

Davis, Wiley Oren

Eldridge, John C.

Engle, William Buchanan "Buck"

Deaton, Joseph

Evans, William Nelson, JR

Everidge, Benjamin

Duke, Peyton M.

Engle, Thomas Sampson

Franklin, Kelly

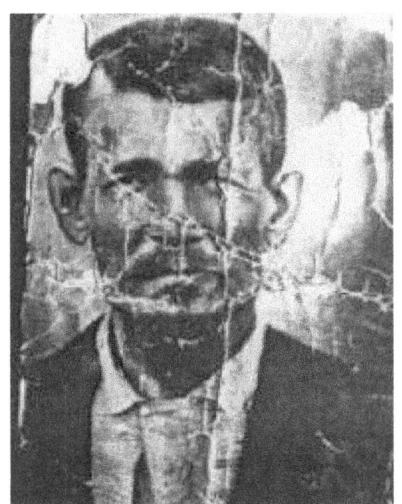
Fugate, John B. "John Blue"

Gayheart, W. Riley

Godsey, Drury S. "Drue"

Fugate, Zachariah

Gayheart, Martin "Mart"

Grigsby, Samuel

Fuller, Elijah "Bunt"

Gearheart, Adam

Guinn, James

**Halcomb,
Oliver Goldsmith**

**Hampton,
Solomon M.**

**Hounshell,
Harvey W.**

Hall, William J.

Hays, Anderson

Hurt, Isaac

**Hammonds,
Archelous "Cheed"**

Hicks, Elijah

**Isaacs, George
Washington**

Isaacs, German

King, Tandy L.

Lewis, John Bowling

Isaacs, Terman

Landrum, Reuben Samuel

Lipps, James D.

Kelly, William E.

Lankford, William P.

Lyttle, George Brittain

Martin, George

McLemore, Benjamin F.

Miller, John S. Jackson "Fatty"

McCray, Benjamin

Meade, Riley

Moore, Cornelius N.

McIntire, Alexander

Miller, Granville Stephen

Moore, James Lewis

Moore, (William) Henderson

Mullins, John A.

Noble, Losson

Mullins, Alexander "Pink"

Mullins, Joseph

Noble, Samuel

Mullins, James T.

Noble, George W.

Noble, William Palmer

Patton, John

Richie, Andrew

Rogers, James Thomas

Pratt, John M. "John Knock"

Richie, Samuel (Company I)

Russell, "App" David Cummings

Pratt, Stephen S.

Richie, Gabriel (Company C)

Sexton, "Hatter" Hatler Hascue

Short, Booker

Slone, Pleasant

Smith, Samuel JR

Slone, James A.

Smith, Daniel

Sparkman, John S.

Slone, John P.

Smith, Reuben Randolph

Stacy, Shadrack Ellsberry

**Strong,
Edward Callahan**

**Walker, "Pete"
Jeremiah**

Webb, Riley

Sumner, John

Watts, Ambrose

**Whipple,
George Sylvester**

Triplett, William M.

**Webb, Andrew
Lewis**

**Whitaker,
Stephen A.**

White, Andrew Jackson

Wright, John Vent

Wright, Hiram

Wright, John Wesley "Bad John"

Wright, Joel

CAUDILL's 13TH KENTUCKY CAVALRY
COLONEL BEN E. CAUDILL, COMMANDING

Throughout the following roster, a substantial number of abbreviations have been used in order to conserve space. The following key is offered to assist the reader in understanding these abbreviations:

abs. = absent	Inf. = Infantry
Adj. = Adjutant	info. = information
aft. = after	KIA = killed in action
AQM = Assistant Quartermaster	Lt. = Lieutenant
Btn. = Battalion	Lt. Col. = Lieutenant Colonel
bef. = before	m. = married
bur. = buried	Maj. = Major
Capt. = Captain	Mtd. = Mounted
capt. = captured	mo. = mouth
Cav. = Cavalry	occ. = occupation
Cem. = Cemetery	poss. = possible, possibly
Co. = Company	pres. = present
Col. = Colonel	prev. = previous, previously
Confed. = Confederate	prob. = probable, probably
Cpl. = Corporal	Pt. = Point
C. S. A. = Confederate States Army	re. = regarding
d. = died	rec. = received
d.c. = death certificate	res. = resident
des. = deserted	s. = son
disc. = discharged	Sec. = Secretary
dtd. = dated	serv. = served, service
enl. = enlisted	Sgt. = Sergeant
Ft. = Fort	s. r. = service record
Gen. = General	U. S. = United States
hosp. = hospital	Vol. = Volunteers

ADAMS, ANDREW ABSALOM "Drewery": (5/17/1843 – 9/17/1897), Co. A, enl. Whitesburg, KY, serv. prev. in Co. F, 5th KY Inf., capt. 12/3/1862 Whitesburg by Harlan Co. Btn., paroled & freed 12/4/1862, res. of Letcher Co. 1860, s. of Randolph & Nancy (Caudill) Adams, m. Saphornia Dotson (1849-1899) 1863, bur. Adams-Brown Cem., Ice, Letcher Co., KY.

ADAMS, BENJAMIN: (3/28/1843 – 4/24/1913), Co. H, enl. Whitesburg, KY 10/18/1862, res. Letcher Co. 1860, s. of Moses & Sarah (Caudill) Adams, m(1) Sarah Lucinda Combs (1847-1878) 1862, (2) Sally Maggard (1845-1913) 1879, bur. Adams Cem., Isom, Letcher Co., KY.

ADAMS, BENJAMIN B.: (5/1828 – 3/28/1901), Co. D, 2nd Lt., enl. Whitesburg, KY 10/4/1862, capt. 7/7/1863 Gladeville, VA, res. Letcher Co. 1860, s. of Benjamin & Nancy (Holbrook) Adams, res. Magoffin Co. 1870, 1880, & 1900, m(1) Sena M. Polly (1835-1876) 1885, (2) Nancy Adams (d. bef.1900)1877 Magoffin Co., d. Magoffin Co., KY.

ADAMS, GEORGE WASHINGTON: (1839 – 1927), Co. D, enl. Whitesburg, KY 10/4/1862, abs. "sick" 8/1863, disc. at close of war (Pension File), res. Letcher Co., KY 1860, s. of Moses & Rebecca (Hall) Adams, res. Letcher Co. 1870 & 1880, moved to VA 1884, rec. Confed. Pension #2861 Wise Co., VA 1913, m. Anna Mullins (1842-1943) 1860, bur. Maple Hill Cem., Bay Center, Pacific Co., WA.

ADAMS, GILBERT: (1/7/1835 – 8/25/1907), Co. A, enl. Whitesburg, KY 9/29/1862, serv. prev. in 5th KY Inf., Co. F, capt. 7/7/1863 at Gladeville, VA, to Kemper Barracks, to Camp Chase Prison 7/20/1863, to Ft. Delaware Prison 3/14/1864, took oath & released 6/9/1865, res. Letcher Co., KY in 1860, s. of Moses & Rebecca (Hall) Adams, m. Elizabeth Collier (1841-1907) 1857, bur. Snodgrass Cem., Norton, Wise Co., VA.

ADAMS, JAMES WEALTH: (9/17/1842 – 3/14/1934), Co. D, joined 13th KY in 1864, serv. prev. in 5th KY Inf., Co. F, rec. clothing 6/29/1864 & 9/7/1864, took oath at Louisa, KY 4/30/1865, wrote of his Confed. serv. in his memoirs, res. Letcher Co., 1860, s. of John B. & Sarah (Craft) Adams, m. Elva Collins (1847-aft. 1930) 1868, res. of Letcher Co. 1870, rec. KY Confed. Pension #1577 1912 Morgan Co., bur. Davis Cem,, West Liberty, Morgan Co., KY.

ADAMS, J. W.: Co. G, enl. 9/26/1862 Perry Co., KY, pres. on Aug.-Dec. 1863 muster roll.

ADAMS, JESSE: (5/1839 – 9/17/1908), Co. H, enl. Whitesburg, KY 10/18/1862, serv. Union 14th KY, Co. M 6/18/1863 to 3/24/1864, res. Letcher Co. 1860, s. of Randolph & Nancy (Caudill) Adams, m. Nancy Elizabeth Dotson (1843-1907), moved to Wolfe Co., KY, Union marker, bur. Adams Cem., Zachariah, Wolfe Co., KY

ADAMS, JESSE B.: (12/25/1821 – 9/14/1907), Co. D, enl. Whitesburg, KY 10/4/1862, res. of Letcher Co., KY in 1860, s. of Benjamin & Nancy (Holbrook) Adams, res. of Letcher Co. 1870 & 1880 (Millstone), m. Margaret Jenkins (1826-1882) 1846, bur. Holbrook-Johnson Cem, Millstone, Letcher Co. KY.

ADAMS, JOHN: (1826 – 2/11/1867), Co. H, enl. Whitesburg, KY 10/18/1862, res. of Letcher Co., KY 1860, s. of Randolph & Nancy Adams, m. (1) Frankie B. Smith (1826-1860) 1846, (2) Nancy Caudill (b. 1837) 1861, bur. Webb Cem., Mayking, Letcher Co., KY.

ADAMS, JOHN W.: (9/1844 – 1/2/1915), Co. E, enl. Whitesburg, KY 10/4/1862, des. 12/24/1862, res. Letcher Co. 1860, s. of William Tolson & Sarah (Hall) Adams, res. Letcher Co. 1870, 1880, 1900, & 1910, m. (1) Sarah Hackworth (1842-1868) in 1867, (2) Altamyra "Alta" Parsons (1847-1943) in1868, Letcher Co. KY, d. Cram Creek, Letcher Co., bur. Blair Cemetery, Ermine, Letcher Co., KY

ADAMS, LOUIS CHAMBERS: (12/4/1836 – 6/12/1903), Co. F, enl. Whitesburg, KY 5/15/1863, serv. prev. 5th KY Inf, Co. A & 2nd Btn. Mtd. Rifles, Co. A, pres. 8/31/1863, res. Morgan Co., KY 1860, m. (1) Deborah (1843-ca 1871), (2) Cynthia Reed (1847-1932) 1873 Morgan Co. KY, bur. Southfork Church Cem., West Liberty, Morgan Co., KY.

ADAMS, MOSES: (4/28/1812 – 5/16/1899), Co. A, enl. Whitesburg, KY 9/29/1862, serv. prev. in 5th KY Inf, Co. F, poss. des. 2/1/1863, res. Letcher Co., KY 1860, s. of Moses & Mary (Garland) Adams, res. of Letcher Co. 1870 &1880, m. Rebecca Hall (1812-1880).

ADAMS, RANDOLPH DIXON: (1841 - 1882), Co. A, enl. Whitesburg, KY 11/1/1862, serv. prev. in 5th KY Inf, Co. F, res. Letcher Co. 1860, s. of Randolph & Nancy (Caudill) Adams, m. Matilda Francis (1846-1918), bur. Carr's Fork Cem., Littcarr, Knott Co., KY.

ADAMS, WATSON ETCHISON: (4/6/1837 – 1/6/1919), Co. H, enl. Whitesburg, KY 10/18/1862, res. Letcher Co. 1860, s. of Randolph & Nancy (Caudill) Adams, m. (1) Rausie Hogg (1843-ca. 1882) 1860, (2) Sarah Caudill (1845-aft. 1910) 1883, bur. Watson Adams Cem, Letcher Co., Whitco, KY.

ADAMS, WILLIAM RILEY: (b. 1840), Co. D, enl. In Whitesburg 10/4/1862, des. and capt. by Union troops in Whitesburg 12/3/1862, paroled and freed 12/4/1862.

ADKINS, SAMUEL (PETER): (10/1844 – d. prob. bef. 1920), Co. C, enl. Whitesburg, KY 10/1/1862, capt. Gladeville, VA 7/7/1863, to Kemper Barracks, to Camp Chase Prison 7/29/1863, to Camp Douglas Prison 8/24/1863, enl. U. S. 5th Vol. 4/6/1865, res. Morgan Co., KY 1860, s. of Absalom Adkins, res. Elliott Co., KY 1870, 1880, 1900 & 1910 (Martinsburg), m. (1) Mary "Polly" Dehart (1844-1900) Morgan Co. 1865, (2) Martha A. 1906.

AKEMON, JOHN: (2/91843 – 9/21-1911) Kash's Co, serv. prev. 5th KY Inf. (Consolidated), Co. B, indicted postwar for murder as member of Kash's Co., res. Breathitt Co. 1860, s. of John & Jane (Little) Akemon, m. (1) Polly Ann Belcher (b. 1855) 1872 divorced, (2) Evaline Raliegh (b. 1864) ca. 1878, bur. Akemon-White Cem., Ashana Rd. off Rt. 28, Barwick, Breathitt Co., KY.

ALBERT, WILLIAM W.: (10/28/1822 – 10/25/1867), Co. K, enl. Lee Co. VA 8/18/1863, pres. Lee Co. 12/31/1863, res. Lee Co. VA, s. of George & Martha Albert, occ. blacksmith, m. (1) Rosanna "Rose" (b. 1824), (2) Mary (1843-1899), d. from typhoid, Lee Co. VA, bur. Albert Cem, Wallens Creek, Lee Co. VA.

ALLEN, ANDREW: (1830 – 7/16/1863), 4th Cpl., Co. G, enl. Perry Co., KY 9/26/1862, poss. serv. prev. 2nd V.S.L. & Diamond's 10th KY Cav., Co. G, res. Breathitt Co.1860, s. of Samuel & Susan (Sizemore) Allen, m. Mary "Polly" Combs (1831-1919) 1851, KIA.

ALLEN, DAVID: (10/22/1844 – 9/26/1919), 4th Sgt., Co. F, enl. Floyd Co., KY 10/14/1862, des. 8/31/1863, enl. Union 39th KY, Co. F 12/29/1863, des. 8/12/1864, res. Floyd Co. 1860, s. of John & Nancy Jane (Click) Allen, m. Susan Joseph (1848-1916) 1861, bur. John Carpenter Cem., Swampton, Magoffin Co., KY.

ALLEN, EMORY: (1835 – 1865), Co. I, enl. Whitesburg, KY 10/18/1862, killed mo. of Drowning Ck. on KY River, res. Perry Co. 1860, s. of Samuel & Susan (Sizemore) Allen, m. Margaret "Peggy" Combs (b. 1843), bur. Confed. Cem., Bibee, Madison Co., KY.

ALLEN, FRANKLIN: (b. 1845), Co. G, enl. Perry Co., KY 9/28/1862, capt. Perry Co. 6/6/1863, to Lexington, KY 6/16/1863, to Camp Chase Prison, to Johnson Island Prison 6/20/1863, to Point Lookout, MD 11/30/1863, enl. Union army 1/25/1864, res. Breathitt Co. 1860, s. of Polly Allen, did not survive war.

ALLEN, GEORGE: (2/1/1836 – 1/16/1918), Co. G, enl. Perry Co., KY 9/23/1862, res. Perry Co. 1860, s. of Samuel & Susan (Sizemore) Allen, m. Rachel Combs (1839-1940), bur. Allen Cem., Rowdy, Perry Co., KY.

ALLEN, GEORGE WESLEY: (1845 – 1918), Co. F, enl. Floyd Co., KY 7/20/1863, also serv. in Diamond's 10th KY Cav., Co. A, pres. 8/31/1863, res. Floyd Co. 1860, s. of Felix & Rhoda (Martin) Allen, m. Rhoda Halbert (1838-aft. 1920), bur. Preston Cem., Warco, Floyd Co., KY.

ALLEN, GRANVILLE: (1/27/1847 – 11/12/1897), Co. C, enl. aft. 6/1864, serv. prev. 10th KY Cav, Co. D, res. Owsley Co.1860, s. of James & Nancy Louise (Roberts) Allen, PWR indictment Perry Co. raid 1/2/1865, m. Salina Bailey (1848-1922), bur. White-Allen Cem., Campton, Wolfe Co., KY.

ALLEN, HEZEKIAH: (1841 – 1898), Co. F, enl. Floyd Co., KY 10/14/1862, rejoined 7/30/1863, res. Floyd Co., s. of Adam & Jemima (Whitt) Allen, m. Polly Hale (b. 1843) 1872 Magoffin Co., bur. Coburn Cem., nr. Handshoe, Floyd Co. KY.

ALLEN, IRA: (1841 – 6/11/1864), 5th Sgt., Co. G, enl. Perry Co., KY 9/26/1862, MIA Battle of Cynthiana 1864, res. Perry Co. 1860, s. of Samuel & Susan (Sizemore) Allen, m. Delila Combs (1846-1912) 1859, memorial marker T-Point Cem., Clayhole, Breathitt Co. KY.

ALLEN, IRVIN: (1838 – 1865), 1st Sgt., Co. G, enl. Perry Co. 9/23/1862, rec. clothing 9/7/1864, killed mo. Drowning Creek on KY River, res. Perry Co. 1860, s. of Samuel & Susan (Sizemore) Allen, m. Elizabeth Noble (b. 1837) 1858, bur. Confed. Cem., Bibee, Madison Co. KY.

ALLEN, JAMES "RIVER JIM": (1824 – 11/6/1864), Co. I, conscripted at Whitesburg, KY 10/18/1862, serv. prev. 5th KY Inf., Co. B (9/13/1862 to 10/7/1862), serv. later 10th KY Cav., Co. D, killed in skirmish with Three Forks Btn., res. Breathitt Co., KY 1860, s. of Samuel & Susan (Sizemore) Allen, m. Nancy Louise Roberts (1826-1912) 1843, memorial marker White-Allen Cem., Campton, Wolfe Co. KY.

ALLEN, JOEL M. "Jr": (1843 – 1922), Co. F, enl. Floyd Co., KY 10/14/1862, serv. later 10th KY Cav, Co. D, res. Floyd Co. 1860, s. of Felix & Rhoda (Martin) Allen, m. (1) Artie Patton (1846-aft. 1880) 1869, (2) Cynthia Patton, bur. Joel Allen Cem., Warco, Floyd Co. KY.

ALLEN, JOEL "Sr": (1832 – 1890), Co. F, enl. Floyd Co., KY 10/14/1862, res. Floyd Co. 1860, s. of David W. & Elizabeth Jane (Martin) Allen, m. Florence (Patton-Leek) Allen (1829-1911), bur. Long Joel Allen Cem., Printer, Floyd Co. KY.

ALLEN, JOHN ALFRED: (1840 – 1865), Co. G, enl. Perry Co., KY 9/28/1862, capt. Gladeville, VA 7/7/1863, to Kemper Barracks, to Camp Chase Prison 7/20/1863, to Camp Douglas Prison 8/24/1863, exch. Point Lookout, MD 2/24/1865, killed mo. Drowning Creek on KY River, res. Perry Co. 1860, s. of Samuel & Susan (Sizemore) Allen, m. Paulina Combs, bur. Confed. Cem., Bibee, Madison Co. KY.

ALLEN, JOHN: (1846) Co. F, enl. Floyd Co. KY 10/14/1862, capt. Aug.-Dec. 1863 muster roll, res. Floyd Co. 1860, s. of George & Rebecca (Stephens) Allen.

ALLEN, JOHN M.: (5/14/1836 – 12/7/1918), 2nd Lt., Co. F, enl. Floyd Co. KY 10/10/1862, capt., resigned w/ poor health 8/11/1863, res. Magoffin Co. 1860, s. of John & Nancy Jane (Click) Allen, res. Floyd Co. 1870, rec. KY Confed. Pension # 1582 Greenup Co. 1912, m. Mary (b. 1840), bur. Methodist Cem., Quincy, Lewis Co. KY.

ALLEN, JOSEPH: (3/29/1839 – 5/21/1913), 2nd Sgt., Co. F, enl. Floyd Co. KY 10/14/1862, capt. Gladeville, VA 7/7/1863, to Kemper Barracks 7/17/1863, to Camp Chase Prison 7/20/1863, to Camp Douglas Prison 8/24/1863, exch. Point Lookout, MD 3/2/1865, res. Floyd Co. 1860, s. of Adam & Mary (Bradley) Allen, PWR: postmaster of Wireman, KY 1912, rec. KY Confed. Pension #2331 1912, widow rec. KY Confed. Widow's Pension #2911 Magoffin Co. 1914, m. Rebecca Wireman (1847-1928) 1866, bur. Joseph Allen Cem., Gapville, Magoffin Co. KY.

ALLEN, JOSEPH B. "Sr": (2/1829 – 1900/1910), Co. F, enl. Floyd Co. KY 10/14/1862, res. Magoffin Co., KY 1860 (Johnson Fork), m. Rebecca (1831-1880/1900), res. Magoffin Co. 1870, 1880, 1900.

ALLEN, REUBEN M.: (7/15/1841 – 2/19/1913), 1st Sgt., Co. F, enl. Floyd Co. KY 10/10/1862, serv. prev. 5th KY Inf., Co. E, also serv. 10th KY Cav., Co. A, res. Floyd Co. 1860, s. of Felix & Rhoda (Martin) Allen, m. Levinia Halbert (1843-1922) 1859, bur. Allen Cem., Warco, Floyd Co. KY.

ALLEN, SAMUEL: (1/1844 – bef. 1910), Co. G, enl. Breathitt Co., KY 10/1/1862, Identified in A. G. Report, b. Perry Co., s. of James & Nancy Louise (Roberts) Allen, on 1890 Powell Co. Special Veterans Census, res. Powell Co. 1900, m. (1) Mary Ann Combs, (2) Margaret Shoemaker.

ALLEN, SAMUEL DAVID: (3/16/1842 – 6/11/1922), Sgt., Co. F, enl. Breathitt Co. KY 10/14/1862, res. Floyd Co. 1860, s. of David W. Allen, res. Floyd Co. 1870, Republic Co. KS 1880, Woods Co. OK 1920, rec. OK Confed. Pension, m. Lucy Jane Keith (1842-aft. 1920), bur. Waynoka Cem., Waynoka City, Woods Co., OK.

ALLEN, STEPHEN FARRIS: (9/4/1848 – 3/26/1930), Co. G, b. Perry Co., KY, s. of James & Nancy (Roberts) Allen, rec. KY Confed. Pension #1583 Wolfe Co. 1912, m. Lydia Ann Shoemaker (1861-1940) Wolfe Co. 1878, bur. Allen Cem., Waynesburg, Lincoln Co. KY.

ALLEN, S. P.: Co. A, serv. prev. 5th KY Inf., Co. G, arrested as disch. Confed. Floyd Co. 10/1/1863, to Louisville Prison, took oath and freed 10/31/1863, ret. serv. w/ 13th KY Cav, res. Floyd Co., KY.

ALLEN, WILLIAM JAMES "JR": (11/1836 – 1916), Co. F, enl. Floyd Co., KY 10/14/1862, capt. Gladeville, VA 7/7/1863, res. Floyd Co. 1860, s. of Felix & Rhoda (Martin) Allen, res. Floyd Co. 1870, 1880 & 1900, m. Sally Hicks (1836-1907) 1856, bur. Allen Cem., Hippo, Floyd Co. KY.

ALLEN, WILLIAM "SR": (1813 – 1888), Co. F, enl. Floyd Co. KY 10/14/1862, res. Floyd Co. 1860, res. Floyd Co. 1870 & 1880, m. Eleander (1832-ca. 1871), bur. Allen & Turner Cem., Eastern, Floyd Co., KY.

ALLEN, WOODSON: (1/20/1842 – 11/24/1911), Co. C, enl. Whitesburg, KY 10/1/1862, res. Magoffin Co. 1860, s. of George & Malinda (Howard) Allen, res. Breathitt Co. 1850, res. Magoffin Co. 1880 & 1900 (Trace Fk.), d. Magoffin Co. (d.c. #29332) m. (1) Rebecca Crager 1864, (2) Martha Dickson (1847-1880/1889) 1870, (3) Delaney Whitaker (1866-1939) 1890, bur. Smith-Allen Cem., Fredville, Magoffin Co., KY.

AMBURGEY, ALFRED: (1813 – 1868), Co. A, enl. Whitesburg, KY 11/1/1862, capt. Gladeville, VA 7/7/1863, to Kemper Barracks 7/18/1863, to Camp Chase Prison 7/20/1863, to Camp Douglas 8/24/1863, exch. Point Lookout, MD 2/24/1865, res. Letcher Co. 1860, s. of William & Lucy (Franklin) Amburgey, res. Floyd Co. 1865, m. Mary "Polly" Hagins (b. 1818) 1833, bur Dewey Reservoir Cem., Auxier, Floyd Co., KY.

AMBURGEY, ANDERSON: (1/3/1842 – 2/13/1923), Co. A, enl. Whitesburg, KY 11/1/1862, disc. 4/14/1863, ret. serv. w/ 10th KY Cav, Co. B, capt. Johnson Co., 6/1864, to Louisville Prison, took oath and freed 7/1/1864, res. Letcher Co. 1860, s. of Humphrey & Fannie (Johnson) Amburgey, res. main Carr 1866, killed James Collins & fled to Mexico, MO 1881, changed name to Major Johnson, m. Jane Amburgey (1844-1916), bur. New Home Bapt. Church Cem., Warsaw, Benton Co. MO.

AMBURGEY, HUMPHREY: (1833 – 1865), Co. A, enl. Whitesburg, KY 9/29/1862, shot & killed in his Confederate uniform at home on Burgey's Ck., res. Letcher Co. 1860, s. of Ambrose & Rebecca (Francis) Amburgey, m. Nancy Mullins (1835-1926) 1854, bur. Carr Fork Cem., Littcarr, Knott Co., KY

AMBURGEY, JOHN JESS "BORX": (4/6/1843 – 3/17/1915), Co. B, enl. Whitesburg, KY 9/15/1862, capt. Gladeville, VA 7/7/1863, to Kemper Barracks 7/18/1863, to Camp Chase Prison 7/20/1863, to Camp Douglas Prison 8/24/1863, exch. Point Lookout, MD 3/2/1865, res. Letcher Co. 1860, s. of Ambrose & Elizabeth (Johnson) Amburgey, res. Russell Co., VA 1865, res. Wise Co. VA 1878, res. Castlewood, VA bef. 1900, rec. VA Confed. Pension 1902, m. Aly Grizzle (1841-1903) 1868, bur. Trammel Gap Cem., Trammel, Dickenson Co. VA.

AMBURGEY, JOHN WALKER: (1837 – 12/31/1893), Co. A, enl. Whitesburg, KY 11/1/1862, serv. prev. 5th KY Inf., Co. F, disc. 4/14/1863, ret. serv., capt. Booneville 8/19/1863, to Louisville Prison, to Camp Chase Prison 9/2/1863, to Rock Island Prison 1/22/1864, released 10/6/1964, serv. as hosp. stewart, res. Letcher Co. 1860, s. of Humphrey & Fannie (Johnson) Amburgey, m. Sarah Huff (1840-ca. 1898) 1866, bur. Walker Amburgey Cem., Leburn, Knott Co. KY.

AMBURGEY, THOMAS H.: (9/17/1844 – 6/29/1927), Co. A, enl. Whitesburg, KY 9/2/1862, rec. clothing 9/7/1864, ordered to stack arms 4/15/1865, res. Letcher Co. 1860, s. of Alfred & Mary "Polly" (Hagins) Amburgey, rec. KY Confed. Pension #1196 Floyd Co. 1912, m. Nancy L. Wheatly (1842-1929), bur. Dewey Reservoir Cem., Auxier, Floyd Co. KY.

AMBURGEY, WILBURN (CHARLES): (5/19/1833 – 11/15/1900), 1st Lt., Co. A, enl. Whitesburg, KY & promoted 2nd Lt. 9/10/1862, capt. Gladeville, VA 7/7/1863, to Kemper Barracks 7/18/1863, to Camp Chase Prison 7/20/1863, to Johnson Island Prison 10/10/1863, to Baltimore, MD 2/9/1864, to Ft. Delaware Prison 6/23/1864, poss. rejoined Caudill's 13th or Diamond's 10th Cav. ca. 9/1864, poss. recapt. 1/6/1865, released 6/12/1865, res. Letcher Co. 1860, s. of Robert & Elizabeth (Fuller) Amburgey, res. Menifee Co. aft. 1866, m. (1) Nancy Cornett, (2) Hannah Cornett, bur. Amburgey Cem., Means, Menifee Co., KY

AMBURGEY, WILLIAM G. "DOGSHIN": (3/14/1835 – 8/4/1921), Co. A, enl. Whitesburg, KY 11/1/1862, serv. prev. 5th KY Inf., Co. F, disch. 4/14/1863, res. Letcher Co. 1860, s. of Humphrey & Fannie (Johnson) Amburgey, res. Montgomery Co. 1880, res. Wise Co. VA 1907, m. Susannah Boggs (1840-1921), bur Huff Cem., Norton, Wise Co. VA.

ANDERSON, AARON: (2/10/1840 – 3/21/1917), Co. D, enl. Whitesburg 10/4/1862, disch. w/ failing health 1864, res. Letcher Co. 1860, s. of John & Elizabeth Anderson, rec. Confed. Pension #510 Letcher Co. 1912, m. Elizabeth Hall (1841-1900/1910), bur. Hall Cem., Fleming, Letcher Co., KY.

ANDERSON, HENRY B.: (3/1834 – 9/13/1913), 2nd Lt., Adjt., Co. E, enl. Whitesburg, KY 10/21/1862, elected Adjt. 8/10/1863, serv. later as Adjt. Diamond's 10th KY Cav., also serv. 1st Btn. KY Mtd. Rifles & 3rd KY Mtd. Rifles, Co. C, capt. Greenville, TN 9/4/1864, to Chatanooga Prison 9/13/1864, to Knoxville & exch., surr. Mt. Sterling 4/30/1865, res. Bourbon Co. 1860, s. of Caroline (Smith) Anderson, res. Mercer Co. 1870, res. Garrard Co. 1880, res. Madison Co. 1900, res. KY Confed. Home Pewee Valley 1907, res. Oldham Co. 1910, bur. Pewee Valley Cem., C.S.A. plot, Pewee Valley, Oldham Co., KY.

ANDERSON, JOHN: (1836 – 1864), Co. D, enl. Whitesburg, KY 10/4/1862, capt. Lawrence Co. 7/20/1863, to McLean Barracks 9/13/1863, released on oath 9/17/1863, res. Letcher Co. 1860, s. of John & Elizabeth Anderson, m. Louisa Quillen (1843-1917), bur. Beaver Dam Cem., Colson, Letcher Co., KY.

ANDERSON, WILLIAM: (5/5/1847 – 12/16/1916), Co. D, enl. Whitesburg, KY 10/4/1862, res. Lee Co., VA, s. of Robert & Elsie (Brewer) Anderson, res. Floyd Co. 1880 & 1900, m. Helen Short (1881-1922) Floyd Co. 1885, bur. Taulbee Cem., Adele, Morgan Co., KY.

ANGEL, ANDREW J.: (1841 – 1899), Co. K, enl. 9/29/1862, serv. prev. 5th KY Inf., Co. D, des. 8/9/1863, enl. Co. K 8/18/1863, capt. 11/12/1863 Cumberland Gap area of Lee Co. VA, spent 10 months Ft. Delaware Prison & released 6/1865 (1890 Lee Co. vet. Census) , res. Breathitt Co., s. of Ephriam & Susanna Angel, res. Lee Co., 1880 & 1890, m. (1) Malvina Gross (1847-1874) Owsley Co. 1868, (2) Catherine Taylor (b. 1848) 1881, bur. Turner Cem., Enoch, Lee Co., KY.

ARTHUR, EDWARD FLETCHER: (6/12/1830 – 3/11/1921), Co. K, enl. Lee Co. VA 8/18/1863, serv. prev. Mexican War, serv. prev. 6th KY Cav, Co. B, pres. Lee Co. 12/31/1863, capt. Dandridge, TN 1/17/1864, to Knoxville 1/27/1864, to Camp Chase 2/4/1864, to Rock Island 2/15/1864, exch. City Point, VA 3/23/1865, ret. serv. 6th KY Cav., surr. Cumberland Gap 4/25/1865, res. Knox Co. 1860, s. of Ambrose & Jane (Fletcher) Arthur, m. Susan Rout (1846-1932), bur. Highland Park Cem., Williamsburg, Whitley Co., KY.

ASHLEY, FRANKLIN M.: (1829 - 1886), Co. B, enl. Whitesburg, KY 9/8/1862, disch. 9/29/1862, res. Letcher Co. 1860, s. of Rev. Jordan & Barbara (Combs) Ashley, m. Lucy Tolliver (1820-1911), bur. Adams Cem., Amburgey, Knott Co. KY.

ASHLEY, HILLARD JESSE: (b. 1842, NC), Co. B, enl. Whitesburg, KY 9/15/1862, disch. 9/29/1862, ret. serv., capt Gladeville, VA 7/7/1863, Union prison record not found, but believed he was taken to Camp Douglas with others captured at Gladeville, and that he died there ca. 1864, on 1850 Perry Co. census, res. Perry Co. 1860, s. of Rev. Jordan & Barbara (Combs) Ashley, bur. Oakwood Cemetery, E. 67th St., Chicago, Cook Co., IL.

ASHLEY, JESSE S.: (1835 – 1862), Co. B, enl. Whitesburg, KY 9/18/1862, serv. record lists as H. S. Ashley, poss. killed on Carr Creek by Union soldiers fall/1862, res. Perry Co., s. of Rev. Jordan & Barbara (Combs) Ashley, m. Elizabeth Cornett (b.1838) Perry Co. 1856, res. Morgan Co. 1900 w/ Cottle family.

ASHLEY, JORDAN TOLLIVER: (1844 – 8/4/1925), Co. I, no s.r., KY Confed. pension #2916: serv. prev. 5th KY Inf., Co. I, enl. 13th fall/1862, disbanded nr. Abingdon, VA, took oath Louisa spring 1865, res. Letcher Co. KY 1860, s. of Franklin M. & Lucy (Tolliver) Ashley, res. Letcher Co. 1880, res. Knott Co. 1900, rec. KY Confed. pension #2916 Knott Co. 1912, m. Sarah Hurt (1836-1925) 1869, bur. Franklin Cem., Amburgey, Knott Co. KY.

ASHLEY, LARKIN SHEPHERD: (b. 1837), Co. B, enl. Whitesburg, KY 9/15/1862, pres. fall 1862, d. during war, res. Perry Co. 1860, s. of Rev. Jordan & Barbara Combs Ashley.

AUSTIN, ANDREW JACKSON: (1839 – 1/28/1864), 4th Sgt., Co. D, enl. Whitesburg, KY 10/4/1862, capt Gladeville, VA 7/7/1863, to Kemper Barracks 7/18/1863, to Camp Chase Prison 7/20/1863, to Camp Douglas Prison 8/24/1863, d. at Camp Douglas, res. Letcher Co. 1860, s. of Jesse & Margaret Austin, m. Lucy Bentley (b. 1847), bur. Oak Wood Cem., Chicago, Cook Co. IL.

AYERS, JOHN: (b. 1836), Co. K, enl. Lee Co., VA 8/18/1863, pres, Lee Co. VA. 12/31/1863, res. Lee Co. VA 1850, s. of Keziah Ayers.

AYERS, WILLIAM: (b. 1834), Co. K, enl. VA 8/18/1863, pres. Lee Co., VA 12/31/1863, res. Lee Co. 1850, s. of Keziah Ayers.

BACK, ALFRED COPE: (7/21/1845 – 12/19/1874), Kash's Co., res. Breathitt Co., KY 1860, s. of John & Elizabeth (Cope) Back, indicted 1865 for murder, killed by former Union men 9 years after war, m. Malissa Strong (1845-1910), bur. Strong Cem., Whick, Breathitt Co., KY.

BACK, DAVID: (4/21/1837 – 1/25/1925), Co. H, enl. Whitesburg, KY 10/18/1862, disc. 10/18/1862, res. Letcher Co. 1860, s. of Henry & Sarah (Maggard) Back, m. (1) Rachel Caudill (1841-ca.1873), (2) Nancy Dixon (1848-6/16/1933) 1875, bur. Back Cem., Blackey, Letcher Co., KY.

BACK, DAVID J.: (2/15/1843 – 12/6/1864), Co. A, enl. Whitesburg 10/18/1862, serv. prev. 5th KY Inf., Co. F, w/ Gen. John H. Morgan at 2nd Battle of Cynthiana, wounded & captured 6/12/1864, to Louisville Prison 7/27/1864, to Camp Douglas Prison 7/30/1864, d. smallpox, res. Letcher Co. 1860, s. of John and Sally (Caudill) Back, bur. Oak Wood Cem, Chicago, Cook Co. IL, memorial marker Nancy Back Cem., Jeremiah, Letcher Co., KY.

BACK, HENRY "HENRY BACK III": (9/29/1822 – 5/28/1877), Co. A, enl. Scott Co., VA 11/1/1862, serv. prev. 5th KY Inf., Co. F, entered from des. 3/4/1863, pres. 8/31/1863, res. Letcher Co. 1860, s. of Henry & Susanna (Maggard) Back, m. (1) Francis Blair (1822-after 1883), (2) Thursa, bur. Rich Whitaker Cem., Letcher, Letcher Co., KY.

BACK, HENRY C. "HITCH": (10/21/1842 – 5/17/1917), Co. A, serv. prev. 5th KY Inf., left 13th 12/29/1863, res. Breathitt Co. KY 1860, s. of Samuel O. & Mary (Caudill) Back, res. Breathitt Co. 1890 (Jackson), m. Catherine (1843-after 1900), bur. Snowden Cem., Jackson, Breathitt Co., KY.

BACK, HENRY J.: (2/27/1846 – 4/7/1901), Co. B, enl. Whitesburg, KY 8/29/1862, served prev. in 5th KY Inf., Co. F, rec. clothing, 9/15/1864, claimed service until 4/1865 on 1890 Veterans Census, res. Letcher Co. 1860, s. of John & Sally (Caudill) Back, widow rec. KY Confed. pension #29 Letcher Co. 1912, m. (1) Polly Sumner (1844-1873) 1867, (2) Anna Adams (b. 1852-4/7/1901) Letcher Co., bur. Nancy Back Cem., Jeremiah, Letcher Co., KY.

BACK, HENRY VINCENT "VENCIL": (12/9/1843 – 12/13/1915), Kash's Co., serv. prev. 5th KY Inf., Co. D (Consolidated), res. Breathitt Co., KY 1860, s. of John & Elizabeth (Cope) Back, indicted for murder in 1865, m. Elizabeth Emma Fletcher (1842-aft. 1920 Madison Co. OH), bur. Jackson City Cem., Jackson, Breathitt Co., KY.

BACK, ISAAC: (1/27/1827 – 6/8/1916), Co. A, enl. Whitesburg, KY 11/1/1862, abs. sick Summer/Fall 1863, capt. & released 1864, res. Letcher Co., s. of Lewis & Margaret (Roberts) Back, rec. KY Confed. pension #1589 Wolfe Co. 1912, m. (1) Mary "Polly" Bolling (1836-1864), (2) Cynthia Walker Holbrook (5/24/1844-12/14/1932) 1865 Magoffin Co., bur. John Back Cem., Seitz, Magoffin Co., KY.

BACK, JAMES C.: (12/15/1843 – 1/14/1915), Co. B, enl. Whitesburg, KY 10/12/1862, pres. Summer/1863, claimed serv. until 1865 on 1890 Veterans Census, res. Letcher Co. 1860, s. of Henry & Susannah (Maggard) Back, rec. KY Confed. pension #2333 Letcher Co. 1912, m., (1) Rachel Cornett (1844-ca1882), (2) Nancy Hampton (1867-2/7/1937), bur. Back-Caudill Cem., Jeremiah, Letcher Co., KY.

BACK, LEWIS: (3/14/1834 – 5/18/1905), Co. A, enl. 11/5/1862, serv. prev. 5th KY Inf., Co. F, finished lost time Spring/1863, disch. 4/14/1863, res. Letcher Co. 1860, s. of Henry & Susannah (Maggard) Back, res. Letcher Co. 1890, m. (1) Winna Winfred Sumner (1837-1880's), (2) Mary Blair Brown (b. 1831), bur. Lewis Back Cem., Letcher, Letcher Co., KY.

BACK, LEWIS CECIL: (2/14/1841 – 4/13/1917), Kash's Co., serv. prev. 5th KY Inf., Co. B (Consolidated), res. Breathitt Co., KY 1860, s. of Solomon & Gency (Fields) Back, rec. KY Confed. pension #2534 Breathitt Co. 1912, m. Samantha Cope (1847-1886) 1865, bur. Lazarus Back Cem., Quicksand, Breathitt Co., KY.

BACK, WILLIAM "BILLY": (2/5/1847 – 12/6/1922), Co. B, joined 4/1865, no s.r., claimed 1 month serv. 1890 Veterans Census, res. Letcher Co, KY 1860, s. of Samuel O. & Rhoda (Day) Back, m. Nancy Caudill (1849-1900), bur. Caudill-Back Cem., Roxanna, Letcher Co., KY.

BACK, WILLIAM CODY: (2/3/1848 – 2/20/1912), Co. B, enl. 1863, no. s.r., res. Letcher Co., KY 1860, s. of John & Sally (Caudill) Back, res. Letcher Co. 1890, widow rec. KY Confed. pension #28 Letcher Co. 1912, m. Celia Sumner (1849-10/25/1924) 1868, bur. Broomsage Point Cem., Carbonglow, Letcher Co., KY.

BACK, WILLIAM H.: (12/4/1840 -2/9/1893), Kash's Co., serv. prev. 5th KY Inf., Co. D, Confed. pension #4626 confirms Kash's Co. serv., res. Breathitt Co. 1860, s. of John & Elizabeth (Cope) Back, m. (1) Susannah Back (1842-1880's), (2) Cassandra Davis (1850-1934), bur. John Back Cem., Noctor, Breathitt Co., KY.

BAILEY, ANDREW JACKSON: (1834 – 1864), Cos. F & K, enl. Floyd Co., KY 10/14/1862, 6'0", grey eyes, light hair, serv. prev. 5th KY Inf., Cos. C & K, capt. Perry Co. 5/10/1863, to Camp Chase Prison 5/31/1863, to Johnson's Island Prison 6/14/1863, to Point Lookout Prison 11/30/1863, released on oath 1/10/1864, res. Magoffin Co. 1860, s. of John Jr. & Dorcas (Bradley) Bailey, m. Nancy Estep (1832-1918), bur. Stephens-Bailey Cem., Gunlock, Magoffin Co., KY.

BAILEY, ELISHA D.: (8/15/1838 - 2/25/1899), 3rd Sgt., Co. K, enl. aft. 6/1864, serv. prev. 64th VA Inf., 2nd Co. F, surr. Cumberland Gap 4/30/1865, res. Harlan Co., KY 1860, s. of Jesse & Polly Bailey, res. Harlan Co. 1870, res. Lee Co., VA 1880, m. Martha Jameson (1836-ca1873 VA) b. 8/15/1838, bur. Pennington-Zion Cem., Dryden, Lee Co., VA.

BAILEY, HENRY (C.): (1825 – 1865), Cos. C & F, enl. Whitesburg, KY 10/1/1862, serv. prev. 5th KY Inf., Co. C, trans. Co. F Whitesburg 10/14/1862, capt. Gladeville, VA 7/7/1863, to Kemper Barracks 7/18/1863, to Camp Chase Prison 7/20/1863, to Camp Douglas Prison 4/6/1865, d. of war-related exposure, res. Magoffin Co. 1860, s. of John & Susan (Patrick) Bailey, m. Cynthia Thornsberry (b. 1821), bur. Bailey Cem., Galdia, Magoffin Co., KY.

BAILEY, JAMES: (5/16/1847 – 5/14/1925), Co. C, enl. Whitesburg, KY 10/1/1862, capt. Gladeville, VA 7/7/1863, to Kemper Barracks 7/18/1863, to Camp Chase Prison 7/20/1863, to Camp Douglas Prison 8/24/1863, enl. 5th U. S. Vols. 4/6/1865, res. Perry Co. 1860, s. of James & Elizabeth (Garrison) Bailey, res. Perry Co. 1870 (McIntosh), res. Leslie Co. 1880, 1900, 1910, & 1920 (Wooten), m. Eliza Baker (1851-1930), bur. Bailey Cem., Wooten, Leslie Co., KY.

BAILEY, JOHN: (1/8/1843 – 11/28/1921), Co. F, enl. Floyd Co., KY 10/14/1862, cut off from his command late 1863, ret. serv. until end of war, capt ca. 2/1865 while foraging, res. Magoffin Co. 1860, a Baptist preacher, s. of Joseph & Jane Bailey, rec. Confed. pension #1592 Magoffin Co. 1912, m. Catherine (1843-1910), bur Tip Top Cem., Tip Top, Magoffin Co., KY.

BAILEY, SAMUEL: (1822 – 3/24/1896), Cos. C & F, enl. Whitesburg, KY 5/15/1863, trans. Co. C to Co. F, capt. Gladeville, VA 7/7/1863, res. Magoffin Co. 1860, s. of John & Susan (Patrick) Bailey, m. Nancy Runyon (1825-1886), bur. Henry Gardner Bailey Cem., Gunlock, Magoffin Co., KY.

BAKER, DAVID S.: (1842 – 1872), Co. K, enl. Whitesburg, KY 3/1863, 5'4", dark hair, eyes & complexion, serv. prev. 5th KY Inf., Co. I, capt. Perry Co. 5/10/1863, to Johnson's Island Prison, to Point Lookout Prison, exch. City Point, VA 2/10/1865, pres. Camp Lee, VA 3/1865, res. Perry Co. 1860, s. of Isaac & Elizabeth Jane "Eliza" (Griffith) Baker, m. Emaline Combs, bur. Combs Cem., Hazard, Perry Co., KY.

BAKER, HENRY C.: (11/8/1808 -1/23/1877), Co. D, enl. Whitesburg, KY 10/4/1862, pres. 2/15/1863, res. Letcher Co. 1860, res. Lawrence Co. 1870 (Louisa), m. Mary "Polly" Privett (b. 1815.

BAKER, IRA D.: (4/21/1829 – 2/27/1901), Co. A, serv. prev. 5th KY Inf, Co. F (Original) & Co. B (Consolidated), des. 5th KY Co B Pike Co. 11/4/1862, des. Caudill's Army Whitesburg 11/20/1862, res. Breathitt Co., m. (1) Matilda (1828-1879 Owsley Co.), (2) Elisa Overbee, (3) Mary Houndshell (b. 1856), bur. Cundiff Cem., Warcreek, Breathitt Co., KY.

BAKER, JOHN: (12/5/1840 – 12/22/1915), Co. K, serv. prev. 5th KY Inf., Co. I, 5'8", grey eyes, dark hair, capt. Perry Co. 5/10/1863, to Camp Chase Prison, to Johnson's Island Prison 6/14/1863, to Point Lookout 11/30/1863, exch. Point Lookout 2/10/1865, res. Perry Co., KY 1860, s. of Isaac & Elizabeth Jane "Eliza" (Griffith) Baker, m. Catherina Dehart (1872-1940), bur. Baker Cem., Hazard, Perry Co., KY.

BANKS, ALFRED: (8/31/1841 – 8/2/1898), Co. B, enl. Whitesburg, KY 9/15/1862, paroled Cumberland Gap 5/2/1865, res. Letcher Co. 1860, s. of William & Nancy (Haney) Banks, res. Lee Co., VA post-war, m. Nancy Hyatt (1834-1910) 1865, bur. Memorial Slemp Cem., Dryden, Lee Co., VA.

BANKS, ELIJAH: (1846 – 1905), Co. H, enl. Whitesburg, KY 10/18/1862, disch. 10/18/1862, re-enl. aft. 9/1863, res. Letcher Co. 1860, s. of Spencer Adams & Cassa Banks, m. Elizabeth Burton (1852-aft. 1910) 1868, bur. Elijah Banks Cem., nr. Kodak, Letcher Co., KY.

BANKS, GEORGE WASHINGTON: (10/9/1847 – 6/30/1913), Co. B, on "artificial unit" as G. Banks, rec. clothing 6/29/1864, res. Breathitt Co., KY 1860, s. of William & Pheba Banks, res. Breathitt Co. 1880, m. Elizabeth Taulbee (1851-1923), bur. Bailey-Banks Cem. Taulbee, Breathitt Co., KY.

BANKS, JAMES H.: (11/8/1837 – 3/18/1926), Co. D, enl. Whitesburg, KY 10/4/1862, pres. Spring/1863, res. Letcher Co. 1860, s. of William & Nancy (Haney) Banks, m. Lucinda Blair (1840-1920) Big Cowan 1856, bur. Banks Cem., Whitco, Letcher Co. KY.

BANKS, ZACHARIAH: (1843 – 1867), Co. B, enl. Whitesburg, KY 8/29/1862, rec. clothing 9/24/1864, res. Letcher Co. 1860, s. of William & Nancy (Haney) Banks, bur. Branson Cem., Letcher, Letcher Co., KY.

BARNES, WILLIAM: (1845 – 10/1/1863), Co. B, enl. Whitesburg, KY 9/12/1862, capt. Gladeville, VA 7/7/1863, to Camp Chase Prison 7/20/1863, to Camp Douglas Prison 8/24/1863, d. lung inflammation, res. of Letcher Co. 1860, b. VA, bur. Oak Wood Cem., Chicago, Cook Co., IL.

BARRETT, HARRISON: serv. prev. 5th KY Cav. Co. B, capt. 7/30/1863, to Louisville 8/3/1863, to Camp Chase 8/6/1863, enl. 13th KY Cav. Co. K, Lee Co., VA 8/18/1863, capt. Cumberland Gap on 11/12/1863, NFR.

BATES, HENRY C.: (1844 – 1889), Co. D, enl. Whitesburg, KY 10/4/1862, rec. clothing 6/29/1864, res. Letcher Co., s. of James & Elizabeth (Adams) Bates, res. Letcher Co. 1870 & 1880, on Letcher Co. tax roll 1888 (Millstone), m. Rachel Lee (b. 1843) 1870, bur. Bates Cem., Kona, Letcher Co., KY.

BEGLEY, ELIJAH R.: (12/11/1827 – 9/2/1899), Cos. I & K, conscripted Co. I Whitesburg, KY 10/18/1862, 6'2", blue eyes, dark hair, light complexion, serv. prev. 5th KY Inf., Co. B, enl. Co. K VA 8/18/1863, requested furlough Lee Co., VA 2/28/1865, surr. Cumberland Gap 4/30/1865, res. Owsley Co. 1860, s. of Henry C. & Elizabeth Roberts Begley, res. Owsley Co. 1890 (Buck Creek), widow rec. KY Confed. pension #4214 Owsley Co. 1923, m. (1) Mary Combs (1833-1881/1883), (2) Rhoda Hamilton (1846-1929) Lee Co., bur. Begley Cem., Welchburg, Jackson Co., KY.

BELCHER, STOKLEY: (1835 – 10/21/1912), Co. K, surr. Cumberland Gap 4/30/1865, res. Harlan Co. KY 1860, s. of David Rogers & Betsy Belcher, widow rec. KY Confed. pension #3191 Harlan Co. 1914, m. Juda Middleton (1839-aft. 1920) Hancock Co., TN, bur. Dale Cem., Dale, Pottawatomie Co., OK.

BENTLEY, AARON RICE: (1836 – 1876), 1st Lt., Co. H, enl. Whitesburg, KY 10/18/1862, 6' 0", dark hair, serv. prev. 5th KY Inf., Co. F, wounded Perry Co. 4/14/1863, capt. Gladeville, VA 7/7/1863, to Camp Chase Prison 7/20/1863, to Johnson's Island Prison 10/10/1863, rel. on oath 5/12/1865, res. Letcher Co., s. of Solomon & Mary Bentley, m. Darcus Hall (1844-1918) 1866, res. Letcher Co. 1870, bur. Bates Cem., Deane, Letcher Co., KY.

BENTLEY, BARRET: (b. 1832), Co. H, enl. Brashearville, KY 4/15/1863, serv. prev. Diamond's 10th KY Cav., Co. E, pres. summer/1863, res. Floyd Co. 1860, s. of Solomon & Mary Bentley, res. Boyd Co. 1870, res. Lawrence Co. 1878, m. (1) Ruth (b. 1843), (2) Lorinda "Manda" McKinney.

BENTLEY, BENJAMIN: (1829 – 1866), Co. H, enl. Whitesburg, KY 10/18/1862, disch. 4/1/1863, res. Letcher Co. 1860, s. of Solomon & Mary "Polly" (Yonts) Bentley, m. Elizabeth Baker (1830-aft. 1900 Letcher Co.) 1849, widow res. Letcher Co. 1870, bur. Bates Cem., Deane, Letcher Co., KY.

BENTLEY, HIRAM: (1847 – 1/11/1899), Co. D, enl. Whitesburg, KY 10/4/1862, pres. 11/20/1862, res. Floyd Co. 1860, s. of Moses & Martha (Blankenship) Bentley, res. Floyd Co. 1870 & 1880 (Antioch), m. Anna Akers (b. 1851-aft. 1910) 1866.

BENTLEY, JOHN Q.: (2/1829 – 10/20/1910), Co. D, enl. Whitesburg, KY 10/4/1862, 6; 2", dark hair & complexion, grey eyes, pres. summer/1863, joined Union 39th, Co. K 11/16/1863, disch. 9/15/1865, res. Letcher Co. 1860, s. of John & Peggy (Hamilton) Bentley, res. Letcher Co. 1880, m. Lucinda Thacker (1835-1917) 1868, bur. John Q. Bentley Cem., Deane, Letcher Co., KY.

BENTLEY, JOHN VENT: (1826 – 8/6/1895), Co. D, enl. Whitesburg, KY 10/4/1862, pres. 11/1/1862, res. Pike Co. 1860, s. of Ben & Elizabeth (Crase) Bentley, m. Anna "Anny" (1831-bef. 1900 Letcher Co.), bur. Green Acres Cem., Ermine, Letcher Co., KY.

BENTLEY, LAFAYETTE: (1841 – 1865), Co. D, enl. Whitesburg, KY 10/4/1862, took leave & ret. serv. spring/1863, paid 5/1/1863, pres. 8/1/1863, killed late in the war, res. Wise Co., VA 1860, s. of James & Sarah (Dockery) Bentley, m. Susan Potter (1835-1914), bur. Bentley Cem., Jenkins, KY (lost to development), memorial marker Potter Cem. Jenkins, Letcher Co., KY.

BENTLEY, MAY: (1840 – 1865), Co. D, enl. Whitesburg, KY 10/4/1862, pres. fall/1862, enl. Union 39th KY, Co. K 1/15/1864, disc. 9/15/1865, shot & killed at home after leaving serv., res. Letcher Co. 1860, s. of Thomas & Margaret (Crase) Bentley, m. Mary Vanover, bur. hollowed-out poplar log, Delaney farm, Adamson, Letcher Co., KY.

BENTLEY, SOLOMON DAVIS: (8/1/1836 – 2/12/1909), Co. D, enl. Whitesburg, KY 10/4/1862, pres. fall/1862, res. Letcher Co. 1860, s. of Thomas Bentley, res. Letcher Co. 1870 & 1880, res. Wise Co., VA 1900, m. Mary (1840-d. aft. 1920), bur. Sam Bentley Cem., Payne Gap, Letcher Co., KY.

BENTLEY, WILLIAM: (b. 1844), Co. D, enl. Whitesburg, KY 10/4/1862, pres. fall/1862, enl. Union 39th KY, Co. K 10/10/1863, des. Floyd Co. 5/30/1864, ret. Union serv. Paintsville 4/3/1865, disc. 9/15/1865, res. Floyd Co. 1860, s. of Moses & Martha (Blankenship) Bentley, res. Floyd Co. 1870, m. (1) Mahalia Jane Akers (b. 1848) Pike Co. 1866, (2) Rebecca Henson Mullins in 1877, on 1880 Floyd Co., KY census.

BERRY, ALBERT SEATON: (5/13/1836 – 1/6/1908), Co. A, enl. 5th KY Inf. Co. G Camp Moccasin, VA 3/24/1862, trans. Co. F, serv. as color bearer, enl. 13th KY Cav., trans. Signal Corp 12/1862, serv. later as 2nd Lt in Confed. Marine Corps, capt. at Sailor's Creek, VA 4/6/1865, res. Campbell Co. 1860, s. of James T. Berry, graduate Miami Univ. 1855, Cincinnati Law School 1858, mayor of Newport five terms, KY Legislator 1876-1901, Campbell County judge, m. Anna S. (1846-1908), bur. Evergreen Cem., Southgate, Campbell Co., KY.

BERRY, EBEN: (b. 1839), Co. K, enl. Lee Co., VA 8/18/1863, Evan Berry on s.r., pres. Lee Co. 12/31/1863 bur. Faulkner Cem., Bradrick, Lawrence Co. OH., res. Estill Co., KY 1860, prob. s. of Levi Berry, m. Martha Francis Broughton (b. 1840) Madison Co. 1858.

BIGGS, WILLOUGHBY: (7/11/1836 – 11/11/1876), Co. F, enl. Floyd Co., KY 10/4/1862, a.k.a. Willy Briggs, pres. 4/30/1863, serv. later Union 39th Inf., Co. F, res. Lawrence Co., s. of Isom & Clarkia (Collins) Biggs, res. Lawrence Co. 1870, m. Martha Dean (b. 1837),

BISHOP, JOHN THOMAS: (1831 – bef. 1870), Capt., Co. F, s.r. in the "Artificial Unit", surr. Cumberland Gap 4/28/1865, res. Nicholas Co., KY 1860, s. of William & Mary Bishop, m. Rhoda Spegel (1829-aft. 1870).

BLANKENSHIP, JOHN W.: (1842 – aft. 1910), Co. D, enl. Whitesburg, KY 10/4/1862, serv. prev. VA State Line, Co. E, enl. Diamond's 10th KY, Co. H, 5/15/1863, pres. 7/23/1863, poss. joined Union 39th, Co. E aft. 7/23/1863, res. Letcher Co. 1860, s. of Barnett & Jenny (Bentley) Blankenship, res. Pike Co. (Knox) 1910, m. Martha (1844- aft. 1910 Pike Co.).

BLANTON, WILLIAM (HARRISON): (7/2/1848 – 7/1/1922), Co. K, rec. clothing 9/7/1864, surr. Cumberland Gap 4/30/1865, res. of Owsley Co. in 1850, s. of Nancy (Baker) Blanton, m. Nancy Ann Burton (1850-1922) in Breathitt Co. in 1868, served as Breathitt Co. Judge & County Attorney, bur. Combs Cem., Jackson, Breathitt Co., KY.

BLEVINS, DAVID: (1832 -1903), 2nd Cpl., Co. K, enl. aft. 7/27/1863, serv. prev. 64th VA, 2nd Co. F, 27th Btn. VA Cav., Co. G & 25th VA Cav., Co. B, surr. Cumberland Gap 4/30/1865, res. Harlan Co, KY 1860, s. of James T. & Susan Blevins, pardoned by Gov. Thomas Bramlett for Harlan Co. war-related murder 1867, widow rec. KY Confed. pension #1220 Harlan Co. 1912, m. Margaret "Peggy" Farley (1847-1926) Harlan Co. 1864, bur. Reds Creek Cem., Dizney, Harlan Co., KY.

BLEVINS, JAMES: (b. 3/1831), Co. K, serv. prev. 64th VA Inf., Co. H, surr. w/ Co. K, 13th KY Cav. Cumberland Gap 4/30/1865, res. Harlan Co. KY 1860, s. of James T. Sr. & Susan Blevins, res. Harlan Co. 1900 & 1910 (Clover Fk.), m. (1) Emiline Eldridge (b. 1829, (2) Mary Kirkam (b. 1864), (3) Nancy (1852-1932) 1895, bur. unmarked Blevins Family Cem., Dizney, Harlan Co. KY.

BLEVINS, JOHN RANSON: (1842 – 3/10/1924), Co. K, enl. Lee Co., VA aft. 8/4/1863, serv. prev. VA State Line & 64th VA Inf., Co. H (3/18/1863-8/4/1863), surr. Cumberland Gap 4/30/1865, res. Harlan Co. KY 1860, s. of James T. Blevins SR, pardon application of 1/31/1867 claims loyalty, pardoned of killing Union soldier Jason Fields in self-defense, m. Lucy Wynn (b. 1842), rec. KY Confed. pension #1219 Evarts, 1912, bur. Bills Creek Cem., Dizney, Harlan Co., KY.

BOGGS, ELIJAH: (1/12/1830 – 1/12/917), Co. D, enl. Whitesburg, KY 10/4/1862, pres. 10/20/1862, serv. later Union Harlan Co. Btn., res. Letcher Co. 1860, s. of Eli & Sarah (Eldridge) Boggs, res. Letcher Co. 1910, m. Juda Smith (1840-1912), bur. Eli Boggs Cem., Eolia, Letcher Co., KY.

BOGGS, HENRY C.: (11/1/1837 – 2/9/1916), Co. D, enl. 10/4/1862, serv. later in Union Army, res. Letcher Co., KY 1860, s. of Eli & Sarah (Eldridge) Boggs, res. Letcher Co. 1900, res. Lee Co., VA 1910, m. (1) Julia Williams (1838-2/2/1912), (2) Mary Jane Melton (1839-aft. 1920 Harlan Co.), bur. Eli Boggs Cem., Oven Fork, Letcher Co., KY.

BOGGS, LEVI: (10/7/1835 – 8/10/1914), Co. D, enl. Whitesburg, KY 10/4/1862, pres. 10/20/1862, res. Letcher Co. 1860, s. of Eli & Sarah (Eldridge) Boggs, m. Elizabeth Calhoun (1833-1917), bur. Old Union Church Cem., London, Laurel Co., KY.

BOLEN, WILLIAM M.: (6/15/1834 – 6/23/1918), Co. C, serv. prev. 5th KY Inf., Cos. A & H, serv. later 13th KY under Maj. Chenoweth, w/ Gen. Morgan on last raid 1864, disbanded 4/1865 in VA en route to Richmond, took oath Louisa 1865, res. Perry Co. 1860, s. of Robert & Polly (Begley) Bolling, res. Knott Co. 1910, rec. Confed. pension #534 Perry Co. 1912, widow rec. Pension #4370 Knott Co. 1925, m. (1) Mary (b. 1846), (2) Sally (1899-aft. 1925), bur. Richie Cem., Talcum, Knott Co., KY.

BOLLING, ALEXANDER L.: (3/9/1836 – 5/11/1912), Co. B, also serv. 7th Btn. Confed. Cav., Co. B, widow claimed serv. in 13th KY Cav., Co. B on pension appl., res. Wise Co., VA 1860, m. Elizabeth (1838-aft. 1910) 1859, bur. Mt. Zion Cem., nr. Pound, Wise Co., VA.

BOLLING, CALEB: (1845 -1863), Co. A, serv. prev. 5th KY Inf., Co. F, enl. 13th KY Cav., Co. A, disch. 4/30/1863, family records claim he was murdered by Union soldiers, res. Letcher Co. KY 1860, s. of Jonathan & Freelove (Mullins) Bolling, bur. Ben Bolling Cem., Flat Gap, Wise Co., VA.

BOLLING, DANIEL BOONE "DAN": (1833 – 1888), 2nd Sgt., Co. A, enl. Whitesburg, KY 9/9/1862, prom. 2nd Sgt. 1/17/1863, abs. sick summer/1863, res. Letcher Co., s. of Jonathan & Freelove (Mullins) Bolling, m. Sarah Caudill (1837-aft. 1880) 1858, bur. Eldridge Cem., Roxanna, Letcher Co., KY.

BOLLING, JESSE: (3/11/1826 – 3/24/1901), Co. D, rec. clothing 6/29/1864 & 9/7/1864, res. Wise Co., VA, s. of Jeremiah & Sally (Ward) Bolling, m. Louisa Short (1831-1907) 1850, bur. Ben Bolling Cem., Flat Gap, Wise Co., VA.

BOLLING, JOHN: (1842 – 1863), 3rd Cpl., Co. A, enl. Whitesburg, KY 11/2/1862, serv. prev. 5th KY Inf., Co. F, capt. Floyd Co. by 39th KY under Major Ferguson 5/20/1863, to Louisa, family records state he was murdered by Union soldiers, res. Letcher Co. 1860, s. of Jonathan & Freelove (Mullins) Bolling, bur. Ben Bolling Cem., Flat Gap, Wise Co., VA.

BOLLING, JOHN D. "NEEDLEHEAD": (1838 – 3/4/1906), Co. D, prob. serv. in Co. D of 13th, then enl. in Co. B 7th Btn. Confed. Cav., widow claimed serv. in pension appl., res. Wise Co., VA 1860, s. of Jeremiah & Providence (Short) Bolling, m. Melvina Craft (1844-1916) 1859, bur. John D. Bolling Cem., Flat Gap, Wise Co., VA.

BOND, STEPHEN P.: (3/27/1841 – 9/16/1916), Co. A, enl. Whitesburg, KY 11/1/1862, capt. Mt. Sterling 6/10/1864, to Louisville Prison 6/19/1864, to Rock Island Prison 6/22/1864, exch. City Point, VA 3/6/1865, res. Wise Co., VA 1860, s. of William J. & Rebecca (Elam) Bond, rec. pension as res. Flatgap, KY, m. Esther Bond (1842-1902), bur. Jayne Cem., Flatgap, Johnson Co., KY.

BOND, WILLIAM ELLINGTON: (5/19/1839 – 8/19/1907, Cos. A & B, enl. Whitesburg, KY 11/1/1862, trans. Co. A to Co. B, capt. Gladeville 7/7/1863, to Camp Douglas, ret. serv, rec. clothing 6/29/1864, 9/7/1864 & 11/19/1864, paroled Cumberland Gap 5/5/1865, widow rec KY Confed. pension #65 Morgan Co. 1912, s. of William J. & Rebecca (Elam) Bond, m. Nancy Lipps (1836-1918) Russell Co.,VA, bur. Farmer Daniels Cem., Dingus, Morgan Co., KY.

BOOTH, ANDREW J.: (12/1825 – 3/20/1874), Ord. Sgt., Cos. I & D, enl. Abingdon, VA 10/31/1862, serv. prev. Bourbon Co. State Militia, serv. prev. 3rd. Btn. KY Mtd. Rifles, rec. clothing 6/29/1864, surr. w/ Co. D Mt. Sterling 4/30/1865, res. Bourbon Co. 1860, occ. hotel clerk, bought & sold property Paris, KY 1871-1873, m. Mary E. Bedford (1827-1877), bur. Paris City Cem., Paris, Bourbon Co., KY.

BOWENS, WILLIAM: (1841 – 1896), Co. H, enl. Whitesburg, KY 10/18/1862, res. Letcher Co., s. of Perran & Anna (Wallen) Bowen, res. Letcher Co. 1880 (Camp Branch), bur. Colson Cem., Colson, Letcher Co., KY.

BOWLING M.: Co. K, enl. Lee Co. VA 8/18/1863, pres. Lee Co. 12/31/1863, res. Clay Co., KY.

BOWMAN, GEORGE W.: (1840 – 1902), Co. K, aka Bownum, aka Bonham, pres. Lee Co. VA 12/31/1863, rec. clothing 9/24/1864, res. Breathitt Co., KY 1860, s. of Joseph & Sytha Bowman, m. Eliza Little (1844-aft. 1900), bur. Jackson City Cem., Jackson, Breathitt Co., KY.

BRADLEY, GEORGE: (1842 – 1883), Co. C., enl. Whitesburg, KY 10/1/1862, abs. on leave spring/1863, res. Breathitt Co. 1860, s. of James & Elizabeth (Hale) Bradley, paralysed 1880, m. Octavia Stacy, (1841-2/5/1916) Hueysville/Floyd Co., bur. George Bradley Cem., Decoy, Breathitt Co., KY.

BRADLEY, JACOB: (12/15/1837 – 2/12/1915), Co. F, enl. Floyd Co., KY 10/14/1862, ret. serv. 3/30/1863, res. Breathitt Co. 1860, s. of George & Susan (Hale) Bradley, res. Breathitt Co. 1880, res. Knott Co. 1900, res. Floyd Co. 1910, m. Barbara Watkins (1842-aft.1920 Middle Ck./Floyd Co.)1862, bur. George Bradley Cem., Decoy, Breathitt Co., KY.

BRADLEY, MILAN J.: Co. G, 5' 11", blue eyes, light complexion, capt. Gladeville, VA 7/7/1863, to Camp Douglas Prison 8/22/1863, rel. on oath 3/27/1865,

BRANSON, JAMES: (1828 – 9/1863), Co. H, enl. Whitesburg, KY 11/15/1862, pres. 4/30/1863, killed by Union troops nr. Letcher P. O., Letcher Co., res. Letcher Co. 1860, s. of Henry & Betsy (Howard) Branson, m. Sallie Howard (1825-1872), bur. Branson Cem. Letcher, Letcher Co., KY.

BRANSON, LEONARD: (1820 – 9/1863), Co. H, no s.r., family history claims serv. and that he was killed by Union troops Letcher Co. ca 9/1863, res. Letcher Co. 1860, s. of Henry & Betsy (Howard) Branson, m. Elizabeth Brashear (6/3/1824-5/26/1897) bur. Branson Cem. Letcher, Letcher Co. KY.

BRANSON, RICHARD A.: (1835 – 6/11/1863), 4th Sgt., Co. B, enl. Whitesburg, KY 8/29/1862, listed on s.r. as R. S. Branson, wounded in skirmish Breathitt County, d. later at home, res. Letcher Co. 1860, s. of Henry & Betsy (Howard) Branson, bur. Branson Cem., Letcher, Letcher Co., KY.

BRASHEAR, EZEKIAL: (1/11/1826 – 6/11/1864), Co. B, enl. Brashearville in Perry Co. 9/12/1862, rec. clothing 4/7/1864, k. Battle of Cynthiana, KY, sent home for burial by Gen. John Hunt Morgan, res. Perry Co. 1860, s. of Sampson & Margaret (Bright) Brashear, m. (1) Nancy Cornett (1830-1857) 1852, (2) Mary Ann Combs (1829-1886) 1859, bur. Branson Cem., Letcher, Letcher Co. KY.

BRASHEAR, HARVEY G.: (4/4/1835 – 3/26/1918), Co. H, enl. Whitesburg, KY 10/18/1862, res. Perry Co. 1860, s. of Sampson & Margaret (Bright) Brashear, moved to St. Paul, AR 1876, m. Polly Ann Cornett (1855-aft. 1910)1875, bur. Brashears Cem., Brashears, Madison Co., AR.

BRASHEAR, HEZEKIAH E.: (1/9/1843 – 12/30/1929), Co. H, enl. Glavdeville, VA 7/17/1863, identified in A. G. Report, res. Perry Co. 1860, s. of Sampson & Margaret (Bright) Brashear, m. Mary Hogg (1852-1912) Letcher Co. 1867, bur. Brashears Cem., Brashears, Madison Co., AR.

BRASHEAR, ISAAC: (6/3/1818 – 1881), Co. B, enl. Whitesburg, KY 8/29/1862, pres. summer/1863, res. Perry Co. 1860, s. of Sampson & Margaret (Bright) Brashear, res. Floyd Co. 1870, res. Greenup Co. 1880, m. Jane Adams (2/21/1821-aft. 1880)1841, bur. Wampler Cem., Argilite, Greenup Co., KY.

BRASHEAR, JAMES N. JR: (8/10/1835 – 4/10/1920), Co. B, enl. Brashearville, KY 9/2/1862, rec. clothing 4/7/1864 and 6/29/1864, w/ Morgan on Last Raid battles 1864, surr. head of Beaver 4/1865, res. Perry Co. 1860, s. of James N. Sr. & Elizabeth (Young) Brashear, m. Elizabeth Pratt (1852-1924), bur. W. C. Brashear Cem., Fusionia, Perry Co., KY.

BRASHEAR, JESSE C.: (8/26/1837 – 11/7/1930), 4th Sgt., Co. H, enl. Whitesburg, KY 9/21/1862, pres. fall/1863, res. Perry Co. 1860, s. of Sampson & Margaret (Bright) Brashear, res. Letcher Co. 1870, m. Betty Jane Hogg (1838-aft. 1910 Madison Co. AR) 1858, bur. Brashears Cem., Brashears, Madison Co., AR.

BRASHEAR, JOHN L.: (1832 – 12/11/1864), Co. H, enl. Whitesburg, KY 10/18/1862, capt. Gladeville, VA 7/7/1863, to Kemper Barracks 7/18/1863, to Camp Chase Prison 7/20/1863, to Camp Douglas Prison 8/24/1863, d. of dysentery Camp Douglas, res. Perry Co. 1860, s. of John & Nancy (Edgeman) Brashear, bur. Oak Wood Cem., Chicago, Cook Co., IL.

BRASHEAR, JOSEPH E.: (1831 – 1864), Co. H, enl Gladeville, VA 7/22/1863, pres. fall/1863, res. Perry Co., KY, s. of Robert & Mary (Everidge) Brashear, m. Caroline Baker (1833-1905) 1854, bur. Edley Cornett Cem., Cornettsville, Perry Co., KY.

BRASHEAR, SAMPSON A. "SAMPSON SR": (3/12/1838 – 12/19/1898), 4th Cpl., Co. B, enl. Whitesburg, KY 9/9/1862, appointed 5/25/1863, wounded Battle of Mount Sterling w/ Gen. John Hunt Morgan 6/9/1864, middle finger of rt. hand amputated as POW Union Army Hospital Lexington 6/9/1864, to Ft. Clay 6/15/1864, to Louisville Prison, to Rock Island Prison 6/24/1864, exch. City Point, VA 3/6/1865, res. Perry Co. 1860, s. of James N. Sr. & Elizabeth (Young) Brashear, m. Mary Ann Combs (1849-1920), bur. W. C. Brashear Cem., Fusonia, Perry Co., KY.

BRASHEAR, SAMPSON "SAMPSON JR": (1844 – 6/9/1864), Co. B, enl. Brashearville 10/12/1862, rec. clothing 4/7/1864, KIA Battle of Mt. Sterling, res. Perry Co. 1860, s. of Isaac B. & Jane (Adams) Brashear, bur. Confed. Cem., Mt. Sterling, Montgomery Co., KY.

BRASHEAR, SAMUEL RAY: (1841 – 1870), Capt., Co. H, enl. Whitesburg, KY 10/16/1862, serv. prev. as Pvt. & musician 5th KY Inf., Co. H, capt. Gladeville, VA 7/7/1863, to Kemper Barracks 7/18/1863, to Camp Chase Prison 7/20/1863, to Johnson's Island Prison 10/10/1863, exch. Pt. Lookout 2/16/1865, to Richmond, VA hosp. 3/4/1865, des. hosp. 3/6/1865, res. Perry Co. 1860, s. of Robert S. & Mary (Everidge) Brashear, tavern operator 1866 & 1867, m. Mary Ann "Martha" Hogg (b. 1831), bur. Edley Cornett Cem., Cornettsville, Perry Co., KY.

BRASHEAR, WILLIAM E.: (12/10/1840 – 9/30/1907), 1st Cpl., Co, B, enl. Brashearville, KY 9/4/1862, rec. clothing 9/24/1864, res. Perry Co. 1860, s. of James N. Sr. & Elizabeth (Young) Brashear, res. Perry Co. 1870 & 1880, m. (1) Polly Hampton (1848-1883) (2) Fannie Lee Elkins (1871-1937) Wolfe Co., bur. Redding Hammock Cem., Greenville, Madison Co., FL.

BRASHEAR, WILLIAM RUTLEDGE: (11/4/1841 – 6/27/1925), 2nd Sgt., Co. H, enl. Whitesburg, KY 9/10/1862, rec. clothing 11/19/1864, res. Perry Co. 1860, s. of Sampson & Margaret (Bright) Brashear, m. Mary Lucinda Sumner AR 1870, bur. Brashears Cem., Brashears, Madison Co., AR.

BRASHEAR, WILLIAM T. B.: (1834 – 2/1/1864), Cos. A & C, enl. Whitesburg, KY 9/21/1862, trans. Co. A to Co. C 9/21/1862, pres. fall/1863, res. Letcher Co. 1860, s. of Robert S. & Mary (Everidge) Brashear, res. Whitesburg post-war, m. Malinda Edwards, bur. Edley Cornett Cem., Cornettsville, Perry Co., KY.

BREWER, JOHN Q.: (1835 – 1895), Co. I, enl. Whitesburg, KY 10/18/1862, res. Perry Co. 1860, s. of Hardy & Nancy Brewer, res. Rockcastle Co. 1880, res. Knott Co. 1890, m. Betty Walker (1836-bef. 1900) 1858, bur. Bush Cem., Pigeon Roost, Perry Co., KY.

BREWER, JOSEPH H.: (1836 – 1897), 1st Sgt., Co. I, conscripted Whitesburg, KY 10/18/1862, 1st Sgt. 12/31/1862 to 3/20/1863, abs. fall/1863, res. Perry Co. 1870 (Troublesome), s. of Hardy & Nancy Brewer, m. Nancy Engle (1838-aft. 1910) 1859, bur. Bush Cem., Pigeon Roost, Perry Co., KY.

BRITTAIN, CHADWELL: (b. 1848), Co. K, enl. Lee Co. VA 8/18/1863, capt. nr. Cumberland Gap fall/1863, surr. Cumberland Gap 4/30/1865, res. Harlan Co. 1860 as Chadwell Noe, s. of Carr & Caroline Britton.

BROOKS, FRANCIS M.: (b. 1843), Co. D, enl. Whitesburg, KY 10/4/1862, pres. fall/1862, serv. Union 39th KY, Co. K 11/16/1862 to 9/15/1865, res. Letcher Co., s. of John & Julia A. Brooks, res. Johnson Co. 1870 (Hoods Ford).

BROWN, DAVID: (9/12/1823 – 1/5/1907), Co. F, enl. Floyd Co., KY 10/14/1862, pres. fall/1862, res. Johnson Co. 1860, res. Johnson Co. 1890, m. (1) Polly "Mary Ann" Johnson (1829-aft.1900)1860, (2) Izenna Pitts (1827-1908), bur. Brown Cem., Fredville, Magoffin Co., KY.

BRYANT, JACOB: (5/2/1840 – 7/4/1920), Co. E, enl. Whitesburg, KY 10/5/1862, capt. Perry Co. 6/6/1863, to Camp Chase Prison, to Johnson's Island Prison, to Point Lookout 11/1863, res. Floyd Co., s. of David & Vina Bryant, m. (1) Elender Roberts (1837-1891), (2) Kizzie Robbins Patton (1832-after 1920), bur. Newman Cem., Price, Floyd Co., KY.

BRYANT, JAMES B.: (8/29/1840 – 5/27/1927), Co. D, enl. Whitesburg, KY 10/4/1862, pres. 11/20/1862, also serv. 4th VA State Line, res. Pike Co. 1860, s. of Joseph & Elizabeth Bryant, m. (3) Matilda Ann Austin Bryant (1835-1919), bur. Jim-Boy Bryant Cem., Pound, Wise Co., VA.

BUERNS, CHARLES: Co. K, surr. Mount Sterling 4/30/1865.

BURGIN, ISAAC: (1844 – 10/19/1934), Co. K, surr. Cumberland Gap 4/30/1865, res. Lee Co., VA 1860, s. of William Burgin, res. Clay Co. KY 1880, d. Manchester, KY d.c #08965, m. Mary Jane Childs (b. 1840) 1864.

BURK, JONATHAN: (b. 1831), Co. E, enl. Whitesburg, KY 10/5/1862, pres. fall/1862, serv. later Diamond's 10th KY Cav., Co. H, did not survive the war, res. Harlan Co. 1860, s. of Robert & Isabelle Burke, m. Ara.

BURTON, ISAAC: (2/13/1845 – 9/13/1924), Co. H, enl. Whitesburg, KY 10/18/1862, rec. clothing 9/7/1864, capt. Wise Co., VA, escaped w/ help of future wife, paroled Cumberland Gap 4/30/1865, res. Perry Co. 1860, s. of Robert & Elizabeth "Betty" Burton, moved Wise Co., VA 1865, rec. VA Confed. Pension #16294 Wise Co, VA (Dooly) 1912, widow rec. VA Confed. Pension 1924, m. Amanda Jane Wampler (1849-aft 1924) 7/27/1865 Wise Co., VA, bur. American Legion Cem., Big Stone Gap, Wise Co. VA.

CALHOUN, JAMES LESTER: (4/10/1834 – 3/10/1899), Kash's Co., res. Breathitt Co., KY 1860, s. of James S. & Mary (Hogg) Calhoun, indicted for murder 1865, m. Elizabeth Williams (1829-1924), bur. Calhoun Cem., Rousseau, Breathitt Co., KY.

CALHOUN, JOHN C.: (1841 – aft. 1912), Co. B, enl. Whitesburg, KY 8/29/1862, capt. Mt. Sterling 6/10/1864, to Louisville Prison 6/20/1864, to Rock Island Prison 6/22/1864, joined U.S. Navy 7/6/1864, initially assigned to *U.S.S. Susquehanna*, res. Letcher Co. 1860, s. of David & Rachel Calhoun, owned Knott Co. property (Troublesome) 1902-1904, res. Handshoe, KY ca. 1912.

CALHOUN, ROBERT: (1846 – bef. 1890), Co. H, enl. Whitesburg, KY 10/18/1862, pres. 11/20/1862, serv. Union 39th KY Infantry, Co. B 4/1863 through 9/1865, res. Letcher Co. 1860, s. of G. W. & Priscilla Calhoun, res. Johnson Co. 1870 & 1880, widow res. Johnson Co. 1890, m. Hannah (1842-aft. 1900).

CALHOUN, SAMUEL C.: (1834 – 1877), 3rd Sgt., Co. A, enl. 11/1/1862, serv. prev. 5th KY Inf., Co. F, prom. 3rd Sgt. 1/17/1863, capt. Booneville, KY 8/19/1863, to Rock Island Prison, enl. frontier service w/ U.S. 2nd Regt. Vols., Co. G 10/6/1864, res. Letcher Co. 1860, s. of David & Eda (Ayers) Calhoun, serv. Ft. Levinworth, KS 1865-1866, m. Martha Hughes (b. 1834), bur. Charlie Logan Gap Cem., Bath, Knott Co., KY.

CALHOUN, THOMAS: (1827 – 1899), Co. A, serv. prev. 5th KY Inf., Co. F, pres. 4/30/1863, res. Letcher Co. 1860, s. of David & Eda (Ayers) Calhoun, res. Letcher Co. 1870, res. Floyd Co. 1880, m. Virginia Jane Music Newsome (b. 1829) Letcher Co. 1848, bur. Calhoun Cem., Water Gap, Floyd Co., KY.

CAMERON, JOHN (THOMAS): (12/1844 – 4/3/1920), Co. D, surr. Mt. Stering, KY 4/30/1865, res. of Bourbon Co. 1860, s. of Lemuel Cameron & Margaret (Smith) Cameron, m. Elizabeth J. Jenkins (1845-1926) 1869, bur. Ruddels Mills Cem., Ruddels Mills, Bourbon Co., KY.

CAMPBELL, ANDREW C.: (1830 – 1913), 2nd Sgt., Cos. G & I, enl. Co. G 10/1/1862, conscripted Co. I Whitesburg KY 10/18/1862, pres. fall/1862, res. Perry Co. 1860, s. of Caleb & Frances (Miller) Campbell, moved TX by 1876, moved Madison Co., AR by 1880, res. Madison Co., AR 1910 (Boston), m. Margaret "Peggy" Napier (b. 1836, d. bef. 1880) 1853, bur. (unmarked) Boston Cem., Boston, Madison Co., AR.

CAMPBELL, CALEB J.: (9/27/1837 – 7/29/1905), Co. C, enl. Whitesburg, KY 10/1/1862, capt. Breathitt Co. 3/8/1864, to Louisville Prison 3/25/1864, to Camp Chase Prison 3/26/1864, to New Orleans Prison 5/2/1865, res. Breathitt Co. 1860, s. of John & Martha "Patsy" (Smith) Campbell, widow rec. KY Confed. Pension #1247 Perry Co. 1913, m. Catherine Smith (1847-1934) Perry Co., bur. Hudson Cem., Rowdy, Perry Co., KY.

CAMPBELL, JOHN C.: (1833 – 1917), Co. C, enl. Whitesburg, KY 10/1/1862, capt. Battle of Cynthiana 6/14/1864, to Rock Island Prison, paroled Richmond, VA 5/1/1865, res. Perry Co. 1860, s. of John & Martha "Patsy" (Smith) Campbell, res. Wolfe Co. 1880, res. Lee Co. 1910 (Shoemaker Ridge), rec. KY Confed. Pension #152 Lee Co. (Fincastle) 1912, m. Martha Williams (1837-1914) 1860, bur. Olinger Cem., Zoe, Lee Co., KY.

CAMPBELL, JOHN C.: (1832 – 1918), Co. B, enl. Whitesburg, KY 8/29/1862, disch. 1/1/1863, res. Letcher Co. 1860, s. of William & Elizabeth (Cornett) Campbell, res. Letcher Co. 1890, m. Harriet Watts (1841-aft. 1910) 1860, bur. Hart Campbell Cem., Ulvah, Letcher Co. KY.

CAMPBELL, JOHN D.: (12/5/1833 – 4/15/1904), Co. G, enl. Perry Co., KY 9/26/1862, wd. & left at home fall/1862, ret. serv. summer/1863, des. Perry Co. 9/15/1863, res. Perry Co. 1860, s. of Caleb & Francis (Miller) Campbell, m. Sally Holliday (1837-1902) 1856, bur. Holliday Cem., Ary, Perry Co., KY.

CAMPBELL, SAMUEL S.: (1843 – 1895), Co. G, enl. Perry Co., KY 9/28/1862, capt. Battle of Cynthiana 6/14/1864, released & joined U.S. forces 10/13/1864, res. Perry Co. 1860, s. of Lewis & Rachel (Allen) Campbell, m. Elizabeth Combs (1845-1903), bur. Campbell-Allen Cem., Rowdy, Perry Co., KY.

CAMPBELL, WILLIAM "BUCK: (3/11/1829 – 6/5/1918), Co. C, enl. Whitesburg, KY 10/1/1862, 5'9", black hair, dark eyes, pres. summer/1863, capt. Breathitt Co. 3/8/1864, to Louisville Prison, to Camp Chase Prison 3/26/1864, released on oath 6/6/1865, res. Perry Co. 1860, s. of Caleb & Francis (Miller) Campbell, m. Polly Allen (1835-1910), bur. Campbell-Napier Cem., Blue Diamond, Perry Co., KY.

CARPENTER, ANDREW: (1834 – 5/10/1879), 3rd Cpl., Co. G, enl. Breathitt Co., KY 9/22/1862, res. Breathitt Co. 1860, s. of William & Sally Carpenter, murdered by gunshot to rt. temple, m. (1) Hetta Gayheart (1831-1870's) 1852, (2) Sarah Miller (1856-1886) 8/4/1878, bur. Carpenter-Howard Cem., Key, Breathitt Co., KY.

CARPENTER, JOHN: (1835 – 1/1878), Co. C, enl. Whitesburg, KY 10/12/1862, res. Breathitt Co. 1860, s. of William & Sally Carpenter, m. Polly Gayheart (b. 1836)1854, bur. Carpenter-Howard Cem., Key, Breathitt Co., KY.

CARPENTER, SAMUEL: (2/14/1840 – 1/2/1899), 2nd Cpl., Co. G, enl. Breathitt Co., KY 9/23/1862, res. Breathitt Co. 1860, s. of William & Elizabeth Carpenter, indicted for murder as member of Co. G 1865, m. Delilah Fugate (1842-bef. 1900)1863, bur. Ed Carpenter Cem. Quicksand, Breathitt Co., KY.

CARTER, LARKIN H.: (10/1840 – 9/5/1918), Co. K, surr. Cumberland Gap 4/30/1865, res. Lee Co. VA 1860, s. of Drury F. & Isabell (Tritt) Carter, m. Margaret Woodard (1856-1926), bur. Reeds Creek Cem., e. of Rt. 776, Purcell, Lee Co., VA.

CASSADY, WILLIAM M.: (7/28/1835 – 11/19/1923), Cos. F & K, enl. Co. F Whitesburg, KY 6/1/1863, trans. Co. K Lee Co., VA 8/18/1863, rec. clothing 6/29/1864, res. Johnson Co. 1860, s. of Benjamin & Juliet Cassady, res. Johnson Co. 1870, res. Martin Co. 1880, m. Tamsy J. (1839-1932), bur. Cassady Cem., Inez, Martin Co., KY.

CAUDILL, ABEL: (2/4/1843 – 7/1/1925), Co. A, serv. prev. 5th KY Inf., Co. F, capt. Booneville, KY 8/19/1863, to Louisville Prison 8/24/1863, to Camp Chase Prison 9/1/1863, to Rock Island Prison 1/22/1864, exch. Pt. Lookout 3/13/1865, res. Letcher Co. 1860, s. of Sam & Sarah (Maggard) Caudill, res. Morehead, KY 1870 (banker & grocer), m. Mary Ann Hall 1869, bur. Caudill Cem., Morehead, Rowan Co., KY.

CAUDILL, ABNER: (7/1835 – 5/21/1886), 2nd Lt., Cos. B & E, enl. Whitesburg, KY 9/12/1862, trans. Co. E 10/5/1862, prom. 2nd Lt. 10/7/1862, resigned, res. Floyd Co. 1860, s. of Abner & Ellender (Johnson) Caudill, res. Floyd Co. 1870, m. (1) Naomi Johnson (b. 1837), (2) Jemimah Hammonds (b. 1835), bur. Caudill Cem., Cranston, Rowan Co., KY.

CAUDILL, ABNER: (1839 – 1863), Co. E, enl. Whitesburg, KY 6/1/1863, res. Letcher Co. 1860, s. of Samuel & Sarah (Maggard) Caudill, widow res. Rowan Co. & remarried 1865, m. Leah Short (1839-1917), memorial headstone Sandlick Cem., Whitesburg, Letcher Co., KY.

CAUDILL, BENJAMIN E.: (1/11/1830 – 2/11/1889), Col., serv. prev. as Capt. 5th KY Inf, Co. F, organized 13th KY Cav. 8/1862, prom. Col. 9/1/1862, capt. Gladeville, VA 7/7/1863, to Kemper Barracks 7/18/1863, to Camp Chase Prison 7/20/1863, to Johnson Island Prison 10/10/1863, to Baltimore 2/9/1864, to Fort Delaware Marine Hosp. 6/15/1864, to Fort McHenry then Hilton Head, SC 6/25/1864, placed on brig ship *Dragoon*, guarded by the gunship *U.S.S. Wabash*, became one of the "Immortal 50", predecessors to the "Immortal 600", exch. 8/3/1864, ret. to command 9/17/1864, res. Letcher Co. 1860, s. of John A. & Rachel (Cornett) Caudill, resident of Alleghany Co. NC postwar, res. Clay Co., KY 1870's, d. Claiborne Co. TN, m. Martha Asberry (7/11/1828-aft. 1880)1848, bur. Slate Hill Cem., Farriston, Laurel Co., KY.

CAUDILL, DAVID: (3/15/1846 – 10/10/1921), Co. B, no s.r., res. Letcher Co. KY 1860, s. of Isom & Elizabeth Back Caudill, rec. KY Confed. Pension #1254 Letcher Co. 1912, m. Peggy Sumner (1846-1928), bur. Caudill Cem., Jeremiah, Letcher Co., KY.

CAUDILL, DAVID D.: (10/22/1848 – 2/21/1927), Co. B, no. s.r. res. Letcher Co., KY 1860, KY Confed Pension application #1634, m. Elizabeth Hampton (1852-aft. 1920)1871, bur. Caudill Cem., Jeremiah, Letcher Co., KY.

CAUDILL, DAVID JESSE "HENRY": (3/9/1839 – 4/9/1907), Lt. Col., Co. B, enl. 27th VA Volunteers, Co. E Rose Hill, VA 5/22/1861, trans. 5th KY Inf. as Pvt. Co. F, enl. 13th KY Cav., prom. to 2nd in command, WIA Battle of Leatherwood Perry Co. 10/19/1862, abs. due to wounds fall/1862, ret. serv. by 4/30/1863, capt 6/13/1863, to Lexington, to Louisville Prison, ret. serv., detached duty beginning 12/15/1864, res. Letcher Co., KY 1860, s. of John A. & Rachel (Cornett) Caudill, committed suicide by hanging at age 67, m. Margaret "Chick" Frizzell (1847-1929) Gladeville, VA 1867, bur. Lindsey Chapel Cem., Grayson, Carter Co., KY.

CAUDILL, EPHRIAM H.: (1841 – 1863), 3rd Sgt., Co. B, enl. Whitesburg, KY 9/12/1862, pres. 4/30/1863, res. Floyd Co., s. of Alfred & Drucilla (Hammonds) Caudill, m. Arty Justice (b. 1837) 1857, bur. Sandlick Cem., Whitesburg, Letcher Co., KY.

CAUDILL, HARVEY: (10/11/1842 – 11/11/1899), 2nd Lt., Cos. B & E, enl. Whitesburg, KY 8/21/1862, 6'1", brown hair, blue eyes, prom. 2nd Lt. Whitesburg 10/7/1862, trans. Co. B to Co. E 6/1/1863, wd. in arm, capt. Gladeville, VA 7/7/1863, ret. serv., capt. Floyd Co. by Capt William Ford Union 39th KY 10/16/1863, to Louisville Prison, released on oath, served two years, wd., left command Whitesburg, ret. from home & serv. until end of war, res. Floyd Co., s. of Abijah & Elizabeth (Slone) Caudill, res. Floyd Co. 1870, res. Pike Co. 1880, widow rec. Confed. Pension, m. Sally Mullins (1843-1918) in Knott Co., bur. Joe Trivette Cem., Myra, Pike Co., KY.

CAUDILL, HENRY C. "HENRY FRANKLIN": (12/9/1828 – 1/7/1882), Co. B, enl. Whitesburg, KY 8/29/1862, disch. 1/1/1863 & ret. home, res. Rowan Co. 1860, s. of Samuel & Sarah (Maggard) Caudill, m. Elizabeth Short (1830-1911), bur. Caudill Cem., Elliottville, Rowan Co., KY.

CAUDILL, HENRY H. "TUSH HENRY": (1821 - 1899), Co. B, enl. Whitesburg, KY 8/29/1862, pres. summer/1863, res. Letcher Co. 1860, s. of Henry & Phoebe (Strailer) Caudill, res. Letcher Co., 1890, claimed serv. until 4/1865, m. Susan Back (1829-aft. 1880) 1846, bur. Nancy Back Cem., Jeremiah, Letcher Co., KY.

CAUDILL, HENRY M.: (1/17/1824 – 4/15/1919), Co. B, enl. Whitesburg, KY 9/3/1862, disch. 9/29/1863, res. Letcher Co. 1860s. of Matthew & Terry (Caudill) Caudill, res. Letcher Co. 1890, m. Mary Elizabeth (1835-aft.1910), bur. Nancy Back Cem., Jeremiah, Letcher Co., KY.

CAUDILL, HENRY R. S.: (2/22/1837 – 3/2/1910), 2nd Lt., Co. H, enl. Whitesburg, KY 10/18/1862, serv. prev. 5th KY Inf., Co. F, capt Gladeville, VA 7/7/1863, to Kemper Barracks 7/18/1863, to Camp Chase Prison 7/20/1863, to Johnson Island Prison 10/10/1863, to Fortress Monroe 9/16/1864, exch. 9/23/1864, res. Perry Co. 1860, s. of Stephen & Elizabeth (Fields) Caudill, m. Mary Branson (1850-aft. 1910), bur. Presbyterian Church Cem., Isom, Letcher Co., KY.

CAUDILL, ISAAC: (3/1846 – 12/13/1920), 2nd Cpl., Cos. B & E, enl. Whitesburg, KY 8/21/1862, also serv. 1st & 2nd Btn. KY Mtd. Rifles, Co. E, trans. from Co. B to Co. E 10/5/1862, prom. 6/1/1863, capt. Breathitt Co. 4/5/1864, to Louisa then to Louisville Prison 4/21/1864, to Camp Morton Prison 4/1864, to Pt. Look for exch. 3/15/1865, res. Letcher Co. 1860, s. of Abijah & Elizabeth "Betsy" (Slone) Caudill, rec. KY Confed Pension #3286 Knott Co. 1912, m. Julia Slone (1844-1930), bur. Alice Slone Cem., Hollybush, Knott Co., KY.

CAUDILL, ISHAM "IKE": (10/10/1847 – 6/4/1916), Co. B, res. Letcher Co., KY 1860, s. of James W. & Elizabeth (Mullins) Caudill, m. Nancy Gilley (1847-1922), bur. Nancy Back Cem., Jeremiah, Letcher Co., KY.

CAUDILL, ISHAM H. "ISOM": (Dec. 1825 – June 13, 1900), Co. B, enl. Whitesburg, KY 8/29/1862, pres. summer/1863, res. Letcher Co. 1860, s. of Henry & Phoebe (Strailer) Caudill, res. Letcher Co. 1890, claimed serv. until 1865, m. Elizabeth Back (b. 1820) 1843, bur. Nancy Back Cem., Jeremiah, Letcher Co., KY.

CAUDILL, JACKSON "JACK": (1844 – 10/10/1922), Co. B, enl. Whitesburg, KY 8/21/1862, 5'8", blue eyes, light hair, fair complexion, abs. sick summer/1863, enl. Union 39th KY, Co. K Louisa 10/19/1863, des. Floyd Co. 12/5/1863, ret. Union serv. 5/2/1864, des. Union serv. Piketon 9/12/1864, arrested 12/23/1864, prisoner Louisa to 6/1865, res. Floyd Co., s. of Alfred & Drucilla (Hammonds) Caudill, court-martialed Lexington 7/15/1865, denied back pay and pension, indicted for 1863 Pike Co. murder while member of 13th KY, d. cancer Floyd Co. (Antioch), m. (1) Louisa Jane (1843-bef. 1870), (2) Mary Ratliff Damron (d. aft. 1920), bur. unmarked Elliott Reynolds Cem. Rt. 979, Floyd Co., KY.

CAUDILL, JAMES AARON: (1841 – 1930), Co. B, enl. Whitesburg, KY 8/29/1862, rec. clothing 9/24/1864, res. Letcher Co. 1850, s. of James & Sarah Elizabeth (Caudill) Caudill, res. AR ca. 1887, res. OK by 1901, rec. OK Confed. Pension #294, widow rec. OK Confed. Pension #7202, m. (1) Eliza Melvina Eldridge (1839-ca. 1880), (2) Sarah Ann Morgan (1861-1944) ca. 1887, bur. Olympus Cem. Grove, Delaware Co., OK.

CAUDILL, JAMES W. "NOAH JIM" or "J.W.": (10/26/1846 – 8/14/1911), Co. A, enl. Whitesburg, KY 11/1/1861, res. Letcher Co. 1860, s. of "Stiller" Bill & Nancy (Dixon) Caudill, res. Letcher Co. 1890, claimed service until 1865, m. Cindy Sumner (1850-1914), bur. Caudill Cem., Blackey, Letcher Co., KY.

CAUDILL, JARVEY: (8/22/1846 – 12/7/1917), Co. D, enl. fall/1863, no. s.r., disbanded Letcher Co. & took oath 3/1865, res. Floyd Co., KY, s. of Abijah & Elizabeth (Slone) Caudill, d. Bonanza nr. Prestonsburg, rec. KY Confed. Pension #2004 Wolfe Co., widow rec. Confed. Pension #3848 1918, m. Louisa Hale/Hall (1847-1925) Magoffin Co. 1867, bur. Bonanza Cem., Bonanza, Floyd Co., KY.

CAUDILL, JESSE H.: (1834 – 1882), 5th Sgt., Cos. A & B, enl. Whitesburg, KY 9/9/1862, serv. prev. 5th KY Inf, Co. F, trans. to Co. B 1/1/1863, appointed 6/24/1863, WIA summer/ 1863, res. Perry Co. 1860, s. of Henry & Phoebe (Strailer) Caudill, res. Wise Co. VA (Richmond) 1880, d. Wise Co., m. Isabell Caudill (1835-1903) in Whitesburg.

CAUDILL, JOHN ASBURY: (3/26/1849 – 5/30/1912), Co. B, no s.r. enl. 1864 age 15, disch. VA, res. Letcher Co. 1860, s. of Col. Ben & Martha (Asbury) Caudill, res. Letcher Co. 1870, res. TX by 1878, m. (1) Alice Reeves (b. 1854) 1868, (2) Catherine Brawner (1847-1924) 1878, bur. Veale's Creek Cem., Ivan, Stephens Co., TX.

CAUDILL, JOHN DIXON: (10/6/1836 – 6/27/1917), 1st Sgt., Co. B, enl. Whitesburg, KY 8/29/1862, rec. clothing 4/7/1864, 6/29/1864 9/7/1864 & 11/19/1864, paroled by Dillard Cumberland Gap 5/3/1865, res. Letcher Co. 1860, s. of John A. & Rachel (Cornett) Caudill, m. Mary A. Green (1838-1920) 1859, bur. Sandlick Cem., Whitesburg, Letcher Co., KY.

CAUDILL, JOHN M.: (3/23/1833 – 4/7/1895), Co. A, serv. prev. 5th KY Inf., Co. F, capt. Gladeville, VA (pension claim) 7/7/1863, to Camp Douglas Prison, res. Letcher Co., s. of Samuel & Sarah (Maggard) Caudill, res. Rowan Co. 1870, widow rec. KY Confed. Pension #3590 Rowan Co. 1912 claiming serv. Co. A,13th KY Cav., m. (1) Jane Boggs (1834-ca. 1865), (2) Fanny Pennington (b. 1840) Elliott Co. 1866, bur. Communtiy Cem., Elliottville, Rowan Co., KY.

CAUDILL, JOHN W.: (2/14/1844 – 7/20/1895), Co. A, serv. prev. 5th KY Inf., Co. F, listed as John M. Caudill on some s.r., capt. Gladeville VA 7/7/1863, to Kemper Barracks 7/18/1863, to Camp Chase Prison 7/20/1863, to Camp Douglas Prison 8/24/1863, exch. Pt. Lookout 2/24/1865, res. Letcher Co. 1860, s. of Wilburn E. & Nancy Caudill, res. Letcher Co. 1890, m. Elizabeth "Betsy" Sumner (1838-1907), bur. Nancy Back Cem., Jeremiah, Letcher Co., KY.

CAUDILL, PRESTON: (1837 – 8/1883), 1st Sgt, Cos. B & E, enl. Whitesburg, KY 8/21/1862, trans. to Co. E 10/5/1862, Union hosp. Lexington, KY 5/21/1865, res. Floyd Co., s. of Abijah & Elizabeth (Slone) Caudill, serv. Floyd Co. as Deputy Sheriff, shot & killed Floyd Co., m. (1) Aray Mullins (1836-ca. 1872) 1854, (2) Martha Osborne (1851-aft. 1880) 1873, bur. Mullins-Caudill Cem., Jacks Creek, Floyd Co., KY.

CAUDILL, SAMUEL B.: (1844 – 1883), Co. B, enl. Whitesburg, KY 10/10/1862, rec. clothing 11/19/1864, res. Letcher Co. 1860, s. of Isom & Elizabeth (Back) Caudill, widow res. Letcher Co. 1890, m. Mary "Polly" Eldridge (1847-aft. 1890), bur. Rich Whitaker Cem., Letcher, Letcher Co., KY.

CAUDILL, SAMUEL C.: (12/29/1831 – 10/29/1907), 2nd Lt., Cos. A & G, serv. prev. 5th KY Inf., Co. F, enl. Co. A & trans. Co. G, prom. 2nd Lt. 2/27/1863, res. Letcher Co. 1860, s. of John A. & Rachel (Cornett) Caudill, m. (1) Mary Anne Greer (1839-bef. 1880) 1854, (2) Letitia Meade (b. 1845), (3) Sarah Hart (1866-aft. 1910) 1885, bur. Hale & Hart Cem., Whitesburg, Letcher Co., KY.

CAUDILL, STEPHEN JACOB: (12/13/1826 – 7/26/1906), Co. B, enl. Whitesburg, KY 8/29/1862, rec. clothing 9/7/1864, paroled Cumberland Gap 5/8/1865, res. Letcher Co. 1860, s. of John A. & Rachel (Cornett) Caudill, m. (1) Elizabeth Adams (6/18/1826-aft. 1880) 1845, (2) Margaret "Peggy" Asbury Caudill, bur. Sandlick Cem., Whitesburg, Letcher Co., KY.

CAUDILL, WILLIAM A.: (1/11/1825 – 1/11/1899), Co. A, enl. Whitesburg, KY 10/3/1862, serv. prev. 5th KY Inf., Co. F, last paid 12/31/1862, disch. by surgeon spring/1863, res. Letcher Co. 1860, s. of John A. & Rachel (Cornett) Caudill, res. Letcher Co. 1870, res. Rowan Co. by 1880, res. Rowan Co. 1895, m. Margaret Asbury (b. 1825) 1844, bur. Old Town Cem., Morehead, Rowan Co., KY.

CAUDILL, WILLIAM B. "COWMOUTH BILL": (4/23/1845 – 6/18/1929), 2nd Cpl., Co. B, enl. Whitesburg, KY 8/29/1862, capt. Gladeville, VA 7/7/1863, to Kemper Barracks 7/18/1863, to Camp Chase Prison 7/20/1863, to Camp Douglas Prison 8/24/1863, exch. Pt. Lookout 2/24/1865, res. Letcher Co. 1860, s. of James W. "Limber Jim" & Elizabeth (Mullins) Caudill, m. Sukie Caudill (1848-1925) 1867, bur. Nancy Back Cem., Jeremiah, Letcher Co., KY.

CAUDILL, WILLIAM J. "STILLER BILL": (7/5/1827 – 11/26/1908), 4th Sgt., Co. B, enl. Whitesburg, KY 8/29/1862, res. Letcher Co. 1860, s. of William C. & Nancy (Craft) Caudill, res. Letcher Co. 1890, claimed serv. through 1865, m. Nancy Dixon (1830-1899) 1847, bur. Caudill Cem., Blackey, Letcher Co., KY.

CAUDILL, WILLIAM W. "WID": (2/13/1839 – 6/22/1920), Co. B, enl. Whitesburg, KY 10/5/1862, disbanded with 13th Newburn, VA 1865, took oath 4/30/1865, res. Letcher Co. 1860, s. of Wilburn E. & Nancy (Caudill) Caudill, res. Letcher Co. 1890, rec. KY Confed. Pension #157 Wolfe Co. 1912, m. (1) Elizabeth Eldridge, (2) Evaline Mullins, bur. Caudill Cem., Campton, Wolfe Co., KY.

CAWOOD, JOHN: (10/29/1844 – 6/6/1865), 2nd Lt., Co. K, enl. Lee Co., VA 8/1863, elected Lt. Lee Co. 12/31/1863, AWOL 12/12/1864, dropped 2/16/1865, reinstated & surr. Cumberland Gap 4/30/1865, successor Elijah Spurlock, res. Owsley Co. 1860, s. of Moses & Emily "Maddy" (Hamlin) Cawood, robbed & murdered 6/6/1865, bur. Cawood Cem, Booneville, Owsley Co., KY.

CHAFFIN, DAVID A.: (1835 – 8/18/1888), 4th Cpl., Co. I, conscripted Whitesburg, KY 10/1/1862, pres. fall/1863, res. Perry Co. when conscripted, res. Lawrence Co. 1870 & 1880, on Lawrence Co. Tax roll 1887, m. Susan J. Rakes (1847-1929), bur. Fallsburg Cem., Fallsburg, Lawrence Co., KY.

CHAFFINS, SAMUEL NELSON "NELSE": (1/2/1833 – 3/18/1914), Co. C, enl. Whitesburg, KY 10/1/1862, serv. prev. 5th KY Inf., Co. E, capt. Floyd Co. 7/26/1863, to Cattlesburg, to Cincinnati 7/3/1863, to Camp Chase Prison 8/24/1863, declared a "bushwhacker" ..."not to be exchanged", exch Pt. Lookout 2/24/1865, paroled Richmond, VA 3/5/1865, took oath Louisa 5/11/1865, res. Floyd Co. 1860, ec. Confed. Pension #133 Floyd Co. (Ballard) 1912, m. Nancy Jane Sutton (1834-1914), bur. Rock Fork Freewill Baptist Church Cem., Rock Fork, Knott Co., KY.

CHAPMAN, DAVID C.: (4/10/1828 – 10/19/1887), Co. A, serv. prev. 5th KY Inf., Co. F, listed on s.r as Chapham, res. Lawrence Co. KY 1860, res. Umatilla Co., OR (Milton) 1880, m. Sarah Jarell (b. 1835) Lawrence Co. 1859, bur. Bowlus Cem., Milton-Freewater, Umatilla Co., OR.

CHENOWETH, THOMAS JOHN: (4/10/1834 – 7/16/1915), Maj., serv. prev. 2nd Lt. 5th KY Inf., Co. B, w. 13th KY in Perry Co. for execution of Gilbert Creech 4/14/1863, capt. Battle of Cynthiana 6/12/1864, to Camp Morton Prison 7/1864, surr. Mt. Sterling 4/30/1865, took oath & released Cincinnati 5/19/1865, res. Hamilton Co., OH 1860, s. of John Smith & Elizabeth (Ross) Chenoweth, graduate of Philadelphia College of Pharmacy, res. Mason Co. 1900 & 1910, drugstore & drug manufacturing facility operator Maysville, KY, chairman of Mason Co. Dem. Party, member of Mason Co. United Confed. Veterans, m. Mary Eliza Pearce (1845-1918) 1868, bur. Maysville-Mason Co. Cem., Maysville, Mason Co., KY.

CHILDERS, ABRAHAM: (1839 – 1864), 4th Sgt., Cos. A & H, enl. Co. A as Pvt., serv. prev. 5th KY Inf., Co. F, trans. Co. H & prom. Sgt. Whitesburg, KY 10/18/1862, disch. 3/1/1863, res. Letcher Co. 1860, s. of Goolsby & Nancy (Johnson) Childers, m. Mary Craft, bur. Childers Cem., Redfox, Knott Co., KY.

CHILDERS, DAVID: (11/30/1837 – 2/26/1910), 4th Cpl., Co. H, enl. Whitesburg, KY 10/18/1862, reinstated 3/2/2863, res. Pike Co. 1860, s. of Goolsby & Nancy (Johnson) Childers, m. Martha Jane Kiser (1842-aft. 1900), bur. Childers Cem., Grayson, Carter Co., KY.

CHILDERS, JAMES M.: (1843 – 1865), 2nd Cpl., Co. H, enl. Whitesburg, KY 9/8/1862, rec. clothing 9/24/1864, res. Letcher Co. 1860, s. of Goolsby & Nancy (Johnson) Childers, bur. Childers Cem. Redfox, Knott Co., KY.

CHRISTIAN, WILLIAM: (8/2/1844 – 1/24/1926), Co. A, enl. Whitesburg, KY 11/2/1862, rec. clothing 4/7/1864, 6/29/1864, 9/1/1864 & 9/15/1864, paroled Cumberland Gap 5/3/1865, res. Letcher Co. 1860, s. of Allen & Abby (Hagins) Christian, bur. Homelake Soldiers & Sailors Cem., Homelake, Rio Grande Co., CO.

CLEMONS, FRANCIS: (1836 – 2/6/1905), Co. C, enl. Whitesburg, KY 10/1/1862, capt. Gladeville, VA 7/7/1863, to Kemper Barracks 7/18/1863, to Camp Chase Prison 7/20/1863, to Camp Douglas Prison 8/24/1863, exch Pt. Lookout 2/24/1865, res. Breathitt Co. 1860, s. of Benjamin & Mary "Polly" Fugate Clemons, to Frankfort, KY State Prison for murder ca. 1896, to Eddyville Prison, on Lyon Co. census 1900, paroled Eddyville "at the point of death" 5/9/1901, ret. Breathitt Co., d. housefire at home, suspected homicide, m. Mary Ann McIntosh (1842-1880) 1857, bur. Laurel Point Cem. Wilstacy, Breathitt Co., KY.

CLEMONS, FRANKLIN: (1818 – 1867), Co. G, enl. Breathitt Co., KY 10/1/1862, res. Breathitt Co. 1860, s. of Benjamin & Polly Hammond Clemons, m. (1) Francis Miller (1819-1854) 1839, (2) Lucinda Mullins (b. 1825) 1855, bur. Laurel Point Cem., Wilstacy, Breathitt Co., KY.

COBURN, GEORGE C.: (10/12/1833 – 11/28/1904), Co. F, enl. Floyd Co. 10/14/1862, pres. 1863, res. Floyd Co. 1860, s. of David & Sarah Morris Coburn, res. Menifee Co. 1869, d. Montgomery Co. (Jeffersonville), m. (1) Louisann (b. 1843), (2) Mary "Polly" Prater (b.1835) 1856, (3) Susan Brown (1845-1918) 1865, bur. Havens Cem., Rothwell, Menifee Co., KY.

COBURN, JAMES POLK: (1846 – 1883), Co. F, enl. Floyd Co. KY 10/14/1862, identified in A. G. report, res. Floyd Co. 1860, s. of John C. & Phoebe (Prater) Coburn, res. Floyd Co. 1870 & 1880, m. Clarinda Nealy (1851-1922), bur. Coburn Cem., Handshoe, Floyd Co., KY.

COBURN, JEREMIAH: (1844 – 1871), Co. F., enl. Floyd Co., KY 10/14/1862, pres. 3/30/1863, res. Floyd Co. 1860, s. of John P. & Agnes Coburn, res. Floyd Co. 1870, bur. Coburn Cem., Handshoe, Floyd Co., KY.

COBURN, JOHN M.: (5/1836 – 9/19/1905), Co. F, (listed incorrectly on some records as John M. Coleman), serv. prev. 5th KY Inf. Co B, joined (Union) 39th KY Inf. In 1862, deserted 7/19/1863 & enl. In 13th KY Cav. 8/20/1863 at Whitesburg (confirmed in Union records), paid 6/1/1864, capt. 8/12/1864 in Floyd Co., to Camp Chase Prison 9/9/1864, admitted to hospital in Richmond, VA 2/20/1865 as paroled prisoner with pneumonia, (some records misfiled in "Artificial Unit"), furloughed 3/21/1865, s. of David & Sarah (Morris) Coleman, res. of Floyd Co. in 1850, res. of Rowan Co. in 1860, m. (1) Mary Ellen Morris (1837-1895) in Morgan Co., (2) Clarinda Osborn (1837-1936) in Carter Co. in 1896, res. of Boyd Co. in 1900, d. 9/19/1905 in Boyd Co., KY.

COBURN, JOSEPH L.: (5/13/1838 – 11/11/1917), 4th Sgt., Co. A, enl. Whitesburg, KY 11/1/1862, prom. 4th Sgt 1/17/1863, capt. Morgan Co. 8/19/1863, to Kemper Barracks 9/2/1863, to Mclean/Cincinnati & released on oath 9/4/1863, res. Floyd Co., s. of David & Sarah (Morris) Coburn, res. Knott Co. 1899 (tax list), res. Knott Co. 1900, applied Confed. Pension Knott Co. 1912, m. Cinthia (1847-1927), bur. Pearl Coburn Cem., Handshoe, Knott Co., KY.

COCKERHAM, DANIEL DUFF: (5/6/1837 – 9/12/1863), Co. K, serv. prev. 5th KY Inf., Co. I, capt. 6/9/1863, to Camp Chase Prison, to Johnson's Island Prison 6/20/1863, d. Johnson's Island Prison, res. Breathitt Co., KY 1860, s. of William & Rhoda Cockerham, m. Orlena Hollon (1838-1919), bur. unmarked Johnson's Island Prison Cem., Marblehead, Ottawa Co., OH.

COLE, SHEPHERD: (2/24/1849 – 10/15/1917), Co. F, res. Magoffin Co., KY 1860, s. of Charles & Charlotte Cole, res. Magoffin Co., 1910, Confed. Pension #1375 Magoffin Co., 1912, claimed serv, in Co. F, m. (1) Mary J. Selvage Magoffin Co. 1869, (2) Deemas McGraw Perkins (1867-1933) Magoffin Co. 1906, bur. unmarked Gose & Risner Cem., Middle Fork, Rt. 3337, Magoffin Co., KY.

COLE, THOMPSON: (1833 – 1869), Co. H, enl. Whitesburg, KY 10/18/1862, pres. 12/12/1862, res. Pike Co. 1860, widow res. Floyd Co. 1870 & 1880, m. America Cole (1841-aft. 1880).

COLEMAN, JOHN M.: Co. F, enl. Whitesburg, KY 8/20/1863, last paid 6/1/1864, capt. Floyd Co. 8/12/1864, to Louisville Prison, to Camp Chase Prison 9/9/1864, to Richmond, VA hospital for pneumonia 2/20/1865, furloughed for 60 days 3/21/1865.

COLLIER, ISOM W.: (1839 – 12/3/1863), 1st. Lt., A.Q.M., Co. A, serv. prev. 5th KY Inf., Co. F, assumed command Co. A from 1/24/1863 to 2/3/1863, predecessor was Capt. Hiram Stamper, signed for horses Ross Ford, TN 3/29/1863, signed for paper shipment for Col. Caudill 3/31/1863, successor was Wilburn Amburgey, capt., d. Johnson's Island Prison 2:30am, res. Letcher Co. 1860, s. of William & Francis (Harrison) Collier, bur. Grave #61, Johnson's Island Prison Cem., Marblehead, Ottawa Co. OH.

COLLIER, JOHN B.: (1831 – 10/22/1863), Co. A, enl. Whitesburg, KY 9/25/1862, serv. prev. 5th KY Inf., Co. F, capt. Gladeville, VA 7/7/1863, to Kemper Barracks 7/18/1863, to Camp Chase Prison 7/20/1863, to Camp Douglas Prison 8/24/1863, d. Camp Douglas, res. Letcher Co. 1860, s. of William & Frances (Harrison) Collier, m. Susannah Blair (1835-aft. 1880), bur. Oak Woods Cem., Chicago, Cook Co., IL.

COLLIER, JOHN HORTON: (1/11/1842 – 6/19/1936), Co. A, identified in A. G. report, also serv. 50th VA Inf., Co. H, res. Letcher Co. 1860, s. Martin D. & Sarah (Horton) Collier, m. Susan V. Slemp (1854-1931) in 1871, bur. Hyatt Cem., Jonesville, Lee Co., VA.

COLLIER, SAMUEL PETER: (10/9/1837 – 9/16/1927), Co. D, enl. Whitesburg, KY 10/4/1862, pres. 10/20/1862, res. Letcher Co. 1860, s. of Rich & Mary (Caudill) Collier, m. Martha Roark (1840-1917) 1860, bur. Collier Cem., Millstone, Letcher Co., KY.

COLLIER, STEPHEN: (10/1834 – 1900 to 1910), Co. H, enl. Whitesburg, KY 10/18/1862, disch. 10/18/1862, res. Letcher Co. 1860, s. of Rich & Mary (Caudill) Collier, res. Letcher Co. 1870, 1880 & 1900, widow Anna res Letcher Co. 1910, m. (1) Patsy Roark 1856, (2) Mary Meade (b. 1847) 1867, (3) Louanna Davis (b. 1833) 1879, bur. unmarked Collier-Meade Cem., Millstone, Letcher Co., KY.

COLLINS, CARTER: (5/24/1837 – 9/23/1903), Co. H, enl. Whitesburg, KY 10/18/1862, pres. 11/6/1862, res. Letcher Co. 1860, s. of Bryant & Mary (Morgan) Collins, res. Letcher Co. 1870, 1872 & 1873, m. Mary Robinson (1836-1934) 1855, bur. Collins Cem. Blaze, Morgan Co., KY.

COLLINS, HIRAM: (1837 – 1869), Co. C, enl. Whitesburg, KY 10/1/1862, res. Breathitt Co. 1860, s. of Shepherd & Polly Collins, m. Barbara Auxier (1838-aft. 1870)) Johnson Co. 1856, bur. Wadkins-Mullins Cem., Evanston, Breathitt Co., KY.

COLLINS, ISAAC: (1843 – 1906), 3rd. Cpl., Co. F, enl. Floyd Co. 10/14/1862, serv. in execution of Union soldier Gilbert Creech Brashearville, Perry Co., avoided capt. Gladeville 7/7/1863, res. Floyd Co. 1860, s. of Elbe Collins, m. Nancy (b. 1831), bur. Collins Cem., Wayland, Floyd Co., KY.

COLLINS, MARSHALL: (1848 – 10/20/1863), Co. F, enl. Floyd Co. 10/14/1862, capt. Gladeville, VA 7/7/1863, to Kemper Barracks 7/18/1863, to Camp Chase Prison 7/20/1863, to Camp Douglas Prison 8/24/1863, d. Camp Douglas w/ lung inflammation, res. Floyd Co. 1860, s. of Elbe Collins, m. Martha (1853-1891), bur. Grave #752, Oak Woods Cem., Chicago, Cook Co., IL.

COLLINS, WILLIAM: (1845 – 1929), Co. F, enl. Floyd Co. KY 10/14/1862, capt. Gladeville, VA 7/7/1863, to Kemper Barracks 7/18/1863, to Camp Chase Prison 7/20/1863, to Camp Douglas Prison 8/24/1863, exch. Pt. Lookout 2/24/1865, res. Floyd Co. 1860, s. of Elbe Collins, bur. Collins Cem., Wayland, Floyd Co., KY.

COLLINSWORTH, EDWARD "EDMOND": (4/15/1832 – 5/10/1917), Co. G, enl. 9/28/1862 in Breathitt Co., res. Breathitt Co. 1860, s. of William & Rachel (Suthards) Collinsworth, m. (1) _____ Harvey, (2) Franky Southwood in 1852, (3) Martha _____, applied for Confed. pension in 1916, bur. Ed Collinsworth Cem., Ned, Breathitt Co., KY.

COLLINSWORTH, JOHN WESLEY: (5/10/1841 – 6/10/1919), Co. G, enl. Breathitt Co. 10/31/1862, enl. Union 40th KY Vol. Mtd. Inf., Co. K Grayson 7/1863, res. Breathitt Co. 1860, s. of William & Lena (Mullins) Collinsworth, aka Collins on some census records, m. Mary "Polly" "Mollie" "Mall" Miller (1842-aft.1920)1864, bur. John Collinsworth Cem., Stacy, Perry Co., KY.

COLLINSWORTH, THOMAS: (6/17/1832 – 10/17/1892), Co. G, enl. Breathitt Co., KY 9/30/1862, res. Perry Co. 1860, s. of William & Rachel (Suthards) Collinsworth, m. Evaline Shortridge (1828-1926), bur. Collinsworth Cem., McCombs, Pike Co., KY.

COLLINSWORTH, WILLIAM: (1837 – 1916), Co. G, enl. Breathitt Co., KY 10/8/1862, serv. prev. 5th KY Inf., Co. F, rec. clothing 6/29/1864, res. Breathitt Co. 1860, s. of William & Rachel (Suthards) Collinsworth, res. Rowan Co. 1870, res. Carter Co. 1900, m. (1) Minerva Combs (1838-bef. 1870) 1856, (2) Hannah (1840-1903 Carter Co.), bur. Underwood Cem., Lawton, Carter Co., KY.

COMBS, ALFRED: (11/22/1844 – 3/18/1933), Co. G, enl. Perry Co., KY 9/23/1862, res. Breathitt Co. 1860, s. of Henry & Tempe (Davis) Combs, res. Menifee Co. 1880, res. of Lexington 1895, started Combs Lumber Co., purchased Swiss Oil Co (now Ashland Oil Co.), Mayor of Lexington 1902, serv. as State Senator, member Good Samaritan Hospital board for 30 years, m. (1) Ester Horton (1850-1895), (2) Alice McClellan (1866-1962), bur. Lexington Cem., Lexington, Fayette Co., KY.

COMBS, AUSTIN G.: (5/13/1850 – 5/27/1942), Co. I, enl. Whitesburg, KY 8/29/1863, pres. fall/1863, youngest man in 13th KY Cav. at 13, on detached service Floyd Co. at close of war, res. Perry Co., s. of Robert & Eliza (Godsey) Combs, res. Perry Co. 1870 & 1880, applied for pension Perry Co. 4/26/1912, moved to Akron, CO for health 1914, shot himself at home 1942, last known 13th man to die, m. Belle Godsey (1849-1941), bur. Akron Cem., Akron, Washington Co., CO.

COMBS, CALVIN: (b. 7/1828), Co. K, serv. prev. 5th KY Inf, 3rd Co. E, (enl. Sullivan Co., TN 2/28/1863, des. GA 9/19/1863), pres. Co. K Lee Co., VA 12/31/1863, surr. Cumberland Gap 4/30/1865, res. Sullivan Co., TN 1860, res. Johnson Co. 1868, 1870, 1880, 1900 & 1910, m. Rosanna (1831-bef. 1900 Johnson Co, KY).

COMBS, DAVID: (8/8/1838 – 3/12/1922), Cos. G & I, enl. Breathitt Co. KY 10/1/1862, 6'2", dark hair, blue eyes, trans. from Co. G to Co. I 4/30/1863, capt. Breathitt Co. (Jackson) 3/8/1864, Union officials claimed he "participated in the ambush and murder of the 6th Kentucky", to Louisville Prison 3/1864, to Camp Chase Prison 3/24/1864, rel. Camp Chase on oath 5/14/1865, res. Perry Co. 1860, s. of Nicholas & Peggy (Smith) Combs, rec. KY Confed. Pension #2940 Perry Co. 1914, d. of influenza, m. Polly Davidson (1838-1921), bur. Combs-Whitaker Cem., Grapevine, Perry Co., KY.

COMBS, DELANEY "DOC": (3/1848 – 1900), Kash's Co., res. Breathitt Co., KY 1860, s. of Alfred & Margaret "Peggy" (Noble) Combs, indicted for murder in 1865 as a member of Kash's Co., res. Breathitt Co. 1880 & 1900, m. Matilda Duff (b. 1851), bur. T-Point Cem., Clayhole, Breathitt Co., KY.

COMBS, ELHANNON L.: (1832 – 11/21/1918), 1st Sgt., Co. I, enl. Gladeville, VA 6/26/1863, res. Perry Co. 1860, s. of Nicholas "Birdeye" & Betts Combs, res. First Creek/Bonnyman 1870, d. on First Ck., m. (1) Harriet Hurt (1844-1880 to 1887), (2) Elizabeth Guinn (1856-aft. 1910) 1887, bur. Combs Cem., Combs, Perry Co., KY.

COMBS, ELIJAH: (10/1/1844 – 4/22/1930), 1st Sgt., Cos. B & I, enl. Co. B, Whitesburg, KY 9/6/1862, trans. to Co. I Whitesburg 1/1/1863, res. Perry Co. 1860, s. of Biram Jr. & Hannah (Owens) Combs, res. Knott Co 1889 (Ball Fork), res. Knott Co. 1900, 1910, & 1920, m. Salina Moore (1853-1925), bur Combs Cem., Softshell, Knott Co., KY.

COMBS, ELIJAH: (11/6/1836 – 5/9/1888), Co. C, enl. Whitesburg, KY 10/1/1862, capt. Gladeville, VA 7/7/1863, res. Perry Co. 1860s. of Jerry & Sarah (Whitley) Combs, m. (1) Nancy Begley (1838-1863 to 1867) 1856, (2) Katherine "Katie" Noble (1841-aft. 1880), bur. Nathan Noble Cem., Watts, Breathitt Co., KY.

COMBS, ENOCH: (3/30/1839 – 2/21/1919), Co. I, conscripted Whitesburg, KY 10/18/1862, pres. 11/1/1862, also serv. Union 14th KY, Co. L aft. 12/1862, then Union Three Forks Btn., res. Letcher Co. 1860, s. of Mason & Matilda Combs, res. Hazard Precinct 1870, res. Knott Co. 1910 (Red Oak), m. Nancy Stacy (1844-1919), bur. Enoch Combs Cem., Garrard, Clay Co., KY.

COMBS, EPHRIAM MASON: (1832 – 1868), Co. G, enl. Perry Co. KY 9/23/1862, pres. 12/8/1862, serv. prev. 5th KY Inf, Co. I, res. Breathitt Co., s. of Stephen & Patsy (Clemons) Combs, m. (1) Eliza "Lizzy" Combs 1854, (2) Millie Large (b. 1844 Russell Co., VA) 1866 Wise Co., VA, bur. Adkins Cem., Caney Ridge, Wise Co., VA.

COMBS, FELIX: (2/13/1826 – 4/9/1912), Co. C, enl. Whitesburg, KY 10/1/1862, capt. Gladeville, VA 7/7/1863, to Kemper Barracks 7/18/1863, to Camp Chase Prison 7/20/1863, to Camp Douglas Prison 8/24/1863, exch. Pt. Lookout 2/24/1865, res. Perry Co. 1860, s. of Moses & Lydia (Hacker) Combs, m. (1) Susannah "Susan" Combs (b. 1829), (2) Chloe "Cloey" Branson Hall Begley (1815-1900) 1858, bur. Ritchie Cem., Fisty, Knott Co., KY.

COMBS, FIELDING: (8/19/1844 – 12/23/1915), Co. C, enl. mo. Montgomery Ck. on Troublesome 10/1/1862, capt. Gladeville, VA 7/7/1863, to Kemper Barracks 7/18/1863, to Camp Chase 7/20/1863, rel. Camp Douglas spring/1865, home on furlough at close of war, forced to take oath at Louisa, KY, res. Perry Co., s. of Biram & Hannah (Owens) Combs, res. Perry Co. (Troublesome) 1870, rec. KY Confed. Pension #2601 Yellow Mt., Mousie, KY 1912, d.c. #30765, m. Cynthia Ann Engle (1845-1901) 1860, bur. Conley Cem., Rock Fork, Knott Co., KY.

COMBS, FRANCIS: (4/28/1832 – 2/6/1918), Co. C, enl. Whitesburg, KY 10/1/1862, pres. fall/1863, res. Perry Co. 1860, s. of George & Nancy (Smith) Combs, res. Perry Co. (Lost Ck.) 1870, m. (1) Raney Holliday (d. 1854), (2) Rhoda Ritchie (1833-1931) 1860, bur. Holliday Cem., Ary, Perry Co., KY.

COMBS, GEORGE A.: (3/3/1842 – 8/10/1926), Co. H, enl. Whitesburg, KY 10/18/1862, res. Letcher Co. 1860, s. of Shadrack & Sarah Adams Combs, m. Millie Maggard (1843-1914) 1864, bur. Presbyterian Church Cem., off Rt. 15, Isom, Letcher Co., KY.

COMBS, GEORGE WASHINGTON: (1/6/1843 – 2/7/1920), Co. G, enl. Breathitt Co., KY 9/28/1862, wd. Battle of Lotts Creek, Perry Co., 1864, disch. due to wounds by Dr. Cox, Whitesburg 8/1864, res. Breathitt Co. 1860, s. of John & Mahalia (Henson) Combs, rec. KY Confed. Pension #574 Ned, KY 1912, m. (1) Unknown, (2) Littie Noble (1840-1919: d.c.11960), bur. Watts & Francis Cem., Lost Creek, Perry Co., KY.

COMBS, GRANVILLE: (12/2/1843 – 3/5/1940), Cos. A & B, enl. Whitesburg, KY 8/21/1862, trans from Co. B to Co. A 1/1/1863, pres. spring/1863, res. Letcher Co. 1860, s. of Mason & Matilda Combs, res. Letcher Co. 1870 & 1880, moved Taney Co., MO 1890, m. Margaret Amburgey (1848-1917) 1864, bur. Patterson Cem., Taneyville, Taney Co., MO.

COMBS, HANBILL: (1831 – 1/19/1924), Co. I, conscripted Whitesburg, KY 10/18/1862, pres. 11/1/1862, serv. Union 14th KY, Co. M until 3/1864, res. Perry Co. 1860, m. (1) Susannah Williams (1847-ca. 1887) ca. 1869, (2) Alice Combs Stacy (1876-1955), bur. W. C. Brashear Cem., Fusonia, Perry Co., KY.

COMBS, HENDERSON M.: (5/1837 – 1/1863), Capt., Co. G, enl. 10/14/1862, ambushed & killed by Union 14th KY Cav., while seated at his breakfast table at home on recruiting furlough, successor was William S. Landrum, res. Breathitt Co. 1860, s. of Alfred & Margaret "Peggy" (Noble) Combs, m. Winnie Allen (b. 1847), bur. McIntosh Cem., Clayhole, Breathitt Co., KY.

COMBS, HENRY DUFF: (4/17/1843 – 10/21/1921), 1st Sgt., Co. I, enl. Hazard, KY 3/22/1863, suceeded Joseph H. Brewer as 1st Sgt., capt. Booneville 8/19/1863, to Louisville Prison 8/24/1863, to Camp Chase 9/1/1863, to Rock Island Prison 2/24/1864, rel. to join Union (2nd U.S. Inf.) 10/6/1864, serv. Union Army in Indian Wars until 11/7/1865, res. Perry Co. 1860, s. of Robert C. & Eliza (Godsey) Combs, practiced law post-war for 25 years, Menifee Co. Clerk for 17 years, pension #1066 witness for Sgt. John S. Sparkman, Menifee Co. 1912, m. Judy Martin (1842-1923) 1867, bur. Combs-Jewell-Day Cem., Frenchburg, Menifee Co., KY.

COMBS, HENRY G.: (1836 – 1862), Co. C, enl. Whitesburg, KY 10/1/1862, res. Perry Co. 1860, s. of Pvt. James & Betty Combs, bur. Sandlick Cem., Whitesburg, Letcher Co., KY.

COMBS, HEZEKIAH: (1826 – 1887), Co. C, res. Perry Co. 1860, s. of Nicholas & Mary Combs Combs, indicted as a regiment member who participated in a raid on Snatch Ck. at Busy in Perry Co. 1/2/1865, res. Perry Co. (Troublesome) 1870, res. Perry Co. (Ball Ck.) 1880, res Perry Co. 1886, widow res. Knott Co. 1889 & 1900, m. Melda Combs (1828-aft. 1900 Knott Co.), prob. bur. Combs Cem., Carrie, Knott Co., KY.

COMBS, HIRAM: (4/4/1842 – 7/9/1923), Cos. C & I, serv. prev. 5th KY Inf., Co. I, enl. 10/1/1862 Whitesburg, witnessed shooting of Wesley Francis early 1864, scouted for Capt. William Smith, served until 4/1865, res. Perry Co. 1860, illegitimate s. of Mason & Nancy (Campbell) Combs, aka Hiram Campbell Perry Co. 1850 & 1860, res. Perry Co. 1870, m. Ceathie (1843-1921), rec. KY Confed. pension #2941 in Knott Co. in 1912 & stated he sered in Co. I, 5th KY Inf. & Co. Cos. C & I, 13th KY Cav., bur. Free Church Cem., Ritchie, Knott Co., KY.

COMBS, HUGH "HUGHEY": (1849 – 1866), Co. G, enl. Whitesburg, KY 8/31/1863, res. Breathitt Co. 1860, s. of Stephen & Patsy (Clemons) Combs, indicted for murders in Perry Co. 1866, bur. McIntosh Cem., Clayhole, Breathitt Co., KY.

COMBS, IRA "UNCLE IRA": (5/29/1844 – 4/8/1934), Co. I, conscripted Whitesburg, KY 10/18/1862, serv. later Union Three Forks Btn., Co. D, res. Perry Co. 1860, s. of Tal & Betty (Ison) Combs, m. (1) Martha Burton (1849-1892) 1865, (2) Matilda Francis (1868-1957), bur. Combs Cem., Jeff, Perry Co., KY.

COMBS, ISAAC: (1841 – 2/26/1865), Co. C, enl. Whitesburg, KY 10/1/1862, capt. Gladeville, VA 7/7/1863, to Kemper Barracks &/18/1863, to Camp Chase Prison 7/20/1863, to Camp Douglas Prison 8/24, 1863, d. Camp Douglas typhoid fever, res. Perry Co. 1860, s. of George & Nancy (Smith) Combs, bur. Oak Wood Cem., Chicago, Cook Co., IL.

COMBS, ISAAC B.: (9/3/1849 – 12/7/1924), Co. C, claimed he enl. in this co. with John Neace in 1863 & serv. until the close of war in Apr., 1865, in KY Confed. pension #4260 for John Neace, s. of Alfred A. Combs & Margaret (Noble) Combs, res. Breathitt Co.1860, m. Mary "Molly" Allen (1853-1891), bur. T-Point Cem., Clayhole, Breathitt Co., KY.

COMBS, JACKSON: (1/1837 – 1903), Capt., Co. G, identified as Capt. this Co. by George W. Noble in *Behold, He Cometh in the Clouds*, took command of Co. G after capt. of Capt. Alexander Noble 1864, res. Perry Co. 1860, s. of Stephen & Patsy (Clemons) Combs, res. Laurel Fork of Little Buckhorn during war, m. (1) Ava Roberts (b. 1840) 1859, (2) Catherine Walters, (3) Martha Ann Cotton (b. 1835), bur. Combs Cem. Dennis, Lawrence Co., KY.

COMBS, JACKSON: (10/6/1835 – 1908), Co. I, conscripted 10/18/1862, disch. 10/24/1862, res. Perry Co., KY 1860, s. of Mason & Matilda (Watts) Combs, res. Letcher Co. 1880, res. Knott Co. 1892, widow res. Knott Co. 1910, m. (1) Mary Ann Young (1843-1890) 1859, (2) Lucinda Combs (1877-aft. 1920, m. Green Cornett) bur. Adams Cem., Amburgey, Knott Co., KY.

COMBS, JAMES: (1840 – 1864), Co. G, enl. Whitesburg, KY 9/26/1862, des. Perry Co. 12/8/1863, res. Breathitt Co. 1860, s. of Stephen & Patsy (Clemons) Combs, bur. McIntosh Cem., Clayhole, Breathitt Co., KY.

COMBS, JAMES: (1843 – 3/10/1863), Co. I, conscripted 10/18/1862, killed Perry Co., KY 3/10/1863, res. Perry Co. 1860, s. of Samuel & Eliza Combs, bur. Combs Cem., Combs, Perry Co., KY.

COMBS, JAMES "JR": (1835 – 1874), Co. C, enl. Whitesburg, KY 10/1/1862, res. Perry Co., s. of George & Nancy (Smith) Combs, bur. Richard Smith Cem., Ary, Perry Co., KY.

COMBS, JAMES "SR": (1810 – 1875), Co. C, enl. Whitesburg, KY 10/1/1862, res. Perry Co. 1860, s. of Harrison & Rachel (Clemons) Combs, res. Perry Co. 1870, m. Elizabeth "Betty" (1810-bef. 1880) Perry Co. 1824, bur. Clear Cr. Church Cem., Lotts Creek, Perry Co., KY.

COMBS, JAMES MAT: (1845 – 1864), 2nd Cpl., Co. I, enl. Whitesburg, KY 10/18/1862, serv. prev. 5th KY Inf., Co. I, prom. Whitesburg 11/18/1862, family history: shot from his horse at mo. of Lotts Ck. by Union's Elijah "Bunt" Fuller of Three Forks Btn. 1864, res. Perry Co. 1860, s. of Robert C. & Eliza (Godsey) Combs, bur. Combs Cem., Hazard, Perry Co., KY.

COMBS, JAMES M.: (1809 – 1890 to 1900), Co. K, enl. Lee Co., VA 8/18/1863, pres. Lee Co., VA 12/31/1863, res. Lee Co., VA 1850-1880, m. Nancy Yeary (1816-1880 to 1900).

COMBS, JAMES PETER: (1846 – 1896), Co. G, enl. Whitesburg, KY 10/1/1862, capt. Gladeville, VA 7/7/1863, to Kemper Barracks 7/18/1863, to Camp Chase Prison 7/20/1863, to Camp Douglas Prison 8/24/1863, exch. Pt. Lookout 2/24/1865, res. Breathitt Co., s. of Byron & Mariah (Messer) Combs, reportedly raised by a Noble family, res. Wolfe Co. 1870 & 1880, widow granted Confed. pension #3644 1914, m. Armina Eversole (1844-1937) Wolfe Co., bur. Combs Cem., Wiliba, Lee Co., KY.

COMBS, JEREMIAH: (1830 – 12/16/1917), Co. C, enl. Whitesburg, KY 10/1/1862, capt. Gladeville, VA 7/7/1863, res. Perry Co. 1860, s. of Andrew & Milly Combs (Johnson) Combs, res. Perry Co. 1870, 1880, & 1900, d. at Hazard, m. Mary "Polly" Williams (1845-1890), bur. Hazard Cem., Hazard, Perry Co., KY.

COMBS, JEREMIAH "JERRY": (3/18/1840 – 2/20/1918), 3rd Sgt., Co. G, enl. Breathitt Co., KY 9/23/1862, capt. Gladeville, VA 7/7/1863, to Kemper Barracks 7/18/1863, to Camp Chase Prison 7/20/1863, to Camp Douglas Prison 8/24/1863, exch. Pt. Lookout 2/24/1865, took oath Mt. Sterling, res. Breathitt Co. 1860, s. of Alfred & Margaret "Peggy" (Noble) Combs, serv. as postmaster Ned, KY, rec. KY Confed. Pension #3108, d. on Cockrells Fork, m. Sarah Ann "Sally" Noble (1840-aft. 1930) 1861, bur. Combs-Neace Cem., Ned, Breathitt Co., KY.

COMBS, JEREMIAH C.: (4/14/1835 – 7/28/1936), Co. I, conscripted 10/18/1862, pres. 11/1/1862, joined Union 14th KY Cav, Co. M, res. Perry Co. KY 1860, s. of Jeremiah & Nancy (Sumner) Combs, has Union marker w/o dates, m. Julia Ann Combs (1841-1933), bur. Jerry Combs Cem., Emmalena, Knott Co., KY.

COMBS, JESSE: (1842 – 10/8/1864), Co. G, enl. Breathitt Co., KY 10/1/1862, capt. Gladeville, VA 7/7/1863, to Kemper Barracks 7/18/1863, to Camp Chase Prison 7/20/1863, to Camp Douglas Prison 8/24/1863, d. of fever at Camp Douglas, res. Breathitt Co., bur. Oak Wood Cem., Chicago, Cook Co., IL.

COMBS, JESSE: (1828 – 8/21/1864), 5th Sgt., Co. I, enl. Whitesburg, KY 10/18/1862, capt. Perry Co. 10/1/1863, to Louisville Prison, to Camp Morton Prison 10/28/1863, d. of pneumonia Camp Morton, res. Perry Co., s. of Rachel Combs, bur. Crown Hill Cem., Indianapolis, Marion Co., IN.

COMBS, JESSE S. SR.: (1824 – 1883), Co. B, enl. Whitesburg, KY 9/6/1862, res. Perry Co. 1860, res. Perry Co. 1870 & 1880, on 1882 Perry Co. tax list, widow on 1883 Perry Co. tax list, m. Nancy (b. 1830), bur. Cornett Cem., Christopher, Perry Co., KY.

COMBS, KENDRICK: (1822 – 1912), Co. C, enl. Whitesburg, KY 10/1/1862, res. Perry Co. 1860, s. of Benton Combs, res. Perry Co. 1880, 1900 & 1910 (Troublesome), m. Elizabeth "Betty" Jones (1834-bef. 1900), bur. Jonathan Jones Cem., Rowdy, Perry Co., KY.

COMBS, KENDRICK: (1834 – 1864), Co. I, conscripted Whitesburg, KY 10/18/1862, capt. Perry Co. 5/16/1863, to Camp Chase Prison 5/31/1863, to Johnson's Island Prison 6/14/1863, to Pt. Lookout Prison 11/30/1863, rel. Pt. Lookout on oath 1/10/1864, d. Jackson, KY while walking home from Pt. Lookout, res. Perry Co. 1860, s. of Nicholas "Birdeye" & Betts Combs, lived & owned land in Perry Co. (First Creek), m. Milly Combs (1839-1910 to 1920, she later married Pvt. Russell Cornett 1870's) 1854, bur. Cardwell Cem. Jackson, Breathitt Co., KY.

COMBS, LORENZO DOW: (1843 – 1900), Co. I, conscripted 10/18/1862, disch. 10/24/1862, res. Perry Co. 1860, s. of Nicholas "Birdeye" & Betts Combs, Perry County Jailor 1880, m. (1) Jency Fields (1836-1870), (2) Polly Combs (1843-1895), bur. Meadowbrook Cem., Airport Gardens, Perry Co., KY.

COMBS, MADISON (JAMES): (1847 – 1902), Co. G, enl. Perry Co., KY 3/15/1863, res. Perry Co. 1860, s. of Jeremiah L. & Sally (Kelly) Combs, res. Perry Co. 1870, res. Knott Co. w/ wife Mary Ann, m. (1) Susan Combs, (2) Mary Ann Smith (1852-1928) 1874, poss. bur. Carrs Fork Cem., Littcarr, Knott Co., KY.

COMBS, MARTIN: listed in Adjt. Gen. Report, no s.r., poss. serv. as Massengill Martin Combs, 1810-1892, m. Betty Combs, bur. Jim Combs Cem., Jeff, Perry Co., KY.

COMBS, MATTHEW: (1832 – 1869), Co. C., enl. Whitesburg, KY 10/1/1862, serv. prev. 5th KY Inf. Cos. B & K, also serv. Fields Partisan Rangers, res. Perry Co. 1860, s. of George & Nancy (Smith) Combs, m. Hannah Adeline Wise (1839-1880 to 1900 Magoffin Co.) Washington Co., AR 1855, bur. Richard Smith Cem., Ary, Perry Co., KY.

COMBS, MILTON J.: (1842 – 1909), 4th Cpl., Co. I, conscripted Whitesburg, KY 10/18/1862, capt. 5/13/1863, ret. serv., pres. fall/1863, res. Perry Co. 1860, s. of Biram L. & Mariah (Messer) Combs, res. Perry Co. 1900 (Campbell), m. Polly Ann Sizemore (1846-1928) 1864, bur. Red Hill Cem., Chavies, Perry Co., KY.

COMBS, NICHOLAS: (10/12/1839 – 8/28/1914), Co. C, enl. Whitesburg, KY 10/1/1862, capt. Gladeville, VA 7/7/1863, to Johnson's Island Prison (re: Pvt. G. W. Noble), res. Perry Co., s. of Jerry & Sarah (Whitley) Combs, res. Wolfe Co. 1890 (Stillwater/Hazel Green), pension witness Lee Co. (Fincastle) 1912, d. heart disease Lee Co. (Fincastle), m. Elizabeth J. Williams (1843-1928), bur. Olinger Cem., Zoe, Lee Co., KY.

COMBS, NICHOLAS: (1843 – 1870), Co. I, enl. Gladeville, VA 7/15/1863, pres. fall/1863, res. Perry Co., 1860, s. of Nicholas "Birdeye" & Betts Combs, res. Hazard 1870, m. Sallie Cornett (b. 1847) 1860, bur. Cornett Cem. Christopher, Perry Co., KY.

COMBS, RUSSELL HACKER "HACK": (3/2/1829 – 6/29/1907), Co. C, identified in Confederate Pension #2948 by John Dobson as being present in this company in 1864, res. Letcher Co. 1860, s. of Shadrack Combs Sr. & Martha Davis Combs, bro. to Pvt. Shadrach Combs, res. Letcher Co. 1870, 1880 & 1900, m. Dicy Polly (b. 1834}, bur. Combs Cem., Ermine, Letcher Co., KY.

COMBS, SAMUEL M.: (1/25/1828 – 3/16/1908), Co. G, no s.r., surr. Mt. Sterling 4/30/1865, res. Perry Co. 1860, s. of Moses & Lydia (Hacker) Combs, res. Perry Co. 1900, m. Sarah Allen (1834-1918), bur. Richie Cem., Fisty, Knott Co., KY.

COMBS, SHADRACH: (6/10/1812 – 8/1/1891), Co. H, enl. at Whitesburg 10/18/1862, l.r. 12/7/1862, s. of Shadrach Combs Sr. & Martha Davis Combs, m. Sarah Adams (b. 1822), father of Pvt. George A. Combs & bro. to Pvt. Russell H. Combs (Co. C), bur. in Combs Cem. Kodak, Perry Co. KY.

COMBS, SHADRACK H. "REBEL SHADE": (7/28/1838 – 1/25/1891), 1st Lt., Co. G, enl. Breathitt Co. 10/14/1862, blue eyes, prom. 2nd Lt. 3/18/1863, prom. 1st Lt. 12/31/1863, des. 10/1864, succeeded by Samuel **Caudill**, paroled Mt. Sterling 5/1/1865, d. Clayhole, KY, res. Breathitt Co. 1860, s. of Alfred & Margaret "Peggy" (Noble) Combs, m. (1) Nancy Ann Davidson (b. 1842) 1861, (2) Sarah Jane Strong (1849-1876) 1874, (3) Lucinda Day (1860-1914) 1876, bur. Strong Cem., Lost Creek, Breathitt Co., KY.

COMBS, SIMEON: (10/13/1843 – 6/11/1932), Co. C, aka Sampson or Simpson Combs, disbanded VA 4/1865, took oath at Louisa, res. Perry Co. 1860, s. of Andrew & Polly (Feltner) Combs, rec. KY Confed. Pension #573, d. Cordia, KY (d.c. #14375), m. Abigail Gayheart (1842-1910) 1869, bur. Clear Fork Reg. Baptist Church Cem., Lotts Creek, Perry Co., KY.

COMBS, STEPHEN SEWELL: (12/18/1841 – 12/19/1916), Kash's Co., res. Breathitt Co. 1860, s. of Henry & Tempe (Davis) Combs, res. Wolfe Co. 1870, 1880 & 1900, res. Madison Co. (Kirksville) 1910, m. (1) Mary J. Rose (1852-aft. 1910 Madison Co., AR), (2) Elizabeth Ann Swango (b. 1858), (3) Nancy Catherine Amyx (1850-1943), bur. Richmond City Cem., Richmond, Madison Co., KY.

COMBS, WASHINGTON: Co. G, see George Washington Combs

COMBS, WASHINGTON: (1842 – 12/19/1927), Co. I, conscripted Whitesburg, KY 10/18/1862, pres. 11/1/1862, later joined Union 14th KY, Co. M, Union marker, res. Perry Co. 1860, s. of Massengil Martin & Elizabeth Combs, m. Marinda Ingram (1850-aft. 1930), bur. Blackhawk Cem., Happy, Perry Co., KY.

COMBS, WAYNE: (3/15/1833 – 8/23/1927), Co. C, serv. prev. 5th KY Inf., Co. I, joined 13th on Morgan's Last Raid, pres. Battles of Mt. Sterling & Cynthiana, res. Perry Co. 1860, s. of Andrew & Polly (Feltner) Combs, applied for KY Confed. Pension Knott Co. 1912, m. Julie Ann Dobson (1843-1927), bur. Bradley Cem., Decoy, Breathitt Co., KY.

COMBS, WESLEY: (1844 – 1865), 1st Sgt., Co. C, enl. Whitesburg, KY 10/1/1862, capt. Gladeville, VA 7/7/1863, to Kemper Barracks 7/18/1863, to Camp Chase Prison 7/20/1863, to Camp Douglas 8/24/1863, exch. Pt. Lookout 2/24/1865, res. Perry Co. 1860, s. of Hezikiah & Melda (Combs) Combs, m. Mary "Polly" Hogg, bur. Combs Cem., Emmalena, Knott Co., KY.

COMBS, WILEY D.: (1823 – 1866), Co. I, conscripted Whitesburg, KY 10/18/1862, disch. Whitesburg 10/23/1862, res. Perry Co. 1860, s. of Henry & Nancy (Brown) Combs, m. (1) Polly Fields (1825- ca. 1858), (2) Lucinda Baker (b. 1841) 1862, remains moved from former Henry Combs Cem., Big Creek, 1960's, bur. Sukey Gap Cem. #1, Busy, Perry Co., KY.

COMBS, WILEY H.: (4/8/1826 – 1/12/1907), Co. K, rec. clothing 9/24/1864, res. Breathitt Co., KY 1860, s. of Samuel & Nancy (Cornett) Combs, m. Eliza Jane Combs (1836-aft. 1910) 1850, bur. Marcum Heights Cem., Jackson, Breathitt Co., KY.

COMBS, WILLIAM BENTON: (1832 – 1927), Co. G, enl. Breathitt Co., KY 10/1/1862, res. Breathitt Co. 1860, s. of Stephen & Patsy (Clemons) Combs, res. Breathitt Co. (Lewis Fk.) 1900, res. Breathitt Co. (Lunah) 1921, m. Susannah Campbell (1837-aft. 1920) 1852, bur. Ritchie & Combs Cem., Ary, Perry Co., KY.

COMBS, WILSON TURK: (2/15/1846 – 8/15/1937), 4th Cpl., Co. G, prom. Whitesburg, KY 10/1/1862, wd. three times, skirmished against Union Capt. Strong's men Breathitt Co. 12/26/1863, capt. w/ 15 men of 13th S. Fork Quicksand 2/22/1864, to Louisa, to Louisville Prison, to Camp Chase Prison, escape attempt failed, isolated & starved, paroled Camp Chase (re: pension statement), res. Breathitt Co. 1860, s. of Stephen & Patsy (Clemons) Combs, indicted for murder as Co. G member, killed Pvt. William Miller & m. his widow, res. Breathitt Co. 1874 (re: land transaction), res. Wolfe Co. (Campton) ca. 1880, res. Powell Co. 1890, res. Forest Co., WI 1897, 1900 & 1910, res. KY 1915, rec. KY Confed. Pension #3838 Morgan Co. (Yokum) 1917, m. Dulcenia Allen Miller (1844-1937), bur. Neal Cem., Cattlesburg, Boyd Co., KY.

CONLEY, JOHN ASHFORD "COON": (5/7/1845 – 12/8/1896), Co. F, enl. Floyd Co., KY 10/14/1862, capt. Gladeville, VA 7/7/1863, to Kemper Barracks 7/18/1863, to Camp Chase Prison 7/20/1863, to Camp Douglas 8/24/1863, exch. Pt. Lookout 2/24/1865, res. Floyd Co., s. of Sampson & Eliza (Morris) Conley, res. Floyd Co. 1870, m. Minda Wood (1851-1880 to 1900) 1869, bur. Conley Cem., Rock Fork, Knott Co., KY.

CONLEY, JOSEPH: (8/16/1832 – 6/27/1912), Co. F, enl. 5/15/1863, serv. prev. 5th KY Inf., Co. H, capt. Gladeville, VA 7/7/1863, to Kemper Barracks 7/18/1863, to Camp Chase Prison 8/24/1863, to Camp Douglas 8/24/1863, exch Pt. Lookout 3/2/1865, res. Magoffin Co. 1860, s. of David & Margaret (Phillips) Conley, widow rec. KY Confed. Widow's Pension #2003 Magoffin Co. 1914, m. (1) Jemima Mullins (d. ca. 1862), (2) Polly Bailey (b. 1842) 1866, bur. Gardner Bailey Cem., Gunlock, Magoffin Co., KY.

CONLEY, THOMAS: (11/20/1835 – 10/23/1891), Co. F, enl. Floyd Co., KY 10/14/1862, serv. prev. 5th KY Inf., Co. H, pres. 4/30/1863, res. Greenup Co. 1860, s. of David & Margaret (Phillips) Conley, res. Breathitt Co. 1880, m. Florence Stone (b. 1838-aft. 1910 Carter Co.) 1858, bur. Anglin Cem. #3, Pactolus, Carter Co., KY.

COOK, JACOB: (7/4/1835 – 6/8/1918), Co. H, enl. Whitesburg, KY 10/18/1862, pres. 11/12/1862, res. Letcher Co. 1860, s. of Anderson Cook, m. (1) Francis Hall (1841-ca. 1881), (2) Mary Malinda Profitt (1865-1928) 1882, bur. Cook Cem., Dry Fork, Letcher Co., KY.

COPE, JAMES DIAL: (11/8/1798 – 4/26/1886), Kash's Co., res. Breathitt Co., KY 1860, indicted for murder as member this Co. 1865, m. Elizabeth Crawford (1803-aft. 1880), bur. Cope Cem., Keck, Breathitt Co., KY.

COPE, JAMES S.: (2/1832 – 1909), Kash's Co., also serv. Union 47th KY Inf., Co. I, poss. James Simpson Cope, s. of James D. & Elizabeth (Crawford) Cope, m. Zurrila Cockrell, bur. Cope Cem., Davis Fk., Davis, Breathitt Co., KY.

COPE, WILLIAM JACKSON: (7/23/1822 – 2/25/1902), Kash's Co., serv. prev. 10th KY Cav., Co. E, res. Breathitt Co. 1860, s. of James P & Mary (Hammonds) Cope, indicted for murder as member this Co. 1865, m. Delilah Strong (1825-aft. 1900), bur. Lazarus Back Cem., Quicksand, Breathitt Co., KY.

CORNETT, CHARLES LEWIS: (10/20/1828 – 4/15/1900), Co. B, enl. Gladeville, VA 8/11/1863, res. Perry Co. 1860, s. of Roger & Mary "Polly" (Lewis) Cornett, m. Polly Creech (1833-1886) 1850, bur. Edley Cornett Cem., Cornettsville, Perry Co., KY.

CORNETT, JAMES C.: (2/24/1841 – 2/26/1918), Co. A, enl. Perry Co., KY 6/6/1863, also serv. Diamond's 10th and Union Three Forks Btn., res. Perry Co. 1860, s. of James & Morning (McKnight) Cornett, m. Louisa Cornett (1843-aft. 1910) 1860, bur. Cornett Cem., Skyline, Letcher Co., KY.

CORNETT, JOHN: (1/28/1828 – 2/16/1904), Co. B, enl. Whitesburg, KY 9/6/1862, dark complexion, grey eyes, dark hair, ill with pleurisy Camp Hope, disch. Gladeville by Col. Ben Caudill 6/5/1863, took oath Louisa 5/5/1865, res. Perry Co. 1860, s. of John C & Rachel (Smith) Cornett, res. AR (Dutton) 1870, m. Nancy Combs (1832-aft. 1920 Dewar, Okmulgee Co., OK), bur. Dutton Cem., Dutton, Madison Co., AR.

CORNETT, JOHN BAXTER "J.B.": (12/16/1837 – 10/1/1910), 5th Sgt., Co. H, enl. Whitesburg, KY 9/29/1862, res. Letcher Co. 1860, s. of Joseph E. & Sarah (Brown) Cornett, m. Mary Elizabeth Hays (1847-1923), bur. Cornett-Brown-Caudill Cem., UZ, Letcher Co., KY.

CORNETT, JOSEPH E.: (4/28/1814 – 5/30/1891), claimed prev. serv. w/ 5th KY Inf., Co. F, family claimed short serv. w/ 13th KY, wd. in hip Letcher Co., left serv. Tazewell Co., VA, res. Letcher Co., 1860, s. of William J. & Mary (Everage) Cornett, post-war res. Letcher Co. (Dry Fork), serv. as Letcher Co. Judge, m. Sarah Brown (1815-1892) 1837, bur. Sandlick Cem., Whitesburg, Letcher Co., KY.

CORNETT, JOSEPH E.: (1843 – 8/10/1863), Co. A, capt. Gladeville, VA 7/7/1863, to Kemper Barracks 7/18/1863, to Camp Chase Prison 7/20/1863, d. Camp Chase of chronic diarrhea 8/10/1863, res. Letcher Co. 1860, s. of Samuel & Mary "Polly" (Adams) Cornett, bur. grave #4, Camp Chase Prison Cem., Columbus, Franklin Co., OH.

CORNETT, RUSSELL: (10/14/1840 – 1899), Co. B, enl. Whitesburg, KY 9/6/1862, pres. spring/1863, res. Perry Co. 1860, s. of John & Rachel (Smith) Cornett, res Perry Co. 1880, m. (1) Ailey Amburgey (1841-1902), (2) Milly Combs (1839-aft. 1910), bur. Cornett Cem., Upper Second Creek, Perry Co., KY.

CORNETT, SAMUEL A.: (7/20/1840 – 5/13/1921), Co. H, enl. Whitesburg, KY 9/17/1862, res. Letcher Co. 1860, s. of Joseph E. & Sarah (Brown) Cornett, m. (1) Lurana "Raney" Whitaker (1840-bef. 1870), (2) Susan Shepherd (1840-aft. 1880), (3) Nan Engle, (4) Alcey Couch, bur. Morgan Cem., Hazard, Perry Co., KY.

CORNETT, WILLIAM A.: (3/12/1836 – 3/23/1911), Co. E, capt. Jonesville, TN 12/17/1863, to Louisville Prison, to Rock Island Prison, exch. Pt. Lookout 2/25/1865, res. Letcher Co. 1860, s. of Samuel "Sam" & Lucy (McDaniel) Cornett, res. Letcher Co. 1870, m. Sarah Caudill (1845-1922), bur. Cornett Cem., Line Fork, Letcher Co., KY.

CORNETT, WILLIAM E.: (1/31/1833 – 7/12/1909), 1st Lt., Co. B, enl. Whitesburg, KY 10/10/1862, prom. from Sgt. to Lt. 6/24/1863, capt. KY 12/1863, res. Letcher Co. 1860, s. of Roger & Mary "Polly" (Lewis) Cornett, m. Matilda Stamper (1836-1890)1856, bur. Edley Cornett Cem., Cornettsville, Perry Co., KY.

CORNETT, WILLIAM G.: (1836 – 1865 to 1870), Co. A, serv. prev. 5th KY Inf., Co. F, capt. Booneville, KY 8/19/1863, to Louisville Prison 8/24/1863, to Camp Chase Prison 9/1/1863, to Rock Island Prison 1/22/1864, disch. near end of war, res. Clay Co. 1860, s. of Samuel & Mary "Polly" (Adams) Cornett, widow res. Jackson Co. (Middlefork) 1870, m. Eliza "Liza" Howard (1844-1919 Menifee Co., d.c. #21851), d. Jackson Co.

COUCH, H. E.: Co. F, enl. Floyd Co. 10/14/1862, pres. summer/1863.

COX, SAMPSON D.: (5/11/1839 – 1926), Co. B, enl. Whitesburg, KY 8/29/1862, capt. Battle of Cynthiana 6/14/1864, to Louisville Prison, to Rock Island Prison 6/24/1864, took oath & exch. City Point, VA 3/6/1865, res. Owsley Co. 1860, s. of Braxton J. & Lydia Cox, rec. Confed. Pension #131 Wolfe Co. 1912, res. Wolfe Co. (Campton/Torrent) 1920, rec pension voucher 11/1926, m. Lucretia Smith (1840-1917), bur. Hatton Cem., Grannie, Wolfe Co., KY.

COX, WILLIAM: (b. 1842), Co. B, serv. prev. 2nd Btn. KY Mtd. Rifles, trans. Johnson's Btn., Co. F 4/3/1863, res. Owsley Co. 1860s. of Braxton J. & Lydia Cox, m. Phoebe Jane (b. 1845), did not survive the war.

CRABTREE, ABRAHAM THOMPSON: (8/25/1833 – 1898), Sgt. Maj., Co. K, enl. Lee Co., VA 8/18/1863, also serv. 4th KY Cav w/ Maj. Gen. Giltner (re: family history), rec. clothing 9/24/1864, serv. as 1st Sgt., surr. as Sgt. Maj. Cumberland Gap 4/30/1865, res. Owsley Co. 1860, res. Estill Co. 1870, res. Cherokee Co. (Galena) 1880, m. (1) Minerva (b. 1838), (2) Delina Lee Estes (1857-1910) Estill Co., bur. Galena Cem., Galena, Cherokee Co. KS.

CRABTREE, DAVID SIMPSON "SIMP": (9/28/1839 – 11/9/1928), 4th Sgt., Co. K, enl. Lee Co., VA 8/18/1863, pres. Lee Co., 12/31/1863, rec. clothing as D. S. Crabtree 9/7/1864 & 9/24/1864, surr. as Pvt. Cumberland Gap 4/30/1865, wd. in hip leading to morphine addiction (re: family history), res. Estill Co. 1860, s. of Jacob & Polly (Yeary) Crabtree, res. Lee Co. 1870, rec. KY Confed. Pension #142 Wolfe Co. 1912, widow rec. KY Confed. Widow's Pension #4541 Lee Co. 1928, m. Elizabeth R. Wilson (1844-1929), bur. Booth & Crabtree Cem., Fixer, Lee Co., KY.

CRAFT, ALLEN: (10/12/1840 – 10/18/1926), Kash's Co., res. Breathitt Co. 1860, s. of John W. & Susannah Hargis Craft, indicted for murder as member this Co. 1865, d. Morgan Co., m. (1) Rachel Oliver (1838-bef. 1880) 1855, (2) Phoebe Jane Collins (1854-aft. 1920) 1880, bur. Craft Cem., Ebon, Morgan Co., KY.

CRAFT, DAVID K.: (1/11/1837 – 5/10/1918), Co. D, enl. Whitesburg, KY 10/4/1862, substitute for John Mullins, res. Wise Co., VA 1860, b. s. of Arch Jr. & Nancy Jane (Polly) Craft, res. Wise Co. 1880, res. Elliott Co. 1890, m. Sarah Maggard (1838-1908) Wise Co., VA 1857, bur. Dr. John W. Hillman Cem., Pound, Wise Co., VA.

CRAFT, ELIJAH: (10/24/1837 – 9/29/1894), Kash's Co., res. Breathitt Co. 1860, s. of John W. & Susannah Hargis Craft, indicted for murder as member this Co. 1865, res. Menifee Co. (Ridge) 1880, d. Breathitt Co. m. Vina (1843-aft. 1910 Liberty, KS), poss. bur. Craft Cem. w/ parents, Guage, Breathitt Co., KY.

CRAFT, ENOCH A. "CHUNK": (2/28/1842 – 2/16/1937), Co. D, enl. Whitesburg, KY 10/4/1862, w/ Gen. John H. Morgan on his last raid through KY, rec. clothing 9/7/1864, res. Letcher Co. 1860, s. of Arch & Letty (Webb) Craft, rec. KY Confed. Pension #2376 Letcher Co. 1912, m. Col. Ben Caudill's sister, Mary Ann "Polly" Caudill (1847-1936) 1867, bur. Uncle Chunk Craft Cem., Millstone, Letcher Co., KY.

CRAFT, JASON L. "BEE": (7/18/1839 – 2/12/1903), 2nd Lt., Co. D, wd. KY 10/20/1864, took 30-day leave, succeeded by James Crutchfield, res. Letcher Co. 1860, s. of Arch & Letty (Craft) Webb, res. Letcher Co. 1870, m. Hennie Ritter Adams (1840-1907), bur. Craft Cem., Millstone, Letcher Co., KY.

CRAFT, JOHN (F.): (b. 1845) Co. D, enl. Whitesburg, KY 10/4/1862, pres. summer/1863, res. Letcher Co. 1860, s. of William Craft & Rachel (Parker) Craft, did not survive the war, NFR.

CRAFT, JOHN HENDERSON: (12/20/1834 – 9/13/1920), 1st Lt., Adjt., Cos. A & C, enl. & prom. Adjt. 11/1/1862, serv. prev. 5th KY Inf., Co. F, capt. Gladeville, VA 7/7/1863, to Kemper Barracks 7/18/1863, to Camp Chase Prison 7/20/1863, to Johnson's Island Prison 10/10/1863, exch. Pt. Lookout 2/16/1865, hosp. Richmond, VA 2/27/1865 to 3/1/1865, res. Letcher Co. 1860, s. of Joseph & Martha (Bates) Craft, Superintendent Letcher Co. Schools post-war, res. Laurel Co. 1887, m. Col. Ben Caudill's sister, Nancy Jane Caudill (1840-1922), bur. Lincks Cem., Larue, Laurel Co. KY.

CRAFT, JOHN LINVILLE: (11/28/1832 – 6/7/1905), 1st Lt., Co. C & Kash's Co., enl. Whitesburg, KY 10/4/1862, capt Gladeville, VA 7/7/1863, res. Breathitt Co. 1860, s. of John W. & Susannah (Hagins) Craft, indicted for murder as member Kash's Co. 1865, m. Nancy Back (1840-1923), bur. Johnston Cem., Dan, Menifee Co., KY.

CRAFT, JOSEPH P.: (2/6/1848 – 10/20/1910), Co. D, capt. Lee Co., VA, paroled Cumberland Gap 5/2/1865, res. Letcher Co, KY 1860, s. of Arch & Letty (Webb) Craft, res. Letcher Co. 1860, res. Letcher Co. 1870, m. Rosy Bagwell (1850-1919) 1869, bur. Thornton Cem., Thornton, Letcher Co., KY.

CRAFT, NEHEMIAH: (7/15/1848 – 8/6/1896), Co. D, enl. Whitesburg, KY 10/4/1862, pres. spring/1863, res. Letcher Co. 1860, s. of Benjamin & Jane (Adams) Craft, m. (1) Nancy Emaline Adams (1852-1900) Letcher Co. 1868, (2) Virginia Prichard (1866-1950), bur. Webb Cem., Mayking, Letcher Co., KY.

CRAFT, NELSON ROBERT: (9/9/1834 – 7/20/1916), 1st Sgt., Co. D, enl. Whitesburg, KY 10/4/1862, pres. summer/1863, res. Letcher Co. 1860, s. of Arch & Letty (Webb) Craft, res. Knott Co. 1890, m. (1) Elizabeth Reynolds (d. aft. 1880) 1855, (2) Julia Parks (1865-1953), bur. Nelson Craft Cem., Mallie, Knott Co., KY.

CRAFT, WILLIAM H.: (1843-1885), Co. I, serv. prev. in 1st /3rd KY Mtd. Rifles, Co. E, on detached service with Capt. Wm. Smith (13th KY., Co. I) 6/1863 – 1/1864, detached with the 13sth KY Cav in East TN 1/1864 & 2/1864, m. Elizabeth C. (1843-1926), s. of William Craft & Rachel (Parker) Craft, res. of Letcher Co. 1860, res. of Scott Co., Val 1870 & 1880, bur. in Craft Cem., Ft. Blackmore, Scott Co., VA.

CRAFT, WILLIAM RICHARDSON: (11/24/1843 – 5/22/1928), 2nd Sgt., Co. D, prom. Sgt. Whitesburg, KY 4/1/1864, res. Letcher Co. 1860, s. of Joseph & Martha (Bates) Craft, res. Letcher Co. 1880, res. Ashe Co., NC 1920, d. reportedly Ashe Co., NC, m. (1) Emily Sergeant (1850-1900 to 1908) 1868, (2) Laura Phillips (1874-1955) Idlewild, Ashe Co., NC, bur. McComas-Crotty Cem., Pinoak, Mercer Co., WVA.

CRAGER, JAMES: (2/1825 – 1910), Co. F, enl. Floyd Co., KY 10/14/1862, res. Floyd Co. 1860, res. Floyd Co. (Dwale) 1900, m. (1) Levisa "Vicey" Sexton (1820-ca. 1868), (2) Elizabeth (1851-living 1920, Wayland, Floyd Co., KY) 1875, bur. Old Herold Cem., Woods, Floyd Co., KY.

CRASE, JAMES M.: (b. 1835), Co. D, aka James Case (s.r.), enl. 10/4/1862, wd. & sent home fall/1862, res. Letcher Co. 1860res. Letcher Co. 1870, m. Elizabeth Stallard (living as widow 1900, Rowan Co. Hogtown Precinct) 1856.

CRAWFORD, ARCHIBALD CALLOWAY: (4/7/1844 – 7/2/1921), Co. K, enl. Lee Co., VA 8/18/1863, serv. prev. 5th KY Inf. (Consolidated), Co. D, pres. Lee Co., VA 12/31/1863, res. Breathitt Co. 1860, s. of Oliver & Elvira (Jett) Crawford, m. Drucilla Brittian (1848-1927 Clark Co.), bur. Crawford Cem., Bryant's Creek, Breathitt Co., KY.

CRAWFORD, GREEN R.: (b. 1843), Co. G or Kash's Co., res. Breathitt Co. 1860, s. of Claborne & Susannah Crawford, indicted for murder as member this Co. 1865, res. Breathitt Co. (Jetts Creek) 1870 m. Peylor (b. 1850), living in Organ, Dona Ana Co., NM, "age 76, single, b. KY, parents b. VA, owns home, able to read & write".

CRAWFORD, WICKLIFFE "WICK": (2/21/1841 – 3/28/1904), Co. K, enl. Lee Co., VA 8/18/1863, serv. prev. 5th KY Inf (Consolidated) Co. D, capt. nr. Cumberland Gap fall/1863, res. Breathitt Co. 1860, s. of Oliver & Elvira Jett Crawford, single in 1880, bur. Crawford Cem. Bryant's Creek, Breathitt Co., KY.

CREECH, FELIX GILBERT: (4/28/1830 – 8/19/1902), 1st Sgt., Co. D, enl. Whitesburg, KY 10/4/1862, pres. fall/1862, res. Letcher Co. 1860, s. of John & Sarah (Smith) Creech, res. Wise Co., VA (Gladeville) 1900, m. (1) Clerinda Sturgill (1833-1893) 1853, (2) Susanna Elizabeth Bond (b.1858 KY) in 1894, bur. Flannery Cem., Wood, Scott Co., VA.

CREECH, HENRY: (4/1839-8/18/1910), Co. G, enl. Gladeville, VA 7/14/1863, s. of William & Sarah (Branson) Creech, nephew of Pvt. Silas Creech, m. (1) Celia Blair (1839-1908), (2) Martha Winstead, res. of Harlan Co. in 1860, bur. Narrow Valley Ch. Cem., Rutledge, Grainger Co., TN.

CREECH, SILAS: (1830 – 1891), Co. G, enl. Wise Co., VA, serv. prev. Union 14th KY Cav., Cos. E & M, paroled Cumberland Gap 5/4/1865, res. Wise Co., VA 1860, s. of Jonathan & Nancy Jane (Blair) Creech, res. Wise Co., VA (Big Stone Gap/Richmond) 1870 & 1880, m. Sarah Dale (b. 1827) 1848, bur. Gosneyville Cem., Walker Luke Rd., Trent, Wolfe Co., KY.

CRUTCHFIELD, JAMES T.: (12/3/1844 – 10/2/1864), 2nd Lt., Co. D, prom. 4/9/1864, KIA Battle of Saltville, VA 10/2/1864, res. Jefferson Co. 1860, s. of Major Edward (CSA Quartermaster) & Susan (Spotts) Crutchfield, bur. Sec. P, Lot 59, Cave Hill Cem., Louisville, Jefferson Co., KY.

CRUTCHFIELD, ROBERT EDWARD: (4/3/1846 – 1/26/1901), Courier, Co. D, enl. fall/1862 (re: pension appl.), listed as courier by 2/6/1863, w/ Maj. Edward Crutchfield in TN 3/16/1863, requested new horse Abingdon, VA for Maj. Crutchfield 8/19/1863, in Abingdon, VA on requisitions 11/10/1863 & 11/30/1863, paid $150 on 11/30/1863, fought bravely during John H. Morgan's Campaign (re: Gen H. Marshall), rec. clothing as member of Co. D 6/20/1864, w/ Gen John H. Morgan Greenville, TN & capt. 9/4/1864 (re: Gen H. Marshall), exch. & requested transfer to Confed. Navy 11/5/1864, appointed midshipman schoolship *Patrick Henry*, left ship on James R., arr. Richmond & left by train guarding Confed. treasure w/ Pres. Davis & Gen. H. Marshall, arr. Washington, GA, never surr, res. Jefferson Co. 1860, s. of Major Edward (CSA Quartermaster) & Susan (Spotts) Crutchfield, res. Meade Co. 1870, res. Louisville, KY 1880, res. Putnam Co., FL 7/1880, d. tuberculosis, widow rec. FL Confed. Pension #03230 1907, "A more gallant soldier never lived" (re: Capt. James T. Rogers, widow's pension appl.), m. Eliza Musgrove (1852-1918) 1870, bur. Westview Cem., Palatka, Putnam Co., FL.

DAVIDSON, EDWARD: (12/23/1838 – 5/17/1903), Co. I, conscripted Whitesburg, KY 10/18/1862, pres. summer/1863, res. Perry Co. 1860, s. of Robert & Nancy (Combs) Davidson, res. Perry Co. 1870 & 1880, res. Knott Co. 1892, res. Breathitt Co. 1900, widow applied KY Confed. Widow's Pension Knott Co. 1912, m. Eliza Walker (1838-aft. 1912) 1858, bur. Hayes Cem., Quicksand, Breathitt Co.,KY.

DAVIDSON, JEREMIAH: (7/29/1829 – 3/18/1899), Co. I, conscripted Whitesburg, KY 10/18/1862, pres. 6/15/1863, also serv. 3rd KY, Co. E 11/1/1864 to 2/17/1865, res. Breathitt Co. 1860, s. of Robert & Nancy (Combs) Davidson, operated store post-war at Canoe in Breathitt Co., after being robbed several times moved to Jackson Co. 1887, m. Mary "Polly" Moore 1850, bur. Link Abram Farm Cem., Welchburg, Jackson Co., KY.

DAVIDSON, JOHN: (2/28/1826 – 10/27/1911), Co. G, enl. Perry Co., KY 3/24/1863, res. Breathitt Co., s. of Robert & Nancy (Combs) Davidson, m. Nancy Ann Morris (1830-aft. 1900), bur. Davidson Cem., Altro, Breathitt Co., KY.

DAVIS, WILEY OREN: (1832 – 1898), Co. G, enl. Breathitt Co., KY 10/1/1862, res. Breathitt Co. 1860, s. of Louis & Elizabeth (Parrish) Davis, believed to have died under suspicious circumstances in James Co., TN, m. Susannah Cunningham (1825-1904) 1853, Confed. memorial marker Strong Cem., Lost Creek, Breathitt Co., KY.

DAY, DAVID: (5/11/1822 – 6/11/1888), Co. B, enl. Whitesburg, KY 8/21/1862, forage master from 9/30/1862, capt. Gladeville, VA 7/7/1863, to Kemper Barracks 7/18/1863, to Camp Douglas Prison 8/24/1863, exch. Pt. Lookout 2/24/1865, res. Letcher Co., 1860, m. Rebecca Back (1825-1875) 1845, bur. Francis-Day Cem., Littcarr, Knott Co., KY.

DAY, WILLIAM: (1837- 1887), Co. A, enl. 5th KY Inf., Co. F 12/18/1861, pres. fall/1863, res. Perry Co., s. of John N. & Levisa Day, res. Perry Co. (Leatherwood) 1870, res Letcher Co. 1880, m. Martha (1837-aft. 1880) Perry Co. 1854, bur. Pendleton Cem., Ice, Letcher Co., KY.

DAY, WILLIAM: (8/21/1821 – 1/28/1884), Co. G or Kash's Co., res. Breathitt Co., 1860, s. of Jesse & Martha Caskey Day, indicted for 1/1865 murder of Duff-Fugate-Milam, Perry Co., res. Breathitt Co. 1870 & 1880, m. (1) Ellen (1824-1860 to 1870), (2) Lourania Cope (1827-aft. 1880) 1863, bur. Boone Fork Cem. off Frozen Creek, Breathitt Co., KY.

DAY, WILLIAM H.: (5/29/1845 – 10/20/1894), Co. H, enl. Whitesburg, KY 10/18/1862, res. Letcher Co. 1860, s. of David & Becky (Back) Day, m. Marinda Francis (1848-1886) bur. Francis-Day Cem., Littcarr, Knott Co., KY.

DEATON, JOSEPH: (1/5/1846 – 11/10/1918), Co. G, enl. Breathitt Co., KY 10/1/1862, also serv. Union 14th KY, res. Breathitt Co., 1860, s. of John & Malinda (Watts) Deaton, m. Ruth Wooten (1847-aft. 1910) 1862, bur. Buck Herald Cem., Talbert, Breathitt Co., KY.

DEATON, WILLIAM "TONY": (1828 – 1898), Co. G, enl. 10/1/1862, pres. spring/1863, also serv. Union Army, Three Forks Btn., Co. E, res. Breathitt Co. 1860, s. of John & Malinda (Watts) Deaton, m. Rachel Raleigh (1828-1891) 1846, bur. Crockettsville Cem., Crockettsville, Breathitt Co., KY.

DEBUSK, CHRISTOPHER: (2/19/1845 – 9/17/1907), Co. K, enl. Lee Co., VA 8/18/1863, serv. prev. 1st Sgt 21st VA Inf., 27th VA Mtd. Rifles & Co. H, 25th VA Cav., pres. w/ 13th pres. Lee Co., VA 12/31/1863, paroled (poss. w/ 25th VA Cav.) upon taking oath 2/29/1864, res. Lee Co., VA 1860, s. of Palser & Sarah (Surber) Debusk, moved from Lee Co., VA to Collin Co., TX 1868, res. Brown Co., TX 1875, res Nolan Co., TX 1898, m. Anna Lavinia McDonough (1847-1925) Collin Co., TX, bur. Sweetwater Cem., Sweetwater, Nolan Co., TX.

DERROW, EQUAL (AQUILLA): (10/4/1846-12/2/1916), Co. D, s. of William & Mary (Furry) Derrow, b. Rockingham Co., VA, serv. prev. in 6th Bttn. Reserves (enl. 4/16/1864 Abingdon, VA), trans. from Abingdon Provost Guards to Co. D, Caudill's command 11/9/1864, (confirmed in letters of J. Stoddard Johnson of Breckinridge's staff), m. Mulhulda N. Thompson (1832-1911) in Lincoln Co., TN in 1867, bur. Mulberry Cem., Mulberry, Lincoln Co., TN.

DIALS, ROBERT: (1841 – 1869), Co. H, enl. Whitesburg, KY 10/18/1862, pres. summer/1863, res. Letcher Co. 1860, s. of Elizabeth "Betsy" Dials, aka "Robert Thacker", raised by Jesse & Nancy Thacker, m. Elizabeth Sparkman (1842-widow in 1880 Letcher Co.) 1859, bur. Slone-Dyer Cem., Leburn, Knott Co., KY.

DINGUS, SAMUEL P.: (8/21/1835 – 7/4/1892), Co. F, enl. Floyd Co., KY 6/1/1863, res. Floyd Co. 1860, s. of William & Mary "Polly" (Green) Dingus, res. Floyd Co. 1870 & 1880, m. Francis Arty Flannery (1837-1899) 1860, bur. Dingus Cem., Alphoretta, Floyd Co., KY.

DIXON, ISAAC D.: (1/1831 – 1903), 3rd Cpl., Co. H, enl Whitesburg, KY 9/29/1862, prom. 3/18/1863, pres. fall/1863, res. Letcher Co. 1860, s. of Thomas & Susan (Profitt) Dixon, res. Letcher Co. 1870, res. Letcher Co. 1900, res. Madison Co., AR 1902, m. (1) Elizabeth Banks (1832-1871) 1855, (2) Mary Whitaker Shepherd (1839-after 1905; remarried G. W. Gray, Madison Co., AR 1905) 1881, bur. Brashears Cem., Brashears, Madison Co., AR.

DOBSON, JOHN R.: (4/9/1836 – 10/22/1918), Co. C, enl. Whitesburg, KY 10/1/1862, escaped capt. Gladeville, VA 7/7/1863, pres. summer/1863, w/ Gen. Morgan Battle of Mt. Sterling 6/9/1864, shot under collar bone, left shoulder in Battle of Cynthiana 6/11/1864, bullet exited right shoulder, taken home per Morgan's orders, ret. serv., disbanded nr. Abingdon, VA, took oath Louisa spring/1865 (re: pension witnesses), res. Breathitt Co. 1860, s. of William & Winney Dobson, res. Knott Co. 1890, rec. KY Confed. Pension #2948 Knott Co. 1912, m. Polly McDaniel (1833-1910/1920), bur. Dobson Cem., Vest, Knott Co., KY.

DOBSON, WILLIAM: (1839 – 5/1923), Co. C, enl. Whitesburg, KY 10/1/1862, pres. Battle of Cynthiana 6/11/1864 (re: pension witness), patient U. S. hosp. Richmond, VA 3/1865, res. Perry Co. 1860, s. of William & Winney Dobson, res. Perry Co. 1870 (Troublesome), res. Knott Co. 1890, appl. Confed. Pension 1912, m. Elizabeth (1846-1918), bur. Dobson Cem., Vest, Knott Co., KY.

DOTSON, THOMAS M.: (1839 – 10/24/1864), Co. A, enl. Whitesburg, KY 10/3/1862, capt. Gladeville, VA 7/7/1863, to Kemper Barracks 7/18/1863, to Camp Chase Prison 7/20/1863, to Camp Douglas Prison 8/24/1863, d. of typhoid & exposure Camp Douglas, res. Russell Co. VA 1850, s. of Andrew J. & Lucinda Jane (Matney) Dotson, m. Ben Caudill's sister, Elizabeth Caudill (1842-remarried William Green, res Letcher Co. 1870 & 1880), bur. Oak Wood Cem., Chicago, Cook Co., IL.

DOWELL, HIBBERT: See Powell, Hibbert.

DRAKE, JOHN E.: (5/9/1843 – 12/12/1927), serv. prev. 5th KY Inf., Co. A & 2nd Cpl. Co. E, 10th KY Cav., scout duty KY from 1/23/1865, attached 13th KY Cav. until surr. 6/1865, res. Wolfe Co. 1870, rec. Confed. Pension #3385 Wolfe Co. 1912, m. (1) Sarah Napier (b. 1848), (2) Rebecca (1853-1931 Menifee Co.), bur. Evans Cem., Campton, Wolfe Co., KY.

DUFF, JOHN L.: (1848 – 1885), Kash's Co., s. of Alex & Catherine Duff, indicted post-war for several 1865 murders as member this company (aka John McDuff), res. Breathitt Co. 1880, m. Dulcena Noble (1857-ca. 1888), she married John Guinn, Breathitt Co. 1888, bur. Strong Cem., Lost Creek, Breathitt Co., KY.

DUFF, MARCUS M. "MACK": (2/1/1846 – 3/22/1916), Co. G & Kash's Co., enl. Co. G Breathitt Co. 10/1/1862, claimed serv. in Kash's Co. (re: pension witness), rec. clothing 4/7/1864, left service at Louisa, 5/1865, res. Breathitt Co. 1860, s. of Alex & Catherine Duff, widow rec. Confed. Widow's Pension Perry Co. 1939, m. (1) Rebecca Wells (1847-1900 to 1906), (2) Tabitha "Bytha" Fugate 1906, bur. T-Point Cem., Clayhole, Breathitt Co., KY.

DUFF, SHADRACK: (1830 – 10/26/1920), Co. A, 5'5", dark hair, blue eyes, serv. prev. 5th KY Inf., capt. Perry Co. 4/13/1864, to Louisville Prison, rel. on oath 4/21/1864, res. Perry Co. 1860, s. of John A. & Polly (Combs) Duff, m. Polly Patrick (1837-1912) 1859, bur. Red Hill Cem., Chavies, Perry Co., KY.

DUKE, JAMES M. "JIM": (1828 – 1889), Co. B, enl. Whitesburg, KY 8/21/1862, capt. Booneville, KY 8/19/1863, to Louisville Prison, rel. to join U.S. 3rd KY Battery 8/25/1863, res. Letcher Co. 1860, s. of John W. & Susan (Brown) Duke, res Montgomery Co. (Levee) 1870, res Harrison Co. (Leesburg) 1880, m. (1) Caroline (1844-bef. 1870), (2) Rachel Madden (m. William Smith Harrison Co. 1883), bur. Jacksonville Cem., Jacksonville, Harrison Co., KY.

DUKE, PEYTON MADISON: (11/3/1833 – 12/26/1894), 1st Lt., Co. B, enl. Whitesburg, KY 8/21/1862, resigned his rank w/ bladder disorder & comp. serv. as Pvt., successor was William Cornett, capt. Battle of Cynthiana 6/14/1864, to Louisville Prison 6/22/1864, to Rock Island Prison 6/24/1864, rel. on oath 5/25/1865, res. Letcher Co. 1860, s. of John W. & Susan (Brown) Duke, res. Letcher Co. 1870, first postmaster of McPherson (now Hindman), m. (1) Rachel Cornett (b. 1843)1858, (2) Nancy Madden (1840-1925) 1872, bur. Duke-Waddle-Kelly Cem., Hindman, Knott Co., KY.

DULANEY, LEWIS B.: (1840 – 12/13/1902), 2nd Lt., enl. 5th KY Inf., Co. H, Camp Moccasin, Scott Co., VA 4/3/1862, 6'2", blue eyes, brown hair, also serv. Co. E, 64th VA Inf. & as 2nd Lt. 13th KY Cav. (re: John B. Wells III), res. Scott Co., VA 1860, s. of Boanerges & Judith (Gilliam) Dulaney, res. Wise Co., VA 1870, res. Scott Co. (Powell) VA 1880, applied Confed. pension Scott Co., VA 1900, widow applied Confed. pension Scott Co. (Blackwater) 1924, m. (1) Sarah Collier (1843-1870 to 1880 Wise Co., VA) 1865, (2) Nancy Madden(1856-aft. 1920 Scott Co., VA) Scott Co., VA 1878.

DYKES, WILLIAM: (b. 12/3/1823), Co. H & Kash's Co., enl. Perry Co. (Brashearville) 3/1/1863, pres. summer/1863, enl. later Kash's Co., res. Perry Co. 1860, s. of Jesse Jr. & Mary (Foster) Dykes, post-war res. Anderson Co., TN (his birthplace), res. Mercer Co., MO 1881, m. Eliza Brashear 1844.

EDWARDS, JAMES (THOMAS): (6/9/1839 - 4/22/1922), Co. B, enl. Whitesburg, KY 9/2/1862, des. 10/10/1862, also serv. 7th Confed. Cav. & 51st A Inf., Co. A, res. Wise Co., VA 1860, b. Carroll Co., TN, s. of John B. & Catherine Edwards, m. Sarah Carrico (1839-1923) in 1860, rec. Confed. Pension Wise Co., VA 1916, bur. Edwards Cem., Herald, Wise Co., VA.

ELDRIDGE, CARR "CARL": (4/11/1845 – 7/27/1932), Co. K, enl. aft. 8/1/1863, serv. prev. 64th VA Inf., Co. H (des. 8/1/1863), surr. Cumberland Gap 4/30/1865, res. Harlan Co. 1860, s. of Hugh & Barthena (Middleton) Eldridge, rec. Confed. Pension #363 Harlan Co., KY, res. Harlan Co. (Frozen) 1930, d.c #16347, m. (1) Martha Hoover, Lee Co., VA 1866, (2) Narcissus Johnson (1844-1900) Harlan Co. 1876, (3) Susan Hensley 1896, (4) Louisa Fields (1867-1943). bur. Middleton Cem., Kildav, Harlan Co., KY.

ELDRIDGE, JAMES: (9/20/1848 – 9/20/1916), Co. K, enl. aft. 8/1/1863, serv. prev. VA State Line & 64th VA Inf., Co. H (enl. 4/18/1863 & des. 8/1/1863), filed claim for a lost horse, surr. Cumberland Gap 4/30/1865, res. Harlan Co. 1860, s. of Hugh & Barthena (Middleton) Eldridge, res. Lee Co. VA (Jonesville) 1870-1910, pension witness at Pennington Gap, VA 1912, rec. VA Confed. Pension, widow rec. VA Confed. Widow's Pension, m. Virginia Jane Johnson (1847-1948) Lee Co., VA 1866, bur. Andrew Reynolds Cem., Pennington Gap, Lee Co., VA.

ELDRIDGE, JOHN C.: (9/5/1833 – 7/29/1910), Co. A, serv. prev. 5th KY Inf., Co F, disc. at expiration of term 4/14/1863, res. Letcher Co. 1860, s. of Levi & Easter (Caudill) Eldridge, res. Letcher Co. 1870, widow rec. KY Confed. Widow's Pension #616 Letcher Co. 1912, m. Elizabeth Caudill (1835-aft. 1912) Perry Co. 1850, bur. Eldridge Cem., Roxanna, Letcher Co., KY.

ENGLAND, ENOCH: (8/1827 – 2/15/1909), Co. H, enl. Whitesburg, KY 10/18/1862, aka Engle & Ingland, listed as Englin at times, joined Union 14th KY Inf., Co. I, res. Letcher Co. 1860, s. of John E. & Elizabeth (Crager) England, res. Magoffin Co. 1870 & 1880, res. Floyd Co. 1900, has Union marker, m. (1) Nancy Collins (b. 1839) Letcher Co. 1855, (2) Margaret Pridemore, (3) Melinda Helton (1845-aft. 1900) 1885, bur. Holbrook Cem., Dotson, Floyd Co., KY.

ENGLAND, RICHARD: (3/16/1843 – 1/10/1917), Co. F, enl. Floyd Co., KY 10/14/1862, pres. fall/1862, res. Magoffin Co. 1860, b. VA, s. of Eliza Crager, res. Floyd Co. 1900, m. Clarinda, d. Magoffin Co., d.c #2303, bur. Montgomery Cem., Swampton, Magoffin Co., KY.

ENGLAND, RUEL: (b. 10/1830), Co. C, capt. Pike Co. KY 7/3/1863, to Kemper Barracks, to Camp Chase Prison 7/20/1863, to Camp Douglas Prison 8/24/1863, exch. Point Lookout 2/24/1865, res. Pike Co. 1860, res. Pike Co. 1870, wife res. Pike Co. 1880, res. Wyoming Co., WV (Huff's Creek) 1900, m. Pricey Clay (b. 1836) 1850.

ENGLE, ENOCH: See ENGLAND, Enoch

ENGLE, HENRY "SR": (1816 – 1872), Co. C, enl. Whitesburg, KY 10/1/1862, pres. spring/1863, furloughed for sickness Hazard, KY 1863, never returned, never took oath, res. Perry Co. 1860, s. of Henry G. & Sarah (Hanson) Ingle, m. Leanna Grigsby (1820-1886) 1839, bur. Engle Cem., Fisty, Knott Co., KY.

ENGLE, HENRY "JR.": (1844 – 1885), Co. C, enl. Whitesburg, KY 10/1/1862, capt. Gladeville, VA 7/7/1863, to Kemper Barracks 7/18/1863, to Camp Chase Prison 7/20/1863, to Camp Douglas Prison 8/24/1863, exch. Point Lookout 4/24/1865, res. Wise Co., VA 1860, s. of Nathanial Thomas & Judith "Juda" (Hall) Engle, res. Perry Co. 1870, widow on Leslie Tax List 1885 & Leslie Co Census 1900, m. Susan Jane "Jincy" Bailey (1843-1922), bur. Hendricks Cem., Wooten, Leslie Co., KY.

ENGLE, HENRY S.: (7/5/1838 – 12/20/1923), Co. C, enl. Whitesburg, KY 10/1/1862, serv. prev. 5th KY Inf, Co. F, res. Perry Co. 1860, s. of William & Nancy (Stacy) Engle, rec. KY Confed. Pension #3115 as res. Perry Co. (Dwarf) 1913, m. Leannah "Leanner" Napier (1843-1921) 1857, bur. Holliday Cem., Ary, Perry Co., KY.

ENGLE, RUEL: See ENGLAND

ENGLE, THOMAS SAMPSON: (1844 – 1902), Co. C, enl. Whitesburg, KY 10/1/1862, pres. spring/1863, res. Perry Co., 1860s. of William & Nancy (Stacy) Engle, m. (1) Elizabeth "Betty" Hoskins (1844-1895) 1865, (2) Rosanna Jones 1897, bur. Engle Cem., Busy, Perry Co., KY.

ENGLE, WILLIAM: See also INGLE, William.

ENGLE, WILLIAM BUCHANAN "BUCK": (1/30/1839 – 12/1/1910), Co. C, aka William C. Engle & William Engle, Sr. on some serv. records, enl. Whitesburg, KY 10/1/1862, gunshot wound resulted in broken arm 1863, left at home by Capt. Anderson Hays, res. Perry Co. 1860, s. of William & Nancy (Stacy) Engle, res. Perry Co. (Troublesome) 1870 & 1880, widow rec. KY Confed. Widow's Pension #2105 Morgan Co. 1912, m. (1) Sallie Grigsby (1841-ca. 1867), (2) Levica "Vicey" McDaniel, (3) Levina "Viney" Fugate (1851-1922) 1875, bur. Elam Cem., Index, Morgan Co., KY.

ESTEP, JONATHAN: (4/13/1837 – 12/8/1918), 2nd Sgt., Co. E, enl. Whitesburg, KY 10/14/1862, pres. summer/1863, res. Letcher Co. 1860, s. of Joel & Rebecca (Hall) Estep, m. (1) Christina Meade (1838-1880 to 1888) 1862, (2) Letha "Letty" Runyon (1847-bef. 1900) Logan Co. WV, 1888, (3) Susan (b.1852) 1900, bur. Estep Cem., Myrtle, Mingo Co., WV.

EVANS, ALFRED: (1833 - 9/17/1870), Co. K, enl. Lee Co. VA 8/18/1863, capt. nr. Cumberland Gap, Lee Co. VA 11/12/1863, to McLean Barracks 11/22/1863, to Camp Chase Prison 11/23/1863, rel. on oath 1/20/1865, res. Jackson Co. 1860 (tavern keeper), s. of William & Mary "Polly" (Stone) Evans, res. Owsley Co. 1870, m. Rebecca Jane Baker (1838-1898), bur. Rock Springs Baptist Ch. Cem., Riceville, Owsley Co., KY.

EVANS, GEORGE STUBBLEFIELD: (4/23/1848 – 11/8/1925), Co. K, reportedly serv. prev. TN Cav. reg., surr. Cumberland Gap 4/30/1865, res. Owsley Co. 1860, s. of William N. Sr. & Elizabeth Evans, m. Virgina Jane Schofield (1861-1942) Webster Co., MO, bur. Thayer Cem., Thayer, Oregon Co., MO.

EVANS, JAMES R.: (1/1830 – 7/30/1920), Co. K, surr. Cumberland Gap 4/30/1865, res. Owsley Co. 1860, b. Claiborne Co., TN, s. of William & Mary "Polly" (Stone) Evans, res. Owsley Co. 1870, 1880 & 1900, m. Margaret Allen (1831-1914), bur. J. R. Evans Cem., Sturgeon, Owsley Co., KY.

EVANS, ROBERT L.: (12/30/1834 – 6/3/1920), Sgt., Co. K, enl. Lee Co., VA 8/18/1863, capt nr. Cumberland Gap fall/1863, ret. serv., rec. clothing 9/7/1864, res. Owsley Co. 1860, s. of William & Mary "Polly" (Stone) Evans, res. Lee Co. VA 1870-1920, m. Sarah Henderson Russell (1836-1921) Lee Co., VA 1865, d. Lee Co. VA (St. Charles).

EVANS, WILLIAM NELSON "SR": (1825 – 3/31/1864), Co. K, enl. Lee Co., VA 8/18/1863, pres. Lee Co. 12/31/1863, capt. Maj. Gen. Thomas' Union forces Dandridge, TN 1/17/1864, to Louisville Prison 2/11/1864, to Rock Island Prison 2/18/1864, d. of pneumonia, res. Owsley Co., 1860, b. Claiborne Co., TN, s. of John Evans, m. Elizabeth (1826-1908), bur. grave #957, Rock Island Confed. Cem., Rock Island, Rock Island Co., IL.

EVANS, WILLIAM NELSON "JR": (9/11/1849 – 11/11/1922), Co. K, enl. 8/1864, serv. until surr. Cumberland Gap 4/30/1865, saw action at Cedar Gap, Crossroads, Bull Gap, Strawberry Plains, Morriston & Wytheville, reached Salem, VA on march to join Gen. Lee when Lee surr., res. Owsley Co. 1860, b. Claiborne Co., TN, s. of William N. Sr. & Elizabeth Evans, moved post-war to Tazewell, TN, to Webster Co., MO 1869, teacher in AR Indian Territory and Texas, ret. MO, Circuit Judge for twenty-six years, member Gen. J. Shelby Camp, UCV, Adjutant Gen. MO E. Div., UDC, (re: Confed. Vet XXXI, p. 106), m. Sarah A. Smith (1853 - 1937), Webster Co., MO 1875, bur. Oak Lawn Cem., West Plains, Howell Co., MO.

EVERIDGE, BENJAMIN: (2/9/1824 – 11/19/1914), Co. A, serv. prev. 5th KY Inf. Co. F, serv. w/ Gen. John Hunt Morgan, Battle of Cynthiana 6/11/1864, disc. w/ unusual illness & fever fall/1864, res. Letcher Co. 1860, s. of Joseph & Sylvania Everidge, rec. KY Confed. Pension #3285, m. Elizabeth Amburgey (1835-1930) 1855, bur. Charlie Logan Cem., Bath, Knott Co., KY.

EVERIDGE, THOMAS: (1832 – 1864), Cos. B & C, enl. Whitesburg, KY 9/3/1862, trans. from Co. B to Co. C, Whitesburg 1/1/1863, killed & bur. by Capt. Thomas Eversole's 3 Fk. Btn. men on Dick's Fk. of Clear Cr., res. Perry Co. 1860, s. of Solomon & Catherine Everidge, m. Rachel Johnson (b. 1860), bur. Ritchie Cem., Ritchie, Knott Co., KY.

EVERIDGE, WILLIAM: (3/21/1845 – 6/19/1929), Co. B, enl. Whitesburg, KY 9/9/1862, des. Gladeville, VA 7/7/1863, disbanded Abingdon, VA spring/1865, never capt., did not take oath, res. Letcher Co. 1860, s. of Solomon & Elizabeth (Turner) Everidge, res. Knott Co. 1890, rec. KY Confed. Pension #2954/#4579 Knott Co. 1912, m. Amelia Walker (1849-1933 Knott Co.) 1866, bur. Everidge Cem., Hindman, Knott Co., KY.

EVERSOLE, IRVIN: (10/15/1829 – 5/24/1932), Co. I, conscripted Whitesburg, KY 10/18/1862, pres. 11/1/1862, res. Perry Co. 1860, s. of Absalom & Elizabeth (Campbell) Eversole, m. (1) Eliza Jane Stacy (1833-ca. 1881) 1848, (2) Amy Huff, (3) Betty Hignite, (4) Elizabeth Bradley Stacy (1848-aft. 1910), bur. Eversole Cem., Bonnyman, Perry Co., KY.

FARLER, FARRIS JR. "FORREST": (4/1829 – 12/20/1901), Co. I, conscripted Whitesburg, KY 10/18/1862, disc. 10/24/1862, res. Perry Co. (land surveyor & timber dealer, rt. fk. Mason's Ck.) 1860, s. of Farris Sr. & Sally (Hutchinson) Farler, res. Perry Co. 1870 & 1880, res. Owsley Co. 1900, widow res. Owsley Co. (Buck Cr.) 1910, m. Nancy Combs (1832-1901) 1857, d. Owsley Co.

FARLER, JOHN A.: 1822 – bef. 1910), Co. I, enl. Whitesburg, KY 10/18/1862, serv. prev. 5th KY Inf, Co. I, rec. clothing 9/15/1864, res. Perry Co. (land surveyor & timber dealer) 1860, s. of Farris Sr. & Sally (Hutchinson) Farler, res. Perry Co. 1870, res. Lee Co. 1880 & 1900, m. Susan Hughes (1845-bef. 1900).

FAULKNER, GEORGE MILLER "Rebel George": (3/8/1846 – 11/6/1917), Co. K, capt. 1/17/1864 Dandridge, TN (w/ 13th KY), to Knoxville 1/27/1864, to Louisville, to Rock Island Prison 2/15/1864, to Pt. Lookout for exchange 2/15/1864, service record misfiled in "Artificial 10th KY", res. of Knox Co. 1850, res. of Grant Co. 1860, s. of Daniel B. & Elizbeth (Tye) Faulkner, m. Caroline Frances Wells (1850-1924), bur. Abner Wells Cem., Artemus, Knox Co., KY.

FELTNER, JOHN: (3/10/1840 – 3/5/1923), Co. I, conscripted Whitesburg, KY 10/18/1862, pres. 11/1/1862, serv. later Union 14th KY, res. Perry Co. 1860, s. of Jacob & Nancy (Grigsby) Feltner, m. Sally Feltner (1840-1880 to 1900), bur. Hardburly Baptist Church Cem., Hardburly, Perry Co., KY.

FELTNER, LEWIS: (2/22/1842 – 3/16/1919), Co. I, conscripted Whitesburg, KY 10/18/1862, pres. 11/1/1862, serv. later Union 14th KY, res. Perry Co. 1860, s. of Jacob & Nancy (Grigsby) Feltner, m. Mahala Napier (1843-1920: d.c. #16992) 1860, bur. Hardburly Baptist Church Cem., Hardburly, Perry Co., KY.

FIELDS, DANIEL B.: (10/20/1844 – 10/13/1927), Co. H, conscripted by Union, serv. until Battle of Lookout Mt., fall/1863, then joined Confed. 13th KY, serv, until 3/1865, res. Letcher Co. 1860, s. of William & Lydia M. (Rice) Fields, res. Letcher Co. 1890, m. Mary Hensley (1861-1944), bur. Mose Whitaker Cem., Roxanna, Letcher Co., KY.

FIELDS, DAVIS STEWART: (10/10/1832 – 3/23/1908), Co. I, serv. prev. 5th KY Inf., Co. F, trans. 13th KY Cav., camped at head of Beaver at time of surr. 4/1865, res. Letcher Co. 1860, b. Perry Co., s. of William & Margaret (Rice) Fields, res. Perry Co. 1880, res. Letcher Co. 1890, widow rec. KY Confed. Widow's Pension #3210, Letcher Co., 1915, m. Nancy Ann Caudill (1835-1918) Letcher Co. 1856, bur. Nancy Back Cem., Jeremiah, Letcher Co., KY.

FIELDS, JAMES H.: (1843 – 1892), Co. K, surr. Cumberland Gap 4/30/1865, res. Harlan Co. 1860, b. TN, s. of Daniel Selena Fields & Patsy, res. Harlan Co. 1870 & 1880, res. Harlan Co. (Clover Fk.) 1891, m. Elizabeth Noe (1841-1923) 1861, bur. unmarked Turner Hill Cem., Kitts, Harlan Co., KY.

FIELDS, STEPHEN H.: (1834 - 1880), Co. H, enl. Whitesburg, KY 10/18/1862, res. Letcher Co. 1860, s. of William & Lydia M. (Rice) Fields, res. Letcher Co. 1870 & 1880, sold land on Big Cowan (n. side of Pine Mt.) 1875, m. Rebecca Day (1835-aft. 1880) 1856, bur. Will Adams Cem., Dongola, Letcher Co., KY.

FITZPATRICK, JAMES B.: (3/10/1835 – 4/5/1900), 1st Lt., Cos. I & E, enl. Whitesburg, KY, Co. E, 10/5/1862, assigned from Co. E to Co. I 10/18/1862, prom. 2nd Lt. 11/2/1862, requested to resign & raise a new Co. in Perry Co. 1/2/1863, request denied, prom. 1st Lt. 4/23/1863, successor was Isaac Smith, severely wd. both shoulders Gladeville, VA, capt. Gladeville 7/7/1863, to Kemper Barracks 7/18/1863, to Camp Chase Prison 7/20/1863, to Johnson's Island Prison 10/10/1863, exch. Point Lookout 2/16/1865, res. Perry Co. 1860, (County Attorney, Hazard, KY), s. of Jacob & Paulina (Brown) Fitzpatrick, moved post-war to Whitesburg, practiced law, elected KY House of Repres.atives 1871, carried mail between Whitesburg & Gladeville, VA 1880-1884, m. (1) Margaret Combs 1861, (2) Martha Brashear May (1845-bef. 1880), (3) Josephine Godsey (1845-1933), bur. Sandlick Cem., Whitesburg, Letcher Co., KY.

FLANERY, JAMES F.: (b. 5/1/1836), Co. F (prob.), serv. prev. 5th KY Inf., Co. E, res. Floyd Co., b. 5/1/1836, s. of John Flanery, res. Grayson Co., TX 1878, res. Grayson Co., TX 1880, res. Denison, TX 1889, applied for pension while living in TX, claiming service in 13th KY Cav., m. Sarah J. Dawson (1840-aft.1930), res. of TX 1910.

FLEMING, JOHN: (8/29/1834 – 1912), Co. D, surr. Mt. Sterling, KY 4/30/1865, no. s.r., s. of John Jackson & Mary Jane (Mullins) Fleming, m. Mary Anne Francis Adams.

FOUCH, ANDREW JACKSON: (1840 – 1864), 4th Cpl., Co. E, enl. Whitesburg, KY 10/5/1862, prom. Cpl. Summer/1863, pres. w/ Andrew & Malon Quillen when they left Frankfort for home 9/12/1864, k. w/ John L. Hall, Marshall Hall & Elisha Mullins, mo. of Nealy Br. on Carr Creek late fall/1864, res. Harlan Co., s. of Woodard Foutch, bur. William D. Hall Cem., Kite, Knott Co., KY.

FRANCIS, GEORGE WASHINGTON: (1841 – 1919), Co. G, enl. Whitesburg, KY 10/14/1862, wd. fall/1863, bullet remained in his leg below the calf the rest of his life, res. Breathitt Co. 1850, s. of William & Polly (Combs) Francis, one of triplets, res. Perry Co. (Lost Creek) 1910, m. Lettie Allen (1840-1919), bur. Watts-Francis Cem., Manuel, Perry Co., KY.

FRANCIS, JOHN WESLEY: (1841 – 8/19/1864), Co. A, enl. 9/29/1862, capt. Gladeville, VA 7/7/1863, to Kemper Barracks 7/18/1863, to Camp Chase Prison 7/20/1863, to Camp Douglas Prison 8/24/1863, d. from smallpox Camp Douglas, res. Letcher Co. 1860, s. of Samuel & Leodicy (Hogg) Francis, m. Elizabeth Mullins (b. 1840) 1859, bur. Oak Wood Cem., Chicago, Cook Co., IL.

FRANCIS, LAWSON: (b. 1831), Co. G, enl. Breathitt Co. 9/23/1862, res. Breathitt Co. 1860, b. VA, s. of James & Rebecca Francis, res. Breathitt Co. 1870, m. Franky McIntosh (b. 1833) 1855.

FRANCIS, PRESTON: (1841 – 12/19/1864), Co. G, enl. Whitesburg, KY 10/1/1862, serv. prev. 5th KY Inf., Co. I & 10th KY Cav., Co. D, capt Gladeville, VA 7/7/1863, to Kemper Barracks 7/18/1863, to Camp Chase Prison 7/20/1863, to Camp Douglas Prison 8/24/1863, d. from debility Camp Douglas, res. Perry Co. 1860, s. of William & Polly (Combs) Francis, bur. Oak Wood Cem., Chicago, Cook Co., IL.

FRANCIS, SAMUEL: (6/25/1843 – 9/16/1922), Co. A, serv. prev. 5th KY Inf., Co. F (re: pension), disbanded Floyd Co. (Beaver) while acting as scout 4/1865, never capt., forced to take oath, Louisa, spring/1865, res. Letcher Co. 1860, s. of Simeon J. & Cassa B. (Smith) Francis, witness for Pension #2713 (widow of W. D. Madden) Knott Co. 1912, rec. KY Confed. Pension #2399 Knott Co. 1912, widow rec. KY Confed. Widow's Pension # 4203 Knott Co. 1922, m. Lettie Mullins (1846-1931) Letcher Co. 1864, bur. Francis Cem., Carr Creek, Knott Co., KY.

FRANCIS, SIMEON: (1843 – 2/4/1864), Co. A, serv. prev. 5th KY Inf., Co. F, w/ Gen. John Hunt Morgan on Ohio & Indiana raid 1863, capt. Buffington Island 7/19/1863, to Camp Douglas Prison, d. from diarrhea, res. Letcher Co. 1860, s. of Samuel & Leodicy (Hogg) Francis, bur. Oak Wood Cem., Chicago, Cook Co., IL.

FRANCIS, SIMEON JUSTICE: (3/25/1818 -9/1/1878), Co. A, enl. 5th KY Inf., Co. F 11/1/1861, enl. 13th KY Cav. Whitesburg, KY 11/2/1862, capt. Gladeville, VA 7/7/1863, to Kemper Barracks 7/18/1863, to Camp Chase 7/20/1863, to Camp Douglas Prison 8/24/1863, res. Letcher Co. 1860, s. of Thomas & Jane (Hammonds) Francis, res. Letcher Co. 1870, d. of ulcers, m. Cassa B. Smith (1825-1902) 1840, bur. Carrs Fork Memorial Cem., Littcarr, Knott Co., KY.

FRANCIS, WESLEY: (3/3/1840 – 2/21/1864), Co. C, enl. Whitesburg, KY 10/1/1862, pres. summer/1863, accidently shot & killed by Samuel Smith while on scout duty on Ball Creek (witnessed by Hiram Combs and Levi Nix), res. Perry Co. 1860, b. VA, s. of James & Rebecca Francis, m. Martha "Patsy" Fugate (1840-1927) Perry Co. 1858, bur. Fugate Cem., Ary, Perry Co., KY.

FRANCIS, WILLIAM: (1832 – 1863), Co. C, enl. Whitesburg, KY 10/1/1862, pres. spring/1863, res. Breathitt Co., b. 1832, s. of Hiram & Sarah Francis, d. 1863, bur. Sandlick Cem., Whitesburg, Letcher Co., KY.

FRANKLIN, JAMES BRANDLEY: (3/18/1839 – 8/8/1865), Co. D, enl. Whitesburg, KY 10/4/1862, pres. fall/1862, also serv. Union 47th KY, res. Letcher Co. 1860, b. Russell Co., VA, s. of Byrd & Agnes (Stallard) Franklin, m. Didemy Collins-Hall (b. 1839).

FRANKLIN, KELLY: (9/9/1844 – 1/27/1921), Co. A, serv. prev. 5th KY Inf., Co. F, pres. 4/14/1863, res. Letcher Co. 1860, s. of James & Eliza (Cornett) Franklin, m. (1) Elizabeth Francis Watts (1841-1900 to 1910) 1867, (2) Matilda Smith Hale Sparkman (1854-1941) Knott Co. 1901, bur. Everidge Cem., Pinetop, Knott Co., KY.

FRAZIER, ANDREW JACKSON "JACK": (2/16/1835 – 12/30/1911), Kash's Co., res. Breathitt Co. KY 1860, b. Russell Co., VA, s. of John & Hannah Haddix Frazier, indicted postwar, Breathitt Co., as member this Co. for 1/1865 Duff-Fugate-Milam murders, res. Breathitt Co. 1870 & 1880, res. Bath Co. 1900, res. Montgomery Co. (Howards Mill Rd.), d. of pneumonia (re: d.c. #32277), m. Margaret Elizabeth Flinchum (1845-1919), bur. Little Slate Cem., Preston, Bath Co., KY.

FRAZIER, JAMES R.: (1841 – 1899), Kash's Co., enl. Breathitt Co. (Frozen Ck.) 10/1863, serv. prev. (1) 5th KY Inf. Co. I, (2) 5th KY Inf., Co. D, res. Breathitt Co. 1860, s. of John & Hannah (Haddix) Frazier, res. Breathitt Co. 1890, m. Mary Henderson (1848-aft. 1920) 1861, bur. Frazier-Clemons Cem., Quicksand, Breathitt Co., KY.

FROST, CORNELIUS S.: (1830 – 1911), 1st Cpl., Co. K, enl. Lee Co., VA 8/18/1863, 5'9", light hair, blue eyes, capt. Jonesville, VA 11/25/1863, to Camp Chase Prison 12/16/1863, rel. on oath 4/21/1865, res. Owsley Co. 1860, b. Hawkins Co., TN, s. of Simeon Frost, res. Owsley Co. (Booneville) 1890 & 1900, m. Catherine Grindstaff (b. 1835), bur. Gilbert-Wilson Cem., Taft, Owsley Co., KY.

FUGATE, ALFRED: (5/17/1844 – 2/14/1918), Co. C, enl. Whitesburg, KY 10/1/1862, pres. spring/1863, res. Breathitt Co. 1860, s. of Henley Sr. & Matilda (Stamper) Fugate, res. Breathitt Co. (Portsmouth) 1912 (re: Sam Noble's pension), m. Rebecca Miller (b. 1837) 1863, bur. Laurel Cem., Press, Breathitt Co., KY.

FUGATE, ANDERSON "ANDY": (1/9/1847 – 4/15/1931), Co. G, enl. Breathitt Co., KY 9/23/1862, serv. prev. 5th KY Inf., Co. B, capt. fall/1862, ret. serv. spring/1863, served until dismandment Gladeville, VA 4/12/1865 (re: pension), res. Breathitt Co. 1860, s. of Anderson "Andrew" & Polly (Napier) Fugate, rec. KY Confed. Pension #3598 Breathitt Co. (Clayhole) 1913, d. Lunah, KY, m. Evaline Harvey (1845-1915), bur. Harvey Bend #2 Cem., Hardshell, Breathitt Co., KY.

FUGATE, BENJAMIN FRANKLIN: (9/1845 – 2/22/1920), Co. G, enl. Breathitt Co. 9/23/1862, res. Breathitt Co., s. of Henley Sr. & Matilda (Stamper) Fugate, m. Matilda Napier (1848-aft. 1920), bur. Henley Fugate Cem., Lost Creek, Breathitt Co., KY.

FUGATE, DANIEL: (1842 – 1864), 1st Cpl., Co. C, enl. Whitesburg, KY 10/1/1862, pres. 9/24/1864, k. during the war, res. Perry Co. 1860, s. of Zachariah "Ball Creek Zack" & Mary "Polly" (Smith) Fugate, m. Louanna Williams (b. 1844) 1861, bur. Fugate Cem., Ary, Perry Co., KY.

FUGATE, DANIEL: (2/14/1841 – 7/17/1864), 1st Cpl., Co. G, enl. Breathitt Co. 9/28/1862, capt. Breathitt Co. (Lost Creek) 6/1/1863, to Camp Chase Prison 6/16/1863, to Johnson's Island Prison 6/20/1863, to Point Lookout Prison 11/3/1863, res. Breathitt Co. 1860, s. of Henley Sr. & Matilda (Stamper) Fugate, bur. Point Lookout Cem., Point Lookout, St. Mary's Co., MD.

FUGATE, GABRIEL: (1838 – 6/11/1876), Co. I, conscripted Whitesburg, KY 10/18/1862, rec. clothing 6/29/1864, res. Perry Co. 1860, s. of Zachariah "Ball Creek Zack" & Mary "Polly" (Smith) Fugate, m. Francis Stacy (b. 1840) 1860, bur. Richard Smith Cem., Ary, Perry Co., KY.

FUGATE, IRA C.: (1842 – 11/11/1877), Co. B, enl. Whitesburg, KY 10/18/1862, capt Booneville 8/15/1863, to Louisville Prison 8/24/1863, to Camp Douglas Prison 10/2/1863, exch. Point Lookout 3/2/1865, res. Letcher Co., res. Scott Co., VA 1850, s. of Ira & Margaret (Haney) Fugate, murdered Letcher Co. 1877, m. Dorthula Greer (b. 1832), bur. Webb Cem., Mayking, Letcher Co., KY.

FUGATE, IRA CHARLEY: (2/9/1847 – 11/3/1895), Co. H, res. Letcher Co., s. of Martin & Elizabeth (Smith) Fugate, m. Nancy Hudson (1838-aft. 1912) Breathitt Co., widow rec. Confed. Pension #2119 Knott Co. 1912, bur. Chestnut Gap Cem., Ary, Perry Co., KY.

FUGATE, JEREMIAH: (2/14/1841 – 2/9/1905), 2nd Cpl., Co. G, enl. Breathitt Co. KY 9/23/1862, prom. Breathitt Co. 10/1/1862, wd. & recovered in hosp., rec. clothing 9/7/1864, res. Breathitt Co. 1860, aka Joseph Fugate, s. of Henley Sr. & Matilda (Stamper) Fugate, applied Confed. Pension Russell Co., VA 1888, m. Malinda Carty (1841-1925) 1866, bur. Jerry Fugate Cem., Motts Creek, off Rt. 71, Russell Co., VA.

FUGATE, JOHN B. "JOHN BLUE": (5/11/1832 – 8/14/1916), Co. C, enl. Whitesburg, KY 10/1/1862, pres. spring/1863, res. Perry Co. 1860, s. of Zachariah "Ball Creek Zack" & Mary "Polly" (Smith) Fugate, res. Perry Co. 1880, moved WV, m. Letty M. Smith (1834-1905), bur. Monroe Slone Cem., West Hamlin, Lincoln Co., WV.

FUGATE, LEVI: (1844 – 1898), Co. C, enl. Whitesburg, KY 10/1/1862, 5'4", dark hair, hazel eyes, capt Breathitt Co. 3/6/1864, to Louisville Prison 3/21/1864, to Camp Chase Prison 3/24/1864, to Memphis, TN & paroled on oath 6/6/1865, res. Perry Co., s. of Martin & Elizabeth (Smith) Fugate, res. Perry Co. 1870 & 1880, res. Knott Co. 1890, widow applied for Confed. Pension, m. Mahala "Cricket" Richie (1854-1922) 1872, bur. Chestnut Gap Cem., Ary, Perry Co., KY.

FUGATE, LEWIS "NAPPER": (4/15/1837 – 1/5/1903), Co. G, enl. Breathitt Co. 9/23/1862, surr. Gladeville, VA, res. Breathitt Co. 1860, s. of Henley Sr. & Matilda (Stamper) Fugate, widow rec. KY Confed. Pension #3118, m. Elizabeth Napier (1840-1918) 1859, bur. Fugate & Smith Cem., Ned, Breathitt Co., KY.

FUGATE, MARTIN: (5/12/1846 – 7/3/1872), Co. C, enl. Whitesburg, KY 10/1/1862, pres. fall/1862, res. Perry Co. 1860, s. of Zachariah "Ball Creek Zack" & Mary "Polly" (Smith) Fugate, m. Cynthia Ann Hudson (1852-1947), bur. Fugate Cem., Ary, Perry Co., KY.

FUGATE, NATHANIAL H. "HUNTER": (1/1834 – 2/7/1918), Co. G, enl. Breathitt Co., KY 9/23/1862, pres. 1/7/1863, res. Breathitt Co. 1860, s. of Eli "Flint" & Mary (Noble) Fugate, m. Anna Neace (1829-1910) 1853, bur. Noble Cem., Leatherwood, Breathitt Co., KY.

FUGATE, WILLIAM BANGER: (1831 – 1920), Co. C, enl. Whitesburg, KY 10/1/1862, serv. prev. 5th KY Inf., Co. I, capt. Perry Co. 6/6/1863, to Lexington, to Camp Chase Prison, to Johnson's Island Prison 6/20/1863, to Point Lookout Prison 11/30/1863, released on oath 4/12/1864, res. Breathitt Co. 1860, s. of Eli "Flint" & Mary (Noble) Fugate, m. Mary "Polly" Noble (1829-1913), bur. Fugate Cem., Stacy, Perry Co. KY.

FUGATE, WILLIAM H.: (1837 – 1879), Co. I, conscripted & disc. Whitesburg, KY 10/19/1862, res. Perry Co. 1860, s. of Anderson "Andrew" & Polly (Napier) Fugate, moved post-war to Clay Co., IN, m. Lucinda "Judy" Campbell (1841-1915) 1858, bur. Poplar Cem., Brasil, Clay Co., IN.

FUGATE, WILLIAM N.: (1825 – 1863), Co. G, enl. Breathitt Co., KY 9/23/1862, pres. 10/1/1863, KIA Union sniper Breathitt Co. (Watts), res. Breathitt Co. 1860, s. of Henley Sr. & Tabitha (McIntosh) Fugate, m. Rachel Neace (1828-aft 1870) 1842, bur. Henley Fugate Cem., Ned, Breathitt Co., KY.

FUGATE, ZACHARIAH JR.: (4/1/1845 – 1/11/1921), Co. C, enl. Whitesburg, KY 10/1/1862, serv. prev. 5th KY Inf., Co. I, serv. as scout & spy, w/ PVT Samuel Smith Jr. winter of 1864, en route to joing Gen. Lee, learned of Lee's surr., disbanded 4/1865, took oath Louisa 5/22/1865, res. Perry Co. 1860, s. of Zachariah "Ball Creek Zack" & Mary "Polly" (Smith) Fugate, rec. KY Confed. Pension #3119 Perry Co. 1913, widow rec. KY Confed. Widow's Pension #4078 Knott Co. 1921, m. Mary "Polly" Campbell (1844-1926), bur. Fugate Cem., Ary, Perry Co., KY.

FUGATE, ZACHARIAH: (1843 – 1864), Co. G, enl. Perry Co, KY 9/26/1862, rec. clothing 4/7/1864, k. by Yankees "after peace was made" (re: G. W. Noble, *Behold, He Cometh in the Clouds*, p.74), res. Breathitt Co. 1860, s. of William N. & Rachel (Neace) Fugate, bur. Henley Fugate Cem., Ned, Breathitt Co., KY.

FULLER, ELIJAH "BUNT": (7/20/1843 – 12/31/1931), Cos. B & C, enl. Whitesburg, KY 9/6/1862, trans. from Co. B to Co. C Whitesburg, 1/1/1863, enl. Union Three Forks Btn. 10/7/1864, res. Perry Co. 1860, s. of Elijah & Elizabeth (Patton) Fuller, res. Perry Co. (Troublesome) 1870 & 1880, res. Knott Co. 1890 & 1900, m. Susan Combs (1836-1929), bur. Napier Cem., Lotts Creek, Perry Co., KY.

FULLER, JESSE ARCHIBALD: (1836 – 1905), Cos. B, C & I, enl. Whitesburg, KY 9/6/1862, trans. from Co. B to Co. C Whitesburg 10/1/1862, pres. fall/1863, res. Perry Co. 1860, s. of Elijah & Elizabeth (Patton) Fuller, res. Knott Co. 1900, d. mo. Clear Creek, widow rec. KY Confed. Widow's Pension #2120 Knott Co. 1912, m. (1) Dicey Couch (1838-1920, (2) Ceiley Fields (d. 1934), bur. Fuller Cem., Emmalena, Knott Co. KY.

FULLER, LEVITACUS: (1837 – 8/21/1864), Co. C, enl. Whitesburg, KY 10/1/1862, capt. Battle of Cynthiana 6/14/1864, to Louisville Prison 6/22/1864, to Rock Island Prison 6/24/1864, d. of dysentery, res. Perry Co. 1860, s. of Elijah & Elizabeth (Patton) Fuller, m. Elizabeth Jane Combs 1859, bur. Grave #1434, Rock Island Confed. Cem. Rock Island, Rock Island Co., IL.

GAYHEART, JACKSON "STONEWALL": (1845 – 1881), 2nd Cpl., Co. C, enl. Whitesburg, KY 10/1/1862, pres. summer/1863, res. Perry Co. 1860, s. of William & Malinda (Mosley) Gearhart, res. Perry Co. 1880, m. Rebecca "Betty" Fuller (1850-aft. 1910), bur. Green Bolen Cem., Softshell, Knott Co., KY.

GAYHEART, JOSEPH: (b. 1833), 3rd. Sgt., Co. C, enl. Whitesburg, KY 10/1/1862, capt. Booneville, KY 8/19/1863, to Louisville Prison 8/24/1863, to Camp Chase Prison 9/2/1863, to Rock Island Prison 1/24/1864, d. from diarrhea, res. Perry Co. 1860, s. of Joseph & Catherine (Picklesimer) Gayheart, m. Margaret Combs (b. 1854) 1857, bur. Rock Island Confed. Cem., Rock Island, Rock Island Co., IL.

GAYHEART, MARTIN "MART": (12/17/1844 – 1927), Co. C, enl. Whitesburg, KY 10/1/1862, pres. summer/1863, res. Perry Co. 1860, s. of Joseph & Catherine (Picklesimer) Gayheart, res. Knott Co. 1900, rec. KY Confed. Pension #1692 Knott Co. 1912, m. Martha (1847-d. aft 1920), bur. Clear Fk. Reg. Baptist Church Cem., Lotts Creek, Perry Co., KY.

GAYHEART, W. RILEY: (1836 – 5/1908), Co. C, enl. Whitesburg, KY 10/1/1862, surr. nr. Abingdon, VA 4/1865, res. Perry Co. 1860, b. Pigeon Roost s. of Joseph & Catherine (Picklesimer) Gayheart, widow rec. KY Confed. Widow's Pension #654 Knott Co. 1912, m. (1) Mary Ann Combs (1844-1870's) 1859, (2) Polly Stacy (1854-aft.1910), bur. Clear Fk. Reg. Baptist Church Cem., Lotts Creek, Perry Co., KY.

GEARHART, ADAM: (1839 – 1890), 1st Lt., Co. F, enl. Floyd Co., KY 10/10/1862, resigned 6/18/1863, res. Floyd Co. 1860, s. of Joseph & Sally (Martin) Gearhart, res. Floyd Co. 1870 & 1880, m. Rebecca Martin (1844-1901), bur. Gearhart Cem. nr. Hueysville, Floyd Co., KY.

GEARHART, ALEXANDER: (1840 – 8/10/1864), 2nd Sgt., Co. D, also serv. Diamond's 10th Cav., Co. D, capt Pike Co. 10/6/1863, to Louisville Prison 10/22/1863, to Camp Morton Prison 10/24/1863, died from typhoid fever, res. Floyd Co. 1860, s. of Allen & Eliza Gearhart, bur. Crown Hill Cem., Indianapolis, Marion Co., IN.

GEARHART, HENDERSON: (b. 1845), Co. C, enl. Whitesburg, KY 10/1/1862, serv. later as Cpl., Union 39th KY Inf. Co. F, res. Breathitt Co. 1860, s. of William & Rachel (Hale) Gearhart, capt. as deserter from 13th KY Cav. Breathitt Co. 6/27/1863, to Richmond, VA & tried 9/23/1863, to Andersonville Prison, d. unk. Date & bur. unm. at Andersonville Prison Cem., Andersonville, GA.

GIBSON, ELIJAH: (1834– 1863), 3rd Cpl., Co. H, enl. Whitesburg, KY 10/18/1862, pres. fall/1863, res. Letcher Co. 1860, s. of John & Charity Gibson, m. Oma Sexton, Camp Branch 1856, bur. Colson Chapel Cem., Colson, Letcher Co., KY.

GIBSON, HIRAM: (11/13/1839 – 11/6/1927), Co. D, enl. Whitesburg, KY 10/4/1862, pres. fall/1862, res. Floyd Co. 1860, s. of Leonard & Nancy Gibson, applied KY Confed. Pension Knott Co. 1912, m. Margaret Holbrook (1842-1923), bur. Gibson Cem., Raven, Knott Co., KY.

GIBSON, ISHAM: (2/28/1842 – 2/8/1919), Co. B, enl. Whitesburg, KY 9/9/1862, pres. summer/1863, s. of Leonard & Nancy Gibson, res. Letcher Co. 1870, widow rec. KY Confed. Widow's Pension #1699 Letcher Co. 1912, m. Purthia Jane Webb (1851-1936) Letcher Co., bur. Haven of Rest Cem., Mayking, Letcher Co., KY.

GIBSON, JESSE J.: (7/14/1831 – 4/14/1919), Co. D, enl. Whitesburg, KY 10/4/1862, serv. later Union 14th KY Cav., Cos. B & L, res. Letcher Co. 1860, s. of John & Charity Gibson, res. Owsley Co. 1870 & 1880, rec. Union pension, Appl. #570595, Cert. #440421 (1884), Appl. #1129387, Cert. #873118 (1919), m. Nancy Manerva Sexton (1844-1922) 1871, d. Sexton Creek, Clay Co., KY.

GIBSON, JOEL: (1809 – bef. 1900), Co. A, enl. 13th KY Cav. aft serv. prev. 5th KY Inf., Co. F, pres. spring/1863, trans. 10th KY Cav., Co. C Pike Co. 2/12/1863, capt. Pike Co. 5/20/186_, to Camp Chase Prison, rel. on oath at age 56 5/15/1865, res. Pike Co. 1860, res. Pike Co. 1870 & 1880, m. (1) Mary (1823-bef. 1870), (2) Rhoda (b. 1836), d. Pike Co.

GIBSON, JOHN P.: (5/1/1844 – 6/1/1916), Co. D, enl. Whitesburg, KY 10/4/1862, serv. prev. 5th KY Inf., res. Floyd Co. 1860, s. of Leonard & Nancy Gibson, appl. KY Confed. Pension Knott Co. 1912, m. Arminta (1870-1923), bur. Gibson Cem., Larkslane, Knott Co., KY.

GIBSON, MILES: (11/13/1839 – 3/20/1900), Cos. A & D, enl. 5th KY, Co. F Whitesburg, KY 11/11/1861, enl. 13th KY Whitesburg, 10/4/1862, trans. from Co. A to Co. D, pres. fall/1863, res. Floyd Co. 1860, s. of Leonard & Nancy Gibson, res. Knott Co. 1889 (re: tax list), widow res. Knott Co. 1900, widow appl. KY Confed. Pension Knott Co. 1912, m. Susannah Holbrooks (1839-1918), bur. Gibson Cem., Raven, Knott Co., KY.

GIBSON, WILLIAM: (4/24/1840 – 6/7/1931), Co. E, enl. Whitesburg, KY 10/5/1862, des. 12/24/1862, ret. serv. (1/1/1863 – 4/30/1863) pres. through 4/30/1863, res. Owsley Co. 1860, Floyd Co. 1870, s. of James Gibson & Parmilia Bethany Britton Gibson, m. Elizabeth Spencer (1842 – 1926), bur. Ashland Cem, Ashland, Boyd Co. KY.

GIBSON, WILLIAM: (b. 1/1844), Co. F, enl. Whitesburg, KY 10/14/1862, pres. 8/31/1863, res. Letcher Co. 1850, res. Pike Co. 1860, s. of Owen Gibson & Sarah (Allen) Gibson, m. Elizabeth Rhoton.

GIBSON, WINSTON: (3/1837 – 1913), Co. B, enl. Whitesburg, KY 9/11/1862, des. Pound Gap 5/19/1863, res. Floyd Co. 1860, s. of Leonard & Nancy Gibson, res. Letcher Co. 1870, res. Knott Co. 1889 (re: tax list), res. Knott Co. 1910, appl. Confed Pension Knott Co. 5/20/1912, m. Nancy Holbrook (1836-aft. 1910), bur. Gibson Cem., Larkslane, Knott Co., KY.

GINES, JOHN: Co. D, enl. Whitesburg, KY 10/4/1862, deserted 10/8/1862, res. of Letcher Co.

GODSEY, AUSTIN CLINTON: (1816 – 11/19/1864), Co. I, enl. Hazard, KY 3/2/1863, 5' 10", light hair, grey eyes, capt. Perry Co. 5/17/1863, to Camp Chase Prison 5/31/1863, to Johnson's Island Prison 6/14/1863, to Point Lookout Prison 11/30/1863, res. Perry Co., b. VA, s. of James & Dicey (Hayes) Godsey, m. (1) Mary Combs (b. 1823), (2) Ursula Combs (b. 1837), bur. Point Lookout Prison Cem., Pt. Lookout, St. Mary's Co., MD.

GODSEY, DRURY S. "Drue": (8/21/1848 – 8/12/1907), 4th Sgt., Cos. B & I, enl. Whitesburg, KY 9/3/1862, capt. fall/1862, ret. serv., trans. Co. B to Co. I Whitesburg, 1/1/1863, surr. Mt. Sterling 4/30/1865, res. Perry Co., s. of Austin Clinton & Mary (Combs) Godsey, res. Wolfe Co. 1870, m. Mary Belle Cockrell (1850-1927), bur. Hazel Green Cem., Hazel Green, Wolfe Co., KY.

GODSEY, JAMES O.: (1845 – 10/7/1863), Co. K, serv. prev. 5th KY Inf., 5' 8", hazel eyes, light hair, Co I, capt. Perry Co. 5/17/1863, to Camp Chase Prison, to Ft. Delaware Prison 7/14/1863, res. Perry Co., s. of Austin Clinton & Mary (Combs) Godsey, d. Pea Patch Island, Ft. Delaware Prison, bur. Finns Point National Cem., Ft. Mott, Salem Co., NJ.

GODSEY, JOHN J.: (6/1/1819 – 3/23/1908), 1st Cpl., Co. I, conscripted Whitesburg, KY 10/15/1862, pres. fall/1863, res. Perry Co. 1860, b. VA, s. of John & Julia A. (Jett) Godsey, res. Perry Co. 1870 (Scuddy), m. Margaret Duff (1826-1902) 1843, bur. Defiance Cem., Scuddy, Perry Co., KY.

GRAY, GEORGE MARION: (2/15/1843 – 3/14/1900), Cos. D & E, enl. Whitesburg, KY 10/4/1862, trans. from Co. D to Co. E, pres. spring/1863, res. Sullivan Co., TN 1850, res. Letcher Co. 1860, s. of George Gray & Sarah (O'Brien), res. Powell Co. 1870, m. Dorothy Wilson, d. Neosha Falls, KS, bur. poss. unmarked nr. Brother John (1847-1935), Cedarvale Cem., Neosha Falls, Woodson Co., KS.

GRAY, OLIVER STEWART: (1839 – 1863), Co. A, enl. Whitesburg, KY 11/1/1862, age 22, AWOL Nov-Dec 1862, entered from des. 3/18/1863, pres. 4/1863, res. Letcher Co. 1860, s. of George & Sarah Gray, bur. Sandlick Cem., Whitesburg, Letcher Co., KY.

GREEN, DANIEL: (1846 – 1884), Co. K, enl. Lee Co., VA 8/18/1863, pres. Lee Co. 12/31/1863, res. Harlan Co. 1860, s. of Lewis III & Telitha Arnett Green, res. Bell Co. (Tom's Creek) 1880. m. Caroline Hoskins (1845-1880's) 1867.

GREEAR, MADISON: (1830 – 12/26/1897), Co. B, enl. Whitesburg, KY 9/9/1862, serv. as blacksmith until 12/1862, capt. Letcher Co., 5/1864, to Louisville Prison, rel. on oath 5/1864, res. Scott Co., VA, s. of Noah & Mary Elizabeth Bonham Greear, owned farms in Morgan Co. KY and in VA, bur. Nicholas Horn Cem., Coeburn, Wise Co., VA.

GREER, JAMES KNOX POLK: (1/4/1846 – 2/3/1910), Cos. F & K, surr. Cumberland Gap 4/28/1865, listed in "Artificial 10th KY" mentions Claiborne Co., TN, serv. w/ 10th KY, Co. F (Co. K) & 2nd TN Cav. Co. D, res. Claiborne Co. TN 1860, s. of William W. & Sallie (Teel) Greer, m. (1) Rosa Ann Shelton (1879-1922), (2) Sarah Kelly (1841-ca. 1873), (3) Mary E. Meyes (b. 1846-bef. 1900) 1874, (4) Josie Jennings (b. 1862) 1899, bur. Greer Cem., Straight Creek, New Tazewell, Claiborne Co., TN.

GRIFFIE, JAMES L.: (1823 – 5/7/1916), Co. C, enl. Whitesburg, KY 10/1/1862, serv. prev. 5th KY Inf., Co. I, capt. Gladeville, VA 7/7/1863, to Kemper Barracks 7/18/1863, to Camp Chase Prison 7/20/1863, to Camp Douglas Prison 8/24/1863, exch. Point Lookout 2/24/1865, res. Perry Co. 1860, b. Floyd Co., s. of Elihu & Betty Griffie, m. Seattie Hays (b. 1817), bur. Combs Cem., Mousie, Knott Co., KY.

GRIGSBY, BENJAMIN FRANKLIN (1829 – 2/8/1900), 5th Sgt., Co. C, conscripted Whitesburg, KY 10/18/1862, 5' 9", light hair, blue eyes, capt. Perry Co. 5/17/1863, to Camp Chase Prison 5/31/1863, to Johnson's Island Prison 6/14/1863, exch. Point Lookout 2/24/1865, res. Perry Co. 1860, s. of John & Patsy (Campbell) Grigsby, moved w/ John Cornett to Dutton, AR 1870, widow's Confed. Pension appl. #13387 Yell Co., AR 1909, m. (1) Polly Terry (1836- bef. 1880 AR), (2) Malissa A. (d. aft. 1911), bur. Rocky Springs Cem., Sugar Grove, Logan Co., AR.

GRIGSBY, BENJAMIN F.: (5/18/1843 – 7/25/1907), 4th Sgt., Co. I, enl. Whitesburg, KY 10/18/1862, 5' 10", black hair, blue eyes, capt. Booneville 8/19/1863, to Louisville Prison 8/24/1863, to Camp Chase Prison 9/2/1863, to Rock Island Prison 1/24/1864, rel. on oath 10/11/1864, res. Perry Co. 1860 (Hazard), s. of Benjamin W. & Winnie (Sizemore) Grigsby, widow rec., KY Confed. Widow's Pension #2653 Perry Co. 1914, m. Elizabeth Feltner (1844-1925) Perry Co. 1868, bur. Balis Napier Cem., Lotts Creek, Perry Co., KY.

GRIGSBY, DAVID: (5/30/1841 – 5/22/1895), 3rd Sgt., Co. C, enl. Whitesburg, KY 10/1/1862, "wd. in arm", rec. clothing 9/24/1864, res. Perry Co. 1860, s. of Benjamin W. & Winnie (Sizemore) Grigsby, m. Lydia Gayheart (1846-1926) 1875, bur. Combs Cem. Lott's Creek, Perry Co., KY.

GRIGSBY, EDWARD: (1834 - 12/9/1863), 2nd Lt., Co. C, enl. Whitesburg, KY 10/1/1862, capt. Gladeville, VA 7/7/1863, to Kemper Barracks 7/18/1863, to Camp Chase Prison 7/20/1863, d. from typhoid fever, res. Perry Co. 1860, s. of Benjamin W. & Winnie (Sizemore) Grigsby, m. Nancy Walker (b. 1836) 1854, bur. Camp Chase Prison Cem., Grave #79, Columbus, Franklin Co., OH.

GRIGSBY, GABRIEL: (5/30/1841 - 1/16/1929), Co. C, enl. Whitesburg, KY 10/1/1862, capt. Battle of Cynthiana 6/14/1864, to Louisville Prison 6/22/1864, to Rock Island Prison 6/24/1864, exch. 3/6/1865, took oath Louisa, KY 4/1865, res. Perry Co. 1860, s. of Benjamin W. & Winnie (Sizemore) Grigsby, res. Perry Co. 1880, res. Knott Co. 1900 (Clear Fork of Lott's Creek), rec. KY Confed. Pension #378 Knott Co. (Cordia, m. (1) Sylvania Everidge (1848-bef. 1910), (2) Leatha Shepherd (1846-aft 1920), bur. Clear Fork Church Cem., Lott's Creek, Perry Co., KY.

GRIGSBY, JOHN JR. "DARB": (2/19/1824 – 1910), Co. I, enl. 10/1/1862, 5' 5", dark hair, blue eyes, capt. Perry Co. 4/25/1864, to Louisville Prison 5/7/1864, to Camp Morton Prison 5/12/1864, rel. on oath 6/12/1865, res. Perry Co. 1860, s. of John & Patsy (Campbell) Grigsby, res. Perry Co. 1870, 1880 & 1900 (Sooks Branch of Lotts Creek), m. (1) Elizabeth Hurt (1828-1880/1900) 1860, (2) Clericy Fields (b. 1845) 1891, bur. Clear Fork Church Cem., Lotts Creek, Perry Co., KY.

GRIGSBY, JOHN L.: (1/16/1837 – 4/21/1924), 1st Sgt., Co. C, enl. Whitesburg, KY 10/1/1862, reportedly serv. prev. 5th KY Inf., serv. as Pvt. In Co. I & as Sgt. in Co. C, disch. due to illness Whitesburg 3/1863, took oath Louisa, KY, res. Perry Co. 1860, s. of William & Jane (Owens) Grigsby, res. Knott Co. 1890, rec. pension Knott Co. (Vest) 1915, m. Melda Ritchie, poss. m. Lucy Engle (b. 1842), poss. m. Elizabeth Gayheart, bur. Grigsby Cem., Vest, Knott Co., KY.

GRIGSBY, LEWIS: (2/19/1824 – 1865), 1st Lt., Co. C, enl. Whitesburg, KY 10/1/1862, 5' 4", light hair, blue eyes, capt. Gladeville, VA 7/7/1863, to Kemper Barracks 7/28/1863, to Camp Chase Prison 7/20/1863, to Johnson's Island Prison 10/10/1863, to Point Lookout 3/21/1865, rel. on oath 6/12/1865, res. Perry Co. 1850 w/ Nancy Campbell & John Grigsby, s. of John & Patsy (Campbell) Grigsby, bur. Clear Fork Church Cem., Lotts Creek, Perry Co., KY.

GRIGSBY, SAMUEL: (8/21/1831 – 7/20/1917), 3rd Sgt., Co. I, conscripted Whitesburg, KY 10/18/1862, pres. summer/1863, res. Perry Co. 1860, s. of John & Patsy (Campbell) Grigsby, m. Eliza Jane Napier (1829-1908), bur. Campbell & Grigsby Cem., Ten Mile, Perry Co. KY.

GRIGSBY, WESLEY: (1841 – 1863), Sgt., Co. C, enl. Whitesburg, KY 10/1/1862, pres. fall/1863, res. Perry Co. 1860, s. of William & Jane (Owens) Grigsby, bur. Sandlick Cem., Whitesburg, Letcher Co., KY.

GRIGSBY, WILLIAM: (1/15/1843 – 8/28/1923), 2nd Sgt., Co. C, capt. Gladeville, VA 7/7/1863, to Kemper Barracks 7/18/1863, to Camp Chase Prison 7/20/1863, to Camp Douglas Prison 8/24/1863, enl. U. S. Navy 5/24/1864, initially assigned to *U.S.S. Susquehanna,* res. Perry Co. 1860, s. of Thomas Grigsby & Francis Owens, m. (1) Dorcus Williams (1847-bef. 1910), (2) Rachel Smith, bur. Richard Smith Cem., Ary, Perry Co., KY.

GUINN, ALLEN: (b. 11/11/1842), Cos. G & I, enl. Breathitt Co. 9/23/1862, trans. from Co. G to Co. I Whitesburg 10/18/1862, capt. Gladeville, VA 7/7/1863, res. Breathitt Co. 1860, s. of John & Sally Guinn, moved AR 1866, res. Washington Co., AR 1880, rec. Confed. Pension Washington Co., AR 8/10/1906, res. Washington Co., AR (Brentwood), 1906, m. Elizabeth Winkle (b. 1829) 1866.

GUINN, DREWERY F.: (1820 – 1865), Co. G, enl. this Co. (re. G. W. Noble: *Behold, He Cometh in the Clouds*), killed while returning home, mo. Drowning Creek 1865, res. Breathitt Co., b. Lee Co., VA, s., of William & Nancy Guinn, m. Virginia "Jennie" "Jane" Noble (1818-1912), bur. Confed. Cem. Bibee, Madison Co., KY.

GUINN, JAMES: (10/19/1831 – 6/22/1914), 1st Lt., Co. I, enl. Whitesburg, KY 10/18/1862, capt. Perry Co. 4/25/1864, successor was Lt. James Fitzpatrick, to Louisville Prison 5/7/1864, to Johnson's Island Prison 5/12/1864, rel. on oath 5/12/1865, res. Perry Co. 1860, b. Lee Co., VA, s. of William & Nancy Guinn, moved Washington Co., AR 1866, m. (1) Martha Napier 1858, (2) Sally (b. 1858), bur. Hazel Valley Cem., Durham, Washington Co., AR.

GUINN, WILLIAM: (1849 – 1863), Co. G (re: G. W. Noble; *Behold, He Cometh in the Clouds*), s. of Drewery & Virginia "Jennie" "Jane" (Noble) Guinn, killed by enemy, Letcher Co. (Line Fork).

HABERN, GEORGE W. H.: (1/20/1838 – 11/1/1901), 1st Sgt., Co. K, serv. prev. 64th VA Inf., Co. A, surr. Cumberland Gap 4/30/1865, res. Lee Co., VA 1860, s. of Benjamin F. Habern, m. Alpha (1836-1893), bur. Wise City Cem., Wise, Wise Co. VA.

HAGANS, ALLEN CHRISTIAN: (7/15/1843 – 5/7/1928), 1st Sgt., Cos. A & E, enl. Whitesburg, KY 10/14/1862, prom Sgt. 1/17/1863, trans. from Co. A to Co. E, rec. clothing 4/7/1864, res. Floyd Co., s. of Gilbert & Leah (Christian) Hagans, res. Floyd Co. 1880, m. (1) Nancy B. Osborne (1843-1882), (2) Annie Patton (1864-1889), (3) Rosa Woods, (4) Rainie Gayheart, (5) Susie Begley, bur. Hagans Cem., Eastern, Floyd Co., KY.

HAGANS, THOMAS C.: (1841 – 8/26/1894), Co. A, enl. Whitesburg, KY 10/14/1862, res. Letcher Co. 1860, s. of Gilbert & Leah (Christian) Hagans, res. Letcher Co. 1880, m. (1) Leodicy Francis, (2) Nancy (b.1842), (3) Susie Begley (1885-aft. 1920), bur. Slone-Dyer Cemetery, Leburn, Knott Co., KY.

HAGINS, DANIEL: (11/22/1807 – 9/17/1866), Kash's Co., indicted post-war for murder as member this co. 1865, m. Elizabeth Stamper (b. 1825), bur. Hagins Cem., Rousseau, Breathitt Co., KY.

HAGINS, HIRAM: (5/14/1841 – 12/1/1897), Kash's Co., res. Breathitt Co. 1860, s. of Daniel & Elizabeth (Stamper) Hagins, indicted post-war for murder as member this co. 1865, res. Breathitt Co. 1880, m. (1) Mary Ann Childers (1838-1909), (2) Christine Spurlock (1853-1888), d. Lyon Co. (Americus Township), KS, bur. Dunlop Cem., Morris Co., KS.

HALCOMB, DAVID WESLEY: (12/25/1842 – 1/22/1911), Co. H, enl. Whitesburg, KY 10/18/1862, rec. clothing 4/7/1864, res. Letcher Co. 1860, s. of Henderson & Sarah (Cornett) Halcomb, m. (2) Rosa Bohannon (b. 1867) 1883, bur. Jerd Halcomb Cem., Line Fork, Letcher Co., KY.

HALCOMB, OLIVER GOLDSMITH: (1/15/1838 – 6/27/1927), 4th Sgt., Co. A, enl. Whitesburg, KY 11/1/1862, serv. prev. 5th KY, Co. F, prom. from Pvt. To Sgt. 1/17/1863, w/ Gen. John Hunt Morgan when Morgan was shot Greenville, TN 1864, continued serv. Russell Co., VA, rec. clothing 9/7/1864, took oath Elliott Co., KY 1866, res. Carter Co. 1860, s. of Henderson & Sarah (Cornett) Halcomb, rec. KY Confed. Pension #2973 Letcher Co. 1912, widow rec. KY Confed. Pension #4475 Letcher Co. 1927, m. Manerva Francis Day (1854-1933) 1872, bur. Halcomb Cem., Line Fork, Letcher Co., KY.

HALCOMB, WILLIAM: (1841 – 3/11/1865), Co. H, enl. Whitesburg, KY 10/18/1862, pres. fall/1862, res. Letcher Co. 1860, s. of Henderson & Sarah (Cornett) Halcomb, bur. Jerd Halcomb Cem., Line Fork, Letcher Co., KY.

HALE, JAMES M.: (4/14/1833 – 3/21/1917), Co. F, enl. Floyd Co., 3/1/1863, pres. spring/1863, res. Magoffin Co. 1860, s. of John Hale, (Am. Legion report says William Hale enl. 13th KY, Co. F 3/1/1863, William M. Hale, res. Magoffin Co. 1860, b. 4/1834 VA, m. Eliza Jane Gullett, res. Magoffin Co. 1900), m. Mary "Polly" Shepherd (1839-1934) Floyd Co., bur. Hale & Shepherd Cem., Gunlock, Magoffin Co., KY.

HALL, ALFRED: (1828 – 1/31/1864), 2nd Cpl., Co. E, enl. Whitesburg, KY 10/5/1862, prom. Cpl 4/30/1863, capt. Floyd Co. 7/7/1863, to Louisville Prison 11/18/1863, to Camp Morton Prison 11/20/1863, d. from pneumonia, res. Floyd Co. 1860, s. of Riley William & Jane "Jennie" (Cook) Hall, m. Temperence Justice (1828-aft. 1880), bur. Crown Hill Cem., Indianapolis, Marion Co., IN.

HALL, ALLEN: (d. 2/14/1930), Co. E, enl. Whitesburg, KY 10/5/1862, serv. prev. 5th KY Inf., Co. E & 7th Btn. Confed. Cav., Co. C, capt. 11/1/1862, res. Floyd Co., b. 3/4/1843 Floyd Co., rec. KY Confed. Pension #3552 Mason Co. (Orangeburg) 1916, m. Luellan (1857-bef 1930), d.c. #04776) bur. Mayseville-Mason Co. Cem., Maysville, Mason Co., KY.

HALL, ALVIN: (5/18/1835 – 8/28/1912), Co. E, enl. Whitesburg, KY 10/5/1862, pres. fall/1862, res. Letcher Co. 1860, s. of Hiram & Lucy (Delph) Hall, res. Letcher Co. 1870, res, Lincoln Co., WV 1880, res. Mingo Co., WV (Harvey) 1900 & 1910, m. Elizabeth Jane King (1836-1900/1910, Mingo Co. WV), bur. Hall Cem., Dingess, Mingo Co., WV.

HALL, ANTHONY: (1830 – 1890), Co. E, enl. Whitesburg, KY 10/5/1862, pres. summer/1863, res. Letcher Co. 1860, s. of James & Sarah (Johnson) Hall, res. Letcher Co. 1870 & 1880, res. Knott Co. 1890 (re: Special Veterans Census; stated he served until the end of the war), m. (1) Dicy Childers (1835-bef. 1880) 1853, (2) Jane Sexton (b. 1857), bur. Beaver Dam Cem., Colson, Letcher Co., KY.

HALL, BENJAMIN: (12/1843 – 3/24/1917), 4th Sgt., Co. D, enl. Whitesburg, KY 10/4/1862, hired as a substitute, pres. summer 1863, serv. later Union 39th KY, Co. K (9/27/1863-9/15/1865), res. Letcher Co. 1860, s. of Reuben & Mahalia (Bentley) Hall, res. Letcher Co. 1870, 1880 & 1900 (Millstone), res. Pike Co. 1910, widow res. Pike Co. 1920, m. (1) Mary Elizabeth Fife (1844-1942, Pike Co.) 1865, Union grave marker, bur. Joe Trivette Cem., Jonancy, Pike Co., KY.

HALL, DAVID (H.): (1837 – 1863), 3rd. Cpl., Co. E, enl. Whitesburg, KY 10/5/1862, pres. summer/1863, res. Letcher Co. 1860, s. of James & Sarah (Johnson) Hall, bur. Beaver Dam Cem., Colson, Letcher Co., KY.

HALL, FIELDING: (1841 – 3/10/1864), Co. E, enl. Whitesburg, KY 10/5/1862, serv. prev. 5th KY Inf., Co. F, capt. Floyd Co. 7/7/1863, to Louisville Prison 11/18/1863, to Camp Morton Prison 11/20/1863, d. from smallpox, res. Letcher Co. 1860, s. of Hiram & Lucy (Delph) Hall, bur. Crown Hill Cem., Indianapolis, Marion Co. IN.

HALL, GREENWAY: (2/6/1831 – 2/25/1914), Co. D, enl. Whitesburg, KY 10/4/1862, pres. summer/1863, res. Wise Co., VA 1860, b. Russell Co., VA, s. of Isham & Jane Hall, res. Letcher Co. 1870 & 1880, res. Johnson Co. (Buffalo) 1900 & 1910, m. Elizabeth Franklin (1837-aft. 1910), bur. Hall Cem., Tomahawk, Martin Co., KY.

HALL, HENRY (CLAY) "HURRY": (1848 – 1896), Co. E, enl. Whitesburg, KY 10/5/1862, pres. spring/1863, res. Floyd Co. 1860, s. of Riley W. & Jane "Jennie" Elizabeth (Cook) Hall, res. Floyd Co. 1870 & 1880 (near Capt. William J. Hall), m. Frankie J. Caudill (1851-aft. 1920 Pike Co.) Floyd Co. 1868, bur. Daughtery & Hall Cem., Freeburn, Pike Co., KY.

HALL, HENRY: (1844 – 1888), Co. F, enl. Floyd Co. 10/14/1862, also serv. Diamond's 10th KY Cav., Co. B, pres. fall/1863, res. Letcher Co. 1850, res. Floyd Co. 1860, s. of Randall & Kate (Johnson) Hall, res. Floyd Co. 1870 & 1880, m. Ellen Stumbo, bur. Hall Cem., Bevinsville, Floyd Co., KY.

HALL, HIRAM: (b. 1827), Co. D, enl. Whitesburg, KY 12/1/1862, b. NC, res. Letcher Co. 1870 & 1880, sons Caloway, Jacob & James res. Johnson Co. 1900, m. Matilda Privett (b. 1820).

HALL, HUGH: (9/5/1832 – 6/10/1899), Co. K, enl. Lee Co., VA 8/18/1863, aka Jehu Hall, pres. Lee Co., VA 12/31/1863, res. Lee Co. VA 1850, res. Claiborne Co., TN 1860, s. of William & Mary Hall, res. Claborne Co., TN 1870, res. Jefferson Co., TN 1880, m. Eliza Nunn (1838-1922), bur. Touchet Cem., Touchet, Walla Walla Co., WA.

HALL, JAMES "STIFF JIM": (3/28/1821 – 10/4/1898), Co. F, enl. Floyd Co., KY 10/14/1862, res. Floyd Co. 1860, s. of William & Margaret (Johnson) Hall, m. (1) Emma Vance 1838, (2) Nancy Davis (1834-aft 1900) 1853, bur. Wilburn Hall Cem., Kite, Knott Co., KY.

HALL, JAMES PRESTON: (3/16/1836 – 6/2/1925), Co. D, enl. Whitesburg, KY 10/4/1862, res. Wise Co., VA 1860, b. Russell Co., VA, s. of Isham & Jane (Mullins) Hall, res. Magoffin Co. 1870, 1880 & 1900, m. Eliza Jane "Louisa" Hall (1834-1930) Letcher Co. 1856, bur. Marion Conley Cem., Minefork, Magoffin Co., KY.

HALL, JOHN: (1832 – 1887), Co. F, enl. Floyd Co. 10/14/1862, pres. fall/1863, res. Letcher Co. 1850, res. Floyd Co. 1860, s. of Randall & Kate (Johnson) Hall, res. Floyd Co. 1870, res. Letcher Co. 1880, m. Margaret King (1832-aft. 1900 Letcher Co.), bur. Hall Cem., Shelby Fk., Deane, Letcher Co., KY.

HALL, JOHN: (3/10/1839 – 5/5/1893), Co. K, enl. Lee Co. VA 8/18/1863, pres. Lee Co. 12/31/1863, res. Harlan Co., KY 1850, res. Lee Co., VA 1860, b. Lynch, KY, s. of Preston & Anne Hall, res. Leslie Co. (Bad Creek) 1880, m. Jane Hall (1832-1916 d.c. #11132), bur. Hall Cem., Asher, Leslie Co., KY.

HALL, JOHN (C.): (1846 – 1890), Co. E, enl. Whitesburg, KY 10/5/1862, res. Letcher Co as John W. Hall 1850, s. of Alexander & Susan Hall, res. Letcher Co. 1880, m. Darcas (Hall) Bentley, widow of Lt. Aaron Bentley (1844-1918), bur. Bates Cem., Beaver Dam, Letcher Co. KY.

HALL, JOHN H.: (3/6/1840 – 12/14/1901), Co. E, enl. 10/5/1862, 5' 8", dark hair, hazel eyes, capt. Letcher Co. 5/18/1864, to Louisville Prison 6/7/1864, rel. on oath 7/1/1864, res. Floyd Co. 1860, s. of James & Emma (Vance) Hall, m. (1) Sarah Johnson (1840-1871) 1859, (2) Lucy Burke (1844-1929 Hartley, Pike Co. KY), bur. Wilburn Hall Cem., Kite, Knott Co. KY.

HALL, JOHN HIRAM "SON": (b. 3/15/1843) Co. E, enl. 8/8/1863, serv. prev. 5th KY Inf. (re: pension), capt. Louisa, KY w/ part of Co. E 1864, to Louisville Prison, paroled on oath, told to stay north of the Ohio River, remained in Ohio for one year, res. Letcher Co. 1860, b. Lee Co., VA, s. of Hiram Sr. & Lucy (Delph) Hall, res. Letcher Co. (poss. Camp Branch nr. P.O.) 1870, rec. Confed. Pension #3976 Letcher Co. 1920, m. Carnelia Hall (1850-bef. 1920) 1869.

HALL, JOHN L. (LAYTON): (1836 – 1864), Co. E, enl. Whitesburg, KY 10/5/1862, killed mo. of Nealy Branch of Carr (then Letcher Co.) fall/1864, res. Floyd Co., s. of David & Anna (Johnson) Hall, bur. William D. Hall Cem., Kite, Knott Co., KY.

HALL, JOHN WASH: (4/18/1829 – 10/28/1915), Co. E, enl. 10/23/1862 Whitesburg, KY, pres. Apr. 1863, res. Floyd Co., s. of William & Margaret (Johnson) Hall, widow applied Confed. Pension 1917, m. Lucinda Hall (1839-1909), bur. Little Cem., Wheelwright, Floyd Co., KY.

HALL, JONATHAN J.: (3/13/1833 – 6/12/1916), Co. A, serv. prev. 5th KY Inf., Co. F, pension states he serv. 5th KY Inf., Co. F and 13th KY Cav., Co. A, that he was disc. in Letcher Co. 1864, & was paroled on 6/3/1865, res. Letcher Co. 1860, b. Floyd Co., s. of Jonathan & Lucinda (Justice) Hall, rec. KY Confed. Pension #675 & #3650 Knott Co. 1912, deacon in Mallett Fork Old Regular Baptist Church, m. Mary "Polly" Cook (1834-1920) 1850, d. Pinetop, bur. Watts-Cook Cem., Pinetop, Knott Co., KY.

HALL, JOSEPH: (3/27/1848 – 3/1/1929), Co. I, enl. Whitesburg, KY 6/1/1863, capt. Gladeville, VA 7/7/1863, to Kemper Barracks 7/18/1863, to Camp Chase Prison 7/20/1863, to Camp Douglas Prison 8/24/1863, exch. Point Lookout 3/14/1865, surr. Danville, VA 4/1865, res. Perry Co., s. of Ezekiel & Cloey (Branson) Hall, rec. KY Confed. Pension #676 Knott Co. (Richie) 1912, m. Mary "Polly" Richie (1855-1930 Covington, Kenton Co. KY) 1872, bur. Ritchie Cem., Fisty, Knott Co., KY.

HALL, LEE: (1838 – 8/10/1864), 2nd Sgt., Co. E, enl. Whitesburg, KY 10/5/1862, prom. Sgt. 4/30/1863, capt. Floyd Co. 11/7/1863, to Louisville Prison 11/18/1863, to Camp Morton 11/21/1863, d. from typhoid fever, res. Floyd Co. 1860, s. of William & Margaret (Johnson) Hall, m. Margaret (b. 1843), bur. Crown Hill Cem., Indianapolis, Marion Co., IN.

HALL, LEWIS: (1844 – 3/28/1865), Co. E, enl. May 1863, "pressed into serv.", capt. Floyd Co. 11/7/1863, to Camp Morton, died of "diarrhea", bur. Crown Hill Cem., Indianapolis, Marion Co., IN, s. of Alfred & Temperence Hall; Confed. mem. marker Francisco Cem., Ashcamp, Pike Co., KY.

HALL, MARSHALL: (1842 – 1864), Co. E, enl. Whitesburg, KY 10/5/1862, rec. clothing 9/1/1864, k. mo. Nealy Branch of Carr, fall/1864 (re: Letcher Co. Family History & The Hall Book), res. Floyd Co., s. of David & Anna (Johnson) Hall, m. Eliza Bates (b. 1836), bur. William D. Hall Cem., Kite, Knott Co., KY.

HALL, MILES: (1835 – 6/15/1885), 2nd. Lt., Co. E, enl. Whitesburg, KY 10/5/1862, resigned 6/8/1863 w/ chronic rheumatism, res. Floyd Co. 1860, s. of William & Margaret (Johnson) Hall, res, Knott Co. (Beaver, w/ son, Joseph), m. Frances Jane (1830-1900), bur. Moore Cem., Topmost, Knott Co., KY.

HALL, REUBEN: (5/1823 – bef. 1910), 1st Cpl., Co. E, enl. Whitesburg, KY 10/5/1862, appointed 1st Cpl 4/30/1863, res. Letcher Co. 1860, s. of Jonathan & Susannah (Elliott) Hall, res. Letcher Co. 1880, res. Letcher Co. (Millstone) 1900, m. Nancy Hall (b. 1828), d. Letcher Co.

HALL, RICHARD: (1843 – 1885), Co. E, enl. Whitesburg, KY 8/1/1863, res. Letcher Co. 1860, s. of Richard & Elizabeth (Wright) Hall, m. (1) Elender, (2) Polly Bryant (1846-1918) 1867, bur. Hall Cem., Fleming, Letcher Co., KY.

HALL, RILEY: (5/13/1824 – 2/24/1911), Co. B, enl. Floyd Co. (Middle Creek) 9/12/1862, 5' 8", dark hair, blue eyes, serv. prev. 5th KY Inf., Co. E, capt. Floyd Co. by Brig. Gen. White, to Louisville Prison, rel. on oath 5/1863, res. Pike Co. 1850, res. Floyd Co. 1860, m. Lucinda Cook (1826-bef. 1910), bur. Robert George Cem., Bays Branch, Floyd Co., KY.

HALL, RILEY: (12/25/1834 – 5/20/1879), Co. E, enl. Whitesburg, KY 10/5/1862, res. Floyd Co. 1860, s. of Riley W. & Jane "Jennie" (Cook) Hall, m. Hannah Justice (b. 1834) Floyd Co. 1855, bur. Limestone Cem., Lawton, Carter Co., KY.

HALL, TALTON "TALT": (1850 – 9/2/1892), Co. B, listed as T. L. Hall on s.r., record misfiled with 10th KY Cav., wd. & capt. On 6/11/1864 at Mt. Sterling, taken to U. S. hosp. at Lexington on 6/12/1864, gunshot wd., right side, ordered to be sent home, age 15, on 7/12/1864; res. Floyd Co. 1850, s. of David Hall & Anna (Johnson) Hall, m. Miranda Triplett (b. 1846) 1868, bur. Wright Cem., Dunham, Letcher Co., KY.

HALL, THOMAS: (12/24/1840 – 6/9/1917), Co. D, enl. Whitesburg, KY 10/4/1862, rejoined from desertion 1/1/1863 & 8/1/1863, later serv. in Union 39th KY., Co. K (9/30/1863-9/15/1865), res. Letcher Co. 1860, s. of Reuben Hall & Mahalia (Bentley) Hall, m. Martha Patricia Whitaker (1840-1929) 1861, bur. Polly Cem., Ermine, Letcher Co., KY.

HALL, WILEY: (b.1838), Co. H, enl. & disc. Whitesburg, KY 10/18/1862, res. Letcher Co. 1860, s. of James & Sarah (Johnson) Hall, res. Letcher Co. 1870, res. Logan Co., WV 1880, m. Sarah Cox. (b. 1840), d. apparently Logan Co., WV after 1900.

HALL, WILLIAM J. "BOLEN BILL": (5/11/1826 – 7/28/1912), Capt., Co. E, enl. Whitesburg, KY 10/23/1862, prom. Sgt. 4/1863, soon elected Capt. to replace Archelous Hammonds, led Co. E in heavy fighting against Lt. Clabe Jones & 14th KY Cav., Letcher Co., spring/1863, serv. until end of war, res. Floyd Co. 1860, s. of William & Margaret (Johnson) Hall, m. Florence Jones (1826-1908) 1850, bur. Hall Cem., Kite, Knott Co., KY.

HALL, WILLIAM J. "JR.": (4/28/1846 – 12/12/1921), Co. E, res. Floyd Co., KY 1860, b. Floyd Co., s. of James & Emma (Vance) Hall, rec. KY Confed. Pension #1372 Knott Co. 1912, widow rec. KY Confed. Widow's Pension #4141 Knott Co. 1922, m. Ritter Bowling (1846-aft. 1922) Letcher Co. 1865, bur. Blue Branch of Jack's Creek, Kite, Knott Co., KY.

HAMBLIN, CHAMP: (6/17/1831 – 4/13/1905), 1st. Lt., Co. K, enl. VA 12/31/1863, appointed 1st Lt. 11/1864, pres. 3/1865, surr. Cumberland Gap 4/30/1865, res. Lee Co., VA 1860, s. of John & Elizabeth Hamblin, m. Jane Sullivan (1842-1922), bur. Hamblin Cem., Ben Hur, Lee Co., VA.

HAMBLIN, GEORGE: (b. 1825), Co. K, enl. Lee Co., VA 8/18/1863, pres. Lee Co. 12/31/1863, res. Knox Co. 1850, res. Harrison, Mercer Co., MO 1870, m. Nancy (b. 1826).

HAMMONS, ARCHELOUS "CHEED": (12/1833 – 1908), Capt., Co. E, enl. Whitesburg, KY 10/5/1862, serv. prev. 5th KY Inf., Co. G, resigned and succeeded by Capt. William J. Hall spring/1863, res. Floyd Co. 1860, s. of William & Sarah (Craft) Hammons, res. Greenbriar Co. (Falling Spring), WV 1870, 1880 & 1900, m. (1) Manerva England (1834-ca.1864), (2) Olivia "Ollie" J. Roberts (1837-aft. 1900) Wyoming Co., WV 1865, bur. Hammons Cem. Falling Spring, Greenbriar Co., WV.

HAMMONS, EPHRIAM THOMAS: (2/14/1831 – 9/10/1916), Co. D, enl. Whitesburg, KY 10/4/1862, res. Letcher Co., s. of Ephriam & Lydia (Adams) Hammons, res. Letcher Co. 1870, 1880 & 1900, res. Knott Co. 1910, m. Drucilla Craft (1826-1930), d.c. #23645, bur. Hale Cem., Bath, Knott Co., KY.

HAMPTON, ABEL: (1/6/1838 – 5/15/1916), Co. D, enl. Whitesburg, KY 10/4/1862, pres. summer/1863, res. Letcher Co. (Millstone) 1860, s. of Joseph & Susannah (Caudill) Hampton, res. Magoffin Co. 1870 & 1880, res. Menifee Co. 1900 & 1910, m. Mary C. Adams (1840-1923) 1856, bur. Back Cem., Dan, Menifee Co., KY.

HAMPTON, JOHN S.: 1st. Cpl., Co. A, enl. Whitesburg, KY 11/1/1862, serv. prev. 5th KY Inf., Co. F, rec. clothing 11/19/1864, res. Letcher Co. 1860, b. 10/30/1838, s. of Wilburn & Phoebe (Caudill) Hampton, m. Mary E. Estep (1842-1920) 1865, d. 12/24/1914, bur. Hampton Cem., Oscaloosa, Letcher Co., KY.

HAMPTON, NELSON: (3/23/1830 – 1907), Co. D, enl. Whitesburg, KY 10/4/1862, pres. summer/1863, res. Letcher Co. 1860, s. of Turner & Mary (Profitt) Hampton, res. Magoffin Co. 1870, res. Wolfe Co. (Hazel Green) 1900, m. Rachel Adams (1838-1914) 1856, bur. Hampton Cem., Trent, Wolfe Co., KY.

HAMPTON, SOLOMON M.: (1833 – 1879), Co. H, enl. Whitesburg, KY 10/18/1862, pres. spring/1863, res. Letcher Co. 1860, s. of Turner & Mary (Profitt) Hampton, widow res Letcher Co. 1890, claimed service until 1865 on Special Census, widow rec. KY Confed. Widow's Pension #683 Letcher Co. 1912, m. Margaret "Peggy" Maggard (1837-aft. 1880) Letcher Co., bur. Rich Whitaker Cem., Letcher, Letcher Co., KY.

HAMPTON, SOLOMON M.: (2/12/1841 – 12/3/1883), 3rd Cpl., Co. B, enl. Whitesburg, KY 9/9/1862, rec. clothing 9/7/1864, paroled Cumberland Gap 5/2/1865, res. Letcher Co. 1860, s. of Wilburn & Phoebe (Caudill) Hampton, m. Athalyle Caudill 1865, bur. Rich Whitaker Cem., Letcher, Letcher Co., KY.

HANDSHOE, ADAM: (1842 – late 1800's), Co. F, enl. Floyd Co. 10/14/1862, reportedly joined Union Army 11/18/1862, rejoined Confed. 13th KY 8/24/1863, res. Floyd Co. 1860, s. of Harrison & Eva (Prater) Handshoe, res. Greenup Co. 1870, res. Boyd Co. 1880, moved to TX & changed name to Hanshaw, widow on 1900 census, m. Margaret (b. 1844), d. Spring Mt., TX, poss. bur. Mt. Olive Cem.

HANDSHOE, ANDREW: (10/15/1833 – 8/24/1907), Co. F, enl. Floyd Co. 10/14/1862, res. Floyd Co. 1860, s. of Harrison & Eva (Prater) Handshoe, res. Greenup Co. 1870 & 1880, moved to TX & changed name to Hanshaw, moved to Araphoe, Custer Co, OK by 1892, m. Susan Bradley (b. 1836), d. Clinton, Custer Co., OK.

HANEY, WILLIAM T.: (1/3/1838 – 7/24/1904), Co. A, enl. 5th KY Inf, Co. F Jeffersonville, VA 6/1/1862, des. 10/10/1862, ret. serv., absent w/ leave 12/1862, res. Morgan Co. 1860, res. Letcher Co. 1890, m. (1) Nancy Gilley, Letcher Co. 1876, (2) Nancy (1847-1920 Letcher Co.), bur. Horse Mill Point Cem., Jeremiah, Letcher Co., KY.

HARRIS, JOHN: (b. 1838), 1st Sgt., Co. E, enl. Whitesburg, KY 10/25/1862, appointed 1st Sgt. 4/3/1863, res. Letcher Co. 1850, res. Floyd Co. (Prestonsburg) 1860, b. VA, s. of Jacob & Jonea Harris.

HARRIS, SQUIRE: (b. 1834), Co. E, enl. Whitesburg, KY 10/5/1862, res. Letcher Co. 1850, res. Floyd Co. 1860, b. Russell Co. VA, s. of Jacob & Jonea Harris, res. Lawrence Co. (Louisa) 1870, m. Nancy Bentley (b. 1832) Letcher Co. 1855.

HART, JAMES H.: (1818 – 1/1873), Co. A, serv. prev. 5th KY Inf., Co. F, one report stated "right arm shot off", capt. Gladeville, VA 7/7/1863, to Kemper Barracks 7/18/1863, to Camp Chase Prison 7/20/1863, to Camp Douglas Prison 8/24/1863, exch. Point Lookout 2/24/1865, res. Letcher Co. 1860, b. NC, res. Letcher Co. 1867, res. Perry Co. (McIntosh) 1870, m. Jane Jones (1822-1917) 1840, bur. Pace Cem., Wooton, Leslie Co., KY.

HART, WILLIAM: (1840 – 1/17/1865), Co. I, serv. prev. 5th KY Inf., Co. H, capt Perry Co. 5/17/1863, to Johnson's Island Prison, to Point Lookout Prison, res. Bath Co. 1860, s. of Samuel & Nancy Hart, bur. Point Lookout Prison Cem., Point Lookout, St. Mary's Co., MD.

HARVEY, BENJAMIN: (5/6/1837 – 6/22/1928), 2nd Sgt., Co. G, enl. Breathitt Co., KY 10/18/1862, serv. later in Union 14th KY, Co. K, res. Breathitt Co., s. of William & Elizabeth Harvey, res. Breathitt Co. 1870, res. Putnam Co. WV 1880, res. Breathitt Co. 1900, res. Wayne Co., WV 1901, d. Perry Co. (Hiner), obituary in Hazard Herald, has Union headstone w/o dates, m. (1) Sarah Clemons (1839-ca. 1861) 1856, (2) Mary (1841-aft. 1900) 1862, bur. Harvey Bend Cem. #1, Harvey Bend, Breathitt Co., KY.

HARVEY, JOHN: (4/22/1833 – 12/8/1910), Co. G, enl. Breathitt Co. 9/23/1862, enl. Union 45th KY, Co. D 10/29/1863, res. Breathitt Co. (HH William & Elizabeth Harvey) 1860, res. Magoffin Co. 1870, 1880 & 1900, m. (1) Catherine Risner (1832-1907), bur. Berry Patrick Cem., Hendricks, Magoffin Co., KY.

HARVEY, SAMUEL: (b. 1834), Co. G, enl. Breathitt Co. KY 9/23/1862, des. Breathitt Co. 12/8/1864, res. Breathitt Co. 1860, s. of Andrew & Sarah Harvey, res. Breathitt Co. 1870, res. Lincoln Co. WV 1880, res. Cabel Co. WV (HH C. Means) 1910, m. Nancy Richie (1835-bef. 1900) 1853.

HARVEY, SIMON "SILAS": (1836 – 1888), Kash's Co., indicted post-war for 1865 murder as member this Co., res. Breathitt Co. 1860, s. of Andrew & Sarah Harvey, res. Breathitt Co. (Jackson) 1870 & 1880, m. Deborah Fields (1842-aft. 1900), bur. Cardwell Cem., Jackson, Breathitt Co., KY.

HARVEY, WESLEY: (6/3/1832 – 1864), Co. G, enl. Breathitt Co., KY 9/23/1862, serv. later Union 14th KY, Co. K, mustered out 3/1864, shot by Union Capt. Bill Strong's men, res. Breathitt Co. 1860, s. of Andrew & Sarah Harvey, m. Martha Jane Bingham (1832-aft. 1880) 1851, bur. Big Andy Noble Cem., Noble, Breathitt Co., KY.

HATTON, HIRAM FRANKLIN: (12/17/1816 – 1888), Co. A, enl. Whitesburg, KY 11/1/1862, paid 6/30/1863, pres. 12/1863, capt. Troublesome Creek 6/10/1864, to Lexington, to Louisville Prison 6/22/1864, to Rock Island Prison 6/24/1864, joined Union Army 10/17/1864, res. Powell Co., b. Montgomery Co., s. of Ephriam & Susannah (Howard) Hatton, m. Susan Louanna Howard (1824-aft. 1880) 1843, bur. Hatton Creek Cem., Stanton, Powell Co., KY.

HAYES, (RICHARD A.) EPPERSON: (5/29/1843 – 3/15/1925), Co. F, enl. Floyd Co. 10/14/1862, 5' 10", brown hair, blue eyes, serv. prev. 5th KY Inf., Co. E, capt Floyd Co. 11/19/1863, to Louisville Prison 12/17/1863, rel. on oath 12/19/1863, res. Floyd Co. 1850 & 1860, s. of Daniel & Mary Hayes, m. Catherine (1847-1908), bur. Hezekiah Hayes Cem., Langley, Floyd Co., KY.

HAYES, JOHN "BUD": (9/26/1845 – 12/7/1924), Co. D, enl. Whitesburg, KY 12/1/1862, also serv. 10th KY, Co. F (re: pension), reported sick w/ measles, surr. Mt. Sterling, KY 4/30/1865, res. Floyd Co. 1860, s. of Daniel & Mary Hayes, res. Floyd Co. 1870, 1880, 1900, 1910 (w/ dau. Catherine), & 1920 (w/ g.d. Edna Newsome), rec. KY Confed. Pension #4210 Floyd Co. (Langley), m. Susan (1854-bef. 1910), bur. Hezekiah Hayes Cem., Langley, Floyd Co., KY.

HAYES, SYLVESTER: (6/1847 – 5/13/1903), Co. C, enl. Whitesburg, KY 10/1/1862, capt. Gladeville, VA 7/7/1863, res. Floyd Co. 1850, s. of John & Mahalia Hayes, m. (1) Anna Martin, (2) Susannah Allen (1862-1919) 1882, bur. Allen Cem., Hueysville, Floyd Co., KY.

HAYS, ANDERSON: (6/10/1820 – 12/24/1909), Capt., Co. C, enl. Whitesburg, KY 10/1/1862, skirmished w/ Union 14th KY Cav. & Lt. Clabe Jones, Perry Co. (mo. Lotts Creek), spring/1863, capt. Gladeville, VA 7/7/1863, to Kemper Barracks 7/18/1863, to Camp Chase Prison 7/20/1863, to Johnson's Island Prison 10/10/1863, to Fortress Monroe Prison 10/6/1864, to Point Lookout Prison 10/11/1864, suffered from chronic diarrhea, exchanged, res. Breathitt Co. 1860, b. Floyd Co., s. of John & Elizabeth Hays, m. Rachel Sizemore (1822-1892) 1839, bur. Hays Cem., Hindman, Knott Co., KY.

HAYS, GEORGE: (5/10/1848 – 3/3/1916), Co. C, claimed enl. 6/1863 in Breathitt Co. in two 13th KY Confed. Pensions, sworn in by G. W. Noble, serv. as recruiting officer and was on Gen. Morgan's 1864 raid cut off at Battle of Mt. Sterling, joined Noble & went south 10/1864, rejoined Co. C at Whitesburg 2/1865, disbanded Gladeville, VA 4/1865, s. of Capt. Anderson Hays, res. of Breathitt Co. 1860, m. Sally Everage (1852-1934), bur. in Hays Cem., Hindman, Knott Co., KY.

HAYS, JAMES: (2/22/1842 – 4/15/1915), Co. C, enl. Whitesburg, KY 10/1/1862, capt Gladeville, VA 7/7/1863, to Kemper Barracks 7/18/1863, to Camp Chase Prison 7/20/1863, to Camp Douglas Prison 8/24/1863, exch. Point Lookout 2/24/1865, in hosp. Richmond, VA 3/24/1865, res. Breathitt Co. 1860, s. of Capt. Anderson & Rachel (Sizemore) Hays, m. Matilda McDaniel 1872, bur. Hays Cem., Hindman, Knott Co., KY.

HELMS, JOHN: (1825 – 1863), Co. I, conscripted Whitesburg, KY 10/18/1862, pres. summer/1863, res. Perry Co. 1860, b. Ireland, m. Malinda (b. 1830), bur. Sandlick Cem., Whitesburg, Letcher Co., KY.

HENDERSON, HANNIBAL: Co. K, enl. Lee Co., VA 8/1863, pres. Lee Co. 12/31/1863.

HENSON, PAUL: (1838 – 4/16/1865), Co. D, enl. Whitesburg, KY 10/4/1862, pres. 4/26/1863, capt. Pike Co. 12/11/1863, to Rock Island Prison, rel. upon joining U.S. 3rd Vol. Inf., Co. A 10/13/1864, d. Mt. Torrence or Mt. Faranee, KS, res. Pike Co. 1860, widow rec. Union Pension & claimed service in 39th VA Cav., m. Mary "Polly" Stewart (b. 1841) Letcher Co. 1856.

HENSON, WILLIAM H: (7/1836 – 1921), Co. D, enl. Whitesburg, KY 10/4/1862, res. Floyd Co. 1860, res. Floyd (nr. Melvin) 1900, res. Floyd Co. 1910, m. Dorcas Bentley (1838-aft. 1920) Letcher Co. 1856, bur. Elliott Cem., Beaver, Floyd Co., KY.

HERD, JAMES: (1830 – 1899), Capt. Co. K, pre-war Clay Co. Sheriff, Hector's Creek & Manchester landowner during war, enl. as Pvt. 5th KY Inf., Co. B Jonesville, VA 5/25/1863, serv. as recruiter, enl. 13th KY Cav. Lee Co., VA 8/4/1863, reported 30 serviceable horses 11/20/1863, detached serv. w/ 64th VA Inf. 11/24/1863 to 12/4/1863, elected Capt. Lee Co., VA 12/31/1863, AWOL 12/10/1864 to 1/6/1865, dropped from roll 2/16/1865, reinstated, signed furlough request for Elijah Begley Lee Co, VA 2/28/1865, surr. Cumberland Gap 4/30/1865, res. Clay Co. 1860, s. of Elijah & Elizabeth (Shootman) Herd, res. Washington Co. (Goodson) 1870 & 1880, ret. Clay Co. & remarried 1892, m. (1) Martha Wilson (1830-aft. 1880) 1851, (2) Amanda Johnson Lucas (1860-aft. 1910) 1894, bur. Herd Cem., Manchester, Clay Co., KY.

HEREFORD, JAMES H.: (12/12/1796 – 2/9/1885), Co. K, serv. prev. Union 39th KY Inf. as Maj. & surgeon, dismissed for unclean hosp. 12/31/1863, soon joined Confed. Cav. w/ son, listed as nurse on detached serv., on clothing receipt 9/24/1864, res. Floyd Co. 1860, s. of John & Elizabeth (Patterson) Hereford, m. (1) Cynthia (1806-1839), (2) Meriba Ratliff (1816-1903), has Union marker, bur. Hereford Cem., Prestonsburg, Floyd Co., KY.

HEREFORD JR., JAMES H.: (5/22/1841 – 11/17/1898), Co. K, serv. prev. 5th KY Inf. Co. E, rec. clothing 9/24/1864, res. Floyd Co. 1860, b. Pike Co., s. of James H. Sr. & Meriba (Ratliff) Hereford, widow rec. KY Confed Widow's Pension #4520 Floyd Co. 1928, m. Mary Florence May (1852-1936) 1869, bur. Hereford Cem., Prestonsburg, Floyd Co., KY.

HICKS, CHARLES "CHARLEY": (2/1842 – 1/10/1901), Co. C, enl. Whitesburg, KY 10/1/1862, shot in the back by Clabe Jones, res. Perry Co. 1860, s. of Charles & Rebecca Hicks, res. Perry Co. (Troublesome) 1870 & 1880, res. Knott Co. 1890 & 1900, m. Mary "Polly" Conley (1842-aft. 1900), bur. Hicks Cem., Softshell, Knott Co., KY.

HICKS, ELIJAH: (6/3/1842 – 11/15/1920), Cos. A & C, serv. prev. 5th KY Inf., Co. F, enl. 13th KY, Co. A, trans. from Co. A to Co. C 10/1/1862, pres. fall/1863, may have operated as a guerilla known as "Capt. Elijah Hicks", surr. nr. Appomatox, VA 4/1865, took oath Lebanon, VA 5/1865, told family "Reckon I killed enough", res. Perry Co. 1860, b. Russell Co., VA, s. of Clabe & Susan Hicks, post-war minister, moved to Rowan Co. for rest of his life, m. Elizabeth Hicks (1840-1907) Breathitt Co. 1862, bur. Eagle Hall Cem., Soldier, Carter Co., KY.

HICKS, HARRISON: (2//171841 – 11/25/1910), Co. I, conscripted Whitesburg, KY 10/18/1862, pres. 2/5/1863, enl. Union 39th KY, Co. F 6/27/1863, res. Perry Co. 1860, s. of Clabourn & Vicy (Sadler) Hicks, res. McDowell Co. (Bradshaw) WV. 1900 & 1910, m. Lilly Harris (1843-1925), bur. in Cole Cem., War, McDowell Co. WVA.

HICKS, JESSE: (4/23/1843 – 11/5/1933), Co. I, conscripted Whitesburg, KY 10/18/1862, pres. 5/10/1863, enl. Union 39th KY, Co. F 6/18/1863, serv. w/ Clabe Jones, reportedly stole a Confed. cannon to gain support of the Union, res. Perry Co. 1860, s. of Clabourn & Vicy (Sadler) Hicks, lived Carter Co. for 27 years, res. 1212 Wade St. (Ashland) 5/1/1931, m. Pearlee (1849-1930 to 1933), Floyd Co. 1865, d.c. #25307, bur. Summit Cem., Summit, Boyd Co., KY.

HICKS, JOHN: (1830 – 1879), Co. C, enl. Whitesburg, KY 10/1/1862, res. Perry Co. 1860, s. of Clabe & Susan Hicks, res. Perry Co. (Troublesome) 1870, widow res. Perry Co. 1880, m. Betsy Casebolt (1840-aft. 1880).

HOGG, GEORGE: (2/22/1844 – 11/25/1924), Capt., Co. B, serv. prev. 5th KY Inf., Co. F, 5' 10 ½" light complexion, dark hair, hazel eyes, capt. Gladeville, VA 7/7/1863, to Kemper Barracks 7/18/1863, to Camp Chase Prison 7/20/1863, to Johnson's Island Prison 10/10/1863, to Ft. Delaware Prison, rel. on oath 6/12/1865, res. Letcher Co. 1860, s. of Stephen & Sintha (Ison) Hogg, moved to TX 1870, moved to Monahans, TX 1905, rec. TX Confed. Pension #20704 & #40713 Ward Co., TX, d. Howard Co. (Big Springs) TX, m. Dicy Trent (1860-1938) 1883, bur. Monahans Memorial Cem., Monahans, Ward Co., TX.

HOGG, HIRAM H (11/15/1833 – 8/29/1916), Co. H, enl. Whitesburg, KY 10/18/1862, rec. clothing 11/19/1864, res. Letcher Co. (tanner) 1860, s. of Hiram & Lavinia (Polly) Hogg, moved post-war Coles Co. IL & Effrugham Co. IL, then Booneville, KY 1870, res. Owsley Co. 1890, claimed he was Capt. Co. K, claimed service until 12/1864 (re: Confed Pension #2783), m. Virginia Snyder (1845-1922) 1859, bur. Booneville Cem., Booneville, Owsley Co., KY.

HOGG, HIRAM WESLEY (1840 – 9/22/1863), 2nd. Sgt., Co. H, enl. Whitesburg, KY 9/2/1862, serv. prev. 5th KY Inf., Co. F, KIA Blountville, TN 9/22/1863, res. Letcher Co. 1860, s. of Kelly & Mary (Ison) Hogg, m. Margaret Brashear 1861, bur. Blountville Cem., Blountville, Sullivan Co., TN.

HOGG, JOHN T.: (8/19/1836 - 11/9/1890) Kash's Co., indicted post-war for 1865 murder as member this Co., res. Harrison Co. 1860, s. of Thomas & Clarissa Hogg, m. Georgia Graves (1843-1929), serv. also in 2nd Mtd. Inf. Co. F, Capt. Kash's wife was from Harrison Co., bur. in Battle Grove Cem., Cynthiana, Harrison Co., KY.

HOGG, STEPHEN: (9/28/1845 – 10/12/1923), Co. B, enl. Whitesburg, KY 9/9/1862, serv. prev. 5th KY Inf., Co. B, pres. summer/1863, res. Letcher Co. 1860, s. of Kelly & Mary (Ison) Hogg, res. Letcher Co. 1890, claimed serv. through 4/1865 (re: Special Veterans Census), rec. KY Confed. Pension #1734 Letcher Co. 1912, m. (1) Millie Stamper (1847-1888) 1864, (2) Larcena Mitchell, bur. Hogg Cem., Roxanna, Letcher Co., KY.

HOLBROOK, JESSE S.: (2/6/1837 – 2/9/1909), Co. D, enl. Whitesburg, KY 10/4/1862, rec. clothing 4/7/1864, res. Letcher Co. 1860, s. of Benjamin & Nancy (Jenkins) Holbrook, res. Letcher Co. 1870, had land surveyed on Barn Br. (Rt. Fork of Millstone) 1883, m. Elizabeth Adams (1848-aft. 1880), bur. Uncle Chunk Craft Cem., Millstone, Letcher Co., KY.

HOLBROOK, RANDOLPH H.: (10/10/1829 - 8/26/1895), Co. D, enl. Whitesburg, KY 10/4/1862, pres. spring/1863, served until close of war, res. Letcher Co. 1860, s. of Ben & Nancy (Jenkins) Holbrook, widow rec. KY Confed. Pension #3898 Letcher Co. (Belvia) 1919, m. Jennie Webb (1831-aft. 1920 Jenkins, KY) Letcher Co. (Bottom Fork) 1848, bur. Webb Cem., Mayking, Letcher Co., KY

HOLBROOK, RANSOM T.: (3/21/1846 – 3/1/1894), Co. D, enl. Whitesburg, KY 10/4/1862, 5' 6", dark hair, hazel eyes, capt. Letcher Co. 4/9/1864, to Louisville Prison, rel. on oath 4/21/1864, res. Letcher Co. 1860, s. of William & Sarah (Adams) Holbrook, m. Elizabeth Ann Hughes (1850-1917) 1866, bur. Ransom Holbrook Cem., Mayking, Letcher Co., KY.

HOLLIDAY, JOHN: (4/12/1843 – 4/12/1893), 3rd Cpl., Co. I, conscripted Whitesburg, KY 10/18/1862, also serv. Union 14th Cav., Co. L 12/16/1862 to 3/24/1864, res. Perry Co. 1860, s. of Tolbert & Rachel (Napier) Holliday, m. Arra Begley (1838-1901), bur. Holliday Cem., Ary, Perry Co., KY.

HOLLIDAY, WILLIAM: (7/10/1824 – 11/1886), Co. I, conscripted Whitesburg, KY 10/18/1862, pres. 5/10/1863, res. Perry Co. 1860, s. of John H. & Alley (Justice) Holliday, m. (1) Polly Sizemore (1828-1869), (2) Peggy Conway (1830-1886) 1870, bur. Holliday Cem., Ary, Perry Co., KY.

HOPE, ROBERT A.: (5/1843 – 6/14/1920), 1st. Lt., Adjt., serv. prev. 5th KY Inf., Co. H, 5' 9", grey eyes, dark hair, prom. Sgt. Major & later 1st Lt. & Adjt, capt. Gladeville, VA 7/7/1863, to Kemper Barracks 7/18/1863, to Johnson's Island Prison 10/10/1863, to Point Lookout Prison 3/21/1865, to Ft. Delaware Prison & released on oath 6/12/1865, res. Bath Co., res. Woodford Co. 1850, s. of William R. Hope, a merchant in Atchinson Co., MO by 1870, traveling salesman in Chicago 1880, res. Douglas Co., NE 1900, salesman for glove factory Spirit Lake, IA, m. Fannie Stitt (1850-1924), bur. Lake View Cem., Spirit Lake, Dickenson Co., IA.

HOUCK, GEORGE W. (12/27/1841 – 4/15/1901), 1st Lt., Co. I, serv. prev. 5th KY Inf., Co. I, grey eyes, light hair, light complexion, capt. Carter Co., KY 11/15/1862, to Louisville Prison, to Vicksburg, MS & exch 11/29/1862, enl. Whitesburg, KY 2/11/1863, on 13th roster Washington Co., VA 1/6/1865, led raid on guerillas Johnson Co. 4/9/1865, seriously wounded three times, remained crippled for life, res. Pike Co. 1850, res. Carter Co. 1860, b. Ashe Co., NC, s. of Jesse Houck, moved TX 1868, widow rec. TX Confed. Widows Pension #26563, m. Laura L. (1848-1928), bur. Buffalo Cem., Buffalo, Leon Co., TX.

HOUNSHELL, HARVEY W: (7/13/1843 – 12/17/1924), Kash's Co., serv. prev. 5th KY Inf., Co. I & 10th KY Cav., Co. E, separated from 10th & joined Kash's Co., 13th KY Cav. 9/1/1864, surr. Louisa 5/9/1865, res. Breathitt Co. 1860, b. Lee Co., VA, s. of Andrew & Lavinia (Bryan) Hounshell, m. Minerva Jane Back (1856-1920), bur. Lazarus Back Cem., Noctor, Breathitt Co., KY.

HOUNSHELL, MARTIN VAN BUREN: (7/17/1837 – 2/8/1918), Co. D, enl. Whitesburg, KY 10/4/1862, pres. spring/1863, res. Lee Co., VA 1850 & 1860, s. of Joseph & Sarah Hounshell, moved to Brown Co., TX by 1900, m. Mary Abigail VanHuss (1849-1939) Lee Co., VA 1873, bur. Smith Cem., Cross Cut, Brown Co., TX.

HOWARD, CHADWELL G.: (3/22/1839 – 5/24/1890), Co. K, surr. Cumberland Gap 4/30/1865, res. Harlan Co. 1860, s. of Samuel & Betsy (Brittain) Howard, m. Elizabeth (b. 1839), bur. Joseph Ely Cem., Pennington Gap, Lee Co., VA.

HOWARD, DANIEL: (1845 – 1916), Co. C, enl. Whitesburg, KY 10/1/1862, vol. to serve in execution of Union soldier Creech, who killed Daniel's brother, pres. spring/1863, res. Breathitt Co. 1860, s. of Green & Margaret (Allen) Howard, res. Breathitt Co. 1880, res. Floyd Co. 1900 & 1910, applied Confed. pension 1915, m. Martha Handshoe (1847-1930) Breathitt Co. 1868, bur. W. Prestonsburg Cem., Prestonsburg, Floyd Co., KY.

HOWARD, JAMES: (1843 – 1863), Co. C, enl. Whitesburg, KY 10/1/1862, pres. spring/1863, res. Breathitt Co. 1860, s. of Green & Margaret (Allen) Howard, bur. Sandlick Cem., Whitesburg, Letcher Co., KY.

HOWARD, MARTIN: (b. 11/24/1838), Co. F, enl. Floyd Co. 10/14/1862, serv. prev. 5th KY Inf., Co. A, res. Breathitt Co. 1860, s. of Green & Margaret (Allen) Howard, m. (1) Susanah Shepherd (1841-1901), (2) Josanna Arnett, d. 4/2/1901, bur. Martin Howard Cem., Pyramid, Floyd Co., KY.

HOWARD, MORGAN: (1836 – 3/6/1863), Co. C, enl. Whitesburg, KY 10/1/1862, killed by Union pickets, res. Breathitt Co. 1860, s. of Green & Margaret (Allen) Howard, m. Susan L. Watkins (1837-aft. 1910) Menifee Co.

HOWERTON, JOHN W.: (1846 – 1903), Kash's Co., indicted post-war for 1865 murder as member this Co., res. Owsley Co. 1860, s. of Jacob & Rebecca (Williams) Howerton, res. Lee Co. 1874, res. Morgan Co. (Caney) 1880, poss. res. Wolfe Co. 1890, res. Bath Co. (nr. Salt Lick), m. Isabelle Elizabeth Menifee (1848-aft. 1900 Bath Co.), bur. Dickerson Cem., Salt Lick, Bath Co., KY.

HUDSON, HANNIBAL: (3/22/1833 – 10/21/1919), Co. K, enl. Osborn's Ford, VA 3/28/1862, 5' 10" grey eyes, black hair, serv. prev. 1st Btn. KY Mtd. Rifles, Co. A, capt. Lee Co., VA 11/12/1863, to Camp Chase Prison, to Johnson's Island Prison, rel. on oath 6/13/1865, res. Clay Co. (Manchester) 1860, b. Clay Co. KY, s. of William & Fanny (Barber) Hudson, rec. KY Confed. Pension #2672 Nicholas Co., KY 1913, res. Pewee Valley Confed Home, admitted Eastern State Mental Hosp. 1917, d.c. #27250, bur. (unmarked) Eastern State Hospital Cem., Lexington, Fayette Co., KY.

HUFF, JAMES A.: (1843- 1864), Co. B, enl. Whitesburg, KY 9/9/1862, pres. summer/1863, res. Floyd Co. (Huff's Br. of Caney Cr.)1860, s. of William & Nancy Huff, bur. Huff Cem. Raven, Knott Co., KY.

HUGHES, GABRIEL: (b. 1844), Co. A, enl. Whitesburg, KY 10/4/1862, serv. prev. 5th KY Inf., Co. F, res. Letcher Co. 1860, b. 1844, s. of James & Jinsa Hughes, res. Letcher Co. 1870, 1880, & 1900, widow res. Buck Creek 1910 & res E. Whitesburg 1930, widow d. Letcher Co. 1936.

HUGHES, GABRIEL: (5/11/1839 – 9/2/1917), Co. D, pres. spring/1863, res. Letcher Co. 1860, s. of John & Matilda (Bentley) Hughes, res. Letcher Co. 1870, m. Nancy Potter (b. 1841), bur. Dunham Cem., Dunham, Letcher Co., KY.

HUGHES, HENRY (C): (1839 – 1925), Cos. A & F, enl. Floyd Co. 10/14/1862, trans. from Co. A to Co. F, serv. prev. 5th KY Inf. Co. F, 5' 9 ¾", grey eyes, dk. brown hair, dk. complexion, scars on each side neck, pres. 4/11/1863, capt. Gladeville 7/7/1863, to Camp Douglas 8/24/1863, enl. U.S. Navy 12/23/1863, initially assigned to *U.S.S. Susquehanna*, res. Letcher Co. 1850, res. Perry Co. 1860, s. of James & Jinsa Hughes, res. Knott Co. (Carr) 1920, m. Mary "Polly" Smith (1839-1923) 1858, bur. Hughes Cem., Mallie, Knott Co., KY.

HUGHES, HENRY (HENDERSON): (1839 – 1916), Co. G, enl. Whitesburg, KY 1/1/1863, pres. fall/1863, res. Floyd Co. 1850, res. Perry Co. 1860, s. of James & Jane Hughes, res. Perry Co. (Troublesome) 1870, bur. Campbell-Allen Cem., Rowdy, Perry Co., KY.

HUGHES, MATHIAS: (1832 – 1901), Co. B, enl. Whitesburg, KY 9/7/1862, disc. 1/1/1863, res. Letcher Co. 1850, res. Perry Co. 1860, s. of James & Jinsa Hughes, res. Perry Co. 1870 res. Knott Co. (hotel keeper in Hindman) 1900, estate settled 1901, m. Elizabeth Hicks (1840-1900 to 1910) 1855, bur. Bob Amburgey Cem., Hindman, Knott Co., KY.

HUGHES, WALTER: (5/1841 – 5/29/1902), Co. F, enl. Floyd Co. 10/14/1862, des. & joined Union 39th, Co. F, 11/18/1862, serv. 11/25/1862 to 9/15/1865, res. Floyd Co. 1860, s. of Daniel & Sarah Hughes, res. Floyd Co. 1870, 1880 & 1900, widow applied Union pension 1902, Union marker w/o dates, m. (1) Oma (b. 1843), (2) Florence Patton (b. 1874) 1892, bur. Allen Cem., Warco, Floyd Co., KY.

HUGHES, WILLIAM EDWARD: (10/17/1847 – 9/4/1931), Co. B, enl. Whitesburg, KY 9/9/1862, pres. spring/1863, res. Letcher Co. 1860, s. of John & Matilda (Bentley) Hughes, m. Mary Ellen Brooks (1852-1939) Lawrence Co. 1868, on 1900 – 1930 Wayne Co. WVA Census.

HURST, DAVID: 1848 – 9/7/1922), Co. K, surr. Cumberland Gap 4/30/1865, res. Claiborne Co. TN 1850, s. of Robert & Sarah Hurst, res. Benton Co., AR 1870, res. Washington Co., AR 1880, res. Madison Co., AR (Mill Creek) 1900, 1910, & 1920, m. Elizabeth (1858-aft. 1930) 1872, AR d.c #00666.

HURST, HILARY: 2/8/1838 – 7/30/1911), Co. K, enl. Lee Co., VA 8/4/1863, pres. Lee Co. 12/31/1863, res. Knox Co. 1860, b. Claiborne Co., TN, res. Bell Co. 1870, res. Sumner Co., KS 1900 & 1901, m. (1) Sarah C. Purcifull (1843-1890), (2) Victoria A. Williams (1841-1928) 1891, bur. Council Hill Cem., Bell Plaine, Sumner Co., KS.

HURST, DAVID UMPHREY: (10/19/1847 – 9/7/1922), Co. K, surr. Cumberland Gap 4/30/1865, res. Claiborne Co., TN 1850, s. of Robert & Sarah Hurst, res. Benton Co., AR 1870, res Madison Co., AR 1900-1920, m. (1) Emma Cook (1859-1880) 1877, (2) Elizabeth Dee Johnson (1859-1922), bur Brashears Cem., St. Pail, Madison Co., AR.

HURST, WILLIAM LANDSAW: 9/25/1844 – 9/7/1913), 1st Lt., Co. K, enl. Lee Co., VA 8/1863, elected 1st Lt. Lee Co. 12/31/1863, resigned 11/3/1864, AWOL since 12/10/1864 on roll 1/6/1865, dropped from roll 2/26/1865, successor-Champ Hamlin, res. Breathitt Co. 1860, s. of Hardin & Dulcina (Landsaw) Hurst, m. Mary C. Childers (1855-1929), bur. Old Maude Miller-Collums Farm Cem., Stillwater, Wolfe Co., KY.

HURT, GEORGE WASHINGTON: (1833 – 1875), serv. prev. 5th KY Inf., Co. I, no s.r. 13th, res. Perry Co., s. of William & Lucy Hurt, widow rec. KY Confed. Pension #734 Knott Co. 1912, m. Susan Combs (1833-1923), bur. G. W. Hurt Cem., Upper Second Creek, Perry Co., KY.

HURT, ISAAC: (1826 – 1910), Co. I, conscripted Whitesburg, KY 10/18/1862, pres. spring/1863, res. Perry Co. 1860, s. of William & Lucy Hurt, m. Polly Little (1836-1910), bur. Hurt Cem., Hazard, Perry Co., KY.

HYLTON, ELISHA ELMER: (8/12/1833 – 1/26/1901), Co. A, serv. prev. 5th KY Inf., Co. F, disc. from 13th KY when term expired 4/30/1863, res. Letcher Co. 1860, moved from Wise Co., VA ca.1855, b. VA, s. of Jesse & Martha Ann (Montgomery) Hylton, res. Carr (Mallet Fk.) during war, sold land to William Huff & moved Estill Co. 1868, moved White River, AR, moved Sweetwater, TX, founded town of Hylton, TX, operated blacksmith shop, postmaster, res. Nolan Co. TX 1880, m. Rebecca Ann Huff (1832-aft. 1910), bur. Hylton Cem., Hylton, Nolan Co., TX.

HYLTON, JESSE B.: 7/31/1831 – 8/17/1897), enl. 1863, wd. Gladeville, VA 6/7/1863 (re: pension), b. Pike Co. KY, s. of William & Catherine (Griffith) Hylton, widow rec. VA Confed. Pension 1904, identified as member this regiment, attested by Rhodes Marion Hylton & Benjamin McLemore of 13th, stated he suffered from wounds & exposure during war, that he served as Capt. of Co. A, 21st VA Cav., d. from chronic bowel trouble, m. Susan Jane White (1841-1916), bur. Phipps Cem. Clintwood, Dickenson Co., VA.

HYLTON, RHODES MARION: 5/25/1842 – 12/11/1911), Co. H, enl. Whitesburg, KY 10/18/1862, capt. Gladeville, VA 7/7/1863, to Kemper Barracks 7/18/1863, to Camp Chase Prison 7/20/1863, to Camp Douglas Prison 8/24/1863, exch. Point Lookout 2/24/1865, res. Letcher Co. 1860, s. of William & Catherine (Griffith) Hylton, res. Letcher Co. 1870, m. Sarah E. Dotson (1852-aft. 1918) 1868, bur. Wise City Cem., Wise, Wise Co., VA.

INGLE, WILLIAM: 1843 – 1904), Co. C, enl. Whitesburg, KY 10/1/1862, capt. Gladeville, VA 7/7/1863, to Kemper Barracks 7/18/1863, to Camp Chase 7/20/1863, to Camp Douglas 8/24/1863, to Point Lookout 2/24/1865, exchanged at Richmond, VA, res. Perry Co. (Troublesome) w/ incorrect age 1860, b. Russell Co., VA (now Wise Co.), s. of Flem & Betty (Hall) Ingle, res. Perry Co. 1880, moved to Rowan Co. (Farmers) aft. 1880, res. Rowan Co. 1900, widow rec. KY Confed. Pension #2633 Rowan Co. 1914, d. Rowan Co. (Farmers), m. Elizabeth Patton (1841-1919 Rowan Co., KY) Perry Co. 1868, bur. Slaty Point Cem., Farmers, Rowan Co., KY.

INGRAM, CLARK J.: 3/4/1836 – 1/4/1910), Co. A, serv. prev. 5th KY Inf., pres. spring/1863, res. Letcher Co. 1860, s. of John & Elizabeth (Ison) Ingram, res. Caudill's Br. during war, moved post-war Big Cowan Cr., res. Letcher Co. 1870, moved Owsley Co. 1882, m. (1) Leodicy Caudill (1840-bef.1894), (2) Lusinda (b. 1852) 1894, bur. Moore Cem., nr. Anville, Jackson Co., KY.

ISAACS, GEORGE WASHINGTON: (3/21/1841 – 2/13/1923), Co. E, enl. Piketon, KY 7/20/1863, serv. prev. 5th KY Inf., Co. F, capt. Pike Co. 10/6/1863, to Louisville Prison 10/22/1863, to Camp Morton Prison 10/24/1863, to Ft. Delaware Prison 3/19/1864, rel. on oath 6/9/1865, res. Floyd Co. b. Floyd Co., s. of William Jr. & Jane (Hall) Isaacs, rec. KY Confed. Pension #3602 Knott Co. 1916 claiming rank of Capt. Co. E, m. (1) Milly Ann Yonts, (2) Sarah Collins (1851-bef. 1885), (3) Nellie Kindred (1858-1929 Cabell Co., WV) 1885, d. 2. Boyd Co. (Pollard), bur. Isaacs Cem., West Hamlin, Lincoln Co., WV.

ISAACS, GERMAN: (2/25/1863 – 4/1/1916), Co. E, enl. Whitesburg, KY 10/5/1862, pres. summer/1863, serv. until disbandment Dublin Depot, VA on New River 4/1865 (re: pension), surr. & took oath Louisa, res. Floyd Co. 1860, s. of Samuel & Malinda (Slone) Isaacs, res. Knott Co. 1890, rec. KY Confed. Pension #1374 Magoffin Co. (Mountain) 1912, m. Jennie King (1860-1925), bur. Johnston Cem., Dan, Menifee Co., KY.

ISAACS, JONATHAN "JONTS": (3/17/1843 – 8/15/1904), Co. E, rec. clothing 9/15/1864, res. Floyd Co. 1860, s. of William Jr. & Sarah (Hall) Isaacs, res. Knott Co. 1890 & 1900, m. (1) Margaret Picklesimmer (1838-bef. 1876) 1865, (2) Lucinda Osborne (1853-1947) 1876, bur. Isaacs Cem., Topmost, Knott Co., KY.

ISAACS, TERMAN: (1/13/1841 – 12/2/1916), Cos. E & F, enl. Whitesburg, KY 10/5/1862, trans. from Co. E to Co. F Floyd Co. 10/14/1862, rec. clothing 9/15/1864, des. jail Abingdon, VA, surr. New River (Dublin Depot) VA 1865, res. Floyd Co. 1860, s. of Samuel & Malinda (Slone) Isaacs, res. Floyd Co. 1870, rec. Ky Confed. Pension #1375 Magoffin Co. (Wheelersburg) 1912, m. (1)_____ (2) Matilda Cantrell (1862-1909) Floyd Co. 1870, bur. Isaac Cem., Flat Fork, Magoffin Co., KY.

ISON, ELIJAH "SR.": (7/13/1832 – 5/24/1877), 1st Sgt., Co. H, enl. Whitesburg, KY 9/2/1862, reduced to ranks 3/18/1863, pres. summer/1863, res. Letcher Co. 1860, s. of Gideon & Rachel (Stamper) Ison, lived Isom, KY (nr. mo. Stamper Br.) m. Margaret "Peggy" Hogg (1841-aft. 1900 Letcher Co.), bur. Presbyterian Church Cem., Isom, Letcher Co., KY.

ISON, ELIJAH C. "JR.": (1839 – 12/12/1885), Co. H, enl. Whitesburg, KY 9/12/1862, pres. spring/1863, res. Letcher Co. 1860, s. of Pvt. George & Lucinda (Combs) Ison, m. Margaret Brashear (b. 1844), bur. Lily Cornett Cem., Skyline, Letcher Co., KY.

ISON, ELISHA: (1841 – 1863), Co. H, KIA fall/1863, res. Letcher Co. 1860, s. of Pvt. George & Lucinda (Combs) Ison, m. Sarah.

ISON, GEORGE: (4/10/1810 – 5/30/1886), Co. H, enl. Whitesburg, KY 10/18/1862, des. 11/10/1862, res. Letcher Co. 1860, s. of George Gideon & Anna (Ingram) Ison, res. Letcher Co. 1880, m. (1) Lucinda Combs (1815-1865), (2) Vina "Polly" Adams (d. bef. 1880) 1871, bur. Lily Cornett Cem., Skyline, Letcher Co., KY.

JACKSON, ROBERT: (1845 – 4/1/1863), Co. H, enl. Whitesburg, KY 10/18/1862, also listed on s.r. as Roland Jackson, KIA, res. Harlan Co. 1860, b. VA, m. Mary Hogston.

JACOBS, LEONARD: (b. 10/1842), Co. B, enl. Whitesburg, KY 9/9/1862, 5' 3", auburn hair, blue eyes, capt. Montgomery Co. 10/15/1862, to Cincinnati, to Camp Chase Prison 10/24/1862, to Cairo Prison 11/20/1862, enl. Union 39th KY, Co. F 1/7/1864, res. Perry Co. 1850, res. Carter Co. 1860, s. of William & Rachel Jacobs, res. Hocking Co., OH 1880, boarder in Barton Co., MO 1900, m. Emily (1842-aft. 1880).

JANE, JOSEPH: Co. F, enl. Floyd Co. 10/14/1862, capt. Floyd Co. 6/9/1863, to Louisville Prison 6/14/1863, to Baltimore Prison (Ft. McHenry) 6/16/1863.

JANE, MARTIN C. (b. 9/12/1846), Co. K, enl. Lee Co., VA 8/18/1863, pres. Lee Co. 12/31/1863, res. Lee Co., VA 1860, s. of James Jr. & Francis Jane, lived in Jonesville, VA, apparently did not survive the war.

JENT, ELIAS: (1817 – 1863), Co. I, res. Perry Co. 1860, b. Russell Co., VA, s. of William B. & Margaret "Peggy" (Robinson) Jent, m. Rachel Elizabeth Cornett (1815-aft. 1870), documentation exists indicating he was killed by Union soldiers on Big Branch of Troublesome and was buried there.

JENT, ELIAS: (1844 – 2/14/1914), Co. I, enl. Gladeville, VA 8/1/1863, res. Perry Co. 1860, s. of Henry & Manda (Messer) Jent, m. Nancy (1852-aft. 1900), bur. Jent Cem., Carcasonne, Letcher Co., KY.

JENT, WILLIAM (M.): (9/10/1844 – 9/15/1894), Co. I, conscripted Whitesburg, KY 10/18/1862, pres. summer/1863, res. Perry Co. 1860, s. of Elias & Rachel Elizabeth (Cornett) Jent, res. Letcher Co. 1870, m. Nancy Smith 1867, bur. Carrs Fork Cem., Littcarr, Knott Co., KY.

JERVIS, JAMES L.: (12/13/1821 – 2/28/1904), Co. E, serv. prev. 5th Sgt., 5th KY Inf., Co. E, serv. 13th KY Cav, Co. E (re: 1890 Veterans' Census), res. Floyd Co. 1860, b. Cecil Co., MD, post-war physician, res. Floyd Co. 1890 & 1900, m. Eva Burchett (1823-1911) 1848, bur. Jervis Cem., Endicott, Floyd Co., KY.

JOHNSON, ABISHA J. "SR." "BISH": (9/28/1839 – 2/6/1926), Co. E, enl. Whitesburg, KY 10/5/1862, res. Floyd Co. (Lackey) 1860, s. of Harvey & Sarah (Caudill) Johnson, rec. KY Confed. Pension #766 Floyd Co. (Rail) 1912, m. Mary Jane (1839-aft. 1910), d.c. #03698, bur. Matthew Tackett Cem., Melvin, Floyd Co., KY.

JOHNSON, ABISHA "JR.": (1842 – 1898), Co. E, enl. Whitesburg, KY 10/5/1862, capt. Gladeville, VA 7/7/1863, to Kemper Barracks 7/18/1863, to Camp Chase Prison 7/20/1863, to Camp Douglas Prison 8/24/1863, exch. Point Lookout 3/2/1865, res. Floyd Co. 1860, s. of Peyton & Elizabeth Johnson, res. Knott Co. 1889 (re: tax list), res. Knott Co. 1890 (re: Special Veterans' Census), m. Nancy A. Stone (1853-aft. 1930 Floyd Co.), bur. Jimmy Slone Cem., Pippa Passes, Knott Co., KY.

JOHNSON, ANDREW J.: (5/11/1842 – 1/6/1929), Co. E, enl. Whitesburg, KY 10/5/1862, serv. prev. 5th KY Inf., Co. E & reportedly 5th KY Inf. (2nd Organization), Co. G, rec. clothing 9/15/1864, disbanded New River, VA 5/1865, took oath at Louisa, KY, res. Floyd Co. 1850, s. of Elisha & Elizabeth Johnson, rec. KY Confed Pension #2682 Knott Co. (nr. Topmost) 1913, m. Rebecca Isaacs (1842-1912), bur. Isaacs Cem., Topmost, Knott Co., KY.

JOHNSON, CALEB C.: (12/10/1843 – 3/25/1937), 5th Sgt., Co. E, enl. Whitesburg, KY 10/5/1862, pres. summer/1863, res. Floyd Co. (Caleb Fk. Left Beaver, Weeksburry) 1860, s. of Harvey & Sarah (Caudill) Johnson, m. (1) Mahalia Justice (1843-1880 to 1900), (2) Polly Whitaker (1875-1964), bur. Johnson Cem., Hartley, Pike Co., KY.

JOHNSON, ELI: (11/20/1837 – 7/25/1913), Co. E, enl. Whitesburg, KY 10/5/1862, pres. summer/1863, furloughed Letcher Co. 1864, paroled Lexington, KY, res. Floyd Co. (Hall) 1860, s. of Harvey & Sarah (Caudill) Johnson, rec. Ky Confed. Pension #769 Floyd Co. (Rail) 1912, d. from heart disease, m. Susanah Elizabeth Keene (1840-1913), bur. Matthew Tackett Cem., Melvin, Floyd Co., KY.

JOHNSON, ELISHA "GROUNDHOG": (11/24/1837 – 1/18/1929), Co. E, enl. Whitesburg, KY 10/5/1862, pres. spring/1863, on sick leave Letcher Co. 1863, took oath 4/1865, res. Floyd Co. 1860, s. of David & Anna (Hall) Johnson, rec. KY Confed. Pension #1756 Floyd Co. (Rail) 1912, m. (1) Marilda Mullins (1840-bef. 1880), (2) Elizabeth "Betty" Hall (1842-aft. 1920), bur. Johnson Cem., Melvin, Floyd Co., KY.

JOHNSON, GILBERT: (b. 1832), 2nd Lt., Co. E, enl. Whitesburg, KY 10/5/1862, prom. 2nd Lt. spring/1863, res. Floyd Co. 1850, b. Floyd Co. 1832, s. of John & Sarah (Hammonds) Johnson, res. Floyd Co. 1870, res. Rowan Co. 1880, res. Collin Co., TX 1900 m. Susan L. (b. 1839).

JOHNSON, HARVEY "PANTHER": (5/18/1835 – 1/20/1922), Co. E, enl. Whitesburg, KY 10/5/1862, res. Floyd Co. 1860, s. of David & Anna (Hall) Johnson, pension witness for Matthew Tackett, Melvin, KY 1912, m. Louisa Cook (1836-1896), bur. Harve Johnson Cem., Melvin, Floyd Co., KY.

JOHNSON, JOAB: (10/6/1842 – 5/9/1914), Co. E, enl. Whitesburg, KY 10/5/1862, capt. Gladeville, VA 7/7/1863, to Kemper Barracks 7/18/1863, to Camp Chase Prison 7/20/1863, to Camp Douglas Prison 8/24/1863, exch. Point Lookout 3/2/1865, paroled Louisa, KY 4/18/1865, res. Floyd Co. 1860, s. of Peyton & Elizabeth Johnson, rec. KY Confed. Pension #770 Floyd Co. (Melvin) 1912, m. Sarah Little, res. Lackey, KY (1844-1921), bur. Little Cem., Wheelwright, Floyd Co., KY.

JOHNSON, JOHN: (1836 – 6/17/1882), Co. E, enl. Whitesburg, KY 10/5/1862, capt. Gladeville, VA 7/7/1863, to Kemper Barracks 7/18/1863, to Camp Chase Prison 7/20/1863, to Camp Douglas Prison 8/24/1863, disc. 7/6/1865, res. Floyd Co. s. of Peyton & Elizabeth Johnson, widow res. Knott Co. 1890, widow rec. KY Confed. Widow's Pension #771 Knott Co. (Mallie) 1912, m. Susannah Slone (1849-1933), lived on Caney Cr., bur. Jimmy Slone Cem., Pippa Passes, Knott Co., KY.

JOHNSON, JOHN: (7/4/1820 – 8/4/1911), 2nd Sgt., Co. G, enl. & prom. Breathitt Co. 9/23/1862, capt. Gladeville, VA 7/7/1863, to Kemper Barracks 7/18/1863, to Camp Chase Prison 7/20/1863, to Camp Douglas Prison 8/24/1863, disc. 5/13/1865, res. Breathitt Co. 1850 & 1860, s. of Thomas Johnson, res. Breathitt Co. 1900, m. (1) Margaret Fugate (b. 1832) 1849, (2) Jane Miller (b. 1831), bur. Richie Cem., Talcum, Knott Co., KY.

JOHNSON, LESLIE: (4/1/1842 – 10/16/1908), Co. B, enl. Whitesburg, KY 8/21/1862, res. Letcher Co. 1860, s. of Washington & Sarah (Francis) Johnson, Letcher Co. Sheriff 1866, res. Letcher Co. 1870 & 1880, res. Knott Co. 1889 (re: tax list), res. Knott Co. 1900, moved to OK bef. 1903, m. (1) Amanda Hart 1860, (2) Frances Hylton (1840-aft. 1900 Knott Co.) 1866, (3) Flora Belle Greear (1875-aft. 1910), bur. Roosevelt Cem., Roosevelt, Kiowa Co., OK.

JOHNSON, MILAN: Q.M. Sgt., Co. G, identified in "Artificial 10th KY Cav." – misfiled, capt. Gladeville, VA 7/7/1863, to Kemper Barracks 7/18/1863, to Camp Chase Prison 7/20/1863, to Camp Douglas Prison 8/24/1863.

JOHNSON, MITCHELL: (6/18/1844 – 6/16/1912), 1st Cpl., Co. K, enl. VA 8/18/1863, rec. clothing 9/7/1864, surr. Cumberland Gap 4/30/1865, res. Lee Co., VA (listed as Michael) 1860, s. of Ephriam & Synthia Johnson, res. Morris Co. KS 1870, 1880, 1900 & 1910, m. (1) Sarah Kirk (1844-bef. 1885) Lee Co., VA 1864, (2) Laura (1855-1900 to 1910) 1885, bur. Diamond Springs Cem., Diamond Springs, Morris Co., KS.

JOHNSON, NATHANIAL G.: (b. 1846), Co. A, serv. prev. 5th KY Inf., pres. 3/30/1863, res. Harlan Co. 1860, b. NC, s. of Rice & Phebe, res. Bell Co. (Calloway, w/ Charles Calloway) 1870, res. Bell Co. (Turkey Creek) 1900 & 1910 (w/ dau. Rhoda, wife of John Emery).

JOHNSON, PRESTON: (1824 – 1/30/1865), Co. C. enl. Whitesburg, KY 10/1/1862, capt. Gladeville, VA 7/7/1863, to Kemper Barracks 7/18/1863, to Camp Chase Prison 7/20/1863, to Camp Douglas Prison 8/24/1863, d. Camp Dougls, res. Perry Co. 1860, m. Milly Combs, bur. Oak Wood Cem. Chicago, Cook Co., IL.

JONES, ANDREW: (4/18/1831 – 4/6/1906), Co. C, enl. Whitesburg, KY 10/1/1862, pres. spring/1863, res. Breathitt Co. 1860, b. VA, s. of Jonathan T. & Lucy Jones, m. (1) Mary Noble (b. 1842), (2) Louranie Grigsby, bur. Jones Cem., Lost Creek, Perry Co., KY.

JONES, DANIEL P.: (1822 – 1870 to 1880), Kash's Co., res. Breathitt Co. 1850 & 1860, res. Menifee Co. 1870, indicted post-war for 1865 murder as member Kash's Co. m. Nancy (b. 1826), d. nr. Denniston, Menifee Co., KY.

JONES, GRANVILLE: (3/14/1833 – 3/20/1911), Co. A, serv. prev. 5th KY Inf., Co. F, serv. later 50th VA Inf. (re: pension), res. Grayson Co., VA 1860, s. of Jordan & Martha "Patsy" (Anderson) Jones, rec. VA Confed. Pension Grayson Co., VA 1902, m. Julia Ann Cress (1836-1911)1858, bur. New Hope Cem., Barton Crossroad, Grayson Co., VA.

JONES, GREENBERRY: (7/13/1846 – 2/13/1928), Kash's Co., claimed serv. w/ Anderson Whitaker in Kash's Co. in Whitaker's Confed. Pension, sworn in Feb. 1864 at Round Bottom, Quicksand, Breathitt Co., serv. until paroled at Louisa 5/9/1865, s. of Wiley C. Jones & Elizabeth (Buttrey Jones, res of Breathitt Co. 1860, m. (1) Arnetta Smith (1853-1888), (2) Polly Smith (b. 1844) 1890, res. Morgan Co. 1910-1920, bur. Jones Cem., Cannel City, Morgan Co., KY.

JONES, JAMES HARRISON: (5/14/1845 – 10/8/1888), Kash's Co., serv. prev. Diamond's 10th KY Cav. Co. E, res. Breathitt Co., KY 1860, b. Breathitt Co., KY, s. of Daniel P. & Nancy Jones, indicted post-war for 1865 murder as member Kash's Co., res. Menifee Co. 1870 & 1880, m. Sarah Gibbs (1849-1920), bur Jones Cem., Tar Ridge, Frenchburg, Menifee Co., KY.

JONES, JOEL: (b. 1843), Cos. B & F, enl. Whitesburg, KY 9/15/1862, trans. from Co. B to Co. F, capt. Floyd Co. 11/11/1862, to Camp Morton Prison, did not survive the war, res. Floyd Co. 1850 & 1860, s. of Claborn & Milly Jones.

JONES, JONATHAN HAMILTON: (11/21/1827 – 7/9/1894), Co. H, enl. Whitesburg, KY 10/18/1862, paroled Cumberland Gap 5/10/1862, res. Letcher Co. 1860, b. Grayson Co., VA, res. Knott Co. 1890, widow rec. KY Confed. Widow's Pension #777 Knott Co. 1912, m. Harriet Elizabeth Draughon (1841-1925) 1856, bur. Jones Cem., Mallie, Knott Co., KY.

JONES, JOSEPH: (1/22/1848 – 1908)), Co. F, enl. Floyd Co., KY 10/14/1862, identified in AG Report, res. Magoffin Co. 1860, s. of Franklin & Sarah (Brown) Jones, res. Greenup Co. 1880 & 1900, m. Elizabeth Puckett (1847-1925), res. of Greenup Co. 1880 & 1900, bur. Chenoa Cem., Chenoa, Mclean Co., IL.

JONES, WILEY WILLIAM: (12/22/1823 – 1/19/1896), 1st Lt., Co. F, enl. Prestonsburg, KY 10/14/1862, listed on s.r. as both William Jones & Wiley Jones, serv. prev. 5th KY Inf., Co. C, sick 12/31/1863, recruiting duty 9/1864, surr. Mt. Sterling, KY 4/30/1865, res. Breathitt Co. 1860, b. Morgan Co., s. of Charles & Jemima Jones, res. Lewis Co. 1870, widow rec. KY Confed. Widow's Pension #3229 Lewis Co. (Quincy) 1913, m. Fanny Allen (b. 1823) Breathitt Co., bur. Jones Cem., Quincy, Lewis Co., KY.

JONES, WILLIAM: (1845 – bef. 1910), Co. E, enl. Floyd Co. 10/5/1862, capt. Greenville, TN 9/27/1863, to McLean Barracks 10/11/1863, rel. 10/16/1863, res. Floyd Co. 1850 & 1860, s. of Claborn & Milly Jones, res. Knott Co. (Beaver) 1900, m. Florence Terry (b. 1856) 1872.

JONES, WILLIAM: (1839 – 1864), Co. F, enl. Floyd Co. 10/14/1862, serv. prev. 5th KY Inf., Co. B (Consolidated) 9-10/1862, KIA KY mountains by Union Home Guards 1864 (re: pension statement by Lt. John M. Allen this Co.), res. Breathitt Co. (w/ B. F. Jackson, S. side Jackson, KY) 1860.

JORDAN, ROBERT: 1844 – 4/10/1923), Co. F, enl. Floyd Co. 10/14/1862, disc. Scott Co., VA 4/22/1865, res. Floyd Co. 1860, s. of Sarah Jordan, rec. KY Confed. Pension #780 1912, m. Naomi Hughes (1850-1928) 1865, bur. Ruben Arnett Cem., Hendricks, Magoffin Co., KY.

JUSTICE, WILLIAM RILEY: (1820 – 1894), Co. E, enl. Whitesburg, KY 10/5/1862, capt. Gladeville, VA 7/7/1863, res. Pike Co. 1850 & 1860, b. Floyd Co., s. of George & Nancy "Polly" (Smith) Justice, res. Pike Co. (Lick Creek) 1870 & 1880, m. Mary Ann Thacker.

KASH, LEVI CALLAWAY: (11/18/1831 – 9/27/1910), Capt., Kash's Co., serv. prev. 5th KY Inf., Co. B, enl. Hargis Fields 9/7/1862, elected 1st Sgt. 9/18/1862, abs. 8/15/1863, left at Emory & Henry College nr. Abingdon, VA, listed as deserted 12/18/1863, but had begun recruiting his company 10/1863, Kash's Co., 13th KY Cav. became fully operational 1/1865, indicted post-war for 1865 murder as commander of Kash's Co., res. Breathitt Co., KY 1860, s. of William & Sarah Cope Kash, moved to Montgomery Co. post-war, m. Mollie O'Rear (1848-1941), d. 4th Ave., Winchester, KY, bur. Winchester City Cem., Winchester, Clark Co., KY.

KASH, WILLIAM: 10/16/1808 – 4/5/1885), Kash's Co., indicted post-war for murder as member this Co., res. Breathitt Co. 1860, m. Sarah Cope (1808-1893), bur. Kash Cem., Quicksand, Breathitt Co., KY.

KEETON, RILEY M.: 5/8/1835 – 4/13/1926), Co. H, capt. Gladeville, VA 7/7/1863, to Kemper Barracks 7/18/1863, to Camp Chase Prison 7/20/1863, to Camp Douglas Prison 8/24/1863, res. Magoffin Co., KY 1860, s. of George W. & Dena (Davis) Keeton, m. Emily J. Sebastian (1836-1883), bur. Keeton Cem., Edna, Magoffin Co., KY.

KEITH, WILLIAM: 5/14/1844 – 8/7/1912), Co. A, enl. 1863, res. Breathitt Co., KY, s. of Hugh Daniel & Phoebe (Counts) Keith, res. Breathitt Co. 1890 & 1900 (Lost Creek), m. (1) Catharine (1832-ca. 1876), (2) Rebecca Haynes (1857-aft. 1910), bur. Elmer Turner Cem., Kragon, Breathitt Co., KY.

KEITH, WILLIAM RILEY: (1830 – 1879), Co. H, enl. & disc. Whitesburg, KY 10/18/1862, res. Letcher Co. 1855 & 1860, b. VA, res. Magoffin Co. 1870, widow res Magoffin Co. 1880, m. Eliza Williams (1836-aft. 1880) 1855, bur. Williams Cem., Mash Fork, Magoffin Co., KY.

KELLER, ISAAC: 11/28/1848 – 5/1/1900), Co. K, no s.r., "shot in right leg during war, walked with a limp rest of his life", surr. Cumberland Gap, KY 4/30/1865, res. Union Co., TN 1850 & 1860, b. Union Co., TN, s. of Joseph & Elis Keller, res. Knox Co., KY 1870, m. (1) Sarah Gilliam (1848-bef. 1900) 1868, (2) Sarah Seale (1848-aft. 1900), bur. Lerose Cem., Lerose, Owsley Co., KY.

KELLY, JOHN (JACKSON) "SR": (10/6/1821 – 6/30/1909), Co. H, enl. Whitesburg, KY 9/20/1862, pres. spring/1863, res. Lee Co. 1850, res. Wise Co., VA 1860, b. Harlan Co., KY, moved w/ parents to Big Stone Gap, VA 1830, s. of Mathias & Abigail (Sturgill) Kelly, res. Wise Co. 1880, m. Virginia Jane Booth (1823-1893), d. Lee Co., VA, bur. Richmond Cem. Turkey Cove, Lee Co., VA.

KELLY, JOHN (JACKSON) "JR": (2/26/1847 – 11/13/1935), Co. H, enl. Whitesburg, KY 10/1862, res. Lee Co., Va 1850, res. Wise Co., VA 1860, s. of John J. Sr. & Virginia Jane (Booth) Kelly, res. Wise Co., VA 1880, 1900, 1920 & 1930, m. Elizabeth (1852-aft. 1930), bur. Wise City Cem., Wise, Wise Co., VA.

KELLY, JOHN T.: (1842 – 1864), 3rd Sgt., Co. H, enl. Whitesburg, KY 9/10/1862, rec. clothing 4/7/1864, KIA Battle of Cynthiana (Harrison Co.), res. Letcher Co. 1850 & 1860, s. of John & Letty (Horton) Kelly, Confed. memorial marker, Sandlick Cem., Whitesburg, Letcher Co., KY.

KELLY, WILLIAM E.: (1/13/1839 – 9/7/1895), Co. H, enl. Whitesburg, KY 9/20/1862, capt. Battle of Cynthiana 6/10/1864, to Louisville Prison 6/22/1864, to Rock Island Prison 6/24/1864, exch. Rock Island 3/6/1865, res. Letcher Co. 1860, s. of John & Letty (Horton) Kelly, serv. as Sheriff late 1860's, res. Letcher Co. 1870, moved Montgomery Co. (Slate Creek) 1891, widow rec. KY Confed. Widow's Pension #1394 Morgan Co. (Grassy Creek) 1912, m. Elizabeth "Eliza" Draughan (1843-1943), d. Menifee Co. bur. Chambers Cem., Means, Menifee Co., KY.

KIDD, HARRISON: (1847 – 8/26/1919), Cos. C & B, enl Co. C 5/11/1863, trans. to Co. B "because nearly all members of these companies were killed or captured, not leaving enough for a whole company of either", w/ Gen. John Hunt Morgan when he was killed in TN 1864, surr. nr. Petersburg, VA, disbanded by Lt. Col. D. J. Caudill, sent to Louisa, KY for parole 5/1865, took oath there, Capt. William "Bolen Bill" Hall was in command of Co. B at that time (re: pension), res. Morgan Co. 1860, b. Morgan Co., s. of Edmund & Amanda Kidd, res. Rowan Co. (physician) 1870, rec. KY Confed. Pension #1397 Rowan Co. (Wagoner) 1912, m. (1) Sarah Jane Brown 1873 (b. 1851 Greenup Co.), divorced bef. 1880, (2) Annabelle Bradley 1899 (Rowan Co.), bur. Jennings Cem., Hamm, Rowan Co., KY.

KILE, ROBERT: Co. F, enl. Floyd Co. 10/14/1862, des. 11/8/1862, joined Union 39th KY, Co. F at Peach Orchard, res. Floyd Co, KY.

KILGORE, GEORGE W.: 6/24/1844 – 5/9/1924), Co. B, enl. Scott Co., VA 1863 or 1864, attached to Co. B, 10th KY Mtd. (13th KY) under Lt. Col. D. J. Caudill, serv. until disc. Roanoke, VA 4/11/1865 (re: pension), res. Wise Co. VA 1860, b. Scott Co., VA, s. of Hiram A. & Anna Elizabeth (Bond) Kilgore, serv. post-war as County Judge & County Attorney of Wise Co, VA & as a State Representative, m. (1) Rhoda Elizabeth Hoback (1845-bef. 1897) 1863 (Wise Co. VA), (2) Nannie (1865-aft. 1930) bur. Wise City Cem., Wise, Wise Co., VA.

KINCER, DAVID G.: 1/1/1835 – 4/21/1914), 3rd Sgt., Co. D, enl. Whitesburg, KY 10/4/1862, pres. spring/1863, res. Letcher Co. 1860, s. of Mary Kincer, m. Henrietta Holbrook (1834-1894) 1855, bur. Webb Cem., Mayking, Letcher Co., KY.

KING, JAMES: (9/3/1939 – 4/11/1921), Co. E, enl. Whitesburg, KY 10/5/1862, pres. summer/1863, disc. Whitesburg 1865, res. Floyd Co., b. Floyd Co., s. of Lewis W. & Eda (Flanary) King, rec. KY Confed. Pension #3920 Knott Co. 1912, m. (1) Sarah Bates (1841-1894) 1866, (2) Drucilla Amburgey (1868-1936) 1895, bur. Strange Cem., Kite, Knott Co., KY.

KING, LEWIS: (1818 – 1898), Co. G, enl. Gladeville, VA 6/14/1863, serv. prev. 2nd KY Mtd. Rifles, Co. A, res. Breathitt Co. KY 1860, s. of Moses King, res. Breathitt Co. 1870, res. Wolfe Co. 1880, m. Sarah Louise Crawford (1822-1880 to 1900), bur. Mary King Cem., Flat, Wolfe Co., KY.

KING, TANDY LEWIS: (1830 – 1900 to 1910), Co. E, enl. Whitesburg, KY 10/5/1862, pres. 10/25/1862, res. Floyd Co.1850, s. of Lewis & Eda (Flanary) King, res. Floyd Co. 1870 & 1880, res. Knott Co. 1889 (re: tax list), res. Knott Co. 1900, widow res. Knott Co. 1910 m. Frances "Fanny" (1835-1913), bur. Nan King Cem., Kite, Knott Co. KY.

LANDRUM, REUBEN SAMUEL: (6/10/1837 – 10/15/1900), Co. G, enl. Gladeville, VA 6/20/1863, serv. prev. 5th KY Inf., Co. I, capt. Gladeville 7/7/1863, to Kemper Barracks 7/18/1863, to Camp Chase Prison 7/20/1863, to Camp Douglas Prison 8/24/1863, exch. Point Lookout 2/24/1865, res. Breathitt Co., s. of Reuben W. & Margaret (Brashear) Landrum, m. (1) Miller, (2) Malitha Jane Hagans (1846-1941), bur. Hagan Cem., Rousseau, Breathitt Co., KY.

LANDRUM, ROBERT BRASHEAR "SWEET": (10/20/1846 – 9/12/1910), Co. G, enl. Gladeville, VA 6/20/1863, res. Breathitt Co., s. of Reuben W. & Margaret (Brashear) Landrum, m. Matilda Jane Campbell (1849-1941), bur. Tharp Cem., Haddix, Breathitt Co., KY.

LANDRUM, WILLIAM SILAS: 6/9/1838 – 9/12/1904), Capt., Co. G, serv. prev. 5th KY Inf., Co. I, prom. Capt 2/23/1863, capt. Gladeville, VA 7/7/1863, to Kemper Barracks 7/18/1863, to Camp Chase Prison 7/20/1863, to Johnson's Island Prison 10/10/1863, exch. Point Lookout 2/16/1865, res. Breathitt Co. 1860, s. of Reuben W. & Margaret (Brashear) Landrum, moved to Andrew Co., MO 1880's, ret. Breathitt Co. by 1898 (re: School Census), bur. Strong Cem., Lost Creek, Breathitt Co., KY.

LANKFORD, DAVID C.: (1842 - 1881), Co. K, serv. prev. 64th VA Mtd. Inf., surr. Cumberland Gap 4/30/1865, res. Harlan Co. 1860, b. TN 1842, s. of Benjamin Lankford & Temperance (Posey) Lankford, m. Miriam K Howard (1847-1927) Harlan Co. 1869, widow rec. KY Confed. Widow's Pension #1404 Harlan Co. 1912, bur. Ball Cem., Harlan, Harlan Co., KY.

LANKFORD, WILLIAM: (3/14/1832 – 4/1/1914), Sgt., Co. K, enl. 1863, surr. Cumberland Gap 4/30/1865, res. Harlan Co. 1860, b. Claiborne Co., TN, s. of Benjamin Lankford & Temperance (Posey) Lankford, m. Mary Lyttle (1839-1895), pardoned by Gov. Thomas Bramlett for war-related murder in Harlan Co. 1867, res. Harlan Co. (Mt. Pleasant) 1870 & 1910, rec. KY Confed. Pension #487 Harlan Co. 1913, bur. in the Ball Cem., Harlan, Harlan Co., KY.

LEACH, CHRISTIAN SHULTZ: (6/26/1842 – 3/20/1914), Sgt. Maj., Field & Staff, capt. & imprisoned Johnson's Island (re: obit.), took oath & surr. Cincinnati 5/19/1865, res. Hamilton Co., OH 1860, bookkeeper for Thomas Chenoweth's business in Cincinnati, s. of Joseph Leach & Julia Anne Lee (Shultz) Leach Chenoweth, res. Mason Co. 1870 & 1880, moved St. Paul, MN by 1889, m. Sarah McCann (1845-1923), d. New Orleans, LA, bur. Maysville-Mason Co. Cem., Maysville, Mason Co., KY.

LEWIS, JAMES S. (L.) "REBEL LEWIS": (2/26/1812 – 9/3/1869), Co. I, enl. 8/31/1862, 5' 10", dark complexion, grey hair, grey eyes, capt. Irvine, KY 5/25/1863, to Louisville Prison 8/1/1863, to Camp Chase Prison 8/6/1863, to Ft. Delaware Prison 2/29/1864, rel. on oath 12/15/1864, res. Perry Co. 1860, s. of James T. Lewis & Sarah Couch, moved to TX post-war, m. (1) Elizabeth Jackson, (2) Nancy McIntosh (b. 1811), bur. Old Dennis Cem., Dennis, Parker Co., TX.

LEWIS, JOHN BOWLING: 6/4/1844 – 1/25/1934), Co. I, enl. Whitesburg, KY 8/31/1862, rec. clothing 9/24/1864, disbanded nr. Richmond, VA, arrested on Big Sandy R. & took oath, res. Breathitt Co., 1860, s. of Zara O. & Chaney (Bowling) Lewis, rec. KY Confed. Pension #2987 Perry Co. (Buckhorn) 1914, m. (1) Nancy Emily Vaughn (1848-1901) 1869, (2) Nancy Akemon (1861-1925), d. Elkatawa, KY, bur. Nick Combs Cem., Turkey, Breathitt Co., KY.

LIPPS, JAMES D.: (10/19/1842 – 2/9/1914), Co. A, enl. Whitesburg, KY 5/1/1863, serv. prev. 50th VA, Co. H 6/3/1861 through 11/1/1861, pres. summer/1863, res. Wise Co., VA 1860, s. of Morgan T. & Elizabeth Lipps, m. Mary J. (1848-aft. 1910), bur. Lipps Cem., Dickenson Co., VA.

LITTLE, EDWARD: (1819 – 1892), Co. F, rec. clothing 4/7/1864 & 9/7/1864, des. Abingdon, VA, paroled Cumberland Gap 5/3/1865, res. Breathitt Co. 1860, s. of Edmund & Nellie Cardwell Little, res. Breathitt Co. 1880, m. Ibbie Abrams (1815-aft. 1880), bur. James Little Cem., Elkatawa, Breathitt Co., KY.

LITTLE, WILLIAM: 6/8/1842 – 6/25/1916), Co. B, enl. Whitesburg, KY 9/9/1860, capt. Gladeville, VA 7/7/1863 (re: pension statement), res. Floyd Co. 1860, b. Floyd Co., s. of Isaac & Lucinda Little, widow rec. KY Confed. Widow's Pension #3610 Floyd Co. 1916, m. Beckie Hall (1844-1928) Floyd Co., bur. Little Cem., Wheelwright, Floyd Co., KY.

LITTLE, WILLIAM N.: (5/1845 – 5/20/1929), Co. G., serv. prev. 5th KY Inf Co. B (Consol.), identified as captured with 13th KY Cav. Co. G 2/1864 during skirmish South Fk. Quicksand, Breathitt Co. in Confed. Pension of Wilson T. Combs, s. of Edmond & Eda L. (Abrams) Little, res. of Breathitt Co. 1860, m. America Hays (1843-1893), bur. Little Cem., Cane Cr., Elkatawa, Breathitt Co., KY.

LYTTLE, GEORGE BRITTAIN: (b. 7/19/1845), Co. K, reportedly served as a courier for the Confed. Army in 1862, enl. Lee Co., VA 8/18/1863, capt. Lee Co., VA nr. Cumberland Gap fall/1863, to McLean Barracks 11/22/1863, to Camp Chase Prison 11/23/1863, rel. on oath 12/21/1863, res. Clay Co. 1860, teacher aka 'Dick Fellows', b. Harlan Co., s. of David Y. & Drucilla (Brittain) Little, moved to CA 1866, robbed a lone rider Los Angeles 1869, attempted to rob Coastline Stage & sent to San Quentin 1/31/1870, rel. 4/4/1874, robbed Los Angeles stage 1875, sent to San Quentin 6/16/1875, rel. 5/1881, moved to Santa Cruz, CA, robbed more stages 1881 & 1882, capt. & escaped several times, sent to Folsom Prison 1882, pardoned in 1908, ret. KY, res. Jefferson Co, KY 1910 (teacher and CSA vet), res. Knox Co. (Barbourville) w/ sister, Sally Lyttle Hatton 1920, res. Clay Co. (Brook View) w/ brother, Carlow B. Lyttle, bur. Cedar Craig Cem., Manchester, Clay Co., KY.

MADDEN, ANDREW JACKSON: (1839 – 10/4/1863), Co. A, serv. prev. 5th KY Inf., Co. F, capt. Gladeville, VA 7/7/1863, to Kemper Barracks 7/18/1863, to Kemper Barracks 7/18/1863, to Camp Chase Prison 7/20/1863, to Camp Douglas Prison 8/24/1863, res. Letcher Co. 1860, b. 1839, s. of George W. & Rachel (Fallin) Madden, d. from typhoid Camp Douglas 10/4/1863, bur. Oak Wood Cem., Chicago, Cook Co., IL.

MADDEN, GEORGE WASHINGTON: (1837 – 2/16/1864), Co. A, serv. prev. 5th KY Inf., Co. F, capt. Gladeville, VA 7/7/1863, to Kemper Barracks 7/18/1863, to Camp Chase Prison 7/20/1863, to Camp Douglas Prison 8/24/1863, res. Letcher Co. 1860, b. 1837, s. of George W. & Rachel (Fallin) Madden, d. chronic diarrhea Camp Douglas Prison 2/16/1864, bur. Oak Wood Cem., Chicago, Cook Co., IL.

MADDEN, JOHN A: (1827 – 1888), Co. A, enl. Whitesburg, KY 8/31/1863, serv. prev. 5th KY Inf., Co. F, capt Gladeville, VA (re: Confed. Pension statement), rec. clothing 9/15/1864, res. Letcher Co. 1860, s. of George W. & Rachel (Fallin) Madden, widow rec. Confed. Widow's Pension #2186 Knott Co. 1912, died & bur. Eastern State Mental Hosp. Lexington, Fayette Co., KY.

MADDEN, WESLEY: (12/15/1833 – 5/13/1917), Co. A, serv. prev. 5th KY Inf., Co. F, stated he serv. 'one year twice', capt. w/ others of 13th Booneville, KY 8/19/1863, to Camp Chase Prison, to Rock Island Prison, exch. James River, VA 3/23/1865, did not take oath, res. Letcher Co. 1860, b. Perry Co. (now Knott), s. of George W. & Rachel (Fallin) Madden, rec. KY Confed. Pension #3404 Knott Co. (Brinkley) 1912, m. Malinda (1842-1925), bur. Madden Cem., Amburgey, Knott Co., KY.

MADDEN, WILLIAM D.: (10/20/1822 – 1865), 1st Sgt., Co. A, serv. prev. 5th KY Inf., Co. F, pres. spring/1863, res. Letcher Co., KY 1860, s. of George W. & Rachel (Fallin) Madden, widow rec. KY Confed. Widow's Pension #2713 Knott Co. 1912, pension states he was killed by "a Yankee", William Mosley, Letcher Co. 1865, m. Christena B. Smith (1832-1920's) 1847, bur. Madden Cem., Amburgey, Knott Co., KY.

MAGGARD, JOHN C.: (4/1843 – 1901), Co. B, enl. Whitesburg, KY 8/31/1862, pres. 9/8/1862, res. Letcher, Co. 1860, s. of Moses & Charlotte (Creech) Maggard, res. Letcher Co. (King's Creek) 1870 & 1900, widow res. 1910 & 1920 Letcher Co, m. Mahalia Rice (1850-aft. 1910) 1871.

MAGGARD, JOHN D.: (9/28/1834 – 3/2/1904), Co. H, enl. & disc. Whitesburg, KY 10/18/1862, res. Letcher Co. 1850, res. Perry Co. 1860, s. of Samuel & Rachel (Sturgill) Maggard, res. Letcher Co. 1870 & 1880, m. Ann Pratt (1831-aft. 1900), bur. Pratt Cem., Garner, Knott Co., KY.

MANUEL, MACK C.: (1835 – 1910), Co. F, enl. Floyd Co. 10/14/1862, enl. 10th KY Cav., Co. D 12/5/1862, res. Floyd Co. 1860, b. VA, res. Floyd Co. 1870, 1880, 1890, 1900, widow res. Floyd Co. 1910, m. Mary "Polly" Shepherd (1839-1911) 1859, bur. John Reffett Cem., Pyramid, Floyd Co., KY.

MARSHALL, MORGAN: (1835 – 1865), 4th Cpl., Co. C, aka Morgan Fugate, enl. Whitesburg, KY 10/1/1862, pres. spring/1863, also serv, Union 14th KY Inf., Co. D 9/21/1863 to 12/1/1863 & 3 Fk. Btn. 4/3/1865 to 7/17/1865, killed by former Confed. soldiers 1865 (re: pension statement Pvt. William J. Marshall), res. Breathitt Co. 1860, s. of Andrew Marshall & Unknown Fugate, ½ bro. to Pvt. William Marshall, bur. Lewis Fork Cem., Noble, Breathitt Co., KY.

MARSHALL, THOMAS JEFFERSON: (4/18/1830 – 4/21/1912), Co. G, enl. Gladeville, VA 1/8/1863, capt. Gladeville 7/7/1863, res. Floyd Co. 1860, b. VA, s. of Hugh & Mary Marshall, res. Floyd Co. 1870, res. Johnson Co. 1910, m. (1) Ann Francis (b. 1830), (2) Lourainie Brown (1861-1947) 1887, d. Johnson Co., d.c. #10469, bur. Whitaker Cem., Whitaker, Floyd Co., KY.

MARSHALL, WILLIAM JEFFERSON: (1/30/1835 - 10/1/1896), Co. G, conscripted Breathitt Co., KY (Buckhorn) 6/29/1863 (re: Federal pension), identified in "Artificial 10th KY Cav." – misfiled records, capt. Gladeville, VA 7/7/1863, to Camp Douglas Prison 8/24/1863, "desires to take oath & join three brothers in Federal forces", enl. U.S. Navy 5/24/1864, initially assigned *U.S.S. Susquehanna*, serv. *U.S.S. Wabash* & *U.S.S. New Hampshire*, res. Breathitt Co. 1860, s. of Andrew & Nancy (Ward) Marshall, res. Greenup Co. 1870, res. Boyd Co. 1880, moved to Carter Co., MO, m. (1) Elizabeth Roberts (1835-aft. 1880) 1855, (2) Ella Pole, bur. Henson Hilltop Cem., Ellsinore, Carter Co., MO.

MARTIN, ADAM: (5/5/1839 – 9/18/1905), Capt., Co. F, enl. Floyd Co., KY 9/21/1862, AWOL 6/1864, successor was Capt. James C. Walker, dropped from roll, res. Floyd Co. 1860, s. of John Sr. & Anna (Gearheart) Martin, m. (1) Emeline Martin (1846-1879), (2) Anna Harris 1880, bur. John Martin Cem., Wayland, Floyd Co., KY.

MARTIN, ALLEN: (1820 – 1885), 4th Sgt., Co. F, enl. Letcher Co., KY 10/14/1862, res. Floyd Co. (Rt. Fk. Beaver nr. mo. Patton Br.) 1860, s. of David & Fanny (Rose) Martin, moved Rowan Co. (Morehead) bef. 1870, m. (1) Catherine Walker (1830-bef. 1868) 1845, (2) Rosanna Slone (1840-bef. 1880) 1868, (3) Quintina Christian of Rowan Co. (b. 1848), widow & children moved Caroll Co., AR & then KS, bur. Community Cem., Elliotville, Rowan Co., KY.

MARTIN, FRANK: Cos. F & G, identified in "Artificial 10th KY Cav. – misfiled records, capt. Gladeville, VA 7/7/1863, 5'8", fair complexion, light hair, to Kemper Barracks 7/18/1863, to Camp Chase Prison 7/20/1863, to Camp Douglas 8/24/1863.

MARTIN, GEORGE: (3/3/1828 – 1/25/1925), Co. F, enl. Floyd Co., KY 10/14/1862, serv. Union 39th KY, Co. F 8/8/1863 to 12/20/1864, res. Floyd Co. 1860, s. of David & Fanny (Rose) Martin, res. Perry Co. (Troublesome) 1870 & 1880, moved Owsley Co. 1890's, m. Caroline Frazier (1834-1899), (2) Easter Cornett (1856-1938), bur. w/ Union marker Mainous Cem. Scoville, Owsley Co., KY.

MARTIN, JAMES: (1/12/1844 – 12/1/1927), Co. F, enl. Floyd Co. 10/14/1862, res. Floyd Co. 1860, s. of Simpson & Elizabeth (Turner) Martin, m. Rosie Frazier (1845-1898) 1869, bur. James Martin Cem., Drift, Floyd Co., KY.

MARTIN, JOSEPH "BIG JOE": (1/26/1844 – 1/14/1923), 1st. Sgt., Co. F, enl. Whitesburg, KY 10/14/1862, serv. prev. 5th KY Inf., Co. G, pres. fall/1863, res. Floyd Co. 1860, s. of John Sr. & Anna (Gearheart) Martin, rec. KY Confed. Pension #1425 Floyd Co. 1912, m. Louisa "Lula" Brashear (1854-aft. 1920) Letcher Co. 1867, bur. Watt Martin Cem., Estill, Floyd Co., KY.

MARTIN, RICHARD: (1832 – 1882), Co. F, enl. Floyd Co., KY 10/14/1862, res. Floyd Co. 1860, s. of Joel & Rebecca (Feltner) Martin, res. Floyd Co. 1870 & 1880, m. Winnie Sizemore (1830-aft. 1880), bur. Combs Cem., Mousie, Knott Co., KY.

MARTIN, TANDY: (1836 – 11/18/1863), Co. F, enl. Floyd Co., KY 10/14/1862, capt. Gladeville, VA 7/7/1863, to Kemper Barracks 7/18/1863, to Camp Chase Prison 7/20/1863, to Camp Douglas Prison 8/24/1863, res. Floyd Co. (Lackey) 1860, s. of James & Milly Martin, d. from measles Camp Douglas, bur. Oak Wood Cem., Chicago, Cook Co., IL.

MARTIN, THOMAS: (1844 – 5/11/1865), Co. D, PWR indicates enl. w/ Lt. Samuel W. Thompson 9/12/1863, serv. SW VA & NE KY as scout late fall/1863, capt. by Union 40th KY Mtd. Inf. 1/8/1864, to Grayson, KY as a "guerilla", to McLean Barracks 2/12/1864, trial held 9/13/1864, res. Greenup Co. 1850, s. of George & Polly Martin, executed McLean Barracks, Cincinnati, bur. St. Joseph New Cem., Cincinnati, Hamilton Co., OH.

MARTIN, WILLIAM J. "BEE": (10/30/1832 – 5/10/1906), Co. F, enl. Floyd Co., KY 10/14/1862, serv. prev. 5th KY Inf., Co. G, res. Floyd Co. (Wayland) 1860, s. of John Sr. & Anna (Gearheart) Martin, m. Helen Martin (1842-1923), bur. Martin Cem., Estill, Floyd Co., KY.

MARTIN, WYATT: (4/17/1817 – 1/15/1901), 4th Cpl., Co. F, enl. Floyd Co., KY 10/14/1862, res. Floyd Co. 1850 & 1860, s. of James & Milly Martin, res. Letcher Co. 1870 & 1880, m. (1) Elizabeth "Betsy" Stumbo (1834-bef. 1866) 1853, (2) Jane "Jenny" Amburgey (1821- d. aft 1900) 1866, bur. Steerfork Cem., Pinetop, Knott Co., KY.

MAY, WILLIAM L. BERRY: (6/11/1834 – 8/12/1907), enl. Breathitt Co., KY 3/23/1863, res. Breathitt Co. 1860, s. of William & Sarah May, m. (1) Adeline Turner (1836-1895) 1857, (2) Mary, bur. Deaton & White Cem., Barwick, Breathitt Co., KY.

McCRAY, BENJAMIN: (1840 – 1911), Co. D, enl. Whitesburg, KY 10/4/1862, 5' 8", dark hair, grey eyes, capt. Johnson Co. 5/31/1864, to Louisville Prison & rel. on oath 7/7/1864, res. Letcher Co. 1850, s. of James & Levicy (Yonts) McCray, m. Mahalia (1842-aft. 1910), bur. Henry Meade Cem., Deane, Letcher Co., KY.

McDANIEL, ELIJAH: (1845 – 11/1882), Co. G, identified as captured with 13th KY Cav. Co. G in skirmish South Fk. Quicksand, Breathitt Co. 2/1864 in Confed. Pension of Wilson T. Combs, s. of Arthur & Mary Polly (Fugate) McDaniel, res. Breathitt Co. 1860, m. Mahala Marcum (1845-1921), died on Pond Creek, Jackson Co., KY.

McDANIEL, WILEY: (b. 1834), Co. C, enl. Whitesburg, KY 10/1/1862, pres. fall/1862, res. Breathitt Co. 1860, s. of John & Hannah (Fugate) McDaniel, res. Knott Co. 1889 (re: tax list), m. Elizabeth Pruett (1824-aft. 1910)1858.

McDANIEL, WILLIAM: (10/1843 – 8/1921), Co. H, enl. Whitesburg, KY 10/18/1862, des. 11/6/1862, serv. Union 47th KY Inf., Co. H 7/4/1863 to 12/26/1864, res. Letcher Co. 1860, res. Letcher Co. 1880, res. Laurel Co. 1890, 1900 & 1910 (Crossroads/Hazel Patch), rec Union Pension #671360. m. Clarinda Smith (1850-aft/ 1920), widow rec. Pension #468179, bur. McDaniel Cem., East Bernstadt, Laurel Co., KY.

McELROY, WILLIAM S.: (1837 - 1867), Co. K, enl. Lee Co., VA 8/18/1863, serv. prev. 64th VA Inf., 2nd Co. F, pres. 12/31/1863, surr. Cumberland Gap 4/30/1865, res. Lee Co., VA 1860, b. Lee Co. VA 1837, m. Lavina C. Orr (b. 1839) Lee Co., VA 1859, Lavina remarried 1870.

McFADDEN, DAVID ALEXANDER: (10/4/1825 – 1/27/1875), Co. K, surr. Cumberland Gap 4/30/1865, res. Scott Co., VA 1860 (tanner), b. VA, s. of Isaac & Margaret McFadden, res. Johnson Co. KY 1870, m. (1) Catherine (1823-1855), (2) Louisa Biddle (1831-1912), "struck & killed by lightning in 1870's" (re: family history), bur Old Paintsville Cem., Paintsville, Johnson Co., KY.

McFADDEN, JOHN HOPKINS: (9/25/1837 – 11/22/1908), Co. K, serv. prev. 37th VA Inf., Co. C, pres. Lee Co., VA 12/31/1863, rec. clothing 9/7/1864, surr. Cumberland Gap 4/30/1865, res. Russell Co. VA 1860, s. of Isaac McFadden, widow applied KY Confed. Pension Johnson Co., KY 1912, m. Florence (1841-1913 Johnson Co.), bur. C. C. Meade Cem., Collista, Johnson, Co., KY.

McINTIRE, ALEXANDER: (4/14/1835 – 5/7/1922), Co. G, enl. Whitesburg, KY 10/18/1862, pres. 12/2/1862, joined Union 14th KY, Co. K Perry Co. (Chavies) after John Gambill & other Confeds. killed there, also serv. Union 6th KY Cav., res. Perry Co. s. of Ben & Sally McIntire, res. Owsley Co. 1890, m. Mary Ann Kelly (1840-1912) 1860, bur. w/ Union marker, Alex McIntire Cem., Vincent, Owsley Co., KY.

McINTIRE, WILLIAM: (3/1835 – 1911), Co. H, enl. Whitesburg, KY 10/12/1862, identified in A. G. Report, Perry Co. (mo. Rockhouse Creek) 1860, s. of Benjamin & Sally McIntire, res. Perry Co. 1880, m. Diana Combs (1842-1911) 1859, bur. Stuart Robinson School Cem., Blackey, Letcher Co., KY.

McINTOSH, FUGATE: (1836 – 4/15/1863), Co. G, enl. Breathitt Co., KY 10/1/1862, des & joined Union 14th KY 12/3/1862, res. Breathitt Co. 1860, b. IN, s. of James & Catherine (Fugate) McIntosh, m. Catherine Thomas (b. 1836) 1854, d. Clark Co. (Winchester).

McINTOSH, VERDAMON: (1840 – 5/11/1863), Co. G, enl. Breathitt Co., KY 9/23/1862, des. & joined Union 14th KY, Co. K, res. Breathitt Co. 1860, s. of Nimrod & Nancy McIntosh, d. from fever Irvine, KY, bur. Grave #2643, Camp Nelson National Cem., Hall, Jessamine Co., KY.

McINTOSH, WILLIAM TURNER: (1834 – 3/4/1865), Co. G, enl. Breathitt Co., KY 9/23/1862, capt. Gladeville, VA 7/7/1863, to Kemper Barracks 7/18/1863, to Camp Chase Prison 7/20/1863, to Camp Douglas Prison 8/24/1863, to Point Lookout Prison for exch. 2/24/1865, res. Breathitt Co. 1860, s. of James & Catherine (Fugate) McIntosh, m. Nancy Combs (b. 1836) 1853, d. from pneumonia U. S. Hosp. Richmond, VA, poss. bur. Richmond, VA.

McKEE (McGEE), ANDREW JACKSON: (1847 -1883), Co. K, identified in "Artificial 10th KY Cav." – misfiled records, 5' 6', fair complexion, auburn hair, grey eyes, capt. Lee Co., VA 11/12/1863, to Mclean Barracks 11/22/1863, to Camp Chase Prison 11/23/1863, to Ft. Delaware Prison 2/29/1864, rel. 6/9/1865, s. of Robert M. & Ester (Berry) McGee, b. Owsley Co., res. Clay Co. 1860, moved to Parker Co., TX, m (1) Virginia Mitchell 1871, (2) Tennessee Mitchell 1875, shot & killed Parker Co., TX 1883.

McKEE (McGEE), GEORGE W.: (b. 1842), 2Lt, Co. K, enl. Lee Co., VA 8/18/1863, elected 3rd Lt. 12/31/1863, reported in error as 'killed in KY' & dropped from roll 2/16/1865, had been capt. Whitesburg, KY 12/29/1864, to Louisville Prison 3/28/1865, to Camp Chase Prison & rel. on oath 4/3/1865, s. of Robert M. & Ester (Berry) McGee, res. Clay Co. 1860, moved to TX by 1869, m. Callie (b. 1850), res. McLennan Co. TX 1870.

McKEE, JACOB: Co. K, also listed as Jacob McGee, enl. Lee Co., VA 8/18/1863, capt. nr. Cumberland Gap fall/1863.

McKEE, JOHN: (2/6/1845 – 11/30/1922), Co. I, conscripted Whitesburg, KY 10/18/1862, serv. prev. 5th KY Inf., Co. I (re: pension statement), rec. clothing 9/24/1864, serv. as scout until disbanding between New River & Abingdon, VA 4/5/1865, took oath at Louisa, KY, rec. KY Confed. Pension #851 Knott Co. 1912, m. Minerva (1835-ca. 1921), bur. Young's Fork Cem., Elic, Knott Co., KY.

McKEE, WILLIAM HARRISON: (7/9/1844 – 1/21/1940), Co. I, conscripted Whitesburg, KY 10/1/1862, serv. prev. 5th KY Inf., Co. I, pres. fall/1863, res. Perry Co. 1860, b. Lincoln Co., KY, s. of John McKee, moved to Andrew Co., MO by 1870, res. Andrew Co. 1880, res. CO by 1900, moved to WA (Lind) 1913, m. Alice Ann Thomas (d. 1918), , bur. Lind Cem., Lind, Adams Co., WA.

McLEMORE, BENJAMIN F.: (1845 – 1923), Cos. G & I, enl. Perry Co., KY 9/26/1862, trans. from Co. G to Co. I, rec. clothing 9/24/1864, res. Perry Co. 1860, s. of Hiram & Marg (Fairchild) McLemore, res. Perry Co. (Lost Creek) 1870, m. Caroline (1843-1907), bur. Wise City Cem., Wise, Wise Co., VA.

McLEMORE, JOSEPH: (9/15/1846 – 4/12/1936), Co. G, also listed as 'Josiah", enl. Whitesburg, KY 8/31/1863, capt. Battle of Cynthiana 6/14/1864, to Louisville Prison 6/22/1864, to Rock Island Prison 6/24/1864, enl. Co. I, 2nd U. S. Volunteers late 1864, res. Perry Co. 1860, s. of Hiram & Marg (Fairchild) McLemore, m. Mary Hughes (d. 1943), bur. McLemore & Noble Cem., Dice, Perry Co., KY.

McNIEL, ALEXANDER CAMPBELL: (1/11/1827 – 9/8/1911), Co. F, identified in "Artificial 10th KY Cav." – misfiled records, paroled at Cumberland Gap 4/26/1865 by Dillard's 34th KY Inf., remarks – Lee County, m. Rhoda Ewing (1829-1897), res. of Lee Co., VA 1860, bur Ewing-McClure Cem., Jonesville, Lee Co., VA.

McQUINN, JEREMIAH: (1845 – 1898), Kash's Co., serv. prev. 5th KY Inf. & Diamond's 10th KY Cav., Co. E, res. Breathitt Co. 1860, s. of Charles & Ester (Howard) McQuinn, PWR indicted for 1865 murder as member Kash's Co., res. Breathitt Co. 1880, suffered mental illness after being kicked in the head by a horse, m. Katherine Allen (1845-1880 to 1900), d. Eastern State Mental Hosp., Lexington, KY, bur. Risner Cem., Guage, Breathitt Co., KY.

McQUINN, WILEY: (1813 – 1865), Co. G, enl. Jackson, KY 2/12/1863, 5' 11" hazel eyes, capt. Magoffin Co. 2/22/1864 (actually, 10 mi. above Jackson on S. Fk. Quicksand), to Louisa, to Ohio R. & to Louisville Prison 3/6/1864, to Camp Chase Prison as a guerilla and a horse thief 3/9/1864, rel. on oath 5/13/1865, res. Breathitt Co. 1860, s. of Charles & Lucy McQuinn, m. Sarah Hayes (b.1810), bur. Hayes Cem., Quicksand, Breathitt Co., KY.

MEADE, JAMES MADISON "MATT": (7/5/1843 – 1/6/1925), Co. E, enl. Whitesburg, KY 10/5/1862, pres. 2/1863, res. Letcher Co. 1860, s. of Thomas & Mary Meade, m. Letisha Wright (1843-1924), bur. Lower Meade Cem., Deane, Letcher Co., KY.

MEADE, RHODES W. (1836 – 1869), 4th Sgt., Co. E, enl. Whitesburg, KY 10/5/1862, appointed Sgt. 4/30/1863, capt. Floyd Co. 7/7/1863, to Louisville Prison 11/18/1863, to Camp Morton Prison 11/20/1863, rel. on oath 5/22/1865, res. Letcher Co., b. Floyd Co., s. of Thomas & Mary Meade, widow rec. KY Confed. Pension #859 Letcher Co. 1912, m. Mary Jane Hall (b. 1842) Letcher Co. 1867, d. Rockhouse nr. Deane P.O. (re: pension), bur. Thomas Meade Cem., Deane, Letcher Co., KY.

MEADE, RILEY: (1841 – 8/24/1864), Co. D, enl. Whitesburg, KY 10/4/1862, serv. later Union 45th KY Inf., Co. C, poss. wd. Battle of Lexington & soon died, res. Letcher Co. 1860, s. of Thomas & Mary Meade, bur. w/ Union marker Lexington Cem., Lexington, Fayette Co., KY.

MEADE, WILLIAM REUBEN: (1833 – 1896), 4th Cpl., Co. E, enl. Whitesburg, KY 10/5/1862, des. & ret. serv, appointed 4th Cpl 4/30/1863, res. Letcher Co. 1860, s. of Thomas & Mary Meade, res. Letcher Co. 1870, res. Floyd Co. 1880, res. Letcher Co. by 1886, m. Malinda Thornsberry (d. 1881), bur. Henry Meade Cem., Deane, Letcher Co., KY.

MESSER, ALEXANDER J.: (1838 -6/24/1923), Co. C, ernl. Whitesburg, KY 10/1/1862, serv. prev. 5th KY Inf., Cos. H & I, pres. Summer/1863, res. Perry Co. 1860, s. of Henry Southern & Haney Messer, m. (1) Elizabeth Bowen, (2) Rosa Patton (b. 1868), indicted 1889 for murder of two McCoy boys related to Hatfield-McCoy feud, sent to Eddyville penitentiary, paroled 1906, res. Knott Co. 1910, arrested for parole violation & threats Rowan Co. 1917, sent to Western State Hospital, bur Western State Cem., Hopkinsville, Christian Co. KY, in memory marker Messer Cem., Quicksand, Knott Co., KY.

MESSER, ELIJAH: (12/17/1840 – 4/14/1900), 4th Sgt., Co. C, enl. Whitesburg, KY 10/1/1862, serv. prev. 5th KY Inf., Co. I, serv. until 4/1865, res. Perry Co. 1860, s. of Henry Southern & Haney Messer, res. Perry Co. (Troublesome) 1870, widow rec. KY Confed. Widow's Pension #865 Knott Co. 1912, m. Sarah Maggard (1846-1930) Perry Co., bur. Messer Cem., Quicksand, Knott Co., KY.

MESSER, JESSE: (1836 – 1874), Co. I, conscripted Whitesburg, KY 10/18/1862, pres. summer 1863, res. Perry Co. 1860, s. of Sally Smith Messer, res. Perry Co. (re: tax list) 1871, widow res. Perry Co. (re: tax list) 1874, m. Martha A. Combs (1835-aft. 1880) 1859, bur. Riverside Cem., Hazard, Perry Co., KY.

MIDDLETON, BENJAMIN FRANKLIN: (6/13/1828 – 7/16/1911), Co. K, surr. Cumberland Gap 4/30/1865, res. Harlan Co. 1860, s. of William & Sarah (Turner) Middleton, pardoned by Governor for two Harlan Co. cases of war-related robbery & larceny 1867, widow rec. KY Confed. Widow's Pension #1437 Harlan Co. 1912, m. Sarah Blevins (1842-1919), bur. Nolan Cem., Baxter, Harlan Co., KY.

MIDDLETON, CARLO "CARR": (12/25/1837 – 12/2/1902), Co. K, surr. Cumberland Gap 4/30/1865, serv. prev. 64th VA Inf., Co. H, "He was shot during the war by his cousins 'Devil Jim' & William Turner; the wound caused him to be crippled the rest of his life" (re: family history), res. Harlan Co. 1860, s. of William & Sarah (Turner) Middleton, res. Harlan Co. 1890, m. Marinda Grey (1835-1903), bur. Bill Creek Cem., Dizney, Harlan Co., KY.

MIDDLETON, GEORGE W.: Cpl., Co. K, rec. clothing 9/7/1864, surr. Cumberland Gap 4/30/1865, res. Harlan Co.

MIDDLETON, WALTER: (2/16/1847 – 8/31/1928), 4th Cpl., Co. K, enl. Lee Co., VA 8/18/1863, rec. clothing 9/7/1864, surr. Cumberland Gap 4/30/1865, res. Harlan Co. 1860, s. of James & Abigail Middleton, m. Nancy Hope (1859-1920), bur. Middleton Cem., nr. Ewing, Lee Co., VA.

MIDDLETON, WILLIAM T.: (5/30/1831 – 12/3/1872), Co. K, serv. prev. 25th VA Cav., furloughed from hosp., ret. home & joined 13th KY 2/3/1865, surr. Cumberland Gap 4/30/1865, s. of Walter & Sarah (Turner) Middleton, pardoned by KY Gov. Thomas E. Bramlett for three cases of war-related robbery 1/22/1867, murdered by cousin James Turner 1872, widow rec. KY Confed. Widow's Pension #868, m. Narcissa Howard (1828-1914), bur. Middleton Cem., Kildav, Harlan Co., KY.

MILES, WILLIAM RILEY: (9/1/1839 – 11/29/1928), Co. H, enl. Whitesburg, KY 10/18/1862, pres. 12/20/1862, res. Letcher Co. 1850, s. of Anderson & Susan Miles, res. Letcher Co. 1863, res. Morgan Co. (coal miner) 1880, m. Lettisha (1838-1922), d. from Bright's Disease, bur. Henry Cem., West Liberty, Morgan Co., KY.

MILLER, ANDREW T. "TEETER": (1841 – 1/3/1921), enl. Perry Co. 9/20/1862, disch. w/ physical disability by Dr. Jason Cox, who reported to Col. Caudill "contracted disease due to starvation, lack of clothes & lung trouble", shot once at home by Yankees, once traveled from Whitesburg to Manuel barefoot in the snow, res. Perry Co. 1860, s. of Andrew & Martha "Patsy" (Noble) Miller, rec. KY Confed. Pension #3002 Perry Co. (Manuel) 1912, m. Malinda "Linda" Neace (1845-aft. 1910), bur. Mudlick Cem., Grapevine, Perry Co., KY.

MILLER, DANIEL: (b. 1843), Co. G, enl. Whitesburg, KY 9/26/1862, rec. clothing 4/7/1864, res. Breathitt Co. (Ned) 1860, s. of John & Sarah (Roberts) Miller.

MILLER, GEORGE W.: (10/11/1842 – 1/4/1934), Co. G, enl. Whitesburg, KY 10/10/1862, pres. summer/1863, res. Breathitt Co. 1860, b. 1844, s. of George & Priscilla (Maloney) Miller, res. Wolfe Co. (Lee City) 1910, m. Cinderella Louisa Shackelford (1848-1927) 1866, bur. Allen-Shoemaker Cem., Waynesburg, Lincoln Co., KY.

MILLER, GEORGE WASHINGTON: (5/9/1835 – 4/5/1905), Co. G, enl. Breathitt Co. 10/1/1862, aka George Washington Helton, pres. summer/1863, res. Breathitt Co. 1860, s. of Francis Helton & Martha "Patsy" Fugate, res. Breathitt Co. (Lanesville) 1890, m. Nancy Jane Fugate (1840-1903) 1855, bur. Flint Ridge Cem., Clayhole, Breathitt Co., KY.

MILLER, GRANVILLE STEPHEN: (5/12/1846 – 5/22/1904), Co. G, enl. Whitesburg, KY 8/31/1862, his 1st cousin-once removed, Union Capt. William Strong killed his father, Hiram B. Miller, 5th KY Inf., Quicksand, 4/17/1864, capt. Perry Co. 4/25/1864, to Louisville Prison 5/7/1864, to Camp Morton Prison 5/12/1864, hospitalized 11/4/1864 to 11/30/1864, exch. 3/15/1865, res. Breathitt Co. 1860, b. Breathitt Co. (Panbowl, nr. Jackson), s. of Hiram B. & Elizabeth (Strong) Miller, serv. as 4-term Judge Executive of Breathitt Co., m. (1) Evaline Williams (1843-1875) 1869, (2) Lucinda Williams (1842-1909) 1877, bur. Jackson Cem., Jackson, Breathitt Co., KY.

MILLER, JAMES: (3/16/1848 – 1/17/1928), Co. B, enl. Whitesburg, KY 9/9/1862, capt. Gladeville, VA 7/7/1863, to Kemper Barracks 7/18/1863, to Camp Chase Prison 7/20/1863, to Camp Douglas Prison 8/24/1863, res. Perry Co. 1860, b. Breathitt Co. (Lost Creek), s. of John C. & Tobitha "Bitha" (McIntosh) Miller, m. Sarah Jane Roberts (1858-1939), bur. McIntosh Cem., Clayhole, Breathitt Co., KY.

MILLER, JOHN B.: (10/5/1846 – 6/10/1926), Co. I, enl. Gladeville, VA 11/20/1863, res. Russell Co., VA 1850, b. VA, s. of John & Polly Miller, res. Letcher Co. 1880, m. Rebecca Caudill (1850-aft. 1920) dau. Ben Caudill & Mary Bowling, bur. Kingdom Come Church Cem., Kingdom Come, Letcher Co., KY.

MILLER, JOHN S. JACKSON "FATTY": (7/11/1838 – 1/10/1929), 3rd Cpl., Co. G, enl. Breathitt Co. 9/23/1862, served under Henderson Combs then W. M. Landrum, capt. Gladeville, VA 7/7/1863, to Camp Chase Prison, to Camp Douglas Prison for 20 months, paroled 3/12/1865, res. Breathitt Co. 1860, s. of William Joseph Jr. & Sarah "Sally" (Noble) Miller, rec. KY Confed. Pension #870 Clark Co. KY 1912, m. (1) Nancy Fugate (1841-1880 to 1900) 1859, (2) Louisa Fugate (1848-1930), bur. Dawson-Miller Cem., Kiddville, Clark Co., KY.

MILLER, LOSSON: (12/24/1842 – 2/21/1906), Co. G, enl. Breathitt Co. 9/23/1862, des. 12/8/1862, serv. later Union 14th KY Inf., Co. K 2/14/1863 to 3/24/1864, res. Breathitt Co. 1860, s. of William Joseph Jr. & Sarah "Sally" (Noble) Miller, res. Estill Co. (Miller's Creek) 1870, res. Powell Co. 1880, m. Dicy Edwards (1844-1927), bur. Johnson-Miller Cem., Zoe, Lee Co., KY.

MILLER, MASON: (12/20/1836 – 5/8/1922), Cos. G & B, enl. date unknown, transf. from Co. G to B, stated he disbanded (with 13th) at Gladeville, VA 4/11/1865, s. of Andrew & Martha "Patsy" (Noble) Miller, res. of Perry Co. 1860, m. Nelly Neace (b. 1845), bur. in Combs-Whitaker Cem., Grapevine, Perry Co., KY.

MILLER, NATHANIAL: (4/15/1840 – 1/31/1938), Co. G, enl. Breathitt Co. 9/23/1862, pres. fall/1862, also serv. Union 14th KY, Co. K 12/3/1862 to 3/24/1864, res. Breathitt Co. 1860, s. of William Joseph Jr. & Sarah "Sally" (Noble) Miller, m. (1) America McIntosh (1838-bef. 1870) 1856, (2) Eveline McIntosh (1844-1904), bur. McIntosh Cem., Clayhole, Breathitt Co., KY.

MILLER, SAMUEL: (1/12/1843 – 10/18/1918), Co. C, enl. Whitesburg, KY 10/1/1862, capt. Gladeville, VA 7/7/1863 (re: pension statement), res. Breathitt Co. 1860, s. of Samuel & Franky (Carpenter) Miller, m. Arty Bailey Miller (1843-1918) 1864, d. from chronic diarrhea (d.c. #26084), bur. Miller Cem., Dock, Floyd Co., KY.

MILLER, WILEY: (1842 – 6/23/1917), Cos. G. & B, enl. Breathitt Co. 9/23/1862, capt Perry Co. (Lost Creek) 6/6/1863, to Camp Chase Prison 6/16/1863, to Johnson's Island Prison 6/20/1863, to Point Lookout Prison 10/30/1863, rel. on oath 4/11/1864, ret. KY w/ G. W. Noble, ret. Co. B 9/1864 & serv. until disbandment Gladeville, VA on march to Richmond 4/11/1865, res. Breathitt Co. 1860, s. of Andrew & Martha "Patsy" (Noble) Miller, res. Perry Co. (Manuel) 1870, rec. KY Confed. Pension #3636 Perry Co. 1912, pension mentions his gray uniform, res. Breathitt Co. (Ned) 1917, m. Elizabeth "Bettie" Gwinn (1844-aft. 1910)1864, bur. Ten Mile Cem., Ten Mile, Perry Co., KY.

MILLER, WILLIAM: (2/1/1831 – 8/22/1912), Co. C, enl. Whitesburg, KY 10/1/1862, res. Perry Co. 1860, s. of Andrew Miller & Martha "Patsy" (Noble) Miller, m. (1) Priscilla Fugate (1839-bef. 1870), (2) Sarah Jane Noble (b. 1845), (3) Sarah Hurt, bur. Millertown Church Cem., Lost Creek, Perry Co., KY.

MILLER, WILLIAM: (4/7/1844 – 10/20/1872), Co. G, enl. Breathitt Co. 9/23/1862, disch. 1/1/1863, res. Breathitt Co. 1860, s. of William Joseph Jr. & Sarah "Sally" (Noble) Miller, Breathitt Co. Court records state that he was killed with a rock by former Cpl. Wilson T. Combs in a quarrel over Miller's wife (Dulcenia Allen) 10/20/1872, Combs was acquitted by an all-ex-Confederate jury and he subsequently married Dulcenia Allen Miller, bur. Ritchie Cem., Hardshell, Breathitt Co., KY.

MITCHELL, HARRISON: (1840 – 11/13/1863), Co. H, enl. Whitesburg, KY 9/12/1862, capt. & taken to Camp Douglas Prison, res. Scott Co., VA 1850, res. Perry Co. 1860, s. of William & Eliza Mitchell, d. Camp Douglas bur. Oak Wood Cem., Chicago, Cook Co., IL.

MOORE, CALVIN G.: (b. 4/1843), Co. E, enl. Whitesburg, KY 10/5/1862, serv. later w/ Diamond's 10th, Co. A & Well's Co., surr. w/ 10th KY 5/1865, res. Floyd Co. 1860, s. of John & Rachel (Bridgeman) Moore, res. Floyd Co. 1870 & 1900, m. Seattie Terry (1848-d. aft. 1910) 1867, bur. unmarked, no dates, nr. wife, Spurlock Cem., Printer, Floyd Co., KY.

MOORE, CORNELIUS N.: (8/28/1841 – 11/8/1915), Co. K, enl. 1863, serv. prev. 2nd Btn. KY Mtd. Rifles, Co. A, surr. Cumberland Gap, took oath, res. Jackson Co., b. Owsley Co., s. of Elias & Sally (Morris) Moore, rec. KY Confed. Pension #2737/3453 Lee Co. (Fillmore), KY, m. Elizabeth Spencer (1845-1924) Wolfe Co. 1864, bur. Neal Moore Cem., Fillmore, Lee Co., KY.

MOORE, DANIEL: (7/18/1831 – 5/21/1892), Co. G, enl. Breathitt Co., KY 10/1/1862, res. Breathitt Co. 1860, s. of Allen & Peggy (Lewis) Moore, killed by his brother, James Lewis Moore, m. Darcus Davidson (1834-1922) 1853, bur. Moore Cem., Altro, Breathitt Co., KY.

MOORE, EDWARD (EDMOND): (3/15/1828 – 10/4/1916), Co. E, enl. Whitesburg, KY 10/5/1862, res. Floyd Co. 1860, b. NC, s. of John & Rachel (Bridgeman) Moore, res. Floyd Co. (Steeles Creek) 1870, 1880 & 1900, m. (1) Rachel Nolan (1832-1881 to 1899) (2) Anna Martin (1830-1911 to 1916), d.c. #25400, bur. Collins Cem., Wayland, Floyd Co., KY.

MOORE, ISAAC: (6/18/1843 – 6/18/1923), Co. E, enl. Whitesburg, KY 10/14/1862, poss. also serv. Diamond's 10th KY Cav., rec. clothing 9/1/1864, res. Floyd Co. 1860, s. of Andrew & Elizabeth (Gearheart) Moore, m. Nancy Bunch (1855-1942), d.c. #14958, bur. Lawson Cem., nr. Princess, Boyd Co., KY.

MOORE, JAMES LEWIS: (7/27/1845 – 10/3/1908), Co. K, serv. prev. 5th KY Inf. Co. A & 5th KY Inf. (Consolidated) Co. B, des. Hansonville, VA 8/10/1863, enl. later 13th KY Cav., surr. Cumberland Gap 4/30/1865, res. Breathitt Co. 1860, s. of Allen & Margaret (Lewis) Moore, m. (1) Fanny Noble (1846-1881 to 1899), (2) Elizabeth Belcher Gay (1846-aft. 1900), bur. Jackson Cem., Jackson, Breathitt Co., KY.

MOORE, JEREMIAH: (b. 1834), Co. E, enl. Whitesburg, KY 10/5/1862, pres. fall/1862, res. Floyd Co., s. of Edmond & Rhoda Moore, res. Floyd Co. (Beaver Cr. w/ parents) 1870, res. Floyd Co. 1900, m. Jane Rule.

MOORE, JOEL: (3/9/1840 – 5/27/1897), Co. E, serv. prev. Diamond's 10th KY, 9/20/1862, enl. Whitesburg, KY 10/5/1862, returned to Diamond's 10th & serv. thru 9/1864, res. Floyd Co. 1860, s. of Andrew & Elizabeth (Gearheart) Moore, bur. unm. Eastern State Hospital Cem., Lexington, Fayette Co., KY.

MOORE, (WILLIAM) HENDERSON: (3/4/1843 – 6/22/1936), Co. E, enl. Whitesburg, KY 10/5/1862, capt. Battle of Cynthiana 6/11/1864 (re: TX Pension), res. Floyd Co. 1850 & 1860, b. Hueysville, KY, s. of Archibald & Sarah Moore, res. Floyd Co. 1870, moved TX late 1870, m. Alice Walker (b. 1859) TX 1877, bur. Rutledge Cem., Poteet, Attascosa Co., TX.

MOORE, WILLIAM TANDY: (8/1844 – 1929), Co. E, enl. Whitesburg, KY 10/5/1862, s.r. lists as Tandy Moore, capt. Gladeville, VA 7/7/1863, res. Floyd Co. 1850, s. of John & Rachel (Bridgeman) Moore, m. (1) Nancy Jane Gearhart (1843-1920) 1862, (2) Virgie (1899-1977), bur. Hall Cem., Dony, Floyd Co., KY.

MOORES, NEWTON: (7/10/1838 – 1/18/1898), Capt. & AQM, s.r. list name as Moore, 5' 10", serv. prev. as Pvt. 1st Btn, Mtd. Rifles, Co. E, enl. Paintsville, KY, letter of recommendation from Col. Ben Caudill to Sec. War re. AQM position dtd. 6/4/1863, capt. Gladeville VA. 7/71863, to Kemper Barracks 7/18/1863, to Camp Chase Prison 7/20/1863, to Johnson's Island Prison 10/10/1863, to Point Lookout Prison 2/21/1865, to Ft. Delaware Prison 4/28/1865, rel. on oath 6/12/1865, some records in "10th KY Artificial Unit" – misfiled records, res. Bath Co. 1850, res. Mason Co. (clerk in merchant Charles Anderson's Maysville home) 1860, s. of Harlan & Mary Ann (Stone) Moores, res. Bath Co. 1874, moved Fleming Co. 1877, moved w/ parents Sumner Co., KS 1880, m. Lydia Cutshell 1890, bur. El Reno Cem., El Reno, Canadian Co., OK.

MORGAN, JACKSON: (3/13/1838 – 7/11/1909), 1st Cpl., Co. F, enl. Floyd Co. 10/14/1862, pres. spring/1863, serv. later Union 39th Inf., Co. F, fair complexion, black hair, blue eyes, 5' 7", res. Johnson Co. 1860, m. (1) Elizabeth Prater 1861, (2) Susan Rothwell (b. 1852) 1891, bur. Wells & Vititoe Cem., Tabor, Menifee Co., KY.

MORGAN, JAMES: (1815 - 1887), Co. D, enl. Whitesburg, KY 10/4/1862, res. Letcher Co. 1860, res. Letcher Co. 1870 & 1880, m. Mary E. Polly (1822-1903) 1839, bur. Thornton Cem., Thornton, Letcher Co., KY.

MORGAN, JOHN: (9/25/1841 – 11/19/1901), Co. H, identified in A. G. Report, enl. 10/18/1862 Whitesburg, KY, s. of James & Mary Emily (Polly) Morgan, res. Letcher Co. 1860, m. Manerva Polly (1844-aft. 1900), bur. John Morgan Cem., Mayking, Letcher Co., KY.

MORGAN, REUBEN SALYER: (1829 – 1/1/1890), Co. C, enl. Floyd Co. 1862, no s.r., pension witnesses stated he serv. in Co. C, was ill w/ fever in Gladeville, VA hosp. & given leave by Col. Ben Caudill, res. Floyd Co. 1850, s. of Wiley & Mary "Polly" (Salyers) Morgan, res. Floyd Co. 1870 & 1880, widow rec. KY Confed. Widow's Pension #3008 Knott Co. (Hindman) 1912, m. (1) Susannah Patton (1828-bef. 1860) 1850, (2) Elizabeth Goodwin (1838-1919), bur. Bob Amburgey Cem., Hindman, Knott Co., KY.

MORRIS, EZEKIEL: (1843 – 10/1873), 3rd Cpl., Co. F, aka Ezekiel Prater, 6' 0", light hair, blue eyes, enl. Floyd Co. 10/14/1862, capt. Floyd Co. spring/1864, to Louisville Prison, joined U.S. forces & gained rel. 4/8/1864, res. Floyd Co. 1860, s. of John Morris & Neomy, res. Floyd Co. 1870, widow applied for Union Pension #567726, m. Sarah Triplett (b. 1842), d. Rowan Co.

MOSLEY, NELSON: (1834 – 1863), Co. C, enl. Whitesburg, KY, abs. & never paid 4/30/1863, res. Perry Co. 1860, s. of Henderson & Polly (Jones) Mosley, bur. Sandlick Cem., Whitesburg, Letcher Co., KY.

MOSLEY, SAMUEL: (2/7/1844 – 10/11/1886), Co. B, enl. Whitesburg, KY 9/9/1862, des. 12/11/1862, serv. Union 39th KY Inf., Co. F 9/23/1863 to 9/15/1865, res. Perry Co. 1860, s. of Henderson & Polly (Jones) Mosley, m. Polly (b. 1840), widow applied Union pension Knott Co. 7/1887, bur. Everage Cem. #1, Emmalena, Knott Co., KY.

MULLINS, ALEXANDER "PINK": (3/20/1837 – 9/10/1921), 1st. Lt., Co. E, enl. Whitesburg, KY 11/2/1862, resigned, successor was James Fitzpatrick, res. Pike Co. 1850 & 1860, s. of Alexander & Margaret "Peggy" (Fleming) Mullins, m. (2) Matilda Osborne (1846-1928) Pike Co., bur. Lick Fork Cem., Beefhide, Pike Co., KY.

MULLINS, AMBROSE "AMIE": (11/7/1839 – 2/2/1915), Co. F, enl. Floyd Co. 10/14/1862, res. Breathitt Co., s. of George Mullins & Susie Slusher, res. Breathitt Co. 1890 & 1900, res. Magoffin Co. 1910, m. (1) Miriam Rowe (1841-bef. 1866) 1861, (2) Barbara Wadkins (1842-1881 to 1889) 1866, (3) Clarinda Wadkins (1865-aft. 1915) 1890, bur. Wadkins-Mullins Cem., Evanston, Breathitt Co., KY.

MULLINS, BOOKER: (12/1832 – 1922), Co. C, enl. Whitesburg, KY 10/1/1862, listed as 'Buckner' on roster, pres. fall/1862, took part in Battle of Mt. Sterling & Battle of Cynthiana 1864 (re: pension), res. Breathitt Co. 1860, s. of Ambrose & Mattie Mullins, res. Knott Co. 1889 (re: tax list), res. Knott Co. 1900, applied for KY Confed. Pension Knott Co. 1912, res. Breathitt Co. (Decoy) 1920, m. Margaret Shepherd (1837-bef. 1920) 1852, bur. Bradley Cem., Decoy, Breathitt Co., KY.

MULLINS, BOWEN (OWEN): (1825 – 1882), Co. C, identified in A. G. Report, enl. Whitesburg, KY 10/1/1862, res. Floyd Co. 1850 & 1860, s. of William & Sarah (Waltrip) Mullins, res. Floyd Co. 1870 & 1880, widow res. Knott Co. (Beaver) 1900, m. Lydia Hall (b. 1826), bur. Mullins Branch Cem., Kite, Knott Co., KY.

MULLINS, ELIJAH: (9/9/1824 – 9/7/1902), Co. C, enl. Whitesburg, KY 3/28/1863, res. Breathitt Co. 1860, res. Breathitt Co. 1890, m. (1) Sarah (1825-bef. 1860), (2) Martha Hicks (1825-1917) 1858, bur. Grassy Gap Cem., Lewis Fork, Little Buckhorn Cr., Breathitt Co., KY.

MULLINS, ELISHA: (1843 – 1864), Co. E, enl. Whitesburg, KY 10/5/1862, AKA 'Elijah' on some records, rec. clothing 9/15/1864, killed at mo. Nealy Br., Carr Cr. (then Letcher Co.) fall, 1864, w/ Pvt. Marshall Hall & Cpl. John Layton Hall, res. Floyd Co. 1850, s. of Owen & Lydia (Hall) Mullins, m. Martha "Patsy" Bates (1842-aft. 1870) 1861, bur. William D. Hall Cem., Kite, Knott Co., KY.

MULLINS, ELLIOTT G.: (b. 1828), 1st Lt., Co. E, enl. Whitesburg, KY 10/5/1862, prom. 7/1/1863, rec. clothing 9/1/1864, res. Floyd Co. 1860, s. of William & Sarah Mullins, res. Floyd Co. 1870, res. McDowell Co., WV 1880, m. Amy (b. 1839).

MULLINS, HIRAM: (9/25/1837 – 1/12/1871), 3rd Sgt., Co. E, enl. Whitesburg, KY 10/5/1862, serv. prev. 5th KY Inf., Co. F, rec. clothing 9/7/1864, res. Floyd Co. 1850, s. of William & Sarah Mullins, m. Elizabeth (1839-1921), bur. Mullins-Caudill Cem., Jack's Creek, Floyd Co., KY.

MULLINS, JAMES T: (3/1847 – 7/25/1925), Co. I, enl. Hazard, KY 3/16/1863, pres. 6/10/1863, serv. Union 3 Forks Bttn. Co. E 1864-1865, res. Breathitt Co. 1860, b. Perry Co., s. of Elijah & Polly (Johnson) Mullins, m. (1) Evaline Moonfield 1876, (2) Mary Ann Lawson (1856-1932) 1877 Menifee Co., bur. James Mullins Cem., Richardson Cr., Ratliff, Menifee Co., KY.

MULLINS, JAMES K. POLK: (2/18/1845 – 9/28/1920), Co. C, enl. Whitesburg, KY 3/28/1863, res. Breathitt Co. 1860, s. of Joseph Gentry Mullins & Joannah, res. Breathitt Co. 1870, 1880 & 1890, res. WI (Florence Co.) 1900, res. Breathitt Co. 1920 as 'Jeems', m. Louisa Lykins (d. bef. 1920) 1866, bur. Wyatt Williams Cem., Bays, Breathitt Co., KY.

MULLINS, JOHN A.: (2/6/1843 – 1863), Co. A, serv. prev. 5th KY Inf., Co. F, on roster 4/1863, killed at home while on sick leave (re: 1974 interview w/ W. T. Francis), res. Letcher Co. 1850, s. of John & Matilda Mullins, bur. Francis Cem., Carr Creek, Knott Co., KY.

MULLINS, JOHN A: (1/23/1832 – 5/1/1913), 4th Sgt., Co. D, serv. prev. 5th KY Inf. (consolidated) Co. B, hired as a substitute 3/10/1863, pres. fall/1863, res. Breathitt Co. 1860, s. of Joshua & Mary "Polly" (Caudill) Mullins, res. Letcher Co. w/ Sela Maggard (1832-1918) 1870, 1890 Letcher Co. Veterans Census, bur. Hampton-Adams Cem., Oven Fork, Letcher Co., KY.

MULLINS, JOSEPH: (6/19/1834 – 7/29/1929), Co. H, enl. Whitesburg, KY 10/18/1862, capt. Gladeville, VA 7/7/1863, to Kemper Barracks 7/18/1863, to Camp Chase Prison 7/20/1863, to Camp Douglas 8/24/1863, records that state he died at Camp Douglas are in error, resident of Letcher Co. (Eolia), s. of Joshua & Mary "Polly" (Caudill) Mullins, m. (1) Mahalia Shepherd (1835-1862), (2) Mazie Parsons (1844-1900) Wise Co., VA 1863, (3) Rachel Holcomb Roberts, (4) Drucilla Smith Church, bur. Dewey Memorial Cem., Pound, Wise Co., VA.

MULLINS, SOLOMON: (b. 1838), Co. D, enl. 10/4/1862 Whitesburg, KY, s. of Joshua Mullins & Mary (Caudill) Mullins, res. Wise Co., VA 1860, m. Rachel Maggard, res. Wise Co., VA 1880.

MULLINS, WILLIAM: (b. 1841), Co. D, serv. prev. 4th VA Line, enl. 13th KY 10/4/1862 Whitesburg, KY, capt. Battle of Cynthiana 6/14/1864, to Louisville, to Camp Morton Prison 6/25/1864, Confed serv. described 1866 lawsuit, s. of Joshua & Mary (Caudill) Mullins, res. Letcher Co. 1860 & 1870.

MUSICK, ABRAM: (1815 – 1899), Co. K, serv. prev. 5th KY Inf., Co. E, 5' 9", blue eyes, gray hair, capt. as a 'discharged Confed. soldier' 5/17/1863, exch. 4/161864, serv. Smith's Btn. VA Cav., Well's Co. & 13th GA Cav., Well's Co., joined 13th KY Cav., Co. K aft. 2/22/1865, surr. Cumberland Gap, KY 4/30/1865, changed his name from Abraham to Abram due to his hatred of Lincoln (re: family history), res. Floyd Co. 1860, s. of John W. Musick, m. (1) Delilah (1813-ca. 1870), (2) Nancy Jane Prewitt (1845-1885) 1871, bur. Auxier Community Cem., Auxier, Floyd Co., KY.

NAPIER, DANIEL: (1841 – 1864), 3rd Sgt., Co. I, enl. Whitesburg, KY 10/18/1862, serv. prev. 5th KY Inf., Co. I, prom. Whitesburg, KY 11/10/1862, pres. fall/1863, res. Perry Co. 1850, res. Breathitt Co. 1860, s. of Samuel & Susan (Combs) Napier, m. Dorcus Baker (1843-aft. 1870) Perry Co. 1861, bur. Eversole Cem., Bonnyman, Perry Co., KY.

NAPIER, JOHN: (5/3/1827 – 3/17/1888), Co. G, enl. Breathitt Co., KY 9/30/1863, records stating he was KIA are in error, res. Perry Co. 1850, res. Breathitt Co. 1860, s. of Samuel & Susan (Combs) Napier, res. Breathitt Co. 1870 & 1880, widow res. Breathitt Co. (Little Buckhorn) 1910, m. Fanny Fugate (1832-aft. 1910) 1860, bur. Lewis Fork Cem., Lewis Fork, Breathitt Co., KY.

NAPIER, McCAGER: (8/19/1843 – 7/30/1899), Co. I, conscripted Whitesburg, KY 10/18/1862, des. 10/24/1862 or 11/1862, serv. later Union 14th KY Cav. Co. L, res Perry Co. 1860, s. of James & Mary Napier, m. Patience Spencer (1845-1917), res. Wolfe Co. 1870, bur Hazel Valley Cem., Hazel Valley, Washington Co., AR.

NAPIER, McCAGER S.: (6/17/1844 -4/12/1910), Co. C, enl. 4/5/1863 Whitresburg, KY, serv. later in Union 47th KY Inf. Co. H, s. of Stephen & Polly (Williams) Napier, res. Perry Co. 1860, widow res. Magoffin Co. 1910, m. Anna Engle (1847-aft. 1920), bur. w/Union marker Powers Cem., Lakeville, Magoffin Co., KY.

NAPIER, McCAGER S.: (4/11/1834 – 5/14/1912), 4th Sgt., Co. G, enl. Perry Co. 9/26/1862, serv. later in Union 14th KY Cav., s. of McCager & Leanna (Lewis) Napier, res. Perry Co. 1860, m. Betty Campbell, bur. in Campbell Cem., Napfor, Perry Co., KY.

NAPIER, TALTON JEROME: (1/5/1829 – 3/8/1901), Co. I, conscripted Whitesburg, KY 10/1/1862, pres. spring/1863, res. Perry Co. 1860, s. of McCager & Leanna (Lewis) Napier, m. Melinda Allen (1835-aft. 1910), bur. Campbell-Napier Cem., Blue Diamond, Perry Co., KY.

NEACE, AUSTIN "LONG AUSTIN" "AUSTIN SR.": (6/3/1829 – 10/26/1919), Co. F, enl. Whitesburg, KY 8/24/1863, capt. w/ Co. G Perry Co. 4/24/1864 (re: pension), to Camp Morton, exch. James River, VA 3/23/1865, res. Perry Co. 1860, s. of Jacob & Polly (Francis) Neace, rec. KY Confed. Pension #2523 Breathitt Co. 1912, m. Katharine Fugate (1830-1912) 1846, bur. Ivy Point Cem., Ned, Breathitt Co., KY.

NEACE, AUSTIN C. "AUSTIN JR" "POP DADDY": (8/1844 – 7/11/1917), Co. G, enl. Perry Co. 9/23/1862, wd. Breathitt Co. (Lost Creek) spring/1863, ret. serv., pres. at Battle of Blountville, TN & Battle of Jonesville, TN 1864, called 'Captain Rush" by fellow soldiers due to his bravery, capt. Perry Co. 4/25/1864, to Louisville Prison 5/7/1864, to Camp Morton Prison 5/12/1864, exch. Camp Morton 3/15/1865, res. Breathitt Co. 1860, s. of Samuel & Nancy (Fugate) Neace, res. Perry Co. (Ned) 1870, rec. KY Confed. Pension #3013 Perry Co. 1913, m. Lucy Ann Noble (1847-aft. 1900), bur. Ivy Point Cem., Ned, Breathitt Co., KY.

NEACE, GEORGE WASHINGTON: (1825 – bef. 1900), Co. I, enl. Hazard, KY 2/20/1863, 5' 8", dark hair, blue eyes, capt. Letcher Co. spring/1864, to Louisville Prison, rel. on oath 5/1864, in jail Abingdon, VA 1864, res. Perry Co. 1860, moved Greenup Co. 1873, res. Greenup Co. (Barn) 1880, moved Mingo Co., WV, m. Jane Sutherland (1836-1920 to 1930).

NEACE, JACOB "GREASY": (1825 – 1898), Co. G, enl. 1862, capt. Gladeville, VA 7/7/1863, to Camp Douglas Prison 8/22/1863, to Point Lookout 3/2/1865, exch. James River, VA 2/12/1865, res. Letcher Co. 1860, b. Russell Co., VA, s. of Henry Neace, res. Perry Co. 1880, moved Letcher Co. 1891, widow rec. KY Confed. Pension #1462 Perry Co. (nr. Ned) 1912, m. Margaret Sexton (1830-1915) Letcher Co., d. Letcher Co. (re: pension), bur. Henry Neace Cem., Colson, Letcher Co., KY.

NEACE, JACOB "RAIL JAKE": (1814 - 1895), Co. I, serv. as pilot during first raid on Eversole cabin 10/14/1862, capt. by Maj. John C. Eversole & company w/ G. W. Noble, s"Banger" Fugate, Wiley Miller, Franklin Allen, Irvin Stacy, Daniel Fugate and 'Timberlake from Covington', Breathitt Co., 6/5/1863, taken to Jackson, to Proctor where Abe Johnson wanted to kill "Rail Jake" for helping bushwhack his brother, to Irvine, to Lexington, to Cincinnati, and finally to Camp Chase, arriving on 6/16/1863 (identified in: *Behold, He Cometh in the Clouds,* pp. 26-37), res. Breathitt Co. 1860, s. of Jacob Neace & Polly Francis (step-mother), post-war resident Breathitt Co., m. Polly Aikman (1825-1909), k. w/ rock over election disagreement, bur. Ivy Point #1 Cem., Ned, Breathitt Co., KY.

NEACE, JOHN: (6/10/1842 – 6/20/1928), Co. G, serv. latter part of war until disbandment at Gladeville, VA, on march to Richmond 4/11/1865, res. Breathitt Co., b. Breathitt Co., s. of Jacob & Polly (Aikman) Neace, res. Breathitt Co. (Ned) 1914, rec. KY Confed. Pension #4260 Breathitt Co. 1915, m. Bithie (1843-1923), bur. Neace Cem., Lost Creek, Breathitt Co., KY.

NELSON, CHARLES: Co. C, enl. Whitesburg, KY 10/1/1862, res. Perry Co.

NEWBERRY, GEORGE W.: (1/1/1849 – 1/3/1919), Co. K, surr. Cumberland Gap 4/30/1865, s. of Stephen & Barbara (Rose) Newberry, res. Blount Co., TN 1860, m. Martha Elizabeth Ferguson (1852-1924) 1869, bur. Cloyd Creek Cem., Greenback, Blount Co., TN.

NEWSOM, GEORGE WASHINGTON: (6/21/1841 – 1873), Co. D, enl. Whitesburg, KY 10/4/1862, pres. fall/1862, res. Pike Co. 1850 & 1860, s.r. says res. Letcher Co., s. of Henry & Martha Newsom, res. Pike Co. 1870, m. Matilda Elkins (b.1842) Pike Co. 1859, bur. Newsom-Roberts Cem., Dorton, Pike Co., KY.

NICKELL, DANIEL BOONE: (3/1847 – 1916), Co. D, identified in Confed. pensions of Harrison Kidd, F. M. Royse & A. J. White, enl. spring 1863 in Rowan Co., s. of Fowler Nickell & Nancy Jane (Brown) Nickell, res. Rowan Co. 1860, m. Mary Crum (1848-1909) 1866, bur. Nickell-Harris Cem., Minor, Rowan Co., KY.

NIX, LEVI: (1843 – 11/13/1915), Co. C, no s.r., limited pension information, enl. Buckhorn (Dan Fork) 10/1863 (re: Zachariah Fugate), pres. at Wesley Francis' death early/1864, pres. Battle of Saltville, VA 1864, disbanded nr. Abingdon, VA 4/1865, took oath Booneville, KY 1865, res. Lincoln Co. 1860, b. 1843, s. of Leonard & Fanny (Fugate) Nix, res. Knott Co. 1910, witnessed pensions for several veterans, rec. KY Confed Pension #2221 Knott Co. (Emmalena) 1912, m. 4 times: (3) Hulda Engle Conaway (1843-1894) 1889, (4) Surrilda (b. 1876) 1895, d. 11/13/1915, bur. Engle Cem., Fisty, Knott Co. KY.

NOBLE, ALEXANDER: Capt., (11/15/1836 – 11/6/1864), Co. G, serv. prev. 5th KY Inf., Co. I, capt. Breathitt Co. (S. Fork Quicksand) 3/8/1864, to Louisville Prison 3/21/1864, to Camp Chase Prison 3/24/1864, described there as 'leader of notorious guerilla band', res. Breathitt Co., KY, s. of William & Lettie (Miller) Noble, m. Winnie Sizemore (1837-aft. 1880), d. Camp Chase Prison, bur. Grave #419, Camp Chase Cem., Columbus, Franklin Co., OH.

NOBLE, DANIEL: (1838 – 1903), Co. G, enl. Breathitt Co., KY 9/23/1862, 5' 8 ½", blue eyes, light hair, fair complexion, two sm. scars on left thigh, capt. Gladeville, VA 7/7/1863, to Kemper Barracks 7/18/1863, to Camp Chase Prison 7/20/1863, to Camp Douglas Prison 8/24/1863, enlisted U.S. Navy 12/23/1863, initially assigned *U.S.S. Susquehanna*, serv. as landsman on *U.S.S. South Carolina* & *U.S.S. Metacomet*, awarded *U.S. Naval Medal of Honor* for actions during Battle of Mobile Bay 8/5/1864, des. New Orleans 1/1/1865, res. Breathitt Co. 1860, s. of Hiram & Sarah (Francis) Noble, res. Wolfe Co. (Hazel Green) 1900, m. (1) Mary "Polly" (1851-ca. 1891) Perry Co. 1860, (2) Martha (1865-1933), bur. Childers Cem., Gilmore, Wolfe Co., KY.

NOBLE, ELIAS: Co. C, enl. Whitesburg, KY 10/1/1862, pres. spring/1863, shot & killed by Union soldiers at Gross farm on Buckhorn spring/1863 (re: family history), res. Perry Co., bur. Gross Cem., Buckhorn, Perry Co., KY.

NOBLE, GEORGE WASHINGTON: (1823 – 1863), Co. C, enl. Whitesburg, KY 3/25/1863, shot & killed by Capt. Bill Strong's Union soldiers of 14th KY Cavalry at his home in Breathitt Co. (now Watts), body was undiscovered for several days, res. Breathitt Co. 1860, s. of Nathan & Virginia Jane (Neace) Noble, m. Phoebe Campbell (1826-1919) 1846, bur. Noble Cem., Watts, Breathitt Co., KY.

NOBLE, GEORGE WASHINGTON: (7/17/1844 – 2/18/1930), enl. aft. serv. prev. 5th KY Inf., Co. I, chosen by Col. Ben E. Caudill to recruit for 13th KY Cav., capt. Perry Co. 6/6/1863, to Lexington Prison 6/16/1863, to Camp Chase Prison 6/20/1863, to Johnson's Island Prison, to Point Lookout Prison where "we had to stay in condemned tents without fire and on half rations, and stand in the water, some nights to our knees. When we slept, we had to lie down on the ground, and some nights had to get out and walk to keep from freezing to death. They put the darkies to guarding us and they began to shoot the prisoners, and we began to take the oath with the intention of coming back to our Command and fight for the cause that we had fought for until we died, if it should be that we had to die.", rel. 4/12/1864, he and his cousin, Wiley Miller, worked, rode the 'cars', and walked from Baltimore, arriving home 6/6/1864, traded for a horse & ret. to serv., nr. New River in VA when news of Lee's surr. arrived, res. Breathitt Co. 1860, s. of William Sr. & Letty (Miller) Noble, rec. Confed. pension as res. of Breathitt Co. (Ned) 1914, wrote the book _Behold, He Cometh in the Clouds_, m. Arrena "Rena" Noble (1851-1927), d. at home of his daughter, Penelope Davidson, at Chavies, KY, two weeks after his clothing caught fire while warming himself before the fireplace, bur. Red Hill Cem., Chavies, Perry Co., KY.

NOBLE, ISAAC: See Nathan Isaac Noble

NOBLE, JOHN L. "JACKSON": (1813 – 1896), 1st Lt., Go. G, enl. 10/14/1862, under arrest & cashiered for stealing money 6/1/1863, successor was Shade Combs, res. Perry Co. 1860, s. of Nathan & Virginia Jane (Neace) Noble, res. Perry Co. (as 'Jackson', nr. Ned) 1880, m. (1) Bertha, (2) Elizabeth "Betty" Davidson (1822-aft. 1900), bur. Nathan Noble Cem., Lost Creek, Breathitt Co., KY.

NOBLE, JOHN WHARTON: (5/14/1823 – 3/7/1878), Co. G, enl. Breathitt Co., KY 9/23/1862, pres. 10/20/1862, res. Breathitt Co. (Lost Creek) 1860, s. of Hiram & Sally (Francis) Noble, m. Virginia Jane Miller (b. 1832), bur. Big Andy Noble Cem., Hardshell, Breathitt Co., KY.

NOBLE, LOSSON: (3/11/1844 – 3/11/1929), Cos. B & C, enl. Whitesburg, KY 9/17/1862, trans. from Co. B to Co. C Whitesburg, KY 1/1/1863, pres. spring/1863, res. Breathitt Co. 1860, s. of Ira & Rachel (Fugate) Noble, m. Rhoda Jane Carpenter (1849-1921 to 1929) 1867, bur. Lawson Cem., Mr. Carmel, Breathitt Co., KY.

NOBLE, NATHAN ISAAC: (b. 1841), Co. I, listed as Isaac Noble on s.r., capt. Perry Co., KY 4/25/1864, to Louisville Prison 5/10/1864, res. Breathitt Co., KY, some records in "10th Artificial Unit" – misfiled records.

NOBLE, SAMUEL: (10/10/1839 – 7/8/1921), Co. G, enl. Breathitt Co., KY 9/23/1862, capt. Breathitt Co. 3/6/1864, to Louisville Prison 3/21/1864, to Camp Chase Prison 3/24/1864, paroled 5/2/1865, res. Breathitt Co. 1850, s. of Ira & Rachel (Fugate) Noble, rec. KY Confed. Pension #905 Breathitt Co., 1912, m. (1) Rachel Fugate (d. bef. 1880), (2) Telitha Jones (1835-1900) 1866, (3) Catherine Collinsworth (b. 1859), bur. Marshall & Noble Cem., Lewis Fork, Breathitt Co., KY.

NOBLE, SIMPSON: (1842 – 6/6/1864 @ 10 AM), Co. G, enl. Whitesburg, KY 9/30/1863, serv. prev. 5th KY Inf., Co. I, KIA Battle of Mt. Sterling serv. Gen. John Hunt Morgan, res. Breathitt Co. 1860, s. of William Sr. & Lettie (Miller) Noble, m. Tabitha Fugate (b. 1845) 1863, bur. Confed. Cem., Mt. Sterling, Montgomery Co., KY.

NOBLE, STEPHEN: (9/17/1837 – 12/23/1903), Co. G, enl. Breathitt Co., KY 9/23/1862, disch. 1/1/1863, res. Perry Co. 1860, s. of Enoch & Leah (Palmer) Noble, res. Perry Co. (Troublesome) 1900, m. (1) Samantha J. Jones (1837-bef. 1880), (2) Martha (1838-bef. 1900), (3) Nancy Stacy (1849-1920), bur. Richard Smith Cem., Ary, Perry Co., KY.

NOBLE, WILLIAM: (1847 – 11/9/1863), Cos. C & G, enl. Whitesburg, KY 10/1/1862, trans. from Co. C to Co. G 3/1/1863, KIA Crane's Nest, Wise Co. VA, res. Perry Co. 1860, s. of John L. & Elizabeth (Davidson) Noble, m. Sinda Campbell 1858 (b. 1840), bur. Crane's Nest Cem., nr. Clintwood, Dickenson Co., VA.

NOBLE, WILLIAM: (b. 1837), Co. F, enl. Floyd Co. 8/24/1863, KIA, res. Breathitt Co. 1860, s. of Lawson & Peggy Noble, m. Dulcena Combs (b. 1840) 1858.

NOBLE, WILLIAM D. (B.): (b. 1832), 4th Sgt., Co. G, enl. Breathitt Co. 9/23/1862, prom. 4/19/1863, pres. 12/8/1863, res. Breathitt Co. 1850, s. of Enoch & Leah (Palmer) Noble, res. Breathitt Co. 1870 & 1880, m. Phoebe Napier Combs (1832-aft. 1910).

NOBLE, WILLIAM MASON: (1836 – 11/28/1862), 2nd Lt., Co. G, enl. Breathitt Co. 10/14/1862, killed by the enemy, res. Breathitt Co. s. of Ira & Rachel (Fugate) Noble, m. Polly Combs (b.1833), memorial marker Marshall-Noble Cem., Lewis Fork, Breathitt Co., KY.

NOBLE, WILLIAM PALMER "PAYNTER": (5/10/1829 – 10/19/1908), Co. G, enl. Breathitt Co., KY 9/23/1862, capt. Gladeville, VA 7/7/1863, to Kemper Barracks 7/18/1863, to Camp Chase Prison 7/20/1863, to Camp Douglas Prison 8/24/1863, exch. Point Lookout 2/24/1865, res. Breathitt Co. 1860, s. of George "Buckeye" & Sarah (Campbell) Noble, widow rec. KY Confed. Widow's Pension #906 Breathitt Co. (Ned) 1912, m. Levina Noble (b. 1834) 1852, bur. Big Andy Noble Cem., Hardshell, Breathitt Co., KY.

NOLAN, LEONARD: (1846 – 3/26/1924), Co. F, enl. Floyd Co., KY 10/14/1862, res. Breathitt Co. 1860, s. of Stephen & Levisa Ann (Gibson) Nolan, m. Margaret Dobson (b.1848) 1870, bur. Elam Cem. (KY d.c. #8230), Princess, Boyd, Co., KY.

NOWELL / NOVELL, JAMES: Co. K, AKA 'Norvell' on roster, enl. Lee Co., VA 8/18/1863, pres. Lee Co. 12/31/1863.

NOWELL NOVELL, N. W.: Co. K, AKA 'Norvell' on roster, enl. Lee Co., VA 8/18/1863, pres. Lee Co. 12/31/1863.

ONEY, BUNYON: (1835 – 1888), Co. F, AKA 'Runyon' on some records, enl. Floyd Co., KY 10/14/1862, capt. Magoffin Co. 9/16/1863, to Louisville Prison, to Rock Island Prison 1/31/1864, described there as "guerilla, highway robber, bandit", joined U. S. Army for frontier service to gain release, res. Floyd Co. 1860, s. of William & Susannah (Coburn) Oney, m. (1) Rachel "Biddy" (b. 1833) 1855, (2) Mary E. Edwards 1865, res. Greenup Co. 1870, res. Carter Co. 1880, died Carter Co.

ONEY, DAVID C.: (b. 1838), Co. F, enl. Floyd Co., KY 10/14/1862, pres. summer/1863, res. Magoffin Co. 1860, b. 1838, s. of William & Susannah (Coburn) Oney, res. Floyd Co. 1880, res. Grayson Co., TX 1900, m. Anna Allen (1835-bef. 1900).

ONEY, DOUGLAS: (1839 – 1889), 2nd Cpl., Co. F, enl. Floyd Co. 1860, disc. 7/1/1863, res. Floyd Co. 1860, s. of Benjamin & Sarah (Allen) Oney, Floyd Co. Constable District 3, res. Floyd Co. 1880, widow & son Hiram res. Greenup Co. 1900, m. Mary Susannah Sizemore (1846-bef. 1900) Floyd Co. 1866, d. Greenup Co. (Flatwoods), KY.

ONEY, JOHN C.: (9/4/1845 - 5/5/1929), 4th Sgt., Co. F, enl. Floyd Co., KY 10/14/1862, capt. Wise Co., VA 6/25/1863, to McLean Barracks 7/18/1863, to Cincinnati hosp. 7/19/1863, to Camp Chase Prison 9/6/1863, to Rock Island Prison 1/14/1864, joined Union Army to gain release & fight Indian Wars, res. Floyd Co. 1860, s. of William & Susannah (Coburn) Oney, m. (1) Larena Conley (1853-1917) 1872, (2) Louisa (b. 1838), (3) Brintha Eleanor Gee (1867-1952) 1927, bur. Bethel Ridge Church Cem., Bethel Ridge, Carter Co., KY.

ONEY, WILLIAM P.: (12/17/1838 – 10/18/1911), Co. F, enl. Floyd Co., KY 10/14/1862, res. Magoffin Co. 1860, b. Tazewell Co., VA, s. of James & Rhoda (Day) Oney, family moved to KY 1857, res. Magoffin Co. 1870 & 1900, m. Purlina Allen (1842-1920) 1861, bur. Oney Cem., White Oak, Morgan Co., KY.

OSBORNE, DAVID EDWARD: (9/1831 – 7/24/1885), Co. F, enl. Floyd Co., KY 8/24/1863, also serv. Union 39th KY Inf., Co. F, res. Floyd Co. 1860, s. of Edward S. & Rhoda Osborne, m. Mary Osborne (1831-1924), bur. w/ Union marker David Osborne Cem., Hite, Floyd Co., KY.

OSBORNE, REPTS B.: (6/17/1832 – 2/5/1909), Co. F, enl. Floyd Co, KY 10/14/1862, capt. Floyd Co. 5/26/1863, to Louisa 5/29/1863, also serv. Union 39th KY Inf., res. Floyd Co. 1860, s. of Edward S. & Rhoda Osborne, bur. Osborne Cem., Hite, Floyd Co., KY.

OSBORNE, WILLIAM THOMAS: (6/15/1841 – 1/20/1913), Co. F, enl. Floyd Co., KY 10/14/1862, capt Floyd Co. 5/26/1863, to Louisa, KY 5/29/1863, serv. later Union 39th KY Inf., Co. F, res. Floyd Co. 1860, s. of Edward S. & Rhoda Osborne, res. Floyd Co. (Arkansas) 1900 & 1910, m. Phoebe L. Osborne (1849-1915), bur. Ice Plant Hollow Cem., Martin, Floyd Co., KY.

OWENS, VINCENT: (5/10/1835 – 1/28/1924), Co. B, enl. Whitesburg, KY, res. Perry Co. 1860, s. of Reece & Mary (Hicks) Owens, applied KY Confed. Pension Knott Co. 1912, m. Lucinda Johnson (1839-1920) 1857, bur. Trace Fork Cem., Pippa Passes, Knott Co., KY.

OWENS, WILLIAM: (1834 – 1890), Co. C, enl. Whitesburg, KY 10/1/1862, res. Breathitt Co. 1860, m. Sarah Mullins (1835-bef. 1890), bur. Slone Cem., Buckeye Station, Floyd Co., KY.

OXLEY, THOMAS J.: (7/1844 – 1909), Cos. F & K, enl. Whitesburg, KY 10/14/1862, enl. Diamond's 10th KY Cav., Co. E Rowan Co. 1/1/1863, pres. 6/30/1863, des., joined 13th KY Cav., Co. K Lee Co., VA 8/18/1863, pres. Lee Co., VA 12/31/1863, ret. Diamond's 10th KY Cav., surr. Carter Co. 5/1/1864, found guilty of being a "guerilla", in Union hosp. with "jaundice" 11/28/1864, took oath 3/26/1865, rel. 6/1865, res. Rowan Co. 1860, s. of Isabel Oxley, m. Cassandra "Cassie" bef. 1880, bur. New Alfrey Cem., Gogswell, Rowan Co., KY.

PARSONS, ELIJAH GREEN: (3/4/1846 – 12/27/1907), Co. K, surr. Cumberland Gap 4/30/1865, res. Lee Co., VA 1850, s. of William & Nancy (Carter) Parsons, res. Lee Co. (Rocky Station), VA 1880, m. Martha W. Horton (b. 1858) 1879, bur. Shelburne Cem., Pennington Gap, Lee Co., VA.

PARSONS, JOHN: (3/10/1847 – 1/26/1916), Co. K, enl. Lee Co., VA 8/18/1863, pres. Lee Co. 12/31/1863, res. Harlan Co., KY 1860, b. Harlan Co., s. of Joel & Hanna Parsons, res. Harlan Co. (Upper Clover Fork) 1910, m. Rhoda (1851-1910 to 1920), bur. Robbins Chapel Cem., Keokee, Lee Co. VA.

PATRICK, ALEXANDER B.: (12/17/1818 – 5/23/1881), Kash's Co., serv. prev. 5th KY Inf. (Consolidated), Co. B 1862-1863, indicted post-war for 1865 murder as member this Co., res. Menifee Co. (Frenchburg) 1880, m. Prudence Haddix (1819-1895), bur. Jackson Cem., Jackson, Breathitt Co., KY.

PATRICK, JAMES: (1820 – 1907), Co. C, enl. Whitesburg, KY 10/1/1862, rec. clothing 9/24/1864, res. Perry Co. 1860, s. of Hugh & Barbara (Bailey) Patrick, m. Elizabeth "Betty" Richie (1825-1920) 1847, bur. Patrick Cem., Bearville, Knott Co., KY.

PATTON, CHRISTOPHER: (1843 – 3/2/1865), Co. I, conscripted Whitesburg, KY 10/18/1862, 6' 0", fair complexion, black eyes, black hair, pres. fall/1862, enl. Union 39th KY, Co. F Lawrence Co. (Peach Orchard), KY 11/5/1862, capt. Breathitt Co. by Confed. Army 6/27/1863, paroled Adkins Landing, VA 8/22/1864, ret. Union serv. w/ 39th, sent to Camp Chase Prison for guard duty 9/14/1864, admitted Gen. Hosp. Lexington, KY w/ smallpox 1/22/1865, res. Breathitt Co. 1860, s. of David & Rebecca Patton, d. from smallpox in Gen. Hosp. Lexington, KY, bur. w/ Union marker Lexington Cem., Lexington, Fayette Co., KY.

PATTON, HENRY: (1843 – 1/11/1864), Co. I, conscripted Whitesburg, KY 10/18/1862, des. 11/1/1862, enl. Union 39th KY, Co. F Lawrence Co. (Peach Orchard), KY 11/25/1862, capt. Breathitt Co. by Confederate Army 6/27/1863, to Richmond, VA & charged w/ deserting Confed. Army & ordered for trial, to Andersonville Prison, back to Richmond & admitted to Gen. Hosp. No. 13, res. Breathitt Co. 1860, s. of David & Rebecca Patton, d. from pneumonia, either Richmond, VA or Andersonville GA (re: conflicting Union records).

PATTON, JAMES P.: (2/14/1842 – 4/22/1916), Co. I, conscripted Whitesburg, KY 10/18/1862, pres. fall/1862, poss. serv. later Union 39th KY, res. Breathitt Co. 1860, s. of David & Rebecca Patton, m. Amanda Allen Bradley (1849-1916 to 1920), bur. Warnock Cem., Warnock, Greenup Co., KY.

PATTON, JOHN FRANKLIN: (1839 – 2/6/1908), Co. F, enl. Floyd Co. 10/14/1862, serv. prev. 5th KY Inf., Co. I, res. Floyd Co. 1860, s. of Henry & Rachel Patton, m. Easter Chambers (1846-1913), bur. Patton Cem., Harold Patton Farm, Wolfe Co., KY.

PATTON, STEPHEN: (7/10/1842 – 11/20/1927), Co. F, enl. Floyd Co., KY 10/14/1862, serv. later Union 39th KY, Co. F 12/8/1862 to 9/15/1865, res. Floyd Co. b. Floyd Co. 7, s. of David & Sarah Patton, res. Greenup Co. 1870, m. Elizabeth (1850-1927) bur. Patton Cem., Greenup, Greenup Co., KY.

PATTON, WILLIAM H.: (1841 – 12/27/1864), 4th Cpl., Co. I, conscripted Whitesburg, KY 10/1/1862, serv. prev. 5th KY Inf., Co. F, en. Union 39th KY Peach Orchard, KY 12/7/1862, capt. by Confeds. Breathitt Co. 6/27/1863, to Richmond, VA to be tried for desertion from Confed. Army 9/23/1863, admitted to hosp. Richmond, VA for smallpox 4/19/1864, to Andersonville Prison 7/8/1864, admitted to Andersonville hosp. 10/19/1864, paroled Savannah 11/14/1864, to Annapolis 11/28/1864, admitted Gen. Hosp. #1 Annapolis 12/4/1864, res. Breathitt Co. 1860, s. of David & Rebecca Patton, d. Annapolis Gen Hosp #1, bur. grave #1466, Sec. D, Annapolis National Cem., Annapolis, Anne Arundel Co., MD.

PENNINGTON, ABEL: (11/9/1843 – 11/6/1915), 2nd Lt., Co. D, enl. 3/1863, capt. & confined as "guerilla" prisoner McLean Barracks 12/10/1863, to Camp Chase 1/27/1864, to Ft. Delaware, rel. after taking oath 6/22/1865, res. Morgan Co. 1860, s. of Elisha & Elizabeth Pennington, m. (1) Margaret Baumgardner Wagner, (2) Rhodempsia J. Reynolds (1860-1944) Fleming Co. 1879, bur. Abel Pennington Cem., Ruin, Elliott Co., KY.

PENNINGTON, JAMES: (8/25/1829 – 2/17/1913), Co. K, poss. serv. prev. Union Harlan Co. Btn., Co. E 10/13/1862 to 1/13/1863, enl. Co. F 6/1/1863, enl. Co. K Lee Co., VA 8/18/1863, pres. Lee Co. 12/31/1863, res. Harlan Co. 1860, s. of William Nelson & Delilah (Caudill) Pennington, res. Carter Co. 1880 & 1900, m. Martha Miller (1846-aft. 1913), d. from heart attack suffered during court six weeks after his son had been shot, bur. Pennington Cem., Willard, Carter Co., KY.

PENNINGTON, JAMES HOLMAN: (3/31/1839 – 9/14/1920), Cos. F & D, enl. 6/1/1863 Co. F, also serv. 7th Bttn. Confed. Cav., joined Co. D (13th), rec. clothing 9/7/1864, s. of Elijah & Elizabeth (Caudill) Pennington, res. Morgan Co. 1860, m. Mary Atilla Baumgardner (b. 1847), res. Elliott Co. 1880 & 1900, bur. Riverside Cem., Ione, Pend Orielle Co., WA.

PENNINGTON, WILLIAM: (1816 – 1895), Co. K, enl. Lee Co., VA 8/18/1863, rec. clothing 9/7/1864, res. Johnson Co. 1860, s. of Joshua & Nancy (Sparks) Pennington, m. Martha "Patsy" Blanton (1816-bef. 1900), bur. Johnson Co. Memorial Cem., Staffordsville, Johnson Co., KY.

PENNINGTON, WILLIAM NELSON, JR.: (1842 – 7/14/1882), Co. K, poss. serv. prev. Union Harlan Co. Btn, Co. E 10/13/1862 to 1/13/1863, enl. Lee Co. VA 8/18/1863, pres. Lee Co. 12/31/1863, res. Lawrence Co. 1850 & 1860, s. of William Nelson & Delilah (Caudill) Pennington, m. Elizabeth Jane Beatty, d. Lawrence Co.

PIGMAN, CAMPBELL: (1/13/1830 – 2/1888), 2nd Lt., Co. A, serv. prev. 5th KY Inf., Co. F, resigned from 13th KY Cav. 3/24/1864, res. Letcher Co. 1860, s. of John W. & Rosanna (Amburgey) Pigman, m. Mary Ann Cornett (1832-1880 to 1900)1847, bur. Campbell Pigman Cem., Mallie, Knott Co., KY.

PIGMAN, JAMES MADISON: (1/12/1830 – 4/30/1892), Co. B, enl. Whitesburg, KY 9/7/1862, disc. 1/1/1863, res. Letcher Co. 1860, s. of John W. & Rosanna (Amburgey) Pigman, first sheriff of Knott Co., KY, m. Rhoda Cornett (1830-1904) 1847, bur. Pigman Cem., Mallie, Knott Co., KY.

PIGMAN, WILLIAM: (12/19/1832 – 1884), Cos. A & B, enl. Whitesburg, KY 11/1/1862, trans. from Co. B to Co. A, pres. Whitesburg 4/10/1863, res. Letcher Co. 1860, s. of John W. & Rosanna (Amburgey) Pigman, widow applied for Confed. Pension, m. Rebecca B. Smith (1838-1929) 1855, bur. Steerfork Cem., Pinetop, Knott Co., KY.

PLUMMER, ISAAC: (b. 1835), 3rd Cpl., Co. K & Kash's Co., enl. Lee Co., VA 8/18/1863, serv. prev. 5th KY Inf., Co. D, des. 5th KY Lee Co., VA 8/9/1863, pres. Lee Co., VA 12/31/1863, res. Breathitt Co., KY 1860, s. of Phillip & Elizabeth Plummer, indicted postwar for 1865 murder as member Kash's Co., moved Johnson Co., MO by 1870, widower in Pettis Co. (Blackwater) MO 1880, m. Sarah Ann Means 1868.

POTTER, REUBEN: (1829 – 1862), Co. D, enl. Whitesburg, KY 10/4/1862, pres. fall/1862, shot for des. by PVT John W. Wright while climbing a fence at home (re: David W. Austin, 4/25/1937), res. Letcher Co. 1860, s. of Benjamin & Susannah Potter, m. Hulda Wright (1833-aft. 1900), bur. Old Sol Wright Cem., Beefhide, Pike Co., KY.

POWELL, HIBIRD: (5/16/1839 – 12/27/1916), Co. K, serv. prev. 5th KY Inf., listed as Hibbert Dowell on 13th s.r., Co. C & 2nd Btn. KY Mtd. Rifles, surr. Cumberland Gap 4/30/1865, res. Powell Co. KY, rec. KY Confed. Pension, m. Elizabeth Crabtree (1829-1921), d.c. #00782, bur. Chop Chestnut Cem., Bowen, Powell Co., KY.

PRATER, BENJAMIN FRANKLIN: (6/18/1848 – 11/14/1925), Co. K, enl. Lee Co. (Larkey), VA 4/21/1864, w/ Gen John Hunt Morgan on his Last Raid & at his death in Greenville, TN 9/4/1864, surr. Cumberland Gap 4/30/1865, res. Campbell Co., TN 1860, s. of David & Nancy (Bratcher) Prater, m. (1) Mary Elizabeth Wright (b. 1851) 1868, (2) Nancy J. Thompson (1852-1929) 1874, res. Barry Co., MO 1900, bur. Bethel Cem., Monett, Barry Co., MO.

PRATER, JOHN: (7/21/1825 – 10/21/1887), Co. F, enl. Floyd Co., KY 10/14/1862, serv. prev. 5th KY Inf., Co. C, res. Floyd Co. 1860, s. of William & Obedience Prater, m. Mary Shepherd (1835-bef. 1900), reportedly bur. Prater Cem., Licking River Rd., Magoffin Co., KY.

PRATER, NEWMAN: (1835 – 1900), Co. F, enl. Floyd Co., KY 6/1/1863, also serv. Union 39th KY Inf., Co. F, res. Floyd Co. 1860 (Prater Fk. /Brush Creek), s. of William & Obedience Prater, m. (1) Martha "Patsy" Daniel (1830-1880 to 1900) 1852, (2) Emma Moore (1850-aft. 1900), bur. w/ Union marker w/o dates, Reffit Cem., Maytown, Floyd Co., KY.

PRATER, RILEY: (6/1837 – bef. 1911), Co. F, enl. Floyd Co., KY 10/14/1862, identified in A. G. report, res. Magoffin Co., KY 1860, s. of Adam Prater, res. Magoffin Co. 1870 & 1900 (w/ George & Nancy Jane Hall), m. Lucretia "Creasy" Shepherd (1838-1911) 1854.

PRATER, THOMAS HARGIS: (1845 – 12/21/1865), Co. K, enl. Lee Co. (Larkey), VA 4/21/1864, w/ Gen. John Hunt Morgan on his Last Raid & at his death in Greenville, TN 9/4/1864, surr. Cumberland Gap 4/30/1865, res. Campbell Co., TN 1850 & 1860, s. of David & Nancy (Bratcher) Prater died Campbell Co., TN.

PRATER, WILLIAM W.: (1820 - 1891), Co. F, enl. Floyd Co, KY 10/14/1862, serv. prev. 5th KY Inf., Co. E, serv. Union 39th KY Inf., Co. F 6/11/1863 to 9/15/1865, s. of William & Obedience Prater, res. Floyd Co. 1860, res. Magoffin Co. (Lakeville) 1870 & 1880 (w/ PVT. Irvin Howard), res Magoffin Co. 1890, rec. Union pension, widow applied Union pension 12/12/1891.

PRATT, HIRAM G.: (3/13/1828 – 2/28/1919), 2nd Lt., Co. B, enl. Whitesburg, KY 8/29/1862, resigned due to illness 2/16/1863, res. Perry Co. KY 1860, s. of Henry & Sally (Gibson) Pratt, m. Rhoda Campbell (1825-1880 to 1900) Floyd Co., bur. Edley Cornett Cem., Cornettsville, Perry Co., KY.

PRATT, JOHN M. "JOHN KNOCK": (11/29/1829 – 3/10/1924), Co. B, enl. Whitesburg, KY 9/9/1862, w/ Gen. John Hunt Morgan on his Last Raid, saw action at Gladeville, Saltville, Marion, & Wytheville, VA, res. Letcher Co. (Rockhouse/Pratt Branch then Lt. Fk. Troublesome) 1860, s. of Henry & Sally (Gibson) Pratt, res. Letcher Co. 1870, later res. Perry Co. (Rt. Fk. Mason's Creek), m. Elizabeth Campbell (1831-1892), bur. Pratt Cem., Viper, Perry Co., KY.

PRATT, STEPHEN S.: (8/15/1838 – 8/9/1897), Co. A, enl. Whitesburg, KY 9/12/1863, serv. prev. 5th KY Inf., Co. F, rec. clothing 6/29/1864, res. Letcher Co. 1860. s. of Henry & Celia (Hampton) Pratt, widow rec. KY Confed. Pension #943 Knott Co. 1912, m. 1) Melvina Watts (1845-1881) Hindman, KY ca. 1862, m. 2) Matilda Francis Adams (1846-1918) Hindman, KY 1889, bur. Pratt Cem., Garner, Knott Co., KY.

PRATT, WILLIAM H: (10/27/1842 – 1/21/1924), Cos. A & B, serv. prev. 5th KY Inf., Co. F, trans. from Co. A to Co. B, rec. clothing 4/7/1864, capt. Battle Cynthiana 6/14/1864, to Louisville Prison 6/22/1864, to Rock Island Prison 6/24/1864, paroled 3/6/1865, res. Letcher Co. (Rockhouse/Pratt Br. Then Lt. Fk. Troublesome) 1860, s. of Henry & Celia (Hampton) Pratt, m. (1) Martha Osborne (1849-1890), (2) Florence Allen (1854-aft. 1924), d.c #5941, bur. Pratt Cem., Maytown, Floyd Co., KY.

PUCKETT, ANDERSON: Kash's Co., indicted post-war for 1865 murder as member this Co.

QUILLEN, ANDREW "DREWERY": (1/1838 – 8/20/1918), Co. D, enl. Whitesburg, KY 10/4/1862, pres. summer/1863, capt. & imprisoned at Pikeville, KY, to Louisa, KY & imprisoned until the end of the war, res. Letcher Co. 1860, b. Perry Co. s. of Henry & Elizabeth (Wright) Quillen, rec. KY Confed. Pension #948 Letcher Co. (Chip/Neon) 1912, m. (1) Susan Burke (b. 1843), (2) Vina Fouts (1846-1880 to 1900), (3) Susan Adams (1863-bef. 1910), bur. Bentley Cem., Neon, Letcher Co., KY.

QUILLEN, MALON: (1844 – 1864), Cos. D & E, enl. Whitesburg, KY 10/4/1862, pres. summer/1863, shot and killed on Carr Creek (mo. Neely Branch) during the war (re: family history), res. Letcher Co. 1860, s. of Henry & Elizabeth (Wright) Quillen, bur. William D. Hall Cem., Kite, Knott Co., KY.

QUILLEN, RICHARD: (1833 – 1869), Co. D, enl. Whitesburg, KY 10/4/1862, pres. fall/1862, res. Letcher Co. 1860, s. of Teague Quillen, widow res. Letcher Co. 1870, m. Catherine Yonts (1833-1914), bur. Tolliver-Quillen Cem., Millstone, Letcher Co., KY.

REEVES, WILLIAM (H): (1828 – 1879), Co. K, enl. Lee Co., VA 8/18/1863, pres. Lee Co. 12/31/1863, so. Of Malachi & Barbara (Glance) Reeves, res. Lee Co, VA 1860, moved to Fulton Co., AR, MO and Putnam Co., TN m. (1) Mahala Gross, divorced & murdered with a brick by second wife Putnam Co., TN (period family letters), bur. (unm.) Whittaker Cem., Monterey, Putnam Co., TN.

REYNOLDS, (WILLIAM) HENRY: (2/28/1837 – 12/8/1890), Co. D, enl. Whitesburg, KY 10/4/1862, 5' 9", dark hair, black eyes, pres. fall/1862, serv. later Union 39th KY Inf., Co. K, res. Letcher Co. 1860, s. of Noah & Mary (Stone) Reynolds, res. Letcher Co. 1870, m. Francis Matilda Baker (1845-aft. 1920) 1859, bur. Quillen-Reynolds Cem., Seco, Letcher Co., KY.

REYNOLDS, JOHN: (12/22/1837 – 3/11/1907), Co. A, serv. prev. 5th KY Inf., Co. F, disc. from 13th KY at term expiration 3/28/1863, res. Letcher Co. 1860, s. of Joseph & Queentena (Amburgey) Reynolds, res. Knott Co. 1890, m. Ruth Hylton (1839-1900 to 1910), bur. John Reynolds Cem., Mallie, Knott Co., KY.

REYNOLDS, STEPHEN N.: (1838 – 1877), 3rd Cpl., Co. D, pres. fall/1862, serv. later Union 39th KY, Co. K, res. Letcher Co. 1860, s. of Noah & Mary (Stone) Reynolds, res. Letcher Co. 1870, m. Drucilla Craft (1838-1876), bur. Quillen-Reynolds Cem., Seco. Letcher Co., KY.

REYNOLDS, THOMAS (E): (8/31/1842 – 5/8/1920), 2nd Cpl., Co. K, enl. Lee Co., VA 8/18/1863, pres. Lee Co. 12/31/1863, serv. also 64th VA Mtd. Inf., s. of Hamilton H. & Catherine Mary (Carr) Reynolds, res. Scott Co., VA 1860, m. (1) Rosanna Jennings (b. 1847), (2) Jaley E. Horne (b. 1835) 1912, widow rec. VA Confed. pension, Scott Co., VA 1927, bur. Reynolds Cem., Clinchport, Scott Co., VA.

REYNOLDS, WILLIAM: (2/8/1835 – 5/3/1905), Co. E, enl. Whitesburg, KY 10/5/1862, capt. Floyd Co. 5/1864, to Louisville Prison, rel. on oath 5/1864, res. Floyd Co. 1860, s. of Hamilton & Malinda (Justice) Reynolds, res. Floyd Co. 1870, 1880 & 1900, m. Mary Hall (b. 1840) 1855, reportedly bur. Reynolds Cem., Clear Creek, Floyd Co., KY.

REYNOLDS, (WILLIAM) HENRY: (2/28/1837 – 12/8/1890), Co. D, enl. Whitesburg, KY 10/4/1862, 5' 9", dark hair, black eyes, pres. fall/1862, serv. later Union 39th KY Inf., Co. K, res. Letcher Co. 1860, s. of Noah & Mary (Stone) Reynolds, res. Letcher Co. 1870, m. Francis Matilda Baker (1845-aft. 1920) 1859, bur. Quillen-Reynolds Cem., Seco, Letcher Co., KY.

REYNOLDS, JOHN: (12/22/1837 – 3/11/1907), Co. A, serv. prev. 5th KY Inf., Co. F, disc. from 13th KY at term expiration 3/28/1863, res. Letcher Co. 1860, s. of Joseph & Queentena (Amburgey) Reynolds, res. Knott Co. 1890, m. Ruth Hylton (1839-1900 to 1910), bur. John Reynolds Cem., Mallie, Knott Co., KY.

REYNOLDS, STEPHEN N.: (1838 – 1877), 3rd Cpl., Co. D, pres. fall/1862, serv. later Union 39th KY, Co. K, res. Letcher Co. 1860, s. of Noah & Mary (Stone) Reynolds, res. Letcher Co. 1870, m. Drucilla Craft (1838-1876), bur. Quillen-Reynolds Cem., Seco. Letcher Co., KY.

REYNOLDS, THOMAS: 2nd Cpl., Co. K, enl. Lee Co., VA 8/18/1863, pres. Lee Co. 12/31/1863.

REYNOLDS, WILLIAM: (2/8/1835 – 5/3/1905), Co. E, enl. Whitesburg, KY 10/5/1862, capt. Floyd Co. 5/1864, to Louisville Prison, rel. on oath 5/1864, res. Floyd Co. 1860, s. of Hamilton & Malinda (Justice) Reynolds, res. Floyd Co. 1870, 1880 & 1900, m. Mary Hall (b. 1840) 1855, reportedly bur. Reynolds Cem., Clear Creek, Floyd Co., KY.

RICHARDSON, DAVID: (1831 – 1865), 2nd Sgt., Co. I, conscripted Whitesburg, KY 10/18/1862, rec. clothing 9/24/1864, killed mo. Drowning Creek on KY River, Estill Co., res. Perry Co. 1850, res. Breathitt Co. 1860, b. TN, s. of Thomas & Elizabeth (Cobb) Richardson, m. Nancy Combs (b. 1834), bur. Confed. Cem., Bibee, Madison Co., KY.

RICHIE, ANDREW: (1/20/1840 – 3/8/1912), Co. I, enl. Whitesburg, KY 10/1/1862, pres. Spring/1863, res. Perry Co. 1860, s. of James Monroe Sr. & Hannah (Fugate) Richie, m. Mahala "Haney" Miller (1837-1922) 1860, bur. Russell Cem., Lunah, Breathitt Co., KY.

RICHIE, ANDREW J.: (2/18/1842 – 9/30/1923), Co. C, conscripted Whitesburg, KY 10/1/1862, wd. N. Fk. KY River Perry Co. 10/1863, foot crippled & inflamed 12 mos. Later, res. Perry Co. 1860, s. of Gabriel & Nancy (Campbell) Richie, moved post-war Johnson Co., rec KY Pension #417 Johnson Co. (Oil Springs) 1912, res Johnson Co. (Big Paint Creek) 1920, m. Mary Ann Hale (1845-aft. 1900), d. George W. Richie's (son) home, bur. Preece Cem., Lousa, Lawrence Co., KY.

RICHIE, BENJAMIN: (1/29/1835 – 3/5/1912), Co. C, enl. Whitesburg, KY 10/1/1862, pres. Summer/1863, res. Perry Co. 1860, s. of Thomas & Kesiah (Smith) Richie, res. Perry Co. (Troublesome) 1870 & 1880, res. Knott Co. (w. son, Thomas) 1900, m. Roseanne "Annie" Combs (1843-1900 to 1910) 1863, KY d.c. #8932, bur James Owens Cem., Richie, Knott Co., KY.

RICHIE, GABRIEL: (3/3/1835 – 8/8/1916), Co. C, enl. Whitesburg, KY 10/1/1862, pres. fall/1862, res. Perry Co. 1860, s. of James Monroe Sr. & Hannah (Fugate) Richie, res. Perry Co. (Lost Creek) 1870 & 1880, applied KY Confed. Pension Knott Co. 1912, m. Mary "Polly" Fugate (1839-1905) 1866, bur. Richie Cem., Talcum, Knott Co., KY.

RICHIE, GABRIEL: (1813 – 4/2/1874), Co. I, enl. Hazard, KY 2/3/1863, pres. summer/1863, res. Perry Co. 1860, s. of Alexander Crockett Sr. & Elizabeth Susan "Betsy" (Grigsby) Richie, moved post-war Madison Co., AR, ret. Magoffin Co. by 1870, m. Nancy Campbell (1818-1918) 1835, bur. Risner Cem., Seitz, Magoffin Co., KY.

RICHIE, HENRY: (9/30/1847 – 11/22/1918), Co. I, enl. Hazard, KY 3/7/1863, pres. summer/1863, res. Perry Co. 1860, s. of Gabriel & Nancy (Campbell) Richie, m. (1) Sarah "Sally" Smith 1865 (d. 1881 to 1884), (2) Lillie Foutch (1863-1933) 1884, bur. Puckett-Prater Cem., Van Cleve, Breathitt Co., KY.

RICHIE, JAMES CROCKETT: (1/8/1839 – 6/16/1930), Co. C, enl. Whitesburg, KY 10/1/1862, rec. clothing 9/7/1864, surr. New River, VA, res. Perry Co. 1860, s. of James Monroe Sr. & Hannah (Fugate) Richie, rec. Confed. Pension, m. Matilda Napier (1857-1927) 1877, bur. Lewis Fork Cem., Lewis Fork, Breathitt Co., KY.

RICHIE, JOHN: (1/24/1846 – 9/22/1920), Co. I, conscripted 10/18/1862, disc. Whitesburg, KY 10/28/1862, res. Perry Co. 1860, s. of James Monroe Sr. & Hannah (Fugate) Richie, m. (1) Mary Napier (b. 1867) 1888, (2) Rindy Hicks (1864-bef. 1920), bur. Richie Cem., Talcum, Knott Co., KY.

RICHIE, JOSHUA: (1/1/1845 – 7/21/1914), Cos. B & I, conscripted Whitesburg, KY 9/7/1862, trans. to Co. I from Co. B 1/1/1863, pres. summer/1863, res. Perry Co. 1860, s. of Thomas & Kesiah (Smith) Richie, res. Perry Co. 1870, res. Knott Co. 1900, m. Nancy Hall (1850-1921) 1866, bur. Joshua Richie Cem., Fisty, Knott Co., KY.

RICHIE, JUSTIN AUSTIN "STILLER AULT": (1834 – 1899), 2nd Lt., Co. C, enl. 10/1/1862, pres. 2/10/1864, refused to surrender, res. Perry Co. 1860, s. of John Sr. & Sylvania "Silva" (Sizemore) Richie, res. Perry Co. (Troublesome) 1870 & 1880, res. Knott Co. (Clear Creek/Richie) 1889 (re: tax list), m. Rachel "Katie" Everidge (1843-1939), bur. Webb Cem., Mayking, Letcher Co., KY.

RICHIE, MARTIN: (6/11/1829 – 7/26/1899), Co. C, enl. Whitesburg, KY 10/1/1862, capt. Gladeville, VA 7/7/1863, to Kemper Barracks 7/18/1863, to Camp Chase Prison 7/20/1863, to Camp Douglas Prison 8/24/1863, exch. Point Lookout 2/24/1865, res. Perry Co. 1860, s. of James Monroe Sr. & Hannah (Fugate) Richie, res. Perry Co. 1880, m. (1) Rebecca Williams (1837-bef. 1874) 1852, (2) Winnie Engle (1841-1873) 1865, (3) Malinda Honeycutt (b. 1840) 1874, bur. Martin Richie Cem., Ball Creek, Talcum, Knott Co., KY.

RICHIE, NICHOLAS: (5/30/1843 – 6/10/1932), Co. C, enl. Whitesburg, KY 10/1/1862, wd. Battle Cynthiana 6/11/1864, recovered at home, re-joined 13th in VA (re: pension witness, John Dobson), w/ 13th at disbandment nr. Abingdon, VA, took oath Louisa, KY, res. Perry Co. 1860, s. of John Sr. & Sylvania "Silva" (Sizemore) Richie, res. Knott Co. 1900, rec. KY Confed. Pension #962 Knott Co. 1912, m. Rachel Sumner (1847-1910) 1871, bur. Clear Fk. Reg. Baptist Church Cem., Lotts Creek, Perry Co., KY.

RICHIE, SAMUEL: (5/1842 – 1921), Co. C, enl. Whitesburg, KY 10/1/1862, pres. summer 1863, res. Perry Co. 1860, s. of Thomas & Kesiah (Smith) Richie, res. Perry Co. 1880, res. Knott Co. 1900, applied KY Confed. Pension Knott Co. 1912, res. Knott Co. 1920, m. (1) Chloe Hall (1845-1900 to 1910) 1860, (2) Cordella Hughes Tignor (1866-aft. 1930), bur. James Owens Cem., Ritchie, Knott Co., KY.

RICHIE, SAMUEL: (1/13/1839 – 12/28/1911), Co. I, enl. Whitesburg, KY 10/1/1862, pres. summer/1863, res. Perry Co. 1860, s. of James Monroe Sr. & Hannah (Fugate) Richie, res. Breathitt Co. 1890, m. Artie Bradley (1850-1945), bur. Clemons-Richie Cem., Press, Breathitt Co., KY.

RIGGS. WILLIAM C.: (7/14/1827 – 7/17/1912), 3rd Sgt., Co. F, enl. Floyd Co. 10/14/1862, 5' 11", dark eyes, dark hair, serv. prev. 5th KY Inf., Co. C, capt. Licking River (Magoffin or Morgan Co.) spring/1863, to Camp Chase 5/10/1863, res. Magoffin Co. 1860, b. Scott Co., VA, s. of John Riggs & Nancy Chaney (re: d.c.), res. Magoffin Co. 1900, res. Greenup Co. 1910, m. (1) Margaret M. (1830-bef. 1865), (2) Lorena Brown (b. 1843), Magoffin Co. 1865, bur. Mt. Olive Cem., Maloneton, Greenup Co., KY.

ROBERTS, ALFRED A.: (12/15/1847 – 11/11/1931), Co. G, also listed on s.r. as Alison J. Roberts, enl. Whitesburg, KY 9/23/1862, capt. Gladeville, VA 7/7/1863, to Kemper Barracks 7/18/1863, to Camp Chase Prison 7/20/1863, to Camp Douglas Prison 8/24/1863, res. Breathitt Co. 1860, s. of Caleb & Delilah (Combs) Roberts, res. Perry Co. 1870, res. Breathitt Co. 1880 to 1930, m. (1) Mary (b. 1851), (2) Elvira Campbell (1847-1949), bur. Alfred Roberts Cem., Lost Creek, Breathitt Co., KY.

ROBERTS, ALLEN J.: (7/13/1839 – 2/4/1918), Co. I, serv. prev. 5th KY Inf., Co. C, rec. clothing 9/7/1864, res. Owsley Co. 1860, s. of John Roberts & Susan Campbell, moved MO & worked as a physician, ret. Breathitt Co. by 1912, witnessed Confed. Pension 1912, bur. Noble sec. Lewis Fork Cem., Lewis Fork, Breathitt Co., KY.

ROBERTS, CALEB: (12/7/1818 – 5/21/1910), 4th Cpl., Co. G & Kash's Co., enl. Whitesburg, KY 10/1/1862, serv. prev. 5th KY Inf. Cos. D & F, issued clothing 4/7/1864 & 6/29/1864, rec. forage request 12/11/1864, paroled Raleigh, NC 4/1865, res. Breathitt Co. 1860, indicted post-war for 1865 murder as member Kash's Co., res. Wolfe Co. 1870 to 1910, widow rec. KY Confed. Pension #2783 Wolfe Co. 1912, m. (1) Delilah Combs (d. ca. 1867), (2) Sallie Tolson (1830-1913), bur. Morgan Spencer Cem., Daysboro, Wolfe Co., KY.

ROBERTS, JOHN COMBS: (7/25/1846 – 4/7/1927), Co. G, enl. Breathitt Co., KY 9/23/1862, capt. Gladeville, VA 7/7/1863, to Kemper Barracks 7/18/1863, to Camp Chase Prison 7/20/1863, to Camp Douglas Prison 8/24/1863, exch. Point Lookout 2/24/1865, res. Breathitt Co. 1860, s. of Caleb & Delilah (Combs) Roberts, m. Bethany Combs (1847-1919), bur. Sego Cem., nr. Pretty Prairie, Reno Co., KS.

ROBERTS, JOHN P.: (12/29/1829 – 2/8/1907), Co. G, enl. Breathitt Co., KY 9/23/1862, surr. Mt. Sterling 4/30/1865, res. Breathitt Co. 1860, m. Lucinda Noble (1833-1910) 1853, bur. Big Andy Noble Cem., Hardshell, Breathitt Co., KY.

ROBERTS, PRESTON: (3/29/1829 – 3/29/1911), Co. H, enl. Whitesburg, KY 9/22/1862, pres. spring/1863, res. Letcher Co. 1860, s. of Sampson Roberts & Hilea Hampton, m. (1) Rebecca Caudill (d. 1859) 1851, (2) Sarah Fields (d. bef. 1910) 1862, d. Breathitt Co. (d.c. #5619), bur. Lazarus Back Cem., Quicksand, Breathitt Co., KY.

ROBERTS, RILEY: (1838 – 1912), Co. B, enl. Whitesburg, KY 9/9/1862, pres. fall/1862, res. Floyd Co. 1860, moved McDowell Co., WV by 1880, m. Matilda Caudill (1844-bef. 1910) Floyd Co. 1862, d. McDowell Co. (Panther Pool), WV.

ROBERTS, THOMAS J.: Co. E, enl. Whitesburg, KY 10/14/1862, capt. Gladeville, VA 7/7/1863, to Kemper Barracks 7/18/1863, to Camp Chase 7/20/1863, to Camp Douglas Prison 8/24/1863, enl. U. S. Navy 12/1863, initially assigned *U.S.S. Susquehanna.*

ROGERS, HUGH WILLIAM: (6/8/1848 – 11/8/1891), Co. D, enl. Lexington, KY 6/8/1864, 5' 9", light hair, blue eyes, wd. & capt. Mays Lick 6/19/1864, treated for severe gunshot fracture elbow rt. arm Lexington, KY, to Louisville Prison 7/1/1864, to Camp Chase Prison 8/3/1864, rel. on oath 1/12/1865, surr. 5/15/1865, res. Fayette Co. 1860, s. of William S. & Henrietta (Roseberry) Rogers, res. Fayette Co. 1870 & 1880, moved Bell Co. by 1890, shot & killed while serving as a U.S. Marshall for Bell & Harlan Cos., KY, bur. Paris Cem., Paris, Bourbon Co., KY.

ROGERS, JAMES THOMAS: (9/5/1841 – 1/21/1920), Capt., Co. D, serv. prev. as Lt. 1st Btn. Mtd. Rifles 10/21/1861 to 7/1862, capt. Greenville, TN when Gen. John Hunt Morgan was killed 9/4/1864, to Knoxville Prison, to Chatanooga Prison 10/14/1864, taken by rail toward KY 10/1864, escaped between Murfreesboro & Nashville by jumping from moving cars at night, walked 150 miles to join Gen. Hood's Army, record states he was "one of the most gallant and daring officers in the army and was well known". res. Bourbon Co. 1850, res. Fayette Co. 1860, s. of William S. & Henrietta (Roseberry) Rogers, moved to SC ca. 1866, serv. as magistrate Greenwood Co., SC, m. (1) Evelyn Eloise Walker (1845-1889), (2) Sue Richardson (1865-1940), bur. Ninety-Six Cem., Ninety-Six, Greenwood Co., SC.

ROSE, EZEKIEL M.: (1837 – 1910), 3rd Sgt., Co. K, enl. Lee Co., VA 8/18/1863, pres. Lee Co. 12/31/1863, also serv. three days Union Three Forks Btn. 7/14 to 7/17/1865, res. Owsley Co. 1860, b. Breathitt Co., s. of Robert & Esther (Moore) Rose, m. Cinthy Jett (1847-1896), bur. Shepherd Cem., Booneville, Owsley Co., KY.

ROSS, JAMES PRESTON: (11/1831 – 1916), Co. B, enl. Whitesburg, KY 8/31/1862, des. 9/10/1862, serv. Union Harlan Co. Btn. (10/12/1862 to 1/13/1863) & Union 39th KY Inf., Co. C (enl. 2/16/1863 & des. 8/12/1864), res. Letcher Co. 1860, b. Grayson Co., VA, s. of William Ross & Milly, res. Grayson Co. (Wilson Creek) 1870, res. Clay Co.(Big Creek), KY 1880 & 1900, m. (1) Rebecca (1837-bef. 1875), (2) Gilly Ann Hensley (1849-1926) 1875, reportedly bur. (unmarked) Samuel Brittain Cem., Eirline, Clay Co., KY.

ROYSE, FRANKLIN M.: (6/14/1848 – 5/22/1922), Co. H, enl. 10/1864, disbanded at saltworks in SW VA upon Lee's surr. 4/1865, res. Rowan Co., b. Morgan Co., res. Rowan Co. 1870, rec. KY Confed. Pension #1872 Rowan Co. 1912, m. Martha Pelfrey (1862-1922), bur. Williams-Turner Cem., Elliottville, Rowan Co., KY.

RUNYON, JOHN COMPTON: (3/8/1833 – 8/28/1915). Co. B, enl. Whitesburg, KY 9/13/1862, des. 9/10/1863, res. Pike Co. 1850, m. (1) Arena Bevin (1832-bef. 1894) 1852, (2) Laura Maynard (b. 1875) 1894, bur. Runyon Cem., on hill across from mo. of Mudlick Fk. of Pond Creek, Pike Co., KY.

RUSSELL, ABSOLOM CROSSMAN, "ABB": (11/7/1835 – 9/21/1914), Co. G, identified as captured with Co. G, in skirmish South Fk. Quicksand, Breathitt Co. 2/1864 in Confed pension of Wilson T. Combs, s. of John & Sarah (Dean) Russell, res. Breathitt Co. 1860, m. Mariam Miller (1835-1908) 1855, bur. McIntosh Cem., Clayhole, Breathitt Co., KY.

RUSSELL, DAVID CUMMINGS, "APP": (6/1840 – 1900), Co. G, enl. Breathitt Co. 2/12/1863, serv. prev. 5th KY Inf., Co. I, pres. fall/1863, capt South Fork Quicksand & taken to Camp Chase Prison 2/1864 (re: Wilson Combs' pension statement), res. Breathitt Co. 1860, s. of John & Sally (Dean) Russell, res. Breathitt Co. 1900, widow res. Breathitt Co. (Lost Creek) 1910, m. (1) Allie Jones (d. bef. 1871), (2) Levina Miller (1845-aft. 1910) 1862, poss. bur. (unmarked) Russell Cem., Russell Fork, Breathitt Co., KY.

RUSSELL, JAMES BURGIN: (1/29/1838 – 2/17/1917), Co. G, serv. prev. 5th KY Inf., Co. I, "serv. w/ 10th KY (13th)" (re: pension statement), res. Breathitt Co. 1860, b. Lee Co., VA, s. of John & Sally (Dean) Russell, m. (1) Lavina Smith (1836-bef. 1896) 1857, (2) Mary McIntosh (b. 1845) 1896, bur. McIntosh Cem., Clayhole, Breathitt Co., KY.

SALLEY, GREEN BERRY: (1825 – 12/20/1894), Co. D, listed as 'Beriah' on s.r., enl. Whitesburg, KY 10/4/1862, pres. fall/1862, res. Letcher Co. 1860, from Lee Co., VA, moved Whitesburg 1860, moved Wolfe Co. post-war, m. Mary Church (b. 1835), bur. Trimble Cem., Hazel Green, Wolfe Co., KY.

SAMMONS, THOMAS: (1/10/1844 – 1/3/1914), Co. F, enl. Whitesburg, KY 10/14/1862, pres. fall/1863, serv. prev. 2nd Bttn. KY Mtd. Rifles & 5th KY Inf. Co. G (per pension), res. Floyd Co. 1860, s. of Thomas & Milly Sammons, m. Julia Webb (1845-1914), rec. KY Confed Pension #1885 in Carter Co. 1912, bur. Sammons Cem. #4, Armstrong Hill, Carter Co., KY.

SAWYERS, WILLIAM: Co. F, enl. Floyd Co., KY 8/24/1863, pres. summer/1863.

SCOTT, DANIEL S. (1839 – 1924), Co. K, serv. prev. 4th KY Cav., Co. G (enl. 9/1/1862), capt. & taken to Camp Butler 1/311/1863, exch. later (date unknown), ret. Floyd Co. & joined Co. K, 13th KY, paroled Cumberland Gap 4/30/1865, res. Owen Co. 1860, res. Floyd Co. 1870, b. 1839, res. Floyd Co. 1870, m. Sarah Hoover (1852-1927), bur. Scott Cem., Garrett, Floyd Co., KY.

SEXTON, ELSBURY "BARRY": (1843 – 4/1/1866), 2nd Cpl., Co. B, enl. Whitesburg, KY 9/8/1862, capt. Gladeville, VA 7/7/1863, to Kemper Barracks 7/18/1863, to Camp Chase Prison 7/20/1863, to Camp Douglas Prison 8/24/1863, exch. Point Lookout 2/24/1865, res. Letcher Co. 1860, s. of William & Ellender (Cook) Sexton, d. Russell Co., VA.

SEXTON, HATLER HASCUE "HATTER": (4/20/1832 – 3/14/1914), 1st Sgt., Co. A, enl. 11/1/1862, serv. prev. 5th KY Inf., Co. F & 8th VA Cav., Co. E, rec. clothing 9/15/1864, wd. from gunshot (re: pension statement), res. Letcher Co. 1860, s. of Hulda Sexton, m. Tabitha Sexton (1838-1918), bur. Sexton Cem., Tacoma, Wise Co., VA.

SEXTON, JOSEPH: (9/24/1844 – 3/31/1926), 2nd Cpl., Co. A, enl. Whitesburg, KY 11/1/1862, serv. prev. 5th KY Inf., Co. F, res. Letcher Co. 1860, s. of William & Nancy (Moore) Sexton, res. Wise Co. VA 1900 to 1920, rec. VA Confed. Pension claiming 'broken arm on march' and 'never left til surrender', m. (1) Polly Reynolds (d. bef. 1870), (2) Ester Emeline Freeman (1853-bef. 1900), bur. Sexton Cem., Tacoma, Wise Co., VA.

SEXTON, NATHANIAL: (4/21/1837 – 1902), 1st Cpl., Co. H, enl. Whitesburg, KY 9/13/1862, rec. clothing 9/24/1864, serv. until 4/1865, res. Letcher Co. 1860, b. Red River (Morgan /Wolfe Cos.), moved Letcher Co. (Camp Branch) bef. 1850, s. of William & Elender (Cook) Sexton, res. Knott Co. 1889-1900, widow rec. KY Confed. Widow's Pension #1182 Letcher Co. 1912, m. Nellie Taylor (1845-1927) Letcher Co. 1866, bur. Sexton Cem., Omaha, Knott Co., KY.

SEXTON, STEPHEN A.: (1829 – 1892), Co. A, serv. prev. 5th KY Inf., Co. F, rec. clothing 9/7/1864, res. Letcher Co. 1860, b. Scott Co., VA, s. of William & Rebecca Sexton, res. Floyd Co. 1870, m. (1) Christena Fields (1820-bef. 1887), (2) Mary Jane Patton 1887, d. Floyd Co. (Hueysville), bur. Martin Cem., Hueysville, Floyd Co., KY.

SEXTON, WILLIAM: (1837 – 1902), Co. H, enl. 10/18/1862, rec. clothing 9/15/1864, res. Letcher Co. 1860, s. of William & Nancy (Moore) Sexton, res. Letcher Co. 1870, widow rec. KY Confed. Widow's Pension #1182 in 1912, m. Verlina Sextron (1842-1918), d. Letcher Co. (Deane), bur. Gibson-Sexton Cem., Colson, Letcher Co., KY.

SEXTON, WILLIAM M.: (1845 – 1900), Co. H, enl. Whitesburg, KY 9/22/1862, pres. spring/1863, res. Letcher Co. 1860, s. of William & Ellender (Cook) Sexton, res. Letcher Co. 1870, m. (1) Lucinda Gibson (1844-bef. 1900) 1858, (2) Abentine Meadows, (3) Jane Collins, bur. Sexton Cem., Colson, Letcher Co., KY.

SHEPHERD, BRISON F "BRICE": (3/31/1841 – 12/22/1926), 5th Sgt., Co. F, enl. Floyd Co. 10/14/1862, serv. prev. 5th KY Inf., Co. C, capt. Gladeville, VA 7/7/1863, to Kemper Barracks 7/18/1863, to Camp Chase Prison 7/20/1863, to Camp Douglas Prison 8/24/1863, exch. Point Lookout 2/24/1865, res. Floyd Co. 1850 & 1860, s. of Jacob & Elizabeth Shepherd, res. Magoffin Co. 1870, m. (1) Nancy, (2) Loueaster Salyer (1849-1908), bur. Shepherd Cem., David, Floyd Co., KY.

SHEPHERD, DANIEL: (1841 – 1/22/1896), Co. F, enl. Floyd Co. 10/10/1862, res. Floyd Co. 1850s. of John & Elizabeth Shepherd, res. Floyd Co. 1870 & 1880, m. Rosa A. (1840-1918), bur. Prater Cem., Bonanza, Floyd Co., KY.

SHEPHERD, DAVID: (1935 – 1863), Co. F, enl. Floyd Co. 10/10/1862, res. Floyd Co. 1850 & 1860, s. of John & Elizabeth Shepherd, m. Nancy Stone (b. 1839) 1857, bur. Shepherd Cem., Handshoe, Knott Co., KY.

SHEPHERD, MARTIN: (1845 – 1894), Co. B, enl. Floyd Co. 9/13/1862, pres. fall/1862, res. Floyd Co. 1850, res. Magoffin Co. 1860, s. of John E. & Sarah (Hale) Shepherd, res. Floyd Co. 1870, res. Magoffin Co. 1880, m. Rhoda Hale (b. 1847).

SHEPHERD, WILLIAM R.: (1/4/1842 – 7/30/1913), Cos. C & F, enl. Floyd Co. 1860, capt. Gladeville, VA 7/7/1863, to Kemper Barracks 7/18/1863, to Camp Chase Prison 7/20/1863, to Camp Douglas Prison 8/24/1863, rel. Point Lookout 5/1865, furloughed, took oath Louisa, KY, res. Floyd Co. 1860, res. Breathitt Co. (Daisey Dale) 1890, moved Magoffin Co. (Swampton), rec. KY Confed. Pension #1507/#2521 Magoffin Co. 1912, m. Amanda Conley (1852-1939) Breathitt Co. 1870, bur. Willie Shepherd Cem., Royalton, Magoffin Co., KY.

SHORT, BOOKER: (3/10/1837 – 8/5/1929), Co. H, enl. Whitesburg, KY 10/18/1862, had horse shot out from under him, trans. 7th Btn. Confed. Cav. under Col. Prentice fall/1863, promoted to Capt., disbanded Salem, VA after news of Lee's surrender 4/7/1865, paroled Charleston, WV 6/1865, res. Letcher Co. (Irishman Creek) 1860, b. Russell Co. VA, s. of David & Polly (Cantrell) Short, left KY post-war, ret. 1/1907, res. Menifee Co. (Ratliff), rec. KY Confed. Pension #3088 Menifee Co. 1912, m. Sarah Madden (1837-bef. 1900) 1857, bur. Toler Cem., Ratliff, Menifee Co., KY.

SHORT, WILSON ESLIN: (8/15/1836 – 2/11/1912), Co. H, enl. Whitesburg, KY 6/21/1863, pres. summer/1863, res. Letcher Co., s. of Charles & Anna (Mullins) Short, res. Letcher Co. 1870, res. Knott Co. 1890, widow applied KY Confed. Widow's Pension Knott Co. 1912, m. (1) Nancy Ann Reynolds (1839-1878), (2) Nancy Slone (1858-1925) 1878, bur. Jackson Slone (Slone-Thacker) Cem., Garner, Knott Co., KY

SHULER, FRANKLIN: (b. 1846), Cos. E & F, enl. Whitesburg, KY 10/5/1862, trans. to Co. F from Co. E Whitesburg 10/10/1862, rec. clothing 9/7/1864, did not survive the war, res. Letcher Co. 1860, b. Grayson Co., VA, s. of Adam & Elizabeth (Hall) Shuler.

SHULER, STEPHEN: (10/1839 – 1928), Cos. E & F, enl. Whitesburg, KY 10/5/1862, trans. to Co. F from Co. E Whitesburg 10/14/1862, rec. clothing 9/7/1864, res. Letcher Co. 1860, b. Grayson Co., VA, s. of Adam & Elizabeth (Hall) Shular, res. Lee Co., VA 1880, 1900 & 1910 (Yokum Station), m. Elizabeth Morefield (1845-aft. 1920) Lee Co., VA 1866.

SINGLETON, JOSHUA B.: (6/1835 – aft. 1900), Co. D, enl. Whitesburg, KY 10/4/1862, res. Letcher Co. (Poor Fork) 1860, b. Russell Co., VA, res. Letcher Co. 1870, res. Poor Fork 1882, res. Wise Co. (Gladeville), VA 1900, m. Susannah Maggard (1835-aft. 1900) 1856.

SIZEMORE, EPHRIAM: (1839 – 10/14/1862), Co. G, enl. Breathitt Co. 10/14/1862, killed at the Eversole house by Union 14th KY soldiers Perry Co. (Krypton) 10/14/1862, res. Perry Co. (w/ stepfather, Wes Conway) 1860, s. of William Sizemore & Ann Asher, bur. Red Hill Cem., Chavies, Perry Co., KY.

SIZEMORE, HIRAM: (1825 – 1864), Co. G, enl. Breathitt Co. 10/14/1862, pres. fall/1863, KIA, res. Breathitt Co. 1860, s. of William & Anna (Asher) Sizemore, m. Juda Noble (b. 1824) 1846, bur. Baker Cem., Cortland, Owsley Co., KY.

SIZEMORE, JEFFERSON: (4/1846 – 1901), Co. G, enl. Breathitt Co. 10/14/1862, rec. clothing 6/29/1864, serv. until end of war, surr. Louisa 5/1865, res. Breathitt Co. 1860, s. of Hiram & Juda (Noble) Sizemore, res. Perry Co. 1880, res. Breathitt Co. 1900, widow rec. KY Confed. Widow's Pension #2808 Breathitt Co. (Stacy) 1913, m. Polly Campbell (1851-aft. 1930) Perry Co. 1866, d. Breathitt Co. (Troublesome), bur. Sizemore Cem., Cockrell's Fk., Perry Co., KY.

SIZEMORE, LEWIS: (8/21/1841 – 8/9/1914), Co. G, enl. Breathitt Co. 10/14/1862, serv. prev. 5th KY Inf., Co. B, pres. spring/1863, res. Breathitt Co. 1860, s. of William & Anna (Asher) Sizemore, m. Sarah Little (b. 1845) 1873, bur. Baker Cem., Cortland, Owsley Co., KY.

SKEEN, HENRY A.: (2/24/1844 – 2/17/1937), Co. I, conscripted Whitesburg, KY 10/18/1862, pres. 5/10/1863, serv. later Union 39th KY Inf. 10/1863 to 9/1865, res. Letcher Co. 1860 but also on Wise Co. VA census 1860, s. of Archibald & Susan (Hammond) Skeen, m. (1) Mary Elizabeth (d. bef. 1900), (2) Alice (1850-aft. 1910), bur. (unmarked) Bellomy Cem., Wayne Co., WV.

SLONE, GEORGE W.: (1839 – 1863), Co. B, enl Whitesburg, KY 9/9/1862, pres. summer/1863, res. Floyd Co. 1860, s. of James & Milly Slone, m. Jane, bur. Sandlick Cem., Whitesburg, Letcher Co., KY.

SLONE, HARDIN: (3/20/1839 – 1/27/1918), Co. E, enl. Whitesburg, KY 10/5/1862, capt. & to Louisville Prison 1863, took oath 1865, res. Floyd Co., b. Floyd Co., s. of William & Sarah (Casebolt) Slone, res. Knott Co. 1900, rec. KY Confed. Pension #3048 Knott Co. (Mallie) 1912, m. Mahalia Johnson (1839-aft. 1918), bur. Jimmy Slone Cem., Pippa Passes, Knott Co., KY.

SLONE, HENRY F. "FARMER": (1843 – 7/29/1864), Cos. D & E, enl. Whitesburg, KY 10/4/1862, trans. to Co. E from Co. D Whitesburg 10/5/1862, capt. Pike Co. 10/6/1863, to Louisville Prison 10/22/1863, to Camp Morton 10/24/1863, res. Floyd Co. 1860, s. of Hiram & Temperance Slone, d. from typhoid fever at Camp Morton Prison, bur. Crown Hill Cem., Indianapolis, Marion Co., IN.

SLONE, ISHAM "ISOM": (10/9/1838 – 10/20/1917), Co. A, enl. 1862, serv. prev. 5th KY Inf., Co. F, capt. Gladeville, VA 7/7/1863, to Kemper Barracks 7/18/1863, to Camp Chase Prison 7/20/1863, to Camp Douglas Prison 8/24/1863, exch. Point Lookout 2/24/1865, res. Floyd Co. 1860, b. Floyd Co., s. of Reuben & Sarah Slone, rec. KY Confed. Pension #1023 Knott Co. 1912, m. Rachel Thornsberry, res. Caney Creek (1848-1937) 1878, bur. Slone-Dyer Cem., Leburn, Knott Co., KY.

SLONE, ISHAM "JAILER ISOM": (4/1842 – 1916), 3rd Cpl., Co. E, enl. Whitesburg, KY 10/5/1862, pres. 3/1863, res. Floyd Co. (Caney Creek) 1860, s. of William & Sarah (Casebolt) Slone, res. Floyd Co. 1870, res. Letcher Co. 1880, res. Knott Co. 1900, first Jailer of Knott Co., res. Pike Co. (Freeburn) 1910, Confed. Pension witness Pike Co. 1912, m. (1) Nancy J. Johnson (1845-aft. 1870) 1858, (2) Franky J. Caudill Hall (1851-aft. 1910), bur. Dotson Cem., Board Tree, Pike Co., KY.

SLONE, JACOB: (1836 – 10/1875), Co. E, enl. Whitesburg, KY 10/5/1862, pres. spring/1863, res. Floyd Co. 1860, s. of James & Milly Slone, res. Floyd Co. 1870, m. (1) Mariah (d. bef. 1870), (2) Hannah Johnson (1834-1914), bur. Alice Slone Cem., Hollybush, Knott Co., KY.

SLONE, JAMES A.: (6/16/1838 – 11/23/1917), Co. A, enl. Whitesburg, KY 11/1/1862, serv. prev. 5th KY Inf., Co. F, pres. spring/1863, disc. Gladeville, VA, not capt., 'afraid to go home...for fear of being killed' (re: pension statement), res. Floyd Co. 1860, s. of William & Sarah (Casebolt) Slone, rec. KY Confed. Pension #2282 Knott Co. (Hindman) 1912, m. Frankie (1836-1908), bur. Trace Fork Cem., Pippa Passes, Knott Co., KY.

SLONE, JASPER: (1843 – 7/30/1864), Co. F, enl. Floyd Co. 10/10/1862, capt. Floyd Co. 11/7/1863, to Louisville Prison 11/18/1863, to Camp Morton Prison 11/20/1863, res. Floyd Co. 1860, s. of Reuben & Sally Slone, d. from typhoid fever Camp Morton, bur. Crown Hill Cem., Indianapolis, Marion Co. IN.

SLONE, JOHN: (1834 – 1863), Co. B, enl 9/9/1862, pres. summer/1863, res. Floyd Co. 1860, s. of Hiram & Temperance Slone, bur. Sandlick Cem., Whitesburg, Letcher Co., KY.

SLONE, JOHN C.: (2/15/1833 – 3/12/1911), Co. E, enl. Whitesburg, KY 10/5/1862, res. Floyd Co. 1860, s. of William & Sarah (Casebolt) Slone, res. Knott Co. 1900, widow applied KY Confed. Widow's Pension Knott Co. 1912, m. Sarah "Sally" Johnson (1832-1920), bur. Milton Owens Cem., Pippa Passes, Knott Co., KY.

SLONE, JOHN P.: (4/6/1846 – 11/27/1917), Co. E, enl. Whitesburg, KY 10/5/1862, pres. summer/1863, serv. later Union KY 39th Inf, Co. E, res. Floyd Co. (Caney Creek) 1860, s. of Reuben & Sally Slone, m. Christine B. Smith (1863-1945), bur. Slone Cem., Mallie, Knott Co., KY.

SLONE, MONROE: (1835 – 1900), 4th Sgt., Cos. E & F, enl. Whitesburg, KY 10/5/1862, trans. to Co. F from Co. E Whitesburg 6/1/1863, pres. fall/1863, res. Floyd Co. 1860, s. of Hiram & Temperance Slone, m. Susannah Vance (1839-1905), bur. Monroe Slone Cem., West Hamlin, Lincoln Co., WV.

SLONE, NATHANIAL: (b. 1843), Co. B, enl. Whitesburg, KY 9/9/1862, pres. spring/1863, res. Floyd Co. 1860, s. of James & Milly Slone, res. Estill Co. 1870, res. Jefferson Co. 1880, m. Susan Lucas (b. 1846) Floyd Co. 1866.

SLONE, PLEASANT: (1834 – 3/9/1912), Co. E, enl. Whitesburg, KY 10/5/1862, serv. until 8/31/1863, res. Floyd Co. 1860, s. of Isom & Polly (Reynolds) Slone, res. Knott Co. 1900, widow rec. KY Confed. Widow's Pension #1022 Knott Co. 1912, m. Minerva Jacobs (1839-1933), bur. Little Bill Adkins Slone Cem., Raven, Knott Co., KY.

SLONE, SHADRACK "FIDDLER SHADE": (4/17/1828 – 5/24/1922), Co. E, enl. Whitesburg, KY 10/5/1862, pres. spring/1863, res. Floyd Co. 1860, s. of William & Sarah (Casebolt) Slone, m. Rachel Owens (1831-1895) 1847, bur. Jimmy Slone Cem., Pippa Passes, Knott Co., KY.

SLONE, SPENCER: (2/1841 – aft. 1912), Co. F, enl. Floyd Co. 10/10/1862, 6' 1" sandy hair, blue eyes, capt Floyd Co. 11/7/1863, to Louisville Prison 11/18/1863, to Camp Morton Prison 11/20/1863, rel. on oath 5/22/1865, res. Floyd Co. (Prestonsburg) 1860, s. of Alexander & Matilda (Martin) Slone, res. Floyd Co. 1870, res. Knott Co. 1900, rec. KY Confed. Pension #1512 Knott Co. (Deinde) 1912, m. Amy/Emily (1842-aft. 1900), bur. Slone Cem., Wayland, Floyd Co., KY.

SLONE, TANDY: (1/1837 – 9/1/1923), 2nd Cpl., Co. F, enl. Floyd Co. 10/14/1862, 6' 1", dark hair, blue eyes, capt. Floyd Co. 10/5/1863, to Louisville Prison 11/18/1863, to Camp Morton Prison 11/20/1863, rel on oath 6/21/1865, res. Floyd Co. (Caney Creek/Raven) 1860, s. of Alexander & Matilda (Martin) Slone, widow rec. KY Confed. Widow's Pension #4276 1923, m. Annie Sammons (1839-1926), bur. Turner Cem., Beaver, Knott Co., KY.

SLONE, LEVI "TRUMBLE": (4/20/1828 – 12/18/1905), Co. E, enl. Whitesburg, KY 10/5/1862, also listed as Tumbo Slone, pres. fall/1862, res. Letcher Co. 1860, poss. s. of Shadrack Johnson, res. Knott Co. w/ son Hardin 1900, m. Hannah (1828-bef. 1900), bur. Hughes Cem., Mallie, Knott Co., KY.

SLUSHER, GARDENER: (1837 – bef. 1910), Co. F, enl. Floyd Co. 10/10/1862, res. Breathitt Co. 1860, s. of Phillip & Mary "Polly" (Howard) Slusher, res. Breathitt Co. 1880, res. Breathitt Co. (Rousseau) 1892 (re: tax list), res. Floyd Co. 1900, m. (1) Isabelle (1837-1870 to 1880), (2) Rebecca Bailey (1865-aft. 1920).

SLUSHER, JOHN: (8/12/1840 – 9/1/1864), Co. F, enl. Floyd Co. 10/10/1862, cap. Gladeville, VA 7/7/1863, to Kemper Barracks 7/18/1863, to Camp Chase Prison 7/20/1863, to Camp Douglas 8/22/1863, res. Breathitt Co. 1860, s. of Phillip & Mary "Polly" (Howard) Slusher, widow rec. KY Confed. Widow's Pension #1039 Floyd Co. 1912, m. Rachel Gibson (1842-aft. 1870) 1856, d. from consumption Camp Douglas, bur. Oak Wood Cem., Chicago, Cook Co., IL.

SMALL, LEMUEL: Co. G, identified in A. G. Report, capt. Gladeville, VA 7/7/1863, to Kemper Barracks 7/18/1863, to Camp Chase Prison 7/20/1863, to Camp Douglas Prison 8/24/1863, exch. Point Lookout 2/24/1865.

SMITH, ANDREW JACKSON B.: (1829 – 2/21/1865), Co. A, serv. prev. 5th KY Inf., Co. F, capt. Letcher Co. 6/18/1864, to Camp Douglas Prison, res. Letcher Co. 1860, s. of William B. & Elizabeth (Childers) Smith, m. Quinteena Pigman (1832-bef. 1859) 1849, (2) Sarah Huff (b. 1844) 1859, d. from chronic diarrhea Camp Douglas, bur. Oak Wood Cem., Chicago, Cook Co., IL.

SMITH, ARCHIE WILLIAM: (12/10/1829 – 9/3/1913), Capt. Field & Staff, serv. as Bvt. 2nd Lt. 4th KY Cav. Co. E, F & S Quartermaster 13th KY Cav. 7/1863, s. of Archer & Cynthia (Conway) Smith, b. Owen Co., res. Trimble Co. 1860, m. (1) Mary E. Calvert (1847-1888), (2) Sophronia Etta Irvine (1866-1937), widow rec. KY Confed. Widow's Pension #4130, Trimble Co. 1921, bur. Com Creek Bapt. Ch. Cem., Milton, Trimble Co., KY.

SMITH, BENJAMIN: (12/1838 – 8/1907), 2nd Sgt., Co. F, enl. Whitesburg, KY 10/14/1862, serv. prev. 5th KY Inf., Co. E, took part in the execution of Gilbert Creech, pres. summer/1863, res. Floyd Co. 1860, s. of Benjamin & Katherine "Katie" Smith, res. Knott Co. (Jones Fork) 1900, m. (1) Jane Martin, (I2) Melissa, (3) Amanda Hays.

SMITH, BENJAMIN: (9/16/1825 – 7/18/1904), 2nd Cpl., Co. I, enl. Whitesburg, KY 10/18/1862, serv. in execution of Union soldier Creech, res. Perry Co. 1860, s. of Thomas & Nancy (Clemons) Smith, res. Knott Co. (Quicksand) 1900, m. Matilda Oliver (1830-1899) 1852, bur. Beverly Cem., Elmrock, Knott Co., KY.

SMITH, DANIEL: (1/25/1840 – 10/17/1920), 3rd Cpl., Co. I, conscripted Whitesburg, KY 10/1/1862, prom. Whitesburg 10/18/1862, pres. fall/1863, in heavy fighting Dandridge/Strawberry Plains, TN with 13th under Giltner's Command 1/16/1864 & 1/17/1864 (re: interview w/ his nephew), res. Perry Co. 1860, s. of Samuel & Nancy (Jones) Smith, res. Perry Co. 1880, rec. KY Confed. Pension #1905 Knott Co. (Hindman) 1912, m. Martha Campbell (1845-1888), bur. Richie Cem., Ritchie, Knott Co., KY.

SMITH, ELIAS: (1832 – 12/20/1863), 5th Sgt., Cos. B & I, conscripted Whitesburg, KY 9/6/1862, trans to Co. I from Co. B Whitesburg, KY 10/18/1862, res. Perry Co. 1860, s. of Thomas & Sarah (Clemons) Smith, m. Betty A. Richie (b. 1838) 1859, d. Wise Co., VA, bur. Pound Gap Camp Cem., Almira, Wise Co., VA.

SMITH, EMORY B: (2/23/1841 – 5/1/1900), Co. A, serv. prev. 5th KY Inf., Co. F, disc. by Hiram Strong (13th KY Surgeon) spring/1863, res. Letcher Co. 1860, s. of William B. & Elizabeth (Childers) Smith, m. Susan Amburgey (1841-1926) 1859, bur. Steerfork Cem., Pinetop, Knott Co., KY.

SMITH, GEORGE: (1837 – 8/30/1902), Co. E, enl. Whitesburg, KY 10/5/1862, res. Floyd Co. 1860, res. Floyd Co. 1870 & 1880, res. Carter Co. 1887 (re: courthouse records), m. America (b. 1840).

SMITH, ISAAC: (1842 – 8/1/1864), 2nd Lt., Co. I, enl. Whitesburg, KY 10/18/1862, KIA Breathitt Co., res. Perry Co. 1860, s. of Samuel & Nancy (Jones) Smith.

SMITH, ISAAC: (5/1841 – 1919), Co. I, enl. Whitesburg, KY 10/1/1862, disc. 1/2/1863, res. Perry Co. 1860, s. of James & Rhoda (Owens) Smith, res. Lee Co. (Proctor) 1870, 1880 & 1893, res. Breathitt Co. 1900 (Frozen Cr.) & 1910, m. (1) Telitha Ross (1839-1901), (2) Vina Howard Carpenter (1859-1920) 1902, bur. Dunn Cem., Willstacy, Breathitt Co., KY.

SMITH, JEREMIAH M. "JAKE": (2/1/1832 – 2/17/1913), Co. H, enl. Whitesburg, KY 10/18/1862, pres. fall/1862, poss. serv. Union 14th KY Cav., Co. L (12/28/1862 to 2/13/1863), res. Letcher Co. 1860, s. of William & Millie (Combs) Smith, m. Elizabeth Stacy (1835-1914) 1854, bur. Carr's Fork Cem., Littcarr, Knott Co., KY.

SMITH, JOHN: (b. 1839), Co. I, enl. Gladeville, VA 7/15/1863, abs. by fall/1863, res. Perry Co., s. of James & Rhoda (Owens) Smith.

SMITH, JOHN: (b. 1846), Co. I, enl. Whitesburg, KY 10/18/1862, serv. prev. 5th KY Inf., res. Perry Co. 1860, s. of Samuel & Nancy (Jones) Smith, KIA Miller Creek of Troublesome, bur. (unmarked) Marshall & Noble Cem., Lewis Fork, Breathitt Co., KY.

SMITH, JOHN H.: Co. A, capt. Breathitt Co., KY 9/30/1863, to Louisville Prison 1/1/1864, to Camp Douglas Prison 7/17/1864, enl. U.S. 6th 3/24/1865.

SMITH, LORENZO DOW: (11/16/1816 – 12/8/1905), Co. I, enl. Whitesburg, KY 8/29/1863, pres. summer/1863, res. Perry Co. 1860, s. of Richard & Alecia (Combs) Smith, m. (1) Sally Fugate (1815-1870's), (2) Frankie Stacy (1838-1914) 1881, bur. Richard Smith Cem., Ary, Perry Co., KY.

SMITH, NICHOLAS: (b. 1829), Co. I, conscripted Whitesburg, KY 10/18/1862, serv. prev. 5th KY Inf., Co. F, res. Perry Co., s. of James & Rhoda (Owens) Smith, m. Elizabeth Slone (b. 1831), KIA Perry Co., 1864.

SMITH, RICHARD: (1833 – 1901), Co. G, enl. Perry Co. 10/14/1862, disc. 1/1/1863, res. Perry Co. 1860, s. of Thomas & Sarah (Clemons) Smith, res. Perry Co. 1880, m. (1) Franky Miller (1829-1883), bur. Stacy & Smith Cem., nr. Decoy, Knott Co., KY.

SMITH, SAMPSON B.: (1/8/1843 – 2/14/1920), 2nd Lt., Co. B, enl. Whitesburg, KY 8/29/1862, elected 2nd Lt. 6/2/1864, wd. & capt. Battle of Cynthiana 6/12/1864, treated for flesh wd. of leg Covington hosp., paroled Camp Chase Prison 1/25/1865, res. Letcher Co. 1860, b. Letcher Co., s. of Reubin & Sarah Smith, rec. KY Confed. Pension #3423 Wolfe Co. 1915, m. (1) Mary Elizabeth Combs (1842-1870 to 1900), (2) Rhoda Bailey Booth (1862-1945), bur. Bailey Cem., Campton, Wolfe Co., KY.

SMITH, SAMUEL "SR": (5/7/1802 – 12/6/1863), Co. I, enl. Gladeville, VA 8/1/1863, shot to death by 18 Union soldiers while asleep at home on Ball Creek, res. Perry Co. 1860, s. of Richard & Alecia (Combs) Smith, m. Nancy Jones, bur. Engle Cem., Dwarf, Perry Co., KY.

SMITH, SAMUEL "JR": (10/4/1844 – 2/27/1937), Co. I, enl. Gladeville, VA 8/1/1863, badly wd. Strawberry Plains, TN 1/17/1864, recovered in VA hosp, ret. serv. (re: interview w/ son), serv. as scout eastern KY winter/1864, ret. to command in VA 6 mo. before being ordered to Richmond, nr. New River, VA when rec. news of Lee's surr., res. Perry Co. 1860, s. of Samuel & Nancy (Jones) Smith, rec. Confed. Pension #1910 Knott Co. 1912, m. (1) Nancy Owens, (2) Nancy Singleton (1881-1956), bur. Smith Cem., Cordia, Knott Co., KY.

SMITH, SHADRACK "SHADE": (1/15/1845 – 3/30/1930), Co. I, enl. Whitesburg, KY 8/29/1863, reportedly also serv. Union Army, res. Perry Co. 1860, s. of Isaac & Sintha (Stacy) Smith, rec. KY Confed. Pension #3051 Knott Co. 1912, m. Mary Holliday (b. 1850), bur. Holliday Cem., Ary, Perry Co., KY.

SMITH, SIMEON: (12/1834 – 1914), Co. I, conscripted Whitesburg, KY 10/1/1862, res. Perry Co. 1860, s. of Nick & Nancy Smith, res. Perry Co. 1870 (Troublesome), & 1880, res. Knott Co. 1900 & 1910 (Jones Fork), applied KY Confed Pension Knott Co. 1912, m. Anna (1839-1904).

SMITH, WILLIAM BRANHAM: (9/20/1836 – 4/14/1922), Cos. A & C, serv. prev. 5th KY, Co. F, 5' 6", dark complexion, light hair, grey eyes, rel. by Capt. Hiram Stamper Leatherwood saltworks Perry Co. 4/1/1863, took oath Louisa, KY 5/6/1865, res. Letcher Co. 1860, b. Letcher Co., s. of William B. & Elizabeth (Childers) Smith, rec. KY Confed. Pension #2285 Knott Co. 1912, m. (1) Rebecca Adams (1841-1864), (2) Dorcas Amburgey (1850-1913) 1869, bur. Steerfork Cem., Pinetop, Knott Co., KY.

SMITH, WILLIAM B.: (4/6/1844 - 1876), Co. B, enl. Whitesburg, KY 9/15/1862, rec. clothing 11/19/1864, res. Letcher Co. 1860, s. of John B. & Sarah (Adams) Smith, m. (1) Susannah Hamilton (1847-1888), d. Knott Co..

SMITH, WILLIAM S.: (1834 – 11/19/1863), 3rd Cpl., Co. I, enl. Whitesburg, KY 10/1/1862, killed by Union troops mo. of Ball Perry Co., res. Perry Co. 1850, s. of James & Rhoda (Owens) Smith, bur. Richard Smith Cem., Ary, Perry Co., KY.

SMITH, WILLIAM W.: (11/12/1834 – 10/30/1886), Capt., Co. I, enl. Whitesburg, KY 10/18/1862, organized Perry Co. conscription Co. I, prom. Capt. 11/2/1862, wd. 12/31/1863, w/ Co. I at disbandment VA 1865, res. Breathitt Co. 1860, b. Perry Co. (Troublesome), s. of Samuel & Nancy (Jones) Smith, widow rec. KY Confed. Widow's Pension #1908 Perry Co. 1913, m. Nancy Hounshell (b. 1839) Lott's Creek 1861, bur. Strong Cem., Lost Creek, Breathitt Co., KY.

SOUTH, MARTIN VAN BUREN: (10/28/1836 – 4/1/1873), Kash's Co., serv. prev. 5th KY Inf., Co. D until 11/1/1863, s. of Jeremiah W. & Mary Magdeline (Cockrell) South, indicted post-war for 1865 murder as member this Co., m. Sophronia "Sophia" Hockensmith (b. 1848), bur. Frankfort Cem., Frankfort, Franklin Co., KY.

SOUTHWOOD, SAMPSON: (1844 – 1863), Co. G, enl. Breathitt Co. 10/14/1862, pres. 5/11/1863, res. Breathitt Co. 1860, b. 1844, s. of Isaac & Polly Southwood, d. 1863, bur. Sandlick Cem. Whitesburg, Letcher Co., KY.

SPARKMAN, JOHN S.: (2/26/1826 – 4/1/1920), 5th Sgt., Co. A, enl. Whitesburg, KY 11/1/1862, serv. prev. 5th KY Inf., Co. F, capt. Gladeville, VA 7/7/1863, to Kemper Barracks 7/18/1863, to Camp Chase Prison 7/20/1863, to Camp Douglas Prison 8/24/1863, exch. Point Lookout 2/24/1865, res. Letcher Co. 1860, b. Line Fork (Perry/Letcher Co), s. of William & Drucilla (Harris) Sparkman, res. Letcher/Knott Co. (Possum Trot) 1859-1887, res. Montgomery Co. 1887, res. Bath Co. 1903, res. Menifee Co. 1912, rec. KY Confed. Pension #1066 Menifee Co. 1912, m. (1) Phebe Amburgey (1828-1858) 1849, (2) Mahalia Amburgey (1839-1891) 1859, (3) Florence Nelson-Knox (1880-1904) 1895, bur. Chambers Cem., Means, Menifee Co., KY.

SPARKMAN, RICHARD: (1836 - 1/24/1865), Co. B, enl. Whitesburg, KY 9/9/1862, capt. Johnson Co. 5/31/1864, to Louisville Prison 6/10/1864, to Rock Island Prison 6/16/1864, joined Union (3rd U.S. Vol. Inf.) to be released to fight in Indian Wars 10/6/1864; but, bef. departing, became ill with chronic diarrhea, d. Rock Island hosp., res. Letcher Co. 1860, b. Coyles Branch of Line Fork, s. of William & Drucilla (Harris) Sparkman, m. Sarah Owens (1835-1916) Perry Co. 1856, bur. w/ Union marker Rock Island National Cem., Rock Island, Rock Island Co., IL.

SPARKMAN, SAMUEL SAMPSON: (10/7/1833 – 10/27/1924), Co. A, serv. prev. 5th KY Inf., Co. F, pres. spring/1863, res. Letcher Co. 1860, b. Line Fork (Perry/Letcher Co.), s. of William & Drucilla (Harris) Sparkman, moved MO (Jacksonville) 1866, m. Eveline Isabel Musick (b. 1835) 1852, bur. Mt. Salem Cem. Excello, Macon Co., MO.

SPARKMAN, THOMAS: (1832 – 1867), Co. B, enl. Whitesburg, KY 9/9/1862, res. Perry Co. 1860, b. Line Fork (Perry/Letcher Co.), s. of William & Drucilla (Harris) Sparkman, m. Nancy Owens (b. 1835) 1854, d. from war wounds (re: grandaughter's statement), bur. Green Bolen Cem., Softshell, Knott Co., KY.

SPARKMAN, WILLIAM: (11/16/1830 – 11/22/1918), Co. H, enl. & disc. Whitesburg, KY 10/18/1862, res. Letcher Co. 1860, b. Line Fork (Perry/Letcher Co.), s. of William & Drucilla (Harris) Sparkman, moved Rowan Co. 1863, m. Martha Stewart (1833-1900 to 1910) Rowan Co. 1865, bur. Dawson Cem., Haldeman, Rowan Co., KY.

SPENCER, JOHN G.: (7/27/1838 – 4/22/1918), Co. K, serv. prev. 2nd Bttn. KY Mtd Rifles, Co. A, serv. later 13th KY Cav. Per pension of Simpson Crabtree, s. of John D. & Phoebe (Sparks) Spencer, m. (1) Seany Wright (b. 1836), (2) Hannah Wiler (b. 1845), res. Owsley Co. 1860, petitioned KY Gov. Bramlette for postwar pardon of robbery indictment relating to war-time charge, bur. Hobbs Cem., Fincastle, Lee Co., KY.

SPURLOCK, ELIJAH: (12/29/1842 – 10/24/1913), 2nd Lt., Co. K, enl. VA 8/18/1863, elected 2nd Sgt. 12/31/1863, prom. 2nd Lt. bef. 3/1865, surr. Cumberland Gap 4/30/1865, res. Clay Co. 1860, b. Clay Co., s. of William & Sarah Spurlock, res. MO (Daviess Co.) 1870, res. MO (Breckinridge Co.) 1880, res. OK (Beckham Co.) 1910, m. Martha Lucinda Snyder (1840-1927) 1867, bur. (unmarked) Fairlawn Cem., Elk City, Beckham Co., OK.

STACY, JAMES "BLOSSOMEYE": (10/5/1830 – 2/28/1901), Co. C, enl. Whitesburg, KY 10/1/1862, pres. summer/1863, res. Perry Co. 1860, s. of James Sr. & Polly (Whitley) Stacy, m. (1) Nancy (1832-1857), (2) Hulda (1844-aft. 1900) 1858, bur. Richard Smith Cem., Ary Perry Co., KY.

STACY, JOHN: (10/1824 – 3/22/1912), Co. I, conscripted Whitesburg, KY 10/18/1862, res. Breathitt Co. 1860, s. of James Sr. & Polly (Whitley) Stacy, m. Cynthia Smith (1824-1892), bur. Richard Smith Cem., Ary, Perry Co., KY.

STACY, JOSEPH P.: (1843 – 1878), Co. C, enl. Whitesburg, KY 10/1/1862, pres. fall/1862, also serv. Union 47th KY, Co. K, res. Perry Co. 1860, s. of James Sr. & Polly (Whitley) Stacy, m. Elizabeth Bradley (1847-aft. 1900), bur. Richard Smith Cem., Ary, Perry Co., KY.

STACY, SHADRACK ELLSBERRY: (1/10/1831 – 1/1/1917), Co. C, enl. Whitesburg, KY 10/1/1862, res. Perry Co. 1860, s. of James Sr. & Polly (Whitley) Stacy, m. Ceatta Bradley (1843-1928) 1861, bur. Stacy & Smith Cem., nr. Decoy, Knott Co., KY.

STAMPER, HIRAM H.: (8/2/1834 – 2/19/1873), Capt., Co. A, serv. prev. 5th KY Inf. Co. F, 6' 1", dark hair, blue eyes, elected Capt. of 13th Co. A, 11/2/1862, capt. nr. Whitesburg by Lt. Clabe Jones Harlan Co. Btn. 1/24/1863, exch. 2/3/1863 for Union Capt. Webb., capt. Gladeville, VA 7/7/1863, to Kemper Barracks 7/18/1863, to Camp Chase 7/20/1863, to Johnson's Island Prison 10/10/1863, to Point Lookout Prison 3/21/1865, to Ft. Delaware Prison 4/28/1865, rel. on oath 6/2/1865, res. Letcher Co. 1860, s. of John W. & Lucinda (Hogg) Stamper, widow rec. KY Confed. Widow's Pension #1057 Knott Co. 1912, m. Anna Francis (1837-1915) 1857, bur. Carr's Fork Cem., Littcarr, Knott Co., KY.

STAMPER, HIRAM W.: (4/7/1841 – 7/5/1884), 5th Sgt., Co. H, enl. Whitesburg, KY 10/18/1862, serv. through 12/18/1862, res. Letcher Co. 1860, s. of Isaac D. & Mary (Adams) Stamper, res. Letcher Co. 1890, m. Susannah Hogg (1838-1916), bur. Hogg Cem., Roxanna, Letcher Co., KY.

STAMPER, JOHN W.: (7/20/1838 – 7/4/1907), 1st Sgt., Co. H, enl. Whitesburg, KY 9/23/1862, prom. To 1st Sgt. 3/18/1863, rec. clothing 11/19/1864, res. Letcher Co. (Mallet Fork of Carr) 1860, s. of John W. & Lucinda (Hogg) Stamper, moved Lewis Co. (Petersville) 1885, m. Margarine (1843-aft. 1900), bur. McEldawney Cem., Petersville, Lewis Co., KY.

STAMPER, WILLIAM RILEY: (5/5/1840 – 4/3/1891), Co. H, enl. Whitesburg, KY 10/18/1862, pres. fall/1862, res. Letcher Co. 1860, s. of John W. & Lucinda (Hogg) Stamper, moved Lewis Co. (Petersville) 1885, m. Louisa Branson (1848-1903), bur. William Stamper Cem., Petersville, Lewis Co., KY.

STEPHENS, GEORGE: (b. 1839), Co. B, enl. Perry Co. (Brashearville), KY 9/9/1862, pres. fall/1862, serv. later Union 47th KY Inf., Co. H, res. Perry Co. 1860, s. of George & Susan (Blevins) Stephens, reportedly did not survive the war, father rec. a Union pension.

STEPHENS, (MORGAN) GREENVILLE: (10/11/1841 – 10/5/1917), Co. F, enl. Floyd Co., KY 10/10/1862, res. Floyd Co. 1860, s. of Sam & Florence (Graham) Stephens, res. Floyd Co. 1860, m. Malinda (1844-1926), bur. Davidson Memorial Gardens, Ivel, Floyd Co., KY.

STEPHENS, RICHARD: (12/25/1824 – 1/10/1881), Co. K, enl. Lee Co., VA 8/18/1863, pres. Lee Co. 12/31/1863, res. Lee Co., VA 1860, b. NC, moved to Pulaski Co., KY post-war (re: family statement), bur. Poplar Grove Cem., Willailla, Rockcastle Co., KY.

STEPHENS, W. H.: 3rd Lt., Co. F, paroled 4/28/1865 Cumberland Gap by Dillard's 34th KY Inf., identified in "Artificial 10th KY Cav."- misfiled records.

STEPHENS, WILLIAM: (b. 1843), Co. B, enl. Fall/1862, pres. fall/1862, serv. Union 14th KY Cav., Co. M (4/20/1863 to 3/24/1864), res. Perry Co. 1860, b. 1843, s. of George & Susan (Blevins) Stephens, res. Owsley Co. 1870, res. Wolfe Co. 1880 & 1900 (Campton), m. Lucy (1847-aft. 1900).

STEPHENS, WILLIAM D.: (1834 – 1899), Co. F, enl. Floyd Co. 10/10/1862, res. Floyd Co. 1860, s. of Sam & Florence (Graham) Stephens, m. Rebecca Bradley (1832-1884) 1857, bur. Stephens Cem., Martin, Floyd Co., KY.

STEWART, JASPER: (1829 – 1914), Co. H, enl. Whitesburg, KY 10/18/1862, pres. fall/1862, res. Letcher Co. 1860, res. Perry Co. 1870, m. Nancy Mullins (1833-1908), bur. Stewart-Stamper Cem., Terry Fork of Ball Creek, Knott Co., KY.

STIDHAM, CALVIN W.: (1/13/1830 – 11/6/1884), 1st Cpl., Co. D, pres. fall/1862, res. Letcher Co. (Colly) 1860, b. NC, res. Letcher Co. 1870, m. Susan (1822-1885), bur. Standifer Cem., Flat Gap, Wise Co., VA.

STINSON, JAMES H.: (7/17/1846 – 6/18/1928), Co. F, enl. Floyd Co. 8/24/1863, res. Floyd Co. 1860, s. of Zachariah & Milly A. (Hamilton) Stinson, m. (1) Mary Coffee, (2) Susannah Seagraves 1881, (3) Almeda Seagraves Johnson (1851-1920 to 1928), bur. W. A. Hay Cem., Mazie, Lawrence Co., KY.

STIVERS, WALTER SCOTT: (2/14/1843 – 7/1/1917), 2nd Lt., Co. K, enl. Lee Co., VA 8/18/1863, elected 2nd Sgt. Lee Co. 12/31/1863, prom. 2nd Lt. bef. 3/1865, surr. Cumberland Gap 4/30/1865, res. Lee Co. VA, b. Madison Co., KY, s. of Absalom Stivers, rec. Confed. Pension #245 Madison Co. (Bybee) 1912, moved IN (Vincennes) ca. 1914, ret. Madison Co. by 1917, widow rec. KY Confed. Pension #3784 Madison Co. 1917, m. Martha Pennington (1842-1925) 1864, bur. Flatwoods Cem., Waco, Madison Co., KY.

STRONG, EDWARD CALLAHAN "RED NED": (11/5/1823 – 2/20/1911), Asst. A.Q.M., serv. prev. 5th KY Inf., Co. B, res. Breathitt Co. 1860, b. Strongville (Clay Co., now Breathitt), s. of William Jr. & Jemima (Deaton) Strong, post-war Breathitt Co. Judge, m. Nancy Haddix (1827-1905) 1846, d. Jackson, KY, bur. Strong Cem., Lost Creek, Breathitt Co., KY.

STRONG, HIRAM F.: (5/28/1819 – 1888), Maj., Surgeon, enl. 11/2/1862, requested trans. 10th KY Cav. 6/29/1864, res. Johnson Co. 1850 & 1860, b. Scott Co., VA, pre-war Postmaster Paintsville, KY, res. Johnson Co. 1870 & 1880, will filed Paintsville, KY 2/1888, m. (1) Phoebe Jane Godsey (1818-ca. 1872) 1841, (2) Nancy M. Perry Preston (1814-1874) 1873, bur. Preston Cem., Paintsville, Johnson Co., KY.

STRONG, JOHN D.: (1/16/1830 – 2/12/1905), Kash's Co., res. Breathitt Co. 1860, s. of William & Jemima Deaton Strong, indicted post-war for 1865 murder as member this Co., res. Breathitt Co. 1900, m. Priscilla Kash (1835-aft. 1910), bur. Lazarus Back Cem., Quicksand, Breathitt Co., KY.

STRONG, JULIUS C.: (1844 – 9/10/1876), Co. H, enl. Perry Co. (Brashearville), KY 4/15/1863, res. Johnson Co. 1850 & 1860, b. Scott Co., VA, s. of Hiram F. & Phoebe Jane (Godsey) Strong, res. (grocer) Sweetwater Co., WY 1870, bur. Lakeview Cem., Cheyenne, Laramie Co., WY.

STURDIVANT, PLEASANT G.: (6/10/1844 – 12/24/1919), Co. C, serv. prev. 5th KY Inf., Co. F, Confed. pension verifies 13th KY Cav. service, res. Letcher Co. (Sandlick) 1860, b. Harlan Co., s. of Thomas & Sarah (Noe) Sturdivant (d.c. lists mother as Lussie Lewis), res. Letcher Co. 1870, moved later Knott Co. (Vest), rec. KY Confed. Pension #1045 Knott Co. 1912, widow rec. Confed. Pension #4433 1926, m. (1) Manerva Hogg (1845-aft. 1900)1864, (2) Mary Jane Patton (1858-1936) Knott Co. 1900, bur. Amburgey Cem., Hindman, Knott Co., KY.

STURDIVANT, THOMAS KENT: (1814 – 7/1869), Co. A, enl. Whitesburg, KY 9/8/1862, serv. prev. 5th KY Inf., capt nr. Whitesburg by Lt. Clabe Jones & Union 14th KY Cav. spring/1863, soon released, pres. fall/1863, res. Letcher Co. 1860, s. of Matthew P. & Agnes (Kent) Sturdivant, m. Sarah Noe (1827-aft. 1887), d. from consumption.

STURGILL, ISAAC: (9/16/1833 – 11/19/1911), Co. D, enl. Whitesburg, KY 10/4/1862, pres. fall/1862, res. Letcher Co. 1860, s. of Francis & Ruth (Gilly) Sturgill, m. (1) Henrietta "Riter" Brown, (2) Susan, d. from dropsy, bur. Eli Boggs Cem., Oven Fork, Letcher Co., KY.

STURGILL, JOHN A.: (4/15/1835 – 10/29/1918), 2nd Cpl., Co. D, res. Letcher Co. 1860, s. of Rachel Sturgill, res. Letcher Co. 1870, m. Margaret Cox (1837-1906), bur. Sturgill Cem., Eolia, Letcher Co., KY.

STURGILL, JOHN G.: (12/29/1829 – 5/28/1915), 3rd Sgt., Co. D, enl. Whitesburg, KY 10/4/1862, pres. fall/1862, res. Letcher Co. (Oven Fork) 1860, s. of Francis & Ruth (Gilly) Sturgill, res. Letcher Co. 1870, res. Wise Co., VA 1880, m. Rachel Adams (1836-1914), d. from cancer, bur. Hampton-Adams Cem., Oven Fork, Letcher Co., KY.

SUMNER, JAMES JR.: (1842 – 1880), Co. B, enl. Perry Co. (Brashearville) 9/4/1862, capt. Gladeville, VA 7/7/1863, to Kemper Barracks 7/18/1863, to Camp Chase Prison 7/20/1863, to Camp Douglas Prison 8/24/1863, exch., Point Lookout 2/24/1865, res. Perry Co. 1860, s. of James & Nancy (Adams) Sumner, m. Sarah Back (1841-aft. 1880), d. from typhoid fever, bur. Sumner Cem., Vicco, Perry Co., KY.

SUMNER, JOHN: (1816 – 8/26/1875), Co. B, enl. Whitesburg, KY, pres. fall/1862, res. Letcher Co. 1860, s. of John & Juda (Stewart) Sumner, m. Nancy Hampton (1823-aft. 1880), murdered by James H. Frazier & Solomon Banks during a special election, bur. Rich Whitaker Cem., Letcher, Letcher Co., KY.

SUMNER, JOHN WESLEY: (1840 – 1870), Co. H, enl. Whitesburg, KY 10/18/1862, pres. 4/15/1863, res. Perry Co. 1860, s. of James & Nancy (Adams) Sumner, res. Perry Co. 1869 (re: tax list), m. Lucinda Craft (1848-1870) 1866, bur. Sumner Cem., Vicco, Perry Co., KY.

SUMNER, STEPHEN: (1837 – 1912), Co. H, enl. Perry Co. (Brashearville) 3/16/1863, pres. 4/5/1863, res. Perry Co. 1860, s. of James & Nancy (Adams) Sumner, res. Perry Co. 1880, 1900 & 1910, m. (1) America Craft (b. 1840), (2) Margaret (1840-bef. 1910), bur. Sumner Cem., Vicco, Perry Co., KY.

SUMNER, WESLEY: (1843 – 11/4/1863), Co. B, enl. Whitesburg, KY 9/9/1862, capt. either at Gladeville, VA 7/7/1863 or Buffington Island 7/19/1863 (re: Union records), to Camp Douglas Prison 8/24/1863, res. Letcher Co. 1860, s. of John & Nancy (Hampton) Sumner, d. from typhoid fever Camp Douglas, bur. Oak Wood Cem., Chicago, Cook Co., IL.

TACKETT, ABNER: (2/8/1845 – 5/31/1920), Co. B, enl. Floyd Co. (Middle Creek) 9/11/1862, serv. prev. 5th KY Inf., Cos. B & F, disc. 9/29/1862, res. Pike Co. 1860, s. of William "Buck" & Sarah (Caudill) Tackett, moved Rowan Co. bef. 1870, m. Elizabeth Caudill (1843-1925), bur. Caudill Cem. Cranston, Rowan Co., KY.

TACKETT, GEORGE W.: (10/27/1837 – 12/13/1906), Co. B, enl. Whitesburg, KY 8/21/1862, 5' 6", light hair, grey eyes, capt. Pike Co. 10/6/1863, to Louisville Prison 10/22/1863, rel. on oath 10/31/1863, res. Pike Co. 1860, s. of William "Buck" & Sarah Caudill Tackett, m. Rachel Caudill (1839-1910), bur. Amil Little Cem., Longfork, Pike Co., KY.

TACKETT, MATTHEW: (3/14/1840 – 4/1/1929), Co. E, enl. Whitesburg, KY 10/5/1862, incorrectly listed as Matthew Tuckett on roster, sent home on furlough at close of war 4/1865, took oath, res. Pike Co. 1860, s. of William "Buck" & Sarah (Caudill) Tackett, rec. KY Confed. Pension #2294 Floyd Co. 1912, widow rec. Confed. Widow's Pension #4598 Floyd Co. 1930, m. Linda Johnson (1844-1931) Pike Co. 1860, bur. Matthew Tackett Cem., Melvin, Floyd Co., KY.

TANDY, GEORGE LINTON: (1839 – 5/22/1929), Co. H, enl. Gladeville, VA 5/27/1863, serv. prev. 1st KY Cav. (Helm's), res. Harrison Co. 1860, s. of William & Catherine Tandy, bur Pewee Valley Cem., C.S.A. plot, Pewee Valley, Oldham Co., KY.

TEETERS, JOHN WESLEY: (d. 1/8/1864), Co. F, enl. Floyd Co., KY 10/10/1862, capt. Floyd Co. 10/15/1863, to Camp Morton, in Camp Morton Prison hosp. w/ pneumonia 11/16/1863, res. Kenton Co.

TERRY, (ISAAC) COUCH: (7/10/1848 – 12/16/1933), Co. K, listed on s.r. as Couch Terry, surr. Cumberland Gap 4/30/1865, res. Breathitt Co. 1860, s. of Isaac & Barbara (Gabbard) Terry, m. Emily Day, bur. Terry Cem., Jetts Creek, Breathitt Co., KY.

TERRY, DANIEL: See Daniel Tyree

TERRY, MILES (W.): (1832 - 1898), Co. K, enl. Lee Co., VA 8/18/1863, 5' 6", blue eyes, fair complexion, light hair, pres. Lee Co. 12/31/1863, capt. Breathitt Co. 5/15/1864, to Johnson's Island Prison, to Point Lookout Prison, rel. on oath 1/10/1865, res. Morgan Co. 1860, s. of Isaac & Rebecca (Osborne) Terry, m. Nancy Carter (1832-1877) Morgan Co. 1864, res. Elliott Co. 1870 & 1880, bur. (unm.) Thornsberry Cem., Rt. Fk. Sheepskin, Fannin, Elliott Co., KY.

TERRY, THOMAS: (b. 1834), Co. F, enl. Floyd Co. 3/10/1863, res. Floyd Co. 1860, s. of Leonard & Mary Terry, res. Floyd Co. 1870, m. Elizabeth Jones.

TERRY, THOMAS: (5/1844 – 9/21/1919), Co. K, AKA Thomas Casebolt, enl. Lee Co., VA 8/18/1863, pres. Lee Co. 12/31/1863, res. Perry Co. 1860, s. of Silas & Jenny (Music) Terry, res. Perry Co. in HH of Pvt. James Patrick 1870, res. Perry Co. 1880, res. Knott Co. 1910, m. Sylvania Patrick (1848-1932), bur. Patrick Cem., Bearville, Knott Co., KY.

TERRY, WILLIAM: (1/1/1837 – 12/28/1909), Co. C, AKA William Casebolt, enl. Whitesburg, KY 10/1/1862, pres. fall/1862, res. Perry Co. 1860, s. of B. Roe Spurlock & Elizabeth Casebolt, raised by Silas & Jenny (Music) Terry, res. Knott Co. (Quicksand) 1900, m. (1) Arminda Combs (b. 1837) 1857, (2) Polly Maggard (b. 1855) ca. 1875, bur. Terry Cem., Softshell, Knott Co., KY.

THACKER, REUBEN: (b. 1837), Co. A, serv. prev. 5th KY Inf., Co. F w/ no s.r., pres. summer/1863, res. Floyd Co. 1860, s. of Reuben & Nancy (Ward) Thacker, res. Floyd Co. 1870, res. Greenup Co. (Yellow Creek) 1880, m. Julia A. (b. 1851).

THACKER, ROBERT: See Robert Dials

THERMAN, CHARLES: Co. K, surr. Cumberland Gap 4/30/1865.

THOMAS, JAMES VERNON: (3/4/1831 – 1/22/917), Co. I, conscripted Whitesburg, KY 10/18/1862, pres. fall/1862, s. of James & Hannah (Griever) Thomas, b. Lee Co., VA, m. Susannah Rouse (1832-1914) 1853, res. Perry Co. 1860, moved to Brown Co., KS by 1870, bur. Netawaka Cem., Netawaka, Jackson Co., KS.

THOMAS, JOSEPH: (3/19/1840 – 1/5/1865), Co. K, serv. prev. 64th VA Inf., 2nd Co. F, pres. Lee Co. VA 12/31/1863, res. Harlan Co., KY 1860, m. Cynthia Parsons (b. 1838) 1859, d. from smallpox East Baton Rouge Parish, LA.

THOMPSON, SAMUEL W.: (1839 – 3/27/1879), 1st Lt., Co. D; Pvt., Cos. F & K; also serv. as Brevet 2nd Lt. 5th KY Inf., Co. B; also serv. as commanding Capt. Thompson's Partisan Rangers; recruited a company attached Patton's Partisan Rangers spring/1863, joined 13th summer/1863, trans to Co. K from Co. F Lee Co., VA, pres. Lee Co. 12/31/1863, paroled Cumberland Gap 5/3/1865, res. Morgan Co. 1850 & 1860, reportedly b. Floyd Co., s. of Matthew & M. J. Thompson, m. Martha Wade Lee Co., VA 1865, widow moved OK (Wanette) 1895 & rec. OK Confed. Widow's Pension 1915, bur. Kentucky Town Cem., nr. Whitewright, Grayson Co., TX.

THORNSBERRY, ENOCH: (1826 – 1881), Co. E, enl. 10/5/1862, pres. 2/1863, res. Floyd Co. 1860, s. of Isaac & Eleanor (McCubbin) Thornsberry, res. Carter Co. 1870, res. Elliott Co. 1880, m. Mahala Adams (1830-1887), bur. Thornsberry Cem., Stark, Elliott Co., KY.

THORNSBERRY, JOHN: (1844 – 1886), Co. B, enl. Whitesburg, KY 9/14/1862, AWOL Fall 1862, but returned to serv., pres. On rolls Jan.-Aug. 1863, m. Jane Webb, s. of George & Rebecca (Pridemore) Thornsberry, res. Floyd Co. 1860, bur. (unm.) Thornsberry Cem., Thornsberry Br., Raven, Knott Co., KY.

THORNSBERRY, MARTIN V.: (1832 – 1900), Co. E, enl. Whitesburg, KY 10/5/1862, pres. 2/1863, res. Floyd Co. 1860, s. of Isaac & Eleanor (McCubbin) Thornsberry, res. Floyd Co. 1870 & 1880, res. Knott Co. 1889 (re: tax list), m. Rutha Hall (d. 1918), bur. Moore Cem., Topmost, Knott Co., KY.

TRIPLETT, WILLIAM M. "BILL": (8/12/1841 – 4/17/1929), 1st Cpl, Co. F, enl. Floyd Co. 10/14/1862, serv. prev. 5th KY Inf., Co. E, capt. Louisa, KY 11/17/1863, to Louisville Prison 12/17/1863, to Rock Island Prison 12/24/1863, res. Floyd Co. (Lackey) 1860, s. of Lee & Rachel (Thornsberry) Triplett, res. Knott Co. 1900, applied for KY Confed. Pension Knott Co. 1912, m. Biddy Oney (b. 1840), bur. Triplett Cem., Lackey, Knott Co., KY.

TUCKER, OLIVER PERRY: (1/1/1826 – 10/2/1897), Co. D, enl. Whitesburg, KY 10/4/1862, pres. fall/1862, res. Letcher Co. 1860, m. Dicy (1837-1898), bur. Tucker Cem. Payne Gap, Letcher Co., KY.

TUCKER, REUBEN: Confused in Adj. General Report with Reuben Thacker

TUGGLE, JAMES TARRANT: (9/26/1836 – 7/23/1885), Co. K, enl. Lee Co., VA 8/18/1863, serv. prev. 6th KY, while in 6th KY he surr. Buffington Island, OH, then escaped by swimming Ohio R. & ret. to serv., pres. Lee Co. 12/31/1863, res. Knox Co. 1860, b. Barbourville, KY, s. of Rich & Mary Tuggle, murdered Knox Co. (Stone Cove School), widow rec. KY Confed. Widow's Pension #2850 Knox Co. (Emanuel) 1913, m. Georgia Susie Davis (1855-1939) Davisboro, GA 1873, bur. Tanyard Cem., Barbourville, Knox Co., KY.

TURNER, MORGAN: (7/12/1831 – 1/2/1909), Co. F, enl. Floyd Co. 10/10/1862, pres. fall 1862, res. Floyd Co. 1860, m. Eleander (Spencer) Turner (1840-1913), bur. Morgan Turner Cem., nr. McDowell, Floyd Co., KY.

TYE, JOSHUA B.: (b. 1839), Co. K, capt. Dandridge, TN /17/1864, to Knoxville, to Nashville, to Louisville, to Rock Island 2/15/1864, described: dark complexion, light hair, blue eyes, 6' 0", age 25, identified in "Artificial Unit 10th KY Cav." Misfiled records, s. of Nelson R. & Obedience Tye, b. Knox Co., KY, res. Whitley Co., KY 1860, m. Lee Ellen (1848-1925), moved to Corvell, TX by 1870, Tarrant Co., TX 1880, Choctaw Nation OK 1900, reportedly d. in MO.

TYRA, DANIEL: (1841 – 1/4/1906), Co. C, listed incorrectly on roster as Daniel Terry, enl. Whitesburg, KY 10/1/1862, pres. summer/1863, res. Breathitt Co. 1860, s. of John & Sally Tyra, res. Brethitt Co., (Frozen Creek) 1890 & 1900, m. Cynthia Peace (1844-1926) 1869, bur. (unm.) Tyra Cem., Blanton Ridge, Frozen, Breathitt Co., KY.

TYREE, JOHN W.: (1842 – 11/7/1862), Co. H, enl. Perry Co. (Brashearville) 11/18/1862, res. Breathitt Co. 1860, s. of John & Sally Tyree, m. Sarah Elizabeth Woods, d. from fever Whitesburg, bur. Sandlick Cem., Whitesburg, Letcher Co., KY.

TYREE, JOSEPH: (1/15/1846 – 3/16/1922), Co. H, enl. Perry Co. (Brashearville) 10/29/1862, capt Gladeville, VA 7/7/1863, to Kemper Barracks 7/18/1863, to Camp Chase Prison 7/20/1863, to Camp Douglas Prison 8/24/1863, enl. U.S. Navy 12/23/1863, initially assigned *U.S.S. Savannah*, res. Letcher Co. 1860, s. of David & Nancy (James) Tyree, m. Rebecca Slone, res. Greenup Co. 1870, Magoffin Co. 1880, Floyd Co. 1900, Pike Co. 1910, bur. Alex Ratliff Cem., Wolfpit, Pike Co., KY.

TYREE, PATTERSON: (1833 – 1/10/1865), Co. H, listed as Patterson Tyree on roster, enl. Perry Co. (Brashearville) 10/18/1862, capt Gladeville, VA 7/7/1863, to Kemper Barracks 7/18/1863, to Camp Chase Prison 7/20/1863, to Camp Douglas 8/22/1863, res. Scott Co., VA 1850, res. Letcher Co. 1860, s. of David & Nancy (James) Tyree, d. Camp Douglas Prison, bur. Oak Wood Cem., Chicago, Cook Co., IL.

UNTHANK, CALVIN: (11/15/1845 – 9/16/1930), Co. K, enl. aft. 8/1/1863, serv. prev. VA State Line, 64th VA Inf., Co. H, & 25th VA Cav., Co. G, rec. clothing 9/7/1864, paroled Cumberland Gap 4/1865, res. Harlan Co. 1860, s. of Ewell Unthank, pardoned by Gov. Thomas E. Bramlett for war-related robbery 1/1867, rec. KY Confed. Pension #255 Harlan Co. 1912, m. Clarkie Kirk (1847-1927), bur. Wix Howard Cem., Loyal, Harlan Co., KY.

VIRES, ELISHA: (b. 1847), Kash's Co., res. Breathitt Co. 1850 & 1860, s. of Randall & Celia (Roberts) Vires, indicted post-war for murder as member this Co. 1865, res. Jackson Co. (Horselick) 1880, m. Mary (b. 1853).

WALKER, JAMES CALHOUN: (7/26/1837 – 12/30/1879), Capt., Co. F, enl. Floyd Co. 10/10/1862, prom. 2 Lt. 11/2/1862, capt. Battle Cynthiana 6/12/1864, to Louisville Prison 7/27/1864, to Johnson's Island Prison 7/29/1864, elected Capt while POW Johnson's Island, to Cincinnati for trial 3/9/1865, escaped McLean Barracks 6/30/1865, res. Floyd Co. 1860, b. Perry Co. (Hazard), s. of John W. & Polly Devers, res. Lamar Co., TX 1870, m. Catherine Martin (1841-1905) Floyd Co. 1861, d. TX (Pecan Gap), bur. Waller Cem., Ben Franklin, Delta Co., TX.

WALKER, JEREMIAH "PETE", "JERRY" A: (5/4/1844 – 1/15/1923), Co. I, enl. Whitesburg, KY 10/18/1862, serv. prev. 5th KY Inf., Co. I, pres. spring/1863, res. Perry Co. (Hazard) 1860, s. of John Jr. & Polly (Combs) Walker, Confed. Pension witness 1912, m. (1) Mahalia Evans (d. bef. 1880), (2) Rebecca Davidson (1847-1912) by 1870, (3) Alley Combs (1847–aft. 1900) 1876, bur. Cornett Cem., Wabaco/Hazard, Perry Co., KY.

WALLACE, RICHARD: (1845 – 1863), Co. F, listed as Richard Wallis on s.r., enl. Floyd Co. 10/10/1862, serv. prev. 5th KY Inf., Co. E, KIA Middle Creek Floyd Co. summer/1863, res. Pike Co. 1850, s. of Solomon Wallace.

WALLEN, ELISHA B.: (1847 – 1/1881), 2nd Sgt., Co. K, surr. Cumberland Gap 4/30/1865, res. Letcher Co. 1850, res. Floyd Co. 1860, s. of Preston H. Wallen & Eleanor (Neal) Wallen, m. Pollyu Griffith (b. 1849), Floyd Co. 1870, d. Plum Br. of Rock Fork (now Knott Co.), bur. unm. Chaffins Cem., Rock Fork, Knott Co., KY.

WALLEN, GREENBURY: (5/14/1847 – 10/8/1893), Co. K, enl. Lee Co., VA 8/18/1863, pres. Lee Co. 12/31/1863, rec. clothing 9/7/1864 & 9/24/1864, surr. Cumberland Gap 5/8/1865, res. Hancock Co., TN 1860, b. Hancock Co., s. of Greenbury Wallen Sr. & Nancy, res. Lee Co., VA 1870 & 1880, m. Rebecca Osborne (1848-aft. 1900), d. Lee Co. (Blackwater) VA, bur. John Osborne Cem., east of Blackwater, Lee Co., VA.

WALLEN, HANSFORD "HAM": (1839 – 1882), Cos. C & F, enl. 10/1/1862 Whitesburg, trans. to Co. F, 8/24/1863 Floyd Co., incorrectly reported KIA 3/6/1863, pres. spring/1863, serv. prev. 5th KY Inf. Co. E, res. Floyd Co. 1860, s. of Preston H. & Eleanor (Neal) Wallen, res. Floyd Co. 1870 & 1880, m. (1) Retter (1836-1870 to 1880), (2) Margaret (1841-aft. 1880), bur. Fitzpatrick & Langley Cem., Prestonsburg, Floyd Co., KY.

WALLEN, SHELBY: (1832 – 1885), Co. C, identified in "10th KY Cav. Artificial Unit" – misfiled records, capt. Gladeville, VA 7/7/1863, to Kemper Barracks 7/18/1863, to Camp Chase Prison 7/20/1863, to Camp Douglas Prison 8/24/1863, exch. Pt. Lookout 2/24/1865, res. Floyd Co. 1860, b. TN, s. of John & Mary (Neil) Wallen, res. Floyd Co. 1880, m. Susannah Hale (b. 1831) 1851, bur. Wallen Cem., Watergap, Floyd Co., KY.

WALTERS, ANDREW J. "ANDY", "COLONEL": (4/11/1824 – 8/11/1872), Kash's Co., res. Morgan Co. 1860, s. of Thomas & Matilda (Wilson) Walters, indicted post-war for murder as member this Co. 1865, m. Minerva McQuinn (1825-1887) Morgan Co. 1844, bur. Walters Cem., Belknap, Wolfe Co., KY.

WALTERS, JOHN CALVIN: (1/2/1807 – 8/15/1880), Co. K, listed as Calvin Walters on s.r., enl. Lee Co., VA 8/18/1863, serv. prev. 5th KY Inf., Co. E, pres. Lee Co. 12/31/1863, surr. Mt. Sterling, KY 4/30/1865, res. Johnson Co. 1860, b. VA, m. Elizabeth (1841-1870 to 1880), bur. Goose Branch Cem., Offitt, Johnson Co., KY.

WALTERS, ROLIN F.: (1844 - 5/22/1907), 2nd Lt., Co. F, serv. prev. 5th KY Inf., Co. F, res. Kenton Co. (Covington) 1850 & 1860, s. of Dr. W.W. Walters & Rosanna, took oath 6/15/1865, res. Webb Co. (Laredo), TX 1900, bur. Texas State Cem., Confed. Sec. 2, Row L, Grave #41, Austin, Travis Co., TX.

WARRICK, JOHN FOUNT: (5/1832 – 1916), Co. D, enl. Whitesburg, KY 10/4/1862, serv. as wagoneer 1/15/1865, res. Pike Co. 1860, b. Grayson Co., VA, s. of Robert & Mary "Polly" (Cannoy) Warrick, moved Wise Co., VA 1851, moved Letcher Co., KY 1858, res. Floyd Co. 1870 & 1880, w/ Lucinda (Arkansas) 1900, m. (1) Susannah Elizabeth Porter, Russell Co., VA 1851, (2) Lucinda "Lucy" Anderson (1832-aft. 1900) Letcher Co. 1862, (3) Emma Rita Nelson aft. 1900, bur. Wallen Cem., Water Gap, Floyd Co., KY.

WATTS, AMBROSE "SR": (1/4/1825 – 6/17/1912), Co. G, enl. Whitesburg, KY 9/23/1862, wounded once, capt. by Union 14th KY Cav. 4/1863, taken to Booneville & rel., serv. as courier at Strawberry Plains, TN, serv. as contact for Col. Caudill to Col. Giltner & Gen. Longstreet until close of war, paroled at Booneville (per pension), KY Confed. Pension #3531 granted Breathitt Co. 1914 on his behalf was likely based largely on falsified info., res. Breathitt Co. 1860, s. of Mason Combs & Matilda Watts, res. Breathitt Co. 1910, m. (1) Matilda Deaton (1830-1921), (2) Charlotte Whitaker (1837-1901), bur. Watts Cem., River Caney, Breathitt Co., KY.

WATTS, AMBROSE "JR": (2/7/1839 – 2/18/1920), Co. I, enl. Whitesburg, KY 10/18/1862, pres. fall/1863, res. Breathitt Co. 1860, s. of Washington & Polly (Mullins) Watts, rec. KY Confed. Pension #1555 Breathitt Co. 1912, m. (1) Polly Ann Noble (1847-1893) 1867, (2) Ortha Noble (1873-1954) 1896, bur. Tharp Cem., Haddix, Breathitt Co., KY.

WATTS, GEORGE WASHINGTON: (1838 – 12/1863), Cos. A & B, enl. Whitesburg, KY 9/2/1862, serv. prev. 5th KY Inf., trans. from Co. B to Co. A 1/1/1863, capt. Gladeville, VA 7/7/1863, to Kemper Barracks 7/18/1863, to Camp Chase Prison 7/20/1863, res. Letcher Co. 1860, s. of Enoch & Sarah (Fields) Watts, m. Lucinda Blair 1860, d. Camp Chase Prison, bur. Camp Chase Prison Cem., Grave #86, Columbus, Franklin Co., OH.

WATTS, JOHN C.: (1838 – 12/29/1863), Cos. A & B, enl. Whitesburg, KY 9/2/1862, serv. prev. 5th KY Inf., Co. F, trans. from Co. B to Co. A 1/1/1863, pres. spring/1863, capt Gladeville, VA 7/7/1863, to Kemper Barracks, to Camp Chase Prison, res. Letcher Co. 1860, s. of Thomas & Nancy (Hagins) Watts, m. Elizabeth Francis who m. (2) PVT Kelly Franklin 1867, d. Camp Chase Prison (re: diary entry by Colonel. Ben E. Caudill), bur. Camp Chase Prison Cem., Columbus, Franklin Co., OH.

WEBB, ANDREW LEWIS: (4/8/1840 – 1/8/1929), 3rd Sgt., Co. D, enl. Whitesburg, KY 10/4/1862, prom. Whitesburg 4/1/1864, paroled Cumberland Gap by Dillard 5/2/1865, res. Letcher Co. 1860, s. of Enoch A. & Susannah (Polly) Webb, res. Letcher Co. 1870, rec. KY Confed. Pension #1975 Letcher Co. 1912, m. Nancy Adams (1845-1929) 1866, bur. Thornton Cem., Thornton, Letcher Co., KY.

WEBB, ARCHELOUS C. "ARCHIE": (11/1/1844 – 6/22/1894), Co. D, enl. Whitesburg, KY 10/4/1862, pres. summer/1863, res. Letcher Co. 1860, s. of Jason L. & Elizabeth (Craft) Webb, m. Nancy Craft (1848-1915) 1865, bur. Webb Cem., Mayking, Letcher Co., KY.

WEBB, ENOCH A. (9/16/1810 – 11/3/1881), Capt., Co. D, enl. Whitesburg, KY 10/4/1862, prom. Capt. 11/2/1862, resigned 7/20/1863, James Rogers successor, paroled Cumberland Gap 5/3/1865, res. Letcher Co. (blacksmith) 1860, s. of Benjamin & Jennie (Adams) Webb, m. (1) Susannah Polly (1812-1867) 1829, (2) Martha Lucas (1845-aft. 1900) 1870, bur. Webb Cem., Mayking, Letcher Co., KY.

WEBB, HENRY M. "CHUNK": (6/151836 – 4/6/1927), Co. D, enl. 1862, paroled Cumberland Gap, KY 5/2/1865, res. Letcher Co., KY 1860, s. of Enoch A. & Susannah (Polly) Webb, rec. KY Confed. Pension #1104 Letcher Co. 1912, m. Frances Adams (1839-1923) 1866, bur. Webb Cem., Mayking, Letcher Co., KY.

WEBB, RILEY: (7/4/1843 – 11/18/1915), 1st Cpl., Co. D, enl. Whitesburg, KY 10/4/1862, prom. Cpl. Whitesburg 4/1/1864, paroled Cumberland Gap, KY 5/2/1865, res. Letcher Co. 1860, s. of Enoch A. & Susannah (Polly) Webb, moved Johnson Co. 1911, rec. KY Confed. Pension #1558 Johnson Co. 1912, widow rec. KY Confed. Pension #3518 Johnson Co. 1916, m. Hester Ann Hackworth (1845-1923) Letcher Co. 1868, (d.c. #27488), bur. Old Grant Trimble Cem., Ivyton, Magoffin Co., KY.

WEDDINGTON, HENRY HARRISON "HARRY": (1839 – 1900), 2nd Lt., Co. K, identified in "10th KY Cav. Artificial Unit" – misfiled records, enl. 10/8/1862, 5' 11", dark hair, grey eyes, serv. prev. 5th KY Inf., Co. G, capt. Gladeville, VA 7/7/1863, to Johnson's Island Prison 10/10/1863, rel. on oath 6/28/1865, res. Pike Co. 1860 (student of medicine), s. of William & Mary (Meade) Weddington, res. Pike Co. (Pikeville) 1870 & 1880, widower res. Mingo Co. (Stafford), WV 1900, m. Emeline "Emily" Mead (1850-1898) 1868, bur. (unm.) Pikeville Cem., Pikeville, Pike Co., KY.

WELLS, JOHN PRESTON: (1815 – 1880), Cos. D, F & K, enl. Lee Co. VA 8/18/1863, serv. prev. 5th KY Inf., Co. E & 2nd Btn. Mtd Rifles, Co. A, trans. to Co. K from Co. K Floyd Co. 9/1/1863, pres. Lee Co. 12/31/1863, rec. clothing as member of Co. D 4/7/1864, moved Lawrence Co., OH 3/1865, surr. Lawrence Co., OH 5/16/1865, res. Johnson Co. (Daniel's Creek) 1860, b. Scott Co., VA, s. of Richard Wells, indicted for 1864 robberies 6/1/1865, pardoned by Gov. (re: Ironton Register, 4/1868) res. Lawrence Co. (Windsor Twp), OH 1870 & 1880, m. Nancy A. Webb (b. 1822), bur. Perkins Ridge Cem., Windsor Twp., Lawrence Co., OH.

WHIPPLE, GEORGE SYLVESTER: (10/2/1817 – 6/19/1881), Maj., Surgeon, enl. 4th KY Cav. 1863, prom Maj. as Regiment's Assistant Surgeon, appointed Surgeon 13th KY Cav. 4/14/1865, serv. w/ 13th until disbandment 4/12/1865, continued w/ 4th until 4/30/1865, surr. Mt. Sterling, KY, res. Carroll Co. 1860, b. Hamilton, MA, bought Carroll Co. (Worthville), KY land 1854, attended Medical School Louisville, KY, moved Louisville, KY postwar & practiced medicine, moved back later to Worthville, m. Ann Elisabeth Bailey (1830-1916) Carroll Co. 1850, d. Worthville, KY, bur. Worthville City Cem., Worthville, Carroll Co., KY.

WHITAKER, ANDERSON: (4/7/1849 – 3/26/1923), Kash's Co., enl. Breathitt Co. 3/1/1864, surr. w/ Kash's Co. Salyersville, also forced to surr. Louisa 5/9/1865, res. Breathitt Co. (mo. Quicksand), s. of William J. & Betty (Smith) Whitaker, Deputy Clerk Breathitt Co. 1891, rec. KY Confed Pension #1016 Breathitt Co. 1912, m. Leanna Napier (1850-bef. 1920) 1867, d. Fayette Co., KY (d.c. #10525), bur. Ben Smith Cem., Willstacy, Breathitt Co., KY.

WHITAKER, ISAAC J.: (10/14/1842 – 6/12/1916), Co. B, enl. Whitesburg, KY 8/29/1862, capt. Gladeville, VA 7/7/1863, to Kemper Barracks 7/18/1863, to Camp Chase Prison 7/20/1863, to Camp Douglas Prison 8/24/1863, exch. Point Lookout 2/24/1865, res. Letcher Co., s. of Isaac & Nellie (Adams) Whitaker, res. Letcher Co. 1890, m. (1) Mary Bentley 1869, (2) Nancy Caudill (1845-bef. 1916) 1870, bur. Mose Ison Cem., Blackey, Letcher Co., KY.

WHITAKER, JOHN "BIG JOHN": (9/7/1837 – 1/31/1904), Co. H, enl. Perry Co. (Brashearville) 3/28/1863, pres. summer/1863, res. Letcher Co. 1860, s. of Esquire & Harriet (Higgins) Whitaker, moved Jackson Co. by 1880, m. (1) Martha Ann Day (1834-bef. 1874), (2) Martha Short (1855-aft. 1900) 1874, res. Letcher Co. 1860, s. of Isaac J. & Nellie (Adams) Whitaker, moved to Jackson Co. by 1880, bur. Millard Halcomb Cem., Welchburg, Jackson Co., KY.

WHITAKER, JOHN W.: (1836-1893), Co. B. enl. Whitesburg, KY 8/29/1862, appointed wagoner 12/17/1862, rec. clothing 4/7/1864, res. Letcher Co. 1860, s. of Isaac J. & Nellie (Adams) Whitaker, res. Letcher Co. 1890, m. Patsy Halcomb (b. 1838), bur. Mose Whitaker Cem., Roxanna, Letcher Co., KY.

WHITAKER, MOSE E.: (10/22/1837 – 3/6/1919), Co. B, enl. Whitesburg, KY 8/29/1862, pres. summer/1863, res. Letcher Co. 1860, s. of Isaac & Nellie (Adams) Whitaker, res. Letcher Co. 1890, m. Anna Ison (1835-1923) 1857, bur. Mose Whitaker Cem., Roxanna, Letcher Co., KY.

WHITAKER, STEPHEN A.: (1831 – 1909), 1st Lt., Cos. B & H, enl. Whitesburg, KY 8/29/1862, trans. from Co. B to Co. H & prom. Lt. Whitesburg 10/18/1862, assumed command of Co. H after capt. of Capt. Samuel Ray Caudill, res. 10/1864, reported sick 12/1864, dropped from roll by order of Sec. of War 2/16/1865, A. R. Bentley successor, res. Letcher Co. 1860, s. of Isaac & Nellie (Adams) Whitaker, Letcher Co. magistrate 28 years, deputy county court clerk, m. Levina Frazier (1831-1885) 1849, bur. Rich Whitaker Cem., Letcher, Letcher Co., KY.

WHITE, ABIJAH "HIGE": (1829 – 1895), Co. K, identified 1890 Breathitt Veterans Census, res. Breathitt Co. 1860, s. of Robin & Rachel (Beckwell) White, res. Breathitt Co. 1890, m. Miranda Campbell (1832-aft. 1910) 1859, bur. Akemon-White Cem., Barwick, Breathitt Co., KY.

WHITE, ANDREW JACKSON: (10/31/1834 – 2/28/1921), Capt., Co. H, serv. prev. 5th KY Cav., Co. H, serv. until disbandment in VA 1865 (re: pension statement), res. Rowan Co. 1860, b. Morgan Co., s. of George White & Eleanor (Nickell) White, rec. KY Confed. Pension #2499 Rowan Co. 1912, m. Nancy Carter (1860-1942), d. Elliottville, KY, bur. White Cem., Elliottville, Rowan Co., KY.

WHITE, JACOB (B.): (8/17/1825 – 11/19/1896), Co. K, surr. Cumberland Gap 4/30/1865, s. of William B. & Sarah Ann (Boy) White, res. Scott Co., VA 1850, Sullivan Co., TN 1860, m. Elizabeth Quails, bur. East Hill Cem., Bristol, Sullivan Co., TN.

WHITE, JAMES: (11/9/1837 – 4/22/1898), Co. I, conscripted Whitesburg, KY 10/18/1862, disc. 4/16/1863, res. Breathitt Co. 1860, s. of Robin & Rachel White, widow rec. KY Confed. Pension #3730 Breathitt Co. 1916, m. Drucilla Moore (b. 1842) Breathitt Co. 1858, bur. White & Deaton Cem., Barwick, Breathitt Co., KY.

WHITE, WILLIAM: (b. 1841), Cos. B & H, enl. Whitesburg, KY 10/18/1862, trans. from Co H to Co. B 1864, rec. clothing 6/29/1864, res. Carroll Co., VA 1850, res. Letcher Co. 1860, b. Wythe Co., VA, s. of David & Sarah (Tipton) White.

WICKER, JOHN: (8/1846 – 1917), Co. F, enl. 8/24/1863, pres. summer/1863, disbanded Whitesburg, KY 4/1865, took oath Louisa 5/1865, res. Floyd Co. 1860, b. Floyd Co., s. of Jesse & Eliza (Hays) Wicker, res. Knott Co. 1900, rec. KY Confed. Pension #2318 Floyd Co. (Lackey) 1913, m. Artie (1868-1918), bur. Four Mile Cem., Mousie, Knott Co., KY.

WICKER, ROBERT "ROBIN": (1844 – 1931), Co. F, enl. Floyd Co. 10/10/1862, serv. prev. 5th KY Inf., Co. E, pres. 6/30/1863, res. Floyd Co. 1860, s. of Jesse & Eliza (Hays) Wicker, res. Floyd Co. 1870 & 1880, res. Knott Co. 1910, 1920 & 1930 (Rock Fork), m. (1) Florence Moore (b. 1843), (2) Della Frasier (d. aft. 1930) 1915.

WILLIAMS, ANDREW: (1839 – 1892), Co. C, enl. Whitesburg, KY 10/1/1862, pres. spring/1863, res. Perry Co. 1860 & 1870, res. Perry Co. (Troublesome) 1891 (re: tax list), m. (1) Margaret "Peggy" Jones (1841-ca. 1868) 1861, (2) Polly (1845-bef. 1900), bur. Williams Cem., Ary, Perry Co., KY.

WILLIAMS, ELIJAH M.: (1844 – 4/9/1865), Co. I, identified in "10th KY Cav. Artificial Unit" – misfiled records, enl. Whitesburg, KY 8/29/1863, capt. Perry or Breathitt Co. 3/8/1864, res. Perry Co. 1850 & 1860, s. of Jeremiah & Ibby Williams, d. Camp Chase Prison, bur. Camp Chase Prison Cem., Grave #1846, Columbus, Franklin Co., OH.

WILLIAMS, (WILLIAM) HENRY: (1844 – 1885), Co. D, enl. Whitesburg, KY 10/4/1862, capt. Letcher Co. by Lt. Clabe Jones & Union 14th KY Cav., rel. after taking oath, res. Letcher Co. 1860, s. of William D. & Elender Williams, res. Letcher Co. 1870, res. Menifee Co. 1880, m. Amanda Gilly (1850-1885), bur. Armitage Cem., Frenchburg, Menifee Co., KY.

WILLIAMS, JOHN H.: (2/1825 – 1906), Co. I, conscripted Whitesburg, KY 10/18/1862, disc. 1/2/1863, res. Perry Co. 1860, s. of Hardy & Sarah (Campbell) Williams, res. Perry Co. 1880, moved Leslie Co. (Cutshin) 1883, m. Mary "Polly" Eversole (b. 1826), bur. Baker Cem., Cutshin, Leslie Co., KY.

WILLIAMS, PHILLIP FILLMORE: (2/1/1826 – 10/25/1912), 2nd Cpl., Co. I, conscripted Whitesburg, KY 10/18/1862, prom. Whitesburg 10/28/1862, pres. 4/1863, res. Perry Co. 1860, s. of Hardy & Sarah (Campbell) Williams, res. Lee Co., KY 1870, 1880, 1900 & 1910, m. Mary Jane Fugate (1824-ca. 1866), bur. Williams Cem., Zoe, Lee Co., KY.

WILLIAMS, ROBERT: (9/16/1823 – 7/24/1910), Co. I, conscripted Whitesburg, KY 10/18/1862, pres. fall/1862, res. Perry Co. 1860, s. of Hardy & Sarah (Campbell) Williams, res. Perry Co. 1880 & 1900, res. Leslie Co. 1910, m. (1) Susannah Eversole 1830-ca. 1869), (2) Leana (b. 1850) 1870, bur. Henry Day Cem., Smilax, Leslie Co., KY.

WILLIAMS, STEPHEN: (3/25/1822 – 4/15/1896), Kash's Co., res. Breathitt Co., 1860, s. of Coleman & Cynthia (Davis) Williams, indicted for murder as member this Co. 1865, post-war surveyor for Breathitt Co., m. Sarah Back (1824-1904), bur. Williams-Hill Cem., Noctor, Breathitt Co., KY.

WILLIAMS, WILLIAM: (b. 1846), Co. F, enl. Floyd Co. 9/1/1863, res. Breathitt Co. (Little Buckhorn) 1860, s. of John Vent & June Williams.

WILSON, ANDREW SR. "BIG ANDY": (1797 – 1868), Kash's Co., indicted post-war for murder as member this Co. 1865, m. Easter (1797-aft.1870 Caney Creek, Morgan Co.) bur. I. S. Wilson Cem., Helechawa, Wolfe Co., KY.

WILSON, ELVIN: (5/14/1830 – 10/15/1867), Kash's Co., res. Morgan Co. 1860, s. of Isaac Shelby Sr. & Rebecca (Kash) Wilson, indicted post-war for murder as member this Co. 1865, m. Hannah May (b. 1841) 1858, bur. I. S. Wilson Cem., Helechawa, Wolfe Co., KY.

WILSON, FREDERICK: (b. 1836), Co. K, enl. Lee Co., VA 8/18/1863, pres. Lee Co. 12/31/1863, res. Russell Co., VA 1860, s. of Richard & Nancy (Honaker) Wilson, m. Mary E. (Vaughn) McGlaughlin (1835-1923) Russell Co., VA 1870, res Russell Co., VA 1880, died before 1910, bur. (unm.) Russell Co. Cem., Tumbez, Russell Co., VA.

WILSON, ISAAC SHELBY: (9/8/1812 – 11/16/1892), Kash's Co., res. Morgan Co., KY 1860, indicted post-war for murder as member this Co. 1865, m. (1) Rebecca Kash (1812-aft. 1870), (2) Delilah Nickel, bur. I. S. Wilson Cem., Helechawa, Wolfe Co., KY.

WILSON, JACKSON R.: (7/13/1825 – 12/13/1895), Kash's Co., res. Morgan Co. 1860, s. of Andrew Sr. & Esther (Hurst) Wilson, indicted for murder as member this Co. 1865, m. Margaret Cope (1833-1892), bur. Cope Cem., Keck, Breathitt Co., KY.

WILSON, PHILLIP: (1835 – 1890), Co. K, enl. Lee Co., VA 8/18/1863, pres. Lee Co. 12/31/1863, surr. Cumberland Gap 4/30/1865, res. Jackson Co. 1850, res. Clay Co. 1860, s. of Phillip Wilson & Christine Rogers, bro. in-law of Capt. James Herd, Co. K, m. Elizabth "Betsy" Herd (1840-bef. 1900) Clay Co. 1854, res. Jackson Co. 1880, killed by Jim Bob Faubus, Jackson Co., bur. (unm.) Wilson Cem., Moores Creek, Jackson Co., KY.

WINES, (WINESETT), ALEXANDER: 2nd Lt., Co. F, identified in "10th KY Cav. Artificial Unit" – misfiled records, paroled 4/28/1865 Cumberland Gap by Dillard's 34th KY Inf., serv. prev. 29th VA Inf., Co. C, res. of southwest VA.

WIREMAN, MORGAN: (7/5/1844 – 7/5/1913), Co. F, enl. Floyd Co. 10/10/1862, capt. Gladeville, VA 7/7/1863, to Kemper Barracks 7/18/1863, to Camp Chase Prison 7/20/1863, to Camp Douglas Prison 8/24/1863, exch. Point Lookout 2/24/1865, res. Magoffin Co. 1860, s. of John & Rebecca Wireman, m. Sarah Allen (1840-1919) 1859, bur. Morgan Wireman Cem. (nr. John Wireman Cem.) mo. Vick Branch, Magoffin Co., KY.

WOODARD, NELSON G.: (9/1844 – 3/8/1906), Co. K, serv. prev. 21st VA & 64th VA Inf. Co. K, deserted 64th VA 5/26/1864 & enl. 13th KY Cav., surr. Cumberland Gap 4/30/1865, res. Lee Co., VA 1850 & 1860, s. of Daniel S. & Ellender (Crusenberry) Woodard, res. Lee Co. 1870 (Jonesville) & 1880 (Rocky Station), m. Mary A. "Polly" Stapleton (b. 1846) Lee Co. 1866, res. Lee Co., VA 1900, d. Domino, VA, widow rec. VA Confed. Pension 1907.

WORKMAN, NATHANIAL: (5/1/1831 – 4/14/1913), Cos. C & F, enl. Floyd Co., KY 9/1/1862, trans. from Co. F to Co. C Whitesburg 10/1/1862, pres. summer/1863, res. Floyd Co. 1860, b. VA, s. of Eli & Mary (Blevins) Workman, res. Floyd Co. 1870 & 1880, res. Carter Co. 1890, 1900 & 1910, m. Martha Wright (1830-1900 to 1910), d. from pneumonia (d.c. #09664), bur. Frazie Cem.

WRIGHT, ANDREW JEFFERSON "JR": (8/15/1837 – 9/19/1903), 2nd Cpl., Cos. A & D, enl. Whitesburg, KY 10/4/1862, serv. prev. 5th KY Inf. Co. F, pres. summer/1863, res. Letcher Co. 1860, s. of John & Mary Ann (Bentley) Wright, moved Elliott Co. bef. 1880, m. Adeline Brickey (1832-1904) Scott Co., VA 1865, bur. Andrew Wright Cem., Sandy Hook, Elliott Co., KY.

WRIGHT, ANDREW JACKSON "SR": (1827 – 12/1/1878), Co. A, serv. prev. 5th KY Inf., Co. F, pres. fall/1862, res. Letcher Co. 1860, b. Perry Co., s. of Joel Martin & Susannah Wright, res. Letcher Co. (McRoberts) 1870, m. Harriet Adams (1830-1900) 1845, bur. McRoberts Cem., McRoberts, Letcher Co., KY.

WRIGHT, BENJAMIN: (1839 – 11/17/1863), Cos. B & D, enl. Whitesburg, KY 9/2/1862, trans from Co. B to Co. D Whitesburg 1/1/1863, pres. spring/1863, killed by Union soldier Alfred Killen Wise Co., VA (Cranes Nest), res. Letcher Co. 1860, s. of John & Mary (Bentley) Wright, m. Surilda (1837-1896), bur. Jesse Austin Cem., nr. Pound, Wise Co., VA.

WRIGHT, HIRAM: (10/1/1839 – 10/5/1917), Co. D, enl. Whitesburg, KY 8/1/1863, pres. summer/1863, res. Letcher Co. 1860, b. Perry Co., s. of John & Mary Ann (Bentley) Wright, res. Letcher Co. 1870 & 1900, rec. KY Confed. Pension #1034 Pike Co. (Dorton) 1912, m. Sarena Bowling (1845-1907) 1867, bur Wesley Wright Cem., Dorton, Pike Co., KY.

WRIGHT, JAMES HARRISON: (1/1842 – 10/9/1930), 4th Cpl., Co. D, pres. spring/1863, res. Letcher Co. 1860, s. of James & Mary (Ingles) Wright, m. Seatta Baldridge (1843-1930) 1864, bur. Wright Cem. Dock, Floyd Co., KY.

WRIGHT, JOEL: (11/1837 – 1901), 2nd Cpl., Co. D, serv. prev. 5th KY Inf., Co. F, res. Letcher Co. 1860, s. of James & Mary (Ingles) Wright, m. (1) Sidney Adams (1833-bef. 1870) 1856, (2) Louanna Pitts (1855- aft. 1931) 1876, bur. Pitts Cem., Pyramid, Floyd Co., KY.

WRIGHT, JOHN VENT: (4/1/1845 – 7/13/1903), Co. G, enl. Whitesburg, KY 9/23/1862, pres. fall/1863, res. Letcher Co. 1860, b. Russell Co., VA (Lebanon), s. of John & Mary Ann (Bentley) Wright, m. Dorinda Baldwin (1847-aft. 1900) Scott Co., VA 1866, bur. Duff Cem., Stickleyville, Lee Co., VA.

WRIGHT, JOHN WESLEY "BAD JOHN": (4/17/1844 – 1/30/1931), Co. D, enl. Whitesburg, KY 10/4/1862, 5' 10", hazel eyes, brown hair, serv. prev. 5th KY Inf., Co. F, part of rebel guard that sought deserters fall/1862, killed Pvt. Reuben Potter for desertion, capt. Gladeville, VA 7/7/1863, escaped & fled to OH, rejoined 13th 6/1864 Battle of Cynthiana where he was wd., joined Union 22nd OH Inf., Co. B Cincinnati 10/25/1864, trans. Ft. Smith, AR & serv. until 8/25/1865, res. Letcher Co. 1860, b. Letcher Co., s. of Joel Ellis & Eliza (Bates) Wright, joined Robinson Circus post-war as trick rider and sharp-shooter w/ uncle M.V.B. Bates (the KY Giant), res. Letcher Co.(Chips/Neon) 1866-1901, res. Letcher Co. (Bentley) 1901-1913, res. Pound, VA 1913-1931, m. (1) Alice Lee Harmon (1818-bef. 1866), (2) Martha "Mattie" Humphrey (1835-1924) 1866, (3) Ellen Saunders (1863-1948) Prestonsburg 1924, bur. John Wright Cem. Pound, Wise Co., VA.

WRIGHT, POWELL: (1844 – 1905), 1st Cpl., Cos. C & F, enl. Whitesburg, KY 10/1/1862, serv. prev. 5th KY Inf., Co. E, trans. from Co. C to Co. F Floyd Co. 10/14/1862, pres. summer/1863, enl. 10th KY Cav, Co. A 1/1/1863, AWOL 6/30/1863, res. Floyd Co., b. VA, res. Floyd Co. 1870 & 1880, res. Rowan Co. (Pearce/Paragon) 1900, m. Elizabeth Sutton (1842-aft. 1880), bur. New Alfrey Cem., Gogswell, Rowan Co., KY.

WRIGHT, SOLOMON H.: (1841 – 6/13/1863), 1st Lt., Cos. B & D, enl. Whitesburg, KY 8/29/1862, prom. Whitesburg 10/4/1862, trans. from Co. B to Co. D, reported sick spring & summer/1863 on 13th rosters, apparently enl. 10th KY Cav., Co. C Pike Co. 3/7/1863, killed by Irvin Hill Wise Co. VA (High Knob), successor S. W. Thompson, res. Letcher Co. 1860, s. of Joel Ellis & Eliza (Bates) Wright, bur. Joel Wright Cem., Payne Gap, Letcher Co., KY.

WRIGHT, WILLIAM: (1834 - 1/14/1886), Cos. A & D, enl. Whitesburg, KY 10/4/1862, serv. prev. 5th KY Inf., Co. F, trans. from Co. A to Co. D 2/1/1863, s. of Joel Martin & Susannah Wright, killed by Sam Wright Chestnut Patch/McRoberts, KY, m. Nancy Hughes (1831-aft. 1880) Letcher Co. 1855, bur. McRoberts Cem. McRoberts, Letcher Co., KY.

WYATT, JONATHAN M.: (9/1846 – 1904), Co. K, surr. Cumberland Gap 4/30/1865, res. Lee Co., VA 1850, s. of Nathanial & Lolena (Jones) Wyatt, m. Dorthula Reasor (1854-1940), bur. Jones Riddle Cem., nr. Seminary, Lee Co., VA.

YEARY, WILLIAM HENRY: (6/20/1843 – 2/1926), Co. K, enl. Lee Co., VA 8/18/1863, pres. Lee Co. 12/31/1863, rec. clothing 9/78/1864, surr. Cumberland Gap 4/30/1865, res. Hancock Co., TN 1860, b. TN, s. of Henry & Eliza Yeary, res. Hancock Co., TN 1870, res. Lee Co., VA (White Shoals) 1880, 1900, 1910 & 1920, m. Martha E. Thompson (1850-1924), d. Lee Co. (Beech Grove), VA.

YONTS, CHARLES: (8/18/1832 – 10/18/1898), Co. D, enl. Whitesburg, KY 10/4/1862, pres. fall/1862, res. Letcher Co. 1860, s. of William Yonts Sr. & Levicy, m. Hannah Houston (1818-1908) 1852, bur. Yonts Cem., Neon, Letcher Co., KY.

YONTS, ELIJAH: (1831 – ca. 1863), Co. D, enl. Whitesburg, KY 10/4/1862, pres. fall/1862, enl. Union 39th KY, Co. K 12/25/1862, res. Letcher Co. (Trace Fork/Boone Creek) 1860, s. of William Yonts & Levicy, m. Eliza Cook (b. 1829) 1856, d. Louisa, KY.

YONTS, JOHN: (4/23/1834 – 2/1/1917), Co. D, serv. prev. 5th KY Inf., Co. F, serv. Co. D 13th KY (re: pension statement), res. Letcher Co. 1860, b. Perry Co., s. of William Yonts Sr. & Levicy, m. Mahalia Blankenship (1840-bef. 1910), bur. Quillen Cem., Deane, Letcher Co., KY.

YONTS, SOLOMON: (9/1835 – 9/23/1913), Co. D, enl. Whitesburg, KY 10/4/1862, pres. fall/1862, enl. Union 39th KY, Co. K 12/27/1862, res. Letcher Co. 1860, s. of William Jr. & Nancy (Frey) Yonts, applied Union pension 1893, m. Frances "Frankie" Whitaker (1836-1922)), bur. Goose Creek, Neon, Letcher Co., KY.

YOUNG, HARVEY BOYD: (7/19/1839 – 1/28/1905), Sgt., Co. K, rec. clothing 9/7/1864 & 9/24/1864, surr. Cumberland Gap 4/30/1865, serv. also confirmed in newspaper obit., s. of Amanda Harvey, res. Russell Co., VA 1860, m. (1) Catherine Young (1847-1878), (2) Adaline Abbott (1853-1913) 1879, bur. Tabor Cem., Olive Hill, Carter Co., KY.

ZION, MATTHEW W.: (8/8/1845 – 4/22/1925), Co. K, surr, Cumberland Gap 4/30/1865, res. Lee Co., VA 1860, s. of Abraham D & Mary "Polly" (Parsons) Zion, res. Lee Co., VA 1912, m. Nancy Jane Yeary (1843-1923), bur. Zion Cem., Pennington Gap, Lee Co., VA.

Epilogue

The research that led to the publication of this book has also been responsible for many other projects undertaken by the Ben E. Caudill SCV Camp. These include locating 13th KY Cavalry veteran's burial locations, as well as veterans' graves who served with other Confederate regiments, the successful marking of Confederate veterans' graves with government-provided military markers, identifying the locations of nearby Confederate hospitals and their accompanying burial grounds, erecting monuments to honor those who served the Confederate cause, and finally, establishing and participating in re-enactments of engagements that took place in southeastern Kentucky and southwestern Virginia.

As of this writing, the Ben Caudill Camp has learned that the men of the 13th KY Cavalry came from 47 different counties, in three states; and the majority called Kentucky "home". From this information, and other information that came to light during the research, the camp has been able to properly mark 1,378 Confederate veterans' graves in 74 counties and 14 states. Of this total, 712 were 13th KY Cavalrymen. This is nearly 73% of the 977 13th graves that have been located. Many of the remainder of those marked served with the 5th KY Infantry or Diamond's 10th Kentucky Cavalry, but other Kentuckians served with either the 1st, 2nd and 3rd Battalions of Kentucky Mounted Rifles, the 4th Kentucky Cavalry, the 9th Kentucky Cavalry, the 11th Kentucky Cavalry, or Field's Company of Kentucky Partisan Rangers. Graves have also been marked for Virginia Confederates who served with either the 8th Cavalry, 15th Infantry, 16th Cavalry, 21st Cavalry, 22nd Cavalry, 23 Infantry, 25th Cavalry, 29th Infantry, 34th Cavalry, 37th Infantry, 48th Infantry, 50th Infantry, 51st Infantry, 63rd Infantry, 64th Mounted Infantry, or Smith's Virginia Cavalry. Also included in the 1,378 were North Carolinians who served either with the 14th Battalion Cavalry, 22nd Infantry, 26th Infantry, or with Thomas' North Carolina Legion. Other Confederates who have been honored with military gravestones, by this camp, served either with the 6th Battalion Confederate Cavalry, 7th Battalion Confederate Cavalry, 4th Georgia Infantry, 37th Georgia Infantry, 32nd Tennessee Infantry, 37th Tennessee Infantry, or Robertson's Missouri Regiment.

On rare occasion, the Camp's research meshes well with the research of others, leading to surprising and rewarding results. Such was the case regarding one of Caudill's men from Breathitt County, KY. Research showed that Daniel Noble had joined the Caudill regiment, been captured at Gladeville, VA and eventually was imprisoned at Camp Douglas in Chicago. From there, he was able to escape the confines of prison by enlisting in the U. S. Navy as a "landsman". It was known that he survived the rest of the war, returned to Kentucky, and died in Wolfe County. The Camp's researchers were able to locate his grave and mark it with an upright Confederate gravestone. Little did the camp's researchers know; that was not the rest of Daniel's story! Our camp's historian got a call from a representative of the Medal of Honor Society, wishing to know the location of Daniel Noble's grave. While with the U. S. Navy at the Battle of Mobile Bay, Daniel's heroic efforts had been rewarded with the presentation of the Navy's version of the Medal of Honor. Requests from the Veteran's Administration for a MOH marker for Noble had been denied on the grounds that he already had a Confederate grave marker. In order to receive a government issued MOH Union marker, his Confederate grave marker would have to be removed. To the Caudill Camp, that was unacceptable. The only other option was to use private funds to produce a reasonable facimile. To the camp's rescue came the Noble Family Association! Now, Private/Landsman Confederate Cavalry/U. S. Navy Daniel Noble has what is probably one of the most unusual and impressive set of grave markers that exists anywhere!

Photos by M. R. Cornett

Many of the Confederate grave markers placed by the Ben Caudill Camp were completed before the turn of this century, years before GPS technology became widely available. Now that GPS devices are common, efforts are underway to record the exact latitude and longitude for every one of those 1,378 Confederate graves marked by the camp. Already, nearly 2,500 Confederate grave locations have been recorded with GPS, providing future generations with the data needed to find their ancestor's burial site.

While 1,378 graves marked may be the most impressive work done by the Ben Caudill Camp, it is not the camp's only noteworthy achievement. The discovery of Confederate hospitals that existed in Whitesburg, KY, at Blountville, TN, and at Almira, Castlewood, Fort Blackmore, Nickelsville, Wise and Holston Springs, VA led to the further discovery of nearby cemeteries. In those cemeteries laid many of our Kentucky Confederates who had their service cut short by disease. Diligent research, blood, sweat, and patience led to:

Five newly marked graves in Blountville, TN and Six in Castlewood, VA.

Seven newly marked graves at Camp Nash, VA and Five at Nickelsville, VA.

Just over the mountain in Almira, VA, four new gravestones were placed on previously unmarked graves. These markers were placed only after the area was cleared of brush and small trees. Only then could the markers be dragged across a delapidated wooden bridge and up the hill to the gravesites. These gravestone placements are not all "tail-gaters"! In fact, the terrain is sometimes so steep and void of any type of trail that ropes and pulleys must be rigged to get the gravestone to a hilltop cemetery. This has taken up to a half-day to place a single Confederate marker!

In the historic Wolfe Confederate Cemetery at Holston Springs, in Scott County, Virginia, 55 graves of Kentucky Confederates were identified and marked. The Wolfe cemetery overlooks the Holston River, where General Humphrey Marshall made his headquarters and where these Kentucky men spent their final days, before losing their lives to disease.

Thanks to local businesses who agreed to receive and store the 55 Confederate headstones, particularly the Magee's in Yuma. And, thanks to a determined crew of volunteers who crossed the mountains from Kentucky, the gravestones were placed with precision, and in short order, on previously unmarked graves. On one remarkable day, 23 of the 55 headstones were set: the last few by the light of the truck's headlights!

A special marker was designed, purchased, and placed in the Wolfe Confederate Cemetery, so that all who pass may know who cared enough to make this difference. The inscription reads: (Front) "Kentucky Confederates who died in the Holston Springs Hospital or at Camp Moccasin. Far from home, nearly forgotten; now we remember their brave sacrifice." (Back) "Colonel Ben Caudill Camp 1629, Sons of Confederate Veterans, Whitesburg, KY".

In the Sandlick Cemetery, also known as the Westwood Cemetery, at Whitesburg, Kentucky, there are now more than 40 marked Confederate graves; these include more than a dozen men of the 13th KY Cavalry who died in the nearby Confederate hospital. The Ben Caudill Camp has erected and dedicated a monument to the Confederate hospital at Whitesburg and to the adjacent Sandlick Cemetery. Both the hospital and cemetery were located on property belonging to John Caudill, the father of Colonel Benjamin E. Caudill, commander of the 13th Kentucky Cavalry.

Also, in the Sandlick Cemetery, are 14 Confederate "In Memory of" headstones that were dedicated to Kentucky Confederates who died in a hospital in Gladeville, VA (now Wise, VA). Their graves were lost due to development as the town grew after the war. Unable to even locate their actual burials, the Veterans' Administration finally agreed, after much negotiation, to allow the Camp to place "In Memoriam" markers in the place where these deceased Confederates may have last seen "home".

In the decades that followed the War of Northern Aggression, the old Sandlick Cemetery had apparently been respected by those who remembered the war; but had gradually been neglected by the generations who did not. When it was determined that a likely Confederate burial ground lay beneath the dense overgrowth, a massive clean-up operation was needed before suspicions could be confirmed. After several strenuous days by Camp members and members of their families, it was found that scores of unmarked male graves lay beneath the surface. Some were Caudill's men and others had likely fallen ill as their units passed through Pound Gap. Today's monuments help tell a part of their story and of their demise.

Since it was learned that many of our local Confederates rode with General John Hunt Morgan on his famed "Last Raid", the camp erected a small monument on KY 15, near the entrance to Carr Creek State Park in Knott County. It is well understood that General Morgan entered Kentucky through Pound Gap and traveled through several counties in southeastern Kentucky on his way to Mount Sterling and Cynthiana in June 1864.

 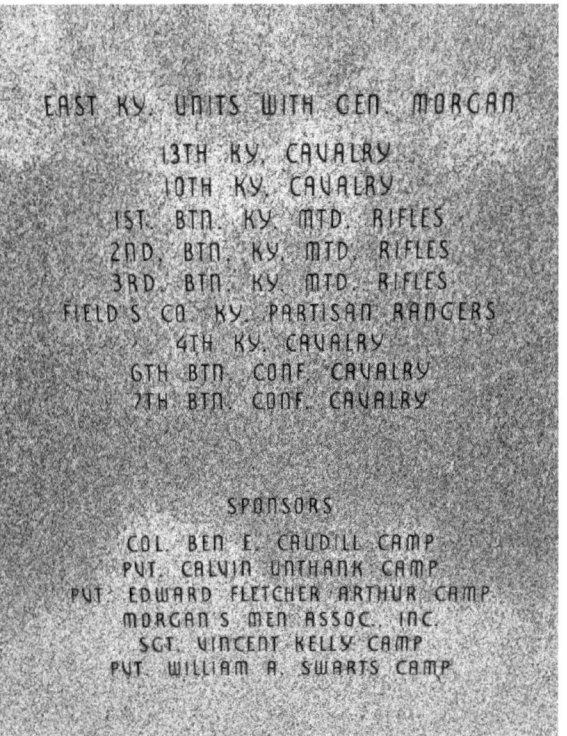

(Front and Back; Photos by F. Sparkman)

Another monument that resulted from of the efforts of the Ben Caudill Camp is the "Brothers Once More" monument located on US 23 at the Kentucky-Virginia state line. The monument is dedicated to the men from southeastern Kentucky and southwestern Virginia who served in the war between 1861 and 1865.

The camp also erected informative signage near Hazel Green, KY where General Humphrey Marshall disbanded the original 5th Kentucky Infantry in October 1862. The metal sign included images of General Humphrey Marshall, commander of the 5th KY Mounted Infantry, and Lieutenant David Swango, one of his officers who hailed from the Hazel Green area. After several years, standing outside a nearby cemetery, the elements began to take their inevitable effects. First, the images of the two officers faded and disappeared, leaving only the central text visible. Then, the supporting treated posts gave way to the wind. The old metal sign was discoverted to be flat on the ground, and still outside the cemetery. Considereate neighbors soon dragged the remains inside the fence.

The Caudill Camp members decided that a suitable replacement was needed. Using funds generated by sales of this book, the camp designed a new granite monument, with text like what had been on the old metal sign. While waiting for the new monument to be produced, the old metal sign was brought back to Perry County to be salvaged. In 2017, the new granite monument was completed, installed in the middle of the cemetery, and then dedicated.

Photos by Mark S. Carroll and Richard M. Smith

When General Marshall disbanded the 5th KY Mounted Infantry, he freed Captain Ben Caudill, Commander of Company F, to go home and begin to assemble a new regiment. Soon, the 10th Kentucky Mounted Rifles would become a reality, and Colonel Benjamin Caudill would serve as its commander. In early 1865, "Caudill's Army" would be redesignated as the 13th KY Cavalry.

When General John Hunt Morgan led his last raid into central Kentucky, accompanied by several members of Caudill's Army, he engaged in battle at Mt. Sterling on June 8, 1864. The Confederates who were killed there were buried nearby, at a location that remained unknown for over a hundred years. Working with local historians and residents, the Ben Caudill Camp located the lost Confederate Cemetery in Mt. Sterling, utilizing documentation from the Montgomery County Courthouse. The long-forgotten burial ground was hidden from view, in an overgrown, wooded area off Reid Street. The Ben Caudill Camp cleared the historic site and placed several Confederate markers to honor the final resting places of soldiers who were known to have been killed in action and buried at this location.

Finally, the research has allowed the Ben Caudill Camp to play the leading role in organizing and maintaining reenactments at Chavies, Leatherwood, and Jenkins. Over the years, these reenactments, along with others in southeast KY and southwest VA have been both educational and entertaining to hundreds who have participated and thousands who have attended.

And now, we are pleased to report that the research continues; understandably at a slower pace, but nevertheless, it continues.

PERSONAL REFLECTIONS

by

Faron Sparkman,

Past Commander and Camp Historian

Researching the lives and service of the men who served in the 13th KY Cavalry, finding their burial sites, and sharing the experience of seeing those sites properly marked, has been a passion of mine since 1995. It was, at that time, that this effort began as a primary mission of the newly formed Colonel Ben Caudill Camp of the Sons of Confederate Veterans, based in Letcher County

That mission involved an intense amount of research throughout Letcher County, neighboring counties, and beyond. Our efforts eventually allowed us to see burial sites of 710 of the 1,148 who served in Caudill's 13th, marked with a Confederate military marker. There were numerous Union markers in our area, most having been set by family members in the early 1900's. Little had been done with Confederate markers before the efforts of the Caudill Camp. For example, Letcher County had a total of four Confederate markers before we began. It now has 175! Perry County previously had just one Confederate marker, and now has 109. Breathitt County had no Confederate markers before our efforts and now has 141. Also of note: we set 146 Confederate markers in Floyd County, 143 in Morgan County, and 127 in Knott County. I had the pleasure of helping to set 691 Confederate markers. Most of these were in small family cemeteries in the mountains of eastern Kentucky; many abandoned over the years, and many in extremely difficult locations to access. Some have required a full day's work to get the heavy upright granite markers up the side of a cliff and over heavily wooded terrain. I am left with memories to treasure forever, with a great sense of satisfaction, having seen each of these honors rightfully bestowed.

Of the 691 Confederate marker placements in which I participated; I have a "top-ten most difficult" list. They include Booker Short and Joseph Cobb in Menifee County, Ambrose Watts in Breathitt County, Charles Hicks and Nathaniel Sexton in Knott County, Jeremiah Roberts and Martin Bailey in Lee County, Caleb Roberts in Wolfe County, Shelby Wallen in Floyd County, and William J. Arrorwood in Johnson County. Each of these required multiple visits just to locate, and at least a full day's effort to get the marker to the grave. I have vivid memories of each, knowing what it took to complete the task. I am also left with a lifetime of memories; locating these sites deep in the woods, some atop extremely steep cliffs, some blocked by streams, and others by rock and deep mud. Someone once remarked that only a squirrel or bird would ever see some of these markers, but that never once deterred me from helping to get it done.

There are also many memories of seeing some of the most beautiful, and largely unknown, terrain in our region, and fond memories of so many unusual circumstances. At the end of one long day of stone-setting in Virginia, with the help of Carlos Brock, we set the marker for John J. Amburgey, traveling a narrow, crooked road, high on a mountain-top at 10:00 at night, in a pouring rainstorm, with only a flashlight. Also with Carlos Brock, we once linked together five come-along pulleys to slowly winch a granite marker for Booker Short up the side of a mountain in Menifee County.

With four others, I helped set a marker for Henry Taylor on a mountain in Floyd County that was accessible only by way of Dewey Lake, using a boat. We borrowed a small johnboat, which we dubbed "Caudill's Navy", placing a sign of its side. Then, we proceeded to nearly sinking the boat once the crew, tools, and the 250-pound stone were brought aboard. I've also been charged by a bull while getting to a hilltop cemetery in Floyd County where Joel Wright was buried.

Driving alone, I went from Kentucky to Texas to set an upright marker for Samuel Thompson, on a day when the ground was as hard as granite and the temperature was 104. One of our comrades, Richard Smith, drove from Kentucky to Colorado to mark one of our 13th KY soldiers with a military marker.

I had the privilege to work with Manton Ray Cornett on many stone-setting adventures. Together, we had the unique honor of researching, locating the previously unmarked grave, and setting a military marker for a rare female Confederate soldier, Mary Ann Wright of the 4th KY Cavalry, in Carroll County, Virginia. There have been countless hours of roster research conducted over the past 27 years with many, including Steve Bowling in Jackson, Kentucky and Larry Combs in Limestone, New York. Thousands of cemeteries have been visited and studied with the help of Carlos Brock, Manton Ray Cornett, Joe Skeens, Buford Caudill, Bill James, Dorothy Hunter, Anita Skaggs, Tim Harp, Richard Smith, Richard Brown, Willis Strong, John and Nancy Bays, Harold and Henrietta McKinney, and Paul and Beverly Estep, among others. I have made countless trips to courthouses and libraries across the state, to study deeds and tax records, to gain insight into the lives and deaths of our soldiers. My research and stone-setting led not only to trips throughout Kentucky, but also to Arkansas, Florida, Missouri, Ohio Oklahoma, South Carolina, Tennessee, and Virginia.

When we began this quest, practically no Confederate soldiers in eastern Kentucky had a military headstone to honor their service. I have had the extreme honor of visiting, to date, 841 of the known 977 burial sites of 13th KY Cavalry soldiers. Many of the soldiers were buried in completely unmarked graves, without any kind of stone. Finding key elderly people in the soldier's family with knowledge of burial sites was paramount. Sadly, many of those key people passed away a short time after our conversations. I am extremely grateful to each one who contributed to the research that led to both marking so many graves and the completion of this book.

It is my hope that others will become interested in this effort, and help to preserve military and family history, and to carry on this valuable research well into the future.

Faron Sparkman

584 Trimble Branch

Prestonsburg, Kentucky 41653

faron.sparkman@gmail.com

BIBLIOGRAPHY

34th Battalion Virginia Cavalry; Cole, Scott C.

50th Virginia Infantry Regimental History; Chapla, John D.; H. E. Howard, Inc.; copyright 1997

64th Virginia Infantry Regimental History; Weaver, Jeffery; H. E. Howard Publisher; copyright 1992

A Family Called Craft; Collier, Joella Craft

A History of Morgan's Cavalry; Duke, Basil; Genesis Publishing Company; copyright 1997

A History of Mt. Sterling, Kentucky; Boyd, Carl & Hazel

A Little Salt with Your Watermelon: The Battle of Leatherwood; Sparkman, Faron; East Kentucky Magazine, July, 2001

Amburgey Ancestry in America; Griffith, Dorothy Amburgey

American Civil War, State of Kentucky

American Civil War Armies: Confederate Troops; Katcher, Phillip

Annals of Floyd County; Wells, Charles C.

A Sifter Full of Bullets; The Story of John S. Sparkman; Sparkman, Faron; 4th Edition, copyright 1997

Battle of Jonesville; Civil War Days Publication; May 31-June2, 2002

Battle of Jonesville; Richmond Sentinel; January 16, 1864

Battle of Jonesville: The Frozen Fight; Brown, Richard & Chaltas, David; Tree Huggin'

Behold, He Cometh in the Clouds; Noble, George Washington

Ben Caudill's Army; Abingdon Virginian; Volume 24; June 1983

Captain Tod Carter of the Confederate States Army: A Biographical Word Portrait; Carter, Rosalie; 1978

Civil War Pension Records

Confederate Pensioners of Kentucky; Abstracted by Lynn, Stephen Douglas; copyright 2000

Confederate Soldiers of Kentucky; Edited by Lynn, Stephen Douglas; copyright 2002

Descendants of Woolery Eversole; submitted by Frazier, Sherry Baker, with notations by the Isatori Family, Boshoven, Kathy, Welch, James & Baker, Lewis G.

Diary of a Bluegrass Confederate: Guerrant, Edward; Louisiana State University Press; copyright 1992

East Tennessee and the Civil War; Temple, Oliver; The Robert Clarke Company; copyright 1899

Eastern Kentucky: Scene of Much Civil War Action; Guerrant, Edward; The Kentucky Explorer; October 1991

Ebersol Families in America; Chestnut, Don

Fights with Guerillas; Tri-Weekly Commonwealth; Frankfort, Kentucky; May 5, 1865

Floyd County Times

Future President Led Civil War Troops in Eastern Kentucky; Mittlebeeler, Emmet; The Kentucky Explorer; September 1988

General Humphrey Marshall's Adjutant Reports, 1862

Harlan County Battalion: Roster-Daily Reports; Harlan Footprints, Volume 1 Footprints

History of the Illinois Central Railroad; Stover, John F.

Kentucky Cavaliers in Dixie; Mosgrove, George; University of Nebraska Press; copyright 1999

Kentucky Census Records: 1850-1930

Letcher County Confederate Veterans; Cornett, James G.

Letcher County's Methodist Heritage; Green, Bob; The Mountain Eagle; September 14, 1994

Life of James Claybourn Jones; Jones, Clabe

Major Benjamin Blankenship Papers

Morgans's Last Raid; Stier, William J.; Civil War Times; December, 1996

Morgan's Raiders; Brown, Dee Alexander

Perry County, Kentucky: A History

Point Lookout Prison Camp for Confederates; Beitzell, Edwin W.

Private Records of the Colonel Ben E. Caudill Camp No. 1629, Sons of Confederate Veterans; copyright 2006

Rebel Raider: The Life of General John Hunt Morgan; Ramage, James;

Records & Rosters of the 10th Kentucky Mounted Rifles; compiled by the Colonel Ben E. Caudill Camp No. 1629, SCV

Regimental History of the 40th Kentucky Mounted Infantry

Report of Brigadier General William E. Jones; C. S. Army Commanding Cavalry Brigade; Headquarters Jones' Cavalry Brigade; Jonesville, Virginia; January 7, 1864

Report of Brigadier General William E. Jones; C. S. Army Headquarters Jones' Cavalry; Morgan's Farm; Lee County, Virginia; March 14, 1864

Stonewall Jackson: The Man, The Soldier, The Legend; Robertson, James I. Jr.; Macmillan Publishing; 1997

Tennesseans in the Civil War; Volume One; Civil War Centennial Commission of Tennessee; copyright 1964

Tenth Kentucky Cavalry, C. S. A.; Prichard, James M. & Wells, John B.

The 7th Battalion Confederate Cavalry; Weaver, Jeffery & Prichard, Jim; 1996-1997

The Battle of Barbourville; Adkins, Ray; Lulu Publishing Company; 2005

The Battle of Ivy Mountain; Scalf, Henry P.

The Battle of Jonesville, Virginia: Parsons, Jerry, Major, 37th Virginia Infantry Re-Enactor

The Battle of Saltville: Massacre or Myth?; Marvel, William; Blue & Gray Magazine; August, 1991

The Battles for Saltville; Marvel, William; H. E. Howard, Inc.; copyright 1992

The Battles of Whitesburg; Brown, Richard & Chaltas, David; East Kentucky Magazine; October 2003; Edietion 5; Volume 3

The Bride and the Bandit; Neff, Robert et al; Private Publication; copyright 1998

The Civil War in Buchanan and Wise Counties: Bushwhacker's Paradise; Weaver, Jeffrey C.; H. E. Howard; Lynchburg, Virginia; 1994

The Civil War in the Big Sandy Valley of Kentucky; Preston, John David; 2nd Edition; copyright 2008

The Civil War in Wise County, Virginia, 1861-1865; Wise County Historical Society; copyright 2004

The Confederate Veteran Magazine

The Defeated Creek Diary; Hall, Eli; copyright pending

The Eversole Farm in Perry County; Eastern Kentucky Magazine; Edition 5, Volume 3; October 2003

The Fight for Middle Creek; Reid, Richard; Sandefur Printing; copyright 1992

The History of the Pound: Sage of Big Laurel Recalls Battles Fought by Armies in Far Southwest; Adams, Taylor James; Roanoke Times, December 10, 1950; edited by Rhonda Robertson and Nancy Clark Brown; The Historical Society of the Pound; 1993

The Life and Campaigns of Major General J. E. B. Stuart; McClellan, Henry B.; Boston; Houghton: 1885

The Mountain, The Miner and the Lord; Caudill, Harry M.

The Partisan; Gen. Humphrey Marshall Camp newsletter

The Union Regiments of Kentucky; (Union Fourteenth Kentucky Cavalry); Speed, Thomas, Captain; Courier-Journal Job Printing Company; Louisville, Kentucky; 1997

The Virginia State Rangers and State Line; Osborne, Randall & Weaver, Jeffrey C.; copyright 1994

To Die in Chicago; Levy, George

War of the Rebellion: Official Records

www.ingramcontent.com/pod-product-compliance
Lightning Source LLC
Chambersburg PA
CBHW062126160426
43191CB00013B/2211